D1569869

VLADIMIR V. KUSIN

FROM DUBČEK TO CHARTER 77

VLADIMIR V. KUSIN

From Dubček to Charter 77

A study of 'normalization'
in Czechoslovakia
1968–1978

ST. MARTIN'S PRESS NEW YORK

All rights reserved. For information, write:
St. Martin's Press, Inc., 175 Fifth Avenue, New York, N.Y.   10010
Printed in Great Britain
Library of Congress Catalog Card Number 78-60995
ISBN 0-312-30717-9
First published in the United States of America in 1978

To Daniela

FOREWORD

This book is an exercise in analysis and argumentation rather than description, narration or exposition. Reasons and conclusions are however mostly arrived at on the basis of primary source materials, and there is a factual backbone in the appraisal.

By the same token an apology is due to the many scholars who have already explored various aspects of the process of 'normalisation' in Czechoslovakia, but whose names and interpretations are not mentioned in this text. This does not signify lack of appreciation for their perceptions, but it has seemed to me that I should not play a vicarious game with other people's concepts. The clean slate approach has therefore been tried. Well, almost clean. With exceptions, I have used secondary literature only to derive from it factual information not easily obtainable elsewhere, or where the writer's concept was felt to be a part of the story, not just a comment on it.

I have set myself the task of explaining the past decade of Czechoslovak politics to the proverbial informed reader. If such a person does indeed exist, he or she would not necessarily be an expert on things Czechoslovak, but perhaps a regular observer of politics, a reader of the foreign news pages in quality newspapers, a journalist for whom background is as important as the news story of tomorrow, a political philosopher, a university student of politics, international relations, Soviet area studies or modern history, someone who may know all about the USSR or Poland or Hungary and has not time for much else, but who would not be averse to learning from just one volume about an akin country where political fortunes have been playing hide and seek so vehemently. But of course I hope that my colleagues who pursue Czechoslovak Studies professionally will not look unkindly on the effort.

The book is constructed as post-reformist 'normalisation' itself has been: the essential girders are erected first, raw and bare, but with sufficient carrying capacity to sustain the weight of burdens yet to come; then, block after beam after joist are added in place, until the edifice acquires strength and form and is ready to accept a coat of whitewash to make it pleasing to the beholder's eye. The reader should have the sense of participation in this building programme; he should be able to identify the individual pieces of masonry as they are brought before his eyes and witness their incorporation into the rising structure.

At several points in the book the reader should be able to pause, look back, survey the work already done and think about what lies ahead. This is particularly true about four moments in time which punctuate the story: April 1969 when the foreman's job was taken away from Dubček, May 1971 when Husák thought the building was solid enough to require some refinement of the rough-and-tumble early methods of its construction, 1976 when an equilibrium seemed to have been reached which kept everything and everyone in place, and 1977 when the Charter opened a chink in the wall. These are the four parts of the book further subdivided to reflect the building progress and cumulating developments as they happened, while flashing back and forward to give a better viewing perspective to the observer.

That is, at least, how I hope this story of ten years in the life of a nation will be read.

The publisher, Peter Chiene, prompted me to write in the first instance and then, when the number of pages coming off my typewriter threatened to surpass the limits of his toleration, accepted the burdern of a bigger volume most helpfully and with grace.

Professor Alec Nove and the University of Glasgow have shown understanding for the subject and the author which is greatly appreciated. Professor Jaroslav Krejčí of the University of Lancaster has kindly given advice and comment on several points. Needless to say, it is the author alone who stands ready to face the critical music.

The Social Science Research Council have provided financial assistance with their customary understanding and efficiency. I am happy to join once again the large number of their grateful beneficiaries.

Glasgow, April 1978.

CONTENTS

LIST OF TABLES

PROLOGUE

Coexistence of democracy with socialism has for Czechoslovakia been a matter of real historical experience and, for many of her inhabitants, the obvious objective towards the attainment of which the state, the society and the individual should work. Next to, and interweaving with, an even older aspiration for national sovereignty, the notions of social equity and of government by the people and for the people have provided a major framework of reference to the nation's politicians for at least six decades.

Just after the war it looked as if communism, that *nullius filius* which had become respectable and awesome, would fit into the pattern of things reasonably well. A reformed communism with a human face seemed possible there and then, under the enlightened presidency of Klement Gottwald and the benign patronage of Iosif Stalin. It was not to be.

A hiatus interposed itself between the past confluence of nationalism, democracy and socialism, and the future. The communist party failed to respond to the traditional challenges after all and modelled its behaviour on the Soviet mono-organisational precept, originally designed to drag an under-developed society to industrial heights at speed. Life under authoritarian rule was proclaimed the best of the best, except for the ultimate objective of communism which was to be still better. It entailed perennial governance by a small self-appointed group of people, with a degree of privilege for their organised followers and disbursement of some benefits to the public in exchange for obedience. Those objecting or seen as natural enemies, were made to bring special sacrifices, some of the ultimate kind. In the irresistible march of history towards an ideal society, old antithetic concepts were being overpowered and shed as the community sought to adapt itself to new prescriptions. A new man of socialism was said to be emerging, caring little for national sovereignty in face of the dominant attraction of proletarian internationalism, contemptuous of political pluralism when the advantages of scientific government by a perennial ruling clique were lavished on him, and scornful of social reformism when contrasted with the surgical immediacy of revolutionary solutions.

Strange as it did seem to the unfading benefactors, not everyone enjoyed the process and the prospect, albeit for different reasons. For the Yugoslavs, bootlicking soon became a perverse mannerism on which to build international solidarity, and then they had enough brain power to experiment in a different social arrangement even if they poured some old wine into the new bottle. Even in the country,

1

where the brave new world was the nearest to completion, did a brave peasant muster enough courage and wisdom to prune the tree which his predecessor implanted into a fertile soil. But he did not dare to sink the saw's teeth too deep into the branch on which he himself was sitting; others were to do it for him some eight years later, still leaving the mighty trunk erect. The Hungarians and the Poles rebelled for nationalist and other reasons and, unlike the Yugoslavs, had to pay a price for the ingratitude: the first in a conflagration and the latter in hopes betrayed. The Albanians opted to go it alone because the new red pope was not popish enough.

The Czechoslovaks were slow in realising that they must seek to adapt the new system before it adapts them. Over a period of twelve years, from 1956 to 1968, they made many steps towards what they started with, a working model of three coexisting ideologies and modes of government—socialism, democracy and nationalism. They were lucky to be able to draw on the experience and theories of others, the Yugoslavs, the Poles and the Hungarians. The pitfalls of the past were to be avoided: not for the Czechoslovaks the complete break with Moscow Yugoslav fashion; not for them the emotional outburst à la the Hungarians; not in their scheme of things to allow a Gomulka to put the clock back once the euphoria died down; and certainly not their cup of China tea to make a revolutionary run for it in the Albanian manner. Theirs was to be an orderly and rational quest for greater economic efficiency, political justice and a measure of freedom. A peaceful transition from communism to socialism with at least some democracy retrieved on the way.

The Prague Spring was made possible by the gradual coalescence of a number of change-seeking groups, especially among economists, social scientists, writers and other artists, Slovaks, students and some progressive party functionaries. They worked through the communist party but in conjunction with, and under pressure from, the population at large. Some were more radical than others, and some were less sceptical than others, but they all believed that doing something was better than doing nothing, and he never fails who never tries.

The reformist alliance was socially composed of all classes in society, but with a clear preponderance of the intellectuals. What especially mattered was the accession to the reformist programme of a strong body of the so-called 'party intelligentsia', men with party cards in their pockets and a history of commitment to the communist cause, but educated in more or less traditional fashion to a multi-track view of the world, more and more often forgetting to put on the ideological blinkers. Some held power in the *apparats*, others were on the fringes of it, and yet others belonged to organisations that claimed autonomy against the party. Loyalties were in conflict, and with increasing frequency homage was being paid to common sense, moral commandment, conscience and even *esprit de corps* rather than to stale dogma and befuddled leaders.

The reform programme relied as much on faith that the circle of communist structures *could* be squared into a democratic frame as on the feeling that things *ought to* start moving and this was just about the only direction they could move in.

The communist party was to be democratised to the point where, while still remaining a vanguard, it would no longer be guided by the principles of democratic centralism.

The political system was to be reorganised to accommodate differing social, professional and political interests and creeds in a spirit of partnership, not under the communist whim.

The country was to be federalised into Czech and Slovak republics, and the other minorities were to receive wide-ranging cultural autonomy.

Human rights were to be guaranteed, popular participation in decision-making enhanced and victims of political persecution re-habilitated on the basis of both amends and reconciliation.

The conduct of the economy was to be separated from the party's sweet will and distanced from the meddling of the state through the endowment of enterprises with enough power to create a wholesome market under the umbrella of macro-economic planning on the one end and entrepreneurial self-management of the working collectives on the other.

Culture was to be free and protected from the two *diktats* of commercialisation and party interference; science was to be liberated from political tutelage.

Externally, Czechoslovakia was to preserve her ties with the USSR and the bloc while pursuing a more active foreign policy, particularly in Europe, with regard to small and medium-sized countries and by projecting Czechoslovak culture abroad; free flow of information and travel across national boundaries was to be safeguarded.

There was to be no ideological or philosophical monopoly; Marx-ism, still recognised as the party's underlying set of beliefs and methodological directives, was to be understood as a *philosophia semper reformanda*, a living organism which can only stay alive if it enriches itself.

When Antonin Novotný could be suffered no more and every other contender in the heavy-weight category ran into an unscalable wall of opposition by all the other contenders jointly and severally, or was simply found wanting against the checklist of indispensible qualities, they anointed an honest man from Slovakia, a villager at heart but also a franc-tireur and a loyal son processed through the Soviet educational system up to the High Party School and seasoned in *apparat* posts. An intelligent if unsophisticated person, a good listener to others, with an

3

open mind, perhaps a little too hesitant in making difficult decisions lest he tread on someone's toes, a trifle overwhelmed by the august office at hand, but with a disposition to apply himself to innovative tasks. We will help you, Sasha, they said. And they did, each in his own way. Smoke rose from the central committee stack to herald the filling of a vacancy, and Prague Spring was under way.

Not quite. It took almost two months before the reformers interested in changing more than just a few rubrics in the personal roster realised that there was really enough room at the top to launch a new course, not just to patch things up. Two other political actors came to the same conclusion almost simultaneously: the Soviet leadership and the Czechoslovak people. Hence the definition of the Prague Spring as an intersection of three force fields: the reformers, the Kremlin and the populus. Not one saw eye to eye with the other two and none was internally united but, as time went by, the divide opened between Moscow and its agents on the one side and the reformers and the public on the other. From a crack it became a crevice, and finally a chasm.

One thing is certain, the Czechoslovak reformers did not want to break away. They knew that the time was not auspicious enough to play a Yugoslavia and they did recall the punishment meted out to Hungary. They thought that the men in Moscow would understand that all they wanted was to make socialism work, communist party and all, in a different way but still in cooperation with Big Brother. Moscow on the other hand saw the logic of reform leading Dubček irretrievably astray and with him a country where the foot of communism had once made an imprint and which could set an example to others. The first golden rule of communist government is that you do not let go what you have. Exceptions are precious few. The second dictum is that you protect from infection what you have. There are various ways how to go about both, but fraternal assistance, otherwise also known as military intervention, is the *ultima ratio*.

Part One

Intervention and compromise

August 1968–April 1969

ONWARD SOVIET SOLDIERS

And so they came, under the cover of darkness in that short August night, rolling over the friendly borders from the Soviet Union, East Germany, Poland and Hungary, and flying in from Bulgaria. The military machine of the Soviet Union, enhanced by contingents from its client armies, became engaged in an active exercise in Eastern Europe for the fourth time in the past quarter century.

The first intervention, sometimes not counted as such and all but forgotten, helped install communist regimes in the area at the end of the war. It was a dual-purpose operation then. Soviet military presence in a territorial belt stretching from the middle of the Baltic coastline down to the southernmost corner of Bulgaria marked the defeat of Nazi Germany. Hitler's *Drang nach Osten* ended in Stalin's *Drang nach Westen*. Historians agree that without it the communist governments would hardly have had a chance in Poland, East Germany, Hungary, Romania and Bulgaria. In Albania Stalin acted through the good offices of his Yugoslav allies. Tito grew powerful enough to enforce an essentially Soviet-type system single-handed, but he too accepted the Red Army's show of strength in Belgrade.

Most of Czechoslovakia was freed from fascism by the Soviet army, and Soviet soldiers stayed for over six months. In their footsteps, as they progressed from East to West, a powerful communist organisation sprang into being, intertwined with emergent local government, to establish a power base for the political struggles to come. Gratitude to the hero in a Soviet military uniform blended with recognition of communist organisational aptitude. The Czechoslovak Communist Party was the party of Stalin whose warriors swept away the local Hitlers and their stooges. By the end of 1945 Soviet troops departed for home, leaving behind a plainclothes army of 800,000 members of the communist party. For good measure, they never let go of Transcarpathian Ruthenia, a part of the pre-war Czechoslovak state, now annexed to the USSR in highly irregular circumstances. That act, a jumping of the gun in view of Edvard Beneš' promise that cession would be effected amicably and in a civilised manner as soon as the native parliament could be told to so decide, is hardly explicable outside a military interventionist framework.

To be sure, Soviet military imposition represented but one, somewhat blurred factor in Czechoslovakia's accession to the emerging bloc. Masses of literature have by now filled library shelves to explain, castigate and excuse the development, but for our purpose it is enough to simply remember that there had been a Soviet military intervention which concerned Czechoslovakia already once before

7

1968.[1] The communist party did all it could, and more, to stress again and again its salutary anti-fascist aspect while shying away from its importance for the communist fortunes of the future. As time went by and one-party rule revealed more of its objectionable face, the memory of Soviet military presence looming over the cradle of post-war East European regimes has left an increasing section of the public, including a number of communists, with a bitter aftertaste or, at least, a mixed feeling about its blessing.

When Soviet armour went into action for the second time, in East Berlin in June 1953, Czechoslovakia was so deeply enmeshed in Stalinism that it did not seem to matter. The grip of Soviet-type communism over the political structure of the country was near total, in spite of the deaths of Stalin and Gottwald a few months earlier. Neither had public opinion any opportunity to express itself; the whole gamut of non-governmental organisations had died a thousand deaths and private reactions could not be gauged in any way. The use of Soviet troops to quell workers protesting against high work norms and miserable working conditions in East Germany sunk into the general collective mind of the Czechs and Slovaks, whatever station in life they occupied, as little more than a confirmation of the firmness with which the bloc was ruled.

Hungary in 1956, a near-conventional warfare against the population on a massive scale, was different because by then a jolt had been administered in the form of Khrushchev's secret speech and the Czechoslovak party-based monolith had begun to show signs of uncertainty. The year 1956 was a watershed for East European communism, and it has never been entirely the same since then. In Czechoslovakia the combined effects of the 20th congress of the Soviet Communist Party, the Polish events and the Hungarian revolution had remarkably little repercussion in the way of direct action. Only the spell was broken and the bell sounded for the beginning of a critical evaluation of communist theory and experience, even if the critics came from the ranks of writers and some social scientists and not, as in Poland and Hungary, of economists or even members of the high party establishment. The main lesson which the budding Czechoslovak reformists were to draw from the seeming success of the Polish 'October' and the abysmal failure of the Hungarian revolt was that cautious manoeuvring brings fruit, but precipitous action invites disaster.

Then a few years later, events in Poland and Hungary took a different turn which invalidated the initial conclusion. Gomulka busily, if gradually, ran down the attainments of 1956 even though he seemed to have been given elbow-room for reform by Moscow, while Kádár healed the wounds inflicted on his people by the dogs of war surprisingly fast, even setting out on a more innovative course.

Rebellion and defeat were perhaps not so disastrous after all. At the turn of the 1950s the experience of the recent past was difficult to appraise: compromise looked like the safer road to liberalisation at first but turned out more dangerous if understood as a sustained policy content; military defeat bore the hallmark of catastrophe initially but eventually gave rise to a slow rebirth of reformism—as if Moscow wanted to make up for the harshness of its previous action. The victors became the vanquished and *vice versa*. As if the Soviet Union repeated the well-publicised American sin of treating its victims with greater magnanimity than its co-victorious allies.

All this speculation, of course, formed a kind of background awareness, or part of it, which made uncertain the outlook of any action which the Czechoslovak reformers might wish to take. The looming presence of Soviet military might on the East European horizon remained unchanged, but by the early 1960s Czechoslovakia had a reform-orientated faction among members of the communist establishment and, above all, times were seen to be changing for the better. The international climate jerkily improved. For all his gambles, Khrushchev, and even his successors, appeared to be pressing for greater efficiency in the running of their systems. Memories of Stalin and of past Soviet military clampdowns were receding. The years of 1945, 1953 and even 1956 seemed to hold little relevance to what the Czech and Slovak reformers were doing in the 1960s. We all were convincing each other that, while circumspection was still advisable, the world had already changed and so had Moscow. Both became more sophisticated. Events in Czechoslovakia acquired a momentum of their own; surely they will result in a new solution, unhaunted by the ghosts of the past.

The ghosts turned out to be real enough when it came to the crunch. Soviet tanks were rolling once again. In the night of 20 August 1968 the largest Soviet military force on the move since the Second World War crossed into Czechoslovakia. The first wave, soon to be followed by another and yet another, consisted of some 100,000 men deployed in Russia, 70,000 from among those stationed in East Germany, about 40,000 Polish troops, 10,000 each of Hungarian and East German soldiers, and 5,000 specially airlifted Bulgarians.[2]

Militarily, the ground was prepared reasonably well and no resistance on the part of the Czechoslovak army was expected. Almost exactly the same number of troops were sent in initially as there were Czechoslovak soldiers in arms. It is a well-established military fact that, even with the advantage of surprise (which after all could not have been total), the attacker has to outnumber the defender to guarantee success, especially if the intention is to complete the operation swiftly and without causing a great mess. But of course the thrust of the Czechoslovak military layout was pointing westwards for over twenty years and no intelligence activity, let alone manoeuvre, had ever been undertaken against a potential enemy in the East. Even a lesser force could occupy the country where the possibility of a shoot-out was virtually nil. And yet, Moscow saw it necessary to go on building up its expeditionary force inside Czechoslovakia for at least a full week following the invasion day, from the initial 230,000 to over half a million. At the same time the invasion troops were being moved about inside the country and some of them withdrawn, both the non-Soviet and the Soviet contingents. Quite obviously, the invasion was an exercise in military overkill which, however, had only limited military aims. Even a simple evaluation of the operation on the basis of troop numbers must lead to the conclusion that, whatever military aspects may have been in the minds of the Soviet leadership, the invasion of Czechoslovakia was a political act.

Some other facts point in the same direction. No case is on record of Warsaw Pact troops trying to force their way into Czechoslovak military compounds in the early invasion days, with the exception of some airfields. The invasion was supported from the air, but only in that advance troops were brought to Prague and logistics personnel was landed at various points to control subsequent operations. Large zones under Czechoslovak military control along the country's borders with West Germany and Austria were initially left un-occupied, presumably to allay Western fears of a spillover. Some of the best-trained Czechoslovak forces were thus unaffected by what was happening in the hinterland for days, which could have been vital if a regrouping for armed resistance had ever been contemplated.

Furthermore, those of us who had witnessed the invading forces first-hand in Prague and elsewhere can tell endless stories about Soviet officers on armoured carriers waving pieces of paper with instructions to locate and seize such highly non-military targets as institutes of the Academy of Sciences and editorial offices of newspapers. Neither did we think very highly of the quality of the equipment used, a point on which Western military experts and scholars disagree with us. And yet, a typical Soviet tank, such as were used *en masse* in Prague, was a formidable enough but still rough-hewn affair with two spare barrel-shaped diesel-oil canisters attached on a wooden plank at the back. The five-odd juggernauts which caught fire in the vicinity of Prague Radio were not shot at by counter-revolutionaries; fuel leaking from the cumbersome vessels was simply set alight, that was all. Many more stories circulated which were more difficult to verify, about failing radio communications between groups of tanks which had to be compensated for by the firing of blanks from the tank guns, and about the uncanny resemblance of submachine guns to those which the Soviet soldiers' forefathers wielded in the last days of the anti-Hitler war. Finally, it soon became apparent that food and sanitary

10

supplies did not keep pace with the hurtling of manpower and armour, either because it was believed that the half-million extra mouths could and would be fed from local sources or simply because someone goofed. Even if the former was the case it points to a serious misreading of the situation. As it turned out, the figure of a Soviet soldier almost reduced to tears by hunger became all too familiar to be easily forgotten.

Much more could be said that was very acutely felt and observed by the Czechs and Slovaks during the invasion week, even though the merciful passage of time has on the one hand consigned some of the experiences into oblivion while elevating others to the realm of folklore where additional embellishment becomes almost as important as the original fact. The real reason for citing eye-witness recollections here is simply to point out that the operation was a political one, with the army being sent in on a mission with a set of non-military instructions as to its behaviour. The troops could no doubt support themselves by simply confiscating food. This they were apparently expressly forbidden to do, and so we can still recall the two Soviet soldiers with dangling submachine guns who walked into a bakery store full of fresh and nice-smelling bread and asked humbly to be given some. When the request was turned down, they walked out again, disappointed and visibly moved by the unmistakable hostility of the customers and staff. The Soviet Union did not wage war on Czechoslovakia in August 1968. It applied its troops as an instrument to resolve a political issue. The Soviet military, unlike in East Germany in 1953 and in Hungary in 1956, was ordered by the party leaders to behave in a non-military fashion, observing rules designed for a political game.

This is not to say that there were no casualties, such as an operation of this magnitude, even if masterminded with utmost restraint and under explicit instruction not to use fire power, must have produced. A typed copy of the official survey of casualties from 20 August to 3 September 1968, which the Czechoslovak government undertook but never published, is in existence. It says that 72 Czechs and Slovaks died as a result of direct action by the invading forces, including 45 shot dead, 25 killed by military vehicles and two of other unspecified causes. Divided by regions, 23 died in Prague, 10 in North Bohemia, nine each in South Moravia and East Slovakia, eight in West Slovakia, six in Central Slovakia, five in Central Bohemia (excluding Prague), and two in South Bohemia. There was no loss of life in West and East Bohemia and North Moravia. In addition 267 persons suffered heavy injuries and 422 were wounded slightly. The invading troops were observed shooting up premises and other inanimate objects in 158 cases; 200 accidents were caused by military vehicles; and there were six fires or explosions. Considering the size of the invasion and the excitable effect it undoubtedly had on both the soldiers and the

Czechoslovak civilians, these figures, while obviously regrettable, are far lower than would have been the case if either shooting orders had been issued or armed resistance offered.

This line of argument can be pursued further. In addition to military objects, another important area which was evidently declared 'no go' for the invading armies were the factories. As far as one can ascertain there was no attempt to scale any factory gate and if a few exceptions to this rule did occur the basic policy directive must be considered proven on the strength of overall experience. An ideological explanation, in addition to political foresight, is easy to deduce: Soviet workers and peasants clad in military uniforms should not be seen battling with their Czechoslovak class brothers because, so the official argument went, the conflict was not between them. Many Czechoslovak workers expected their factories to be occupied and in fact locked themselves in, ready to offer resistance. Others went into the streets where they joined the throngs of people and in doing so they became undistinguishable from the 'counter-revolutionaries' with other class origins on whom blame was laid for the invasion in the first place. So, not only was the invasion not to be a 'military war'; it was not to be an internecine war within one and the same class either, again unlike Budapest in 1956.

All over the country, and in Prague more than elsewhere, people talked to the first contingent of Warsaw Pact soldiers in an effort to persuade them about the wrongness of the invasion. Many spoke Russian and where words failed, gestures and chalk signs became expressive enough. The Bulgarians, incidentally, were said to be the most difficult to get the message through to. Not that the Russians were keen on debates, although one heard about feelings of remorse and shame being vented by some, and stories about suicides and executions of waverers were plentiful. Mostly they listened impassively, repeated stock phrases about counter-revolution and fascism, often in connection with West German imperialistic designs, quite a few produced copies of *Pravda* from which they were willing to read out long justifications, and some called their officers and political commanders to do the talking on their behalf. Then, two or three days later the citizens of Prague noticed that new faces had been brought in, with a far greater proportion of non-Russian features, presumably Central Asian or Siberian, and with a lesser knowledge of the Russian language or at least that version of it which the Czechs were capable of mustering. No one quite knows why the Czechoslovaks began the futile debating exercise in the first place, although once it started the loyal communication media endorsed it, but from the Soviet reaction it became clear that the troops had not been sent in as roving ambassadors of the one and only true communist cause, enjoined to explain it to the deviationists. The invasion may have been political but it was not to be a dialogue.

In fact, come to think of it, the military arm which the Soviet might projected into Czechoslovakia was remarkably inactive. It did not fight and it did not talk. Even the alleged wave of arrests, feared so much in those days, remained confined to relatively few individuals. Contrary to reports and rumours circulating in Czechoslovakia, neither the dreaded military police nor the KGB hunted for suspects behind the protective cover of military armour. Soviet and East German news media wrote scarifyingly that 40,000 counter-revolutionaries were loose in Czechoslovakia and had to be rendered harmless, but the net cast to apprehend them was so wide that only less than a dozen top party leaders got caught in it. The invasion was not a police raid as it is normally understood.

Once again, the Czechoslovak government's confidential survey of casualties and incidents, cited above, records cases of arrest, detention and kidnapping of Czechoslovak citizens by the invading forces. There were 172 such cases in the whole of the country between 20 August and 3 September 1968, but only eight individuals remained unreleased on the latter date.

Little shooting, little talking, few arrests. An army of 500,000 was transferred from one part of the communist orbit into another, to do what? Just to be there and be seen to be there? Perhaps the list of premises which the troops actually occupied will provide a clue. First and foremost, the operation was obviously directed against three centres, all in Prague, which in a communist system comprise the peak of the pyramid of power—the party secretariat, the Prime Minister's office and the Ministry of the Interior. Almost simultaneously, but not quite, the buildings of the communications media were seized, beginning with the radio and the party newspapers and followed by others. At the same time, the various intellectual strongholds became the target, such as the social science institutes and the writers' union. On the other hand, the castle (the president's seat) and the National Assembly remained free, although surrounded. The post office was taken almost *en passant*, but the automatic telephone exchange continued to work. Military presence was set up at railway stations and airports but disruption to traffic was either slight or short-lived except to international connections.

The rationale which seems to be emerging from the actual conduct of the invasion points to a high degree of instrumentality. Armed forces were used as a means towards the achievement of essentially non-military objectives, namely the removal from power of a small group of people from among the top party and state leadership circle, while at the same time disseminating physical fear in the population, especially the intellectual community, in a vigorous and overwhelming way, yet without actually inflicting or provoking bloodshed.

13

A group of commandos could have achieved the first goal perhaps more effectively and certainly at lesser expense, but of course it could not intimidate the public and convince large segments of it that any real continuation of the reformist course was futile. The main purpose of stopping reform required *both* the elimination of change-orientated leaders *and* discouragement of others. As a logical consequence, military invasion should have been followed by the installation of a new leadership, willing to reverse the reformist policies.

Moscow must have been aware of the widespread popularity and commitment to the reformist cause not only among the population but also in the machinery of power. As close and anxious observers of the Czechoslovak scene, especially since the liberalisation course gathered momentum around the mid-1960s, the men in the Kremlin also knew that old-timers, with vested interest in the orthodoxy of politics, had not been completely eliminated from the organs of the party and the state. It was therefore only natural that they would expect the post-reformist leadership to emerge from their ranks. Nevertheless, once-and-for-all surgery was probably not intended because, unlike Dubček and his five colleagues from the party praesidium, reformist politicians in regions and districts were not being removed in the first invasion days. The idea must have been that of a period of transition from reformism to a more orthodox form of governance under a new domestic leadership responsive to Moscow's interpretation of what reform was, and was not, tolerable. The more committed reformers in the lower echelons of the hierarchy would be either brought to heel later or gradually replaced.

On the strength of what eventually happened after the installation of the Husák regime in April 1969, one cannot escape the conclusion that this was not such a bad plan and it would have probably worked. The reformist programme had still been a rather shaky edifice, much of it on the drawing board. Many functionaries in regions and districts had joined the reformist alliance only half-heartedly and because they had been used to obey orders from Prague anyway. One suspects that there would not be a shortage of willing hands ready to help dismantle the half constructed building of Reform Communism. If only there did not have to be a military intervention!

But the invasion could not be dispensed with because the expectations of the nation, as against the *apparats*, had already reached a point from which even the most skilful group of leaders could not stage a return without an accompanying show of force. Moscow was right in concluding that the party-state apparatus was no longer the sole governor of the country; the people had attained a measure of erratic and emotional participation in public matters of which they could only be deprived by a large-scale display of force and widespread experience of fear.

The Soviet leadership resorted to armed intervention not because of inherent bloodthirst but because it saw no other way of arresting the development of the Czechoslovak political system into a non-Soviet variety.

The Dubček leadership kept assuring Moscow that the end result of systemic reforms would still be a kind of socialism, friendly to and allied with the Soviet Union. Moscow saw no guarantee that this would be so, feared the contrary, and of course no guarantees could anyway be given and the fears could not be dispelled.

The limits of tolerance applied by Moscow to its East European client states must ultimately remain a matter for speculation, and they will always depend on a number of factors peculiar to country and time, and on the nature of the leadership of the day in the Kremlin. One has the feeling that Moscow is prepared to tolerate a great deal in the way, for example, of economic reform, style of government, level of western influence on popular taste and pastime, even ideological benevolence. But certain things are kept out of bounds and even discussing them in a mild and innocuous manner must make Mr Brezhnev raise his impressive eyebrows in suspicion. To this category belong changes which lead to a relaxation (let alone abandonment) of the leading role of the party, including all and sundry forms of self-management and 'partnership' with non-party organisations and institutions. Almost equally imprecatory are those human rights and freedoms which permit the public to receive and import un-authorised information, including free discussion of basic political and systemic issues, although obviously there are different shades of liberality to which the communist party of a Soviet type is prepared and allowed to go in this respect.

Unfortunately for them, Czechoslovaks chose precisely the impermissible as the pillars of their reform and there was no way in which they could convince Brezhnev that the system would remain socialist. What, after all, is socialist for them need not be socialist for him. He already had had thoughts about detente prompted by a complex variety of reasons with which the moral commandments of the Czechoslovak 'socialists with a human face' were not even remotely connected, and he knew full well that a process of international relaxation and wheeling-dealing would make it more difficult to keep an aberrant Czechoslovakia straight. He could not afford to wait much longer.

In this light it is almost superfluous to indulge in speculation about the possible outcome of the Prague Spring without a military intervention. Would it or would it not evolve into a democratic, yet communist-run state? Is such an animal at all possible, or, to put it differently and more to the point, is it possible for an East European country to evolve into such a system while remaining in the Soviet orbit? Ten years later the Communist Parties of Italy, Spain, Japan, France, Britain, to name but a few, are posing for their members and the world at large target images of a social arrangement which is not dissimilar from the basic desiderata of the Prague Spring reformers. The cardinal difference lies in the points of departure: Soviet suzerainty for the Czechoslovaks in 1968, western democracy for the Italians *et al.* of today. Thus Eurocommunism is and at the same time is not the same thing as the Prague Spring, and what was impossible for the older of the two may be achievable for the younger one. Both are the illegitimate offspring of a scandalous marriage between democracy and communism. One of the parents strangled the first-born but has hands not long enough to lay them on the other.

THE ACTORS ACT

Warsaw Pact soldiers were of course not the only actors in the unfolding drama but for some time they were to remain in the centre of the stage, for all the world to see. Their confrontation with the Czechoslovak public was shaping history in a way which their political masters in the Kremlin had not expected. The nation was not immediately afraid, only embittered and furious. But the real issues were to be decided elsewhere, behind the facade of futility which the military saturation had painted red.

We do not know the details of the Soviet scenario or the fall-back plans and in most of the explanations offered so far, some of them diligently and painstakingly put together from a minute investigation of the chronology of the fatal night and the ensuing few days, there are weak spots inviting counter-argument.

If, as most students of the period suggest, the diehard faction in the Czechoslovak Communist Party praesidium had foreknowledge of the invasion and if it had been programmed to ouvote Dubček simultaneously with the start of the occupation in order to issue an official 'invitation' to the troops, then it must be said that they acted with curious lack of energy and determination. Adequate records exist of the praesidium meeting on 20 August to show that *before* the news of the invasion reached the praesidium members at about 11.40 p.m., the pro-Moscow faction had largely confined itself to pressing for a change of the agenda. Admittedly, the Situation Report and the special Kolder-Indra position paper which they wanted to discuss would have given them opportunity to criticise the Dubček line, but it is doubtful that such a discussion could have led to the First Secretary's replacement by someone with command over enough votes in the praesidium to effect such a momentous decision as a formal go-ahead to the juggernaut. If the Kremlin believed in the likelihood of this course, it had most certainly been misinformed about the real balance of forces and states of mind.

The notion that a precipitous change of policy and change of cadres could be effected *after* the news of the invasion had come, seems also to be disproved by actual events in the praesidium meeting room. Smrkovský's later description is detailed enough, and another authoritative version became available two days after the event, to permit a fairly safe judgement.[3] For about an hour after Černík heard the news on telephone and broke it to the praesidium, the debate was chaotic. At no point did however anyone from the diehard faction propose Dubček's replacement and a *post hoc* legitimation of the invasion, a course of action which they were supposed to advance according to the

17

many interpretations of the Soviet scenario in the West. Bilak, Kolder, Jakeš and the others (non-praesidium members were free to speak, but not to vote) were procrastinating, according to Smrkovský's account. This I believe to be the clue to what the real plans were: the issue was to be decided elsewhere while the praesidium was stalemated.

The praesidium of the Czechoslovak Communist Party did no longer matter much, it had by then been discounted by the engineers of the invasion as an unreliable body. Moscow's agents in and around the praesidium were just putting obstacles in the way of a forthright condemnation of the invasion, but they were not positively striving to shape events, and had evidently not been asked to do so. When it came to voting on the condemnatory resolution, drafted by Mlynář, they objected to the section which called the invasion an infringement of the Warsaw Pact and of the international legal norms, not apparently to the first paragraph stating that the troops had invaded the country without the knowledge of the constitutional and party organs, although eventually their four votes (Bilak, Kolder, Švestka and Rigo) were cast against the entire resolution. (Seven members of the praesidium were in favour.) Some half-hearted attempts were made by the pro-Soviet Minister of Telecommunications, the director of the Press Agency and the editor of *Rudé právo* (Švestka) to block the dissemination of the praesidium statement, but to no avail and in a lonely-wolf fashion, unsupported by the muscle which would have been necessary to get an alternative statement through the media. In fact, Švestka left the praesidium for the *Rudé právo* office (less than five minutes' walk away) almost immediately after the condemnatory vote, but a workers' delegation from *Rudé právo* arrived at the Central Committee about an hour later and informed Smrkovský that Švestka ordered the presses *which were already printing the praesidium's statement* to be stopped and *was sitting in his office and formulating a new statement*. Moscow's men in the Czechoslovak praesidium did not even have a statement of their own![4]

In fact, several pro-invasion statements existed: a Soviet official one (though issued by TASS, not the praesidium of the Soviet Communist Party), a proclamation addressed to the population by the commanding officer of the invading forces, and an unsigned alleged invitation on behalf of Czechoslovak 'communists-internationalists', not to mention authoritative and lengthy articles in the Moscow *Pravda*. They were, however, publicised outside the official Czechoslovak channels and Moscow's allies in the Czechoslovak party's praesidium appeared to be blissfully ignorant of them.

What kind of a political solution did, then, Moscow have in store, and who were the people to push it through? The key name in context appears to be that of Alois Indra, not a member of the praesidium but a party central committee secretary in charge of the apparatus in regions, districts and localities. His name crops up in several critical situations.

He disappeared from the central committee building when the condemnatory statement had been adopted, at about 1.30 a.m. and repaired to the Soviet Embassy. If the anti-Dubček coup was to be engineered through the Czechoslovak Communist Party, Indra's place at that critical moment would surely be at the telex centre in the central committee headquarters, commanding the various levels of the party *apparat*.

Indra's name was invoked as the person in charge of a revolutionary tribunal to pass judgement on the 'revisionists' when Dubček, Smrkovský and others were arrested by a group of Czech secret service agents under the protective eye of Soviet army officers.

And he personally, in the company of others, called on President Svoboda on 21 or 22 August to seek an appointment of a 'workers' and peasants' government' with himself at the head. He was recognised by others as Moscow's choice for this key post, albeit grudgingly by some, for example Oldřich Pavlovský. Indra himself was asked about the 'worker-peasant government' when he recovered from his illness (at the end of the Moscow talks on 25 August) and spoke at a semi-public party meeting in the Pilsen Škoda Works on 3 February 1969. (The quotation is from a transcript of the proceedings made by a Dubček sympathiser; it has not been published in full.) Indra said: 'After only some of the party secretaries remained in Prague on 21 August, we took part in a meeting in the Praha Hotel. There we resolved that a party congress should not be convened. In the afternoon we went to the Soviet Embassy for information. Then we went to see President Svoboda with a proposition that the government and a section of the party representatives should join forces and constitute a worker-peasant government. The president is entitled by constitution to authorise such a thing. He, however, decided otherwise'.

In the light of this the most likely political scenario to accompany the military thrust could be summarised as follows:

1. The praesidium of the Czechoslovak Communist Party was to be rendered ineffective by bringing to a head internal strife between its 'conservative' and 'progressive' members.

2. A new power centre was to be created under the nominal leadership of Alois Indra, either with the passive or active cooperation of President Svoboda.

3. This centre was to be styled 'a government' rather than a new party praesidium but was to include willing collaborators from among members of the party praesidium and the old government. Its creation should be followed by the formation of similar centres in regions, districts and localities, where Indra hoped to rely on his influence over the party hierarchy. A pro-Soviet change of the balance of forces in the

old party praesidium would presumably be effected only after the 'worker-peasant government' became operational.

4. The secret branch of the police was to form the main operative arm of the new power centre for the initial day or two, but it would be used sparingly and selectively against just the most proscribed reformers.

5. An effort was to be made to preserve constitutional continuity while gradually identifying and isolating 'counter-revolutionary' elements. The blank (unsigned) 'request for assistance' kept the door open to such continuity by presenting the party and the state as essentially 'sound', by not naming names (either of the purported right-wingers or the internationalists, thus showing how uncertain its Moscow authors had been about who was going to do what in the fluid and emotionally charged situation), by conceiving the proclamation as a rallying point for 'all patriotic forces', and by providing an escape hatch for troubled consciences in that it accepted the 'progressive January [i.e. reform-orientated] ideas that will lead us to the creation of a truly modern, rejuvenated and humane socialist society'.

Pelikán[5] says that I. Udaltsov, counsellor of the Soviet Embassy in Prague, had obtained the provisional consent of a group of people some weeks before the invasion that they would legalise the intervention *ex post facto* if and when Moscow decided to carry it out. This would explain why coordination was lacking between the Kremlin and its agents in the Czechoslovak Communist Party praesidium. They had been told that there was likely to be an invasion, but not when and what exactly they were to do. A rather curious way of running a show of this kind.

On many occasions, in the invasion week and later, the Soviet leaders and their allies in the Czechoslovak party stressed the theme of unity and avoidance of a fratricidal conflict. They did so with a varying measure of clumsiness and lack of tact, but the intention seemed clear. Everyone could still become a counter-reformer, or just about everyone. The reversal of radical reformism was to be accomplished briskly but painlessly, as a collective change of mind. Under the impact of the occupation—but without bloodshed!—and with the prodding from a somewhat reorganised party-state chain of command, the population would be induced to opt for the new course, if only because there was no alternative. Had this happened, it would have seemed to a casual observer that the nation simply shifted its loyalty a little. Indra and his colleagues would still call themselves reformers, only more circumspect and loyal ones.

That is why the troops did not shoot. That is why there were so few arrests and drastic acts of vengeance. That is why an early normalisation and withdrawal of troops were promised from the start. And that is how Moscow would have liked it to be.

It was not such a bad plan, benign in its disregard of democratic niceties, moderate in comparison with Hungary in 1956, and tolerant in its essential intolerance. A Brezhnev solution, not Stalin's or even Khrushchev's. But Moscow must have known that it was touch and go, a tightrope act. It came to grief over four factors which had either not been taken fully into account or got out of hand. Firstly, President Svoboda was found ready to go a long way towards adapting himself to the new situation, but not quite the whole way. Secondly, the reformist reconditioning of the party-state machinery had progressed far enough to make the *apparatchiki* resist the temptation of jumping back on the orthodox bandwagon with unseemly haste. Thirdly, the community of reform-seeking intelligentsia was able to speak out loud and clear through the communications media and in this way turn the tables on the normalisation planners: it was the pro-Moscow agents who became isolated rather than the purported 'right-wing extremists'. And fourthly, the identification of the public with the reformist course and the shedding of old customs of blind and uninformed obedience were much more complete than Moscow envisaged, and this identification transcended practically all class boundaries to the point where reclaimed orthodoxy lacked any usable social basis.

In the dead of night of 20 August, the first Moscow scenario was, however, still being acted out and the seeds of its failure were only being sown. The first phase entailed the incarceration of Alexander Dubček and five of his colleagues from the praesidium, Josef Smrkovský, Oldřich Černík, František Kriegel, Josef Špaček and Bohumil Šimon (a candidate member).[6] This in itself was a strange episode which tallies with the overall contours of what we have called the first version of the Soviet plan, but still poses as many questions as it provides answers when examined in detail.

The invasion by ground forces began at 11 p.m. on 20 August but a Soviet signal plane (or two) had been at Prague airport from 8.30 or 10 p.m. at the latest (reports vary). And yet airborne troops were landed only at 1.30 a.m. and Soviet Embassy cars guided military armour (and a Czech police group) to the Central Committee building as late as after 4 a.m. It takes at the most 40 minutes to drive from the airport to the embankment where the party headquarters are situated, especially at night when the streets are empty. If a group of marines—or whatever they are called in the Soviet army—had been despatched to corral the six hapless members of the praesidium at midnight, there would have been no condemnatory resolution from the highest party quarters which caused the invaders so much headache. Moreover, Černík was arrested in the government building, five minutes away from the Central Committee, at least an hour earlier, at 3 a.m. What kept them? Did they not know where the wanted men were? What sort of coordination was it with the diehards in the praesidium who were left to their own devices and did not even muster enough brains to pass the word to the Soviet Embassy that they were unable to reverse or block a public anti-Soviet statement? Or did Indra only manage to bring the bad news at, say, 2 a.m. and had Moscow to be contacted before any action against Dubček was undertaken? If this was so, another version of the initial plan is likely. The plan would hinge on Dubček's attitude to the news of the invasion. Had it been one of accommodation, albeit reluctant, he might have been left in charge and the slow strangulation of reformism would be masterminded through him, not through any new 'worker-peasant government'. This is what eventually happened anyway, and may be it was on the books from the start. Sasha Dubček (as he was known affectionately) would crumble and accept the inevitable. But Sasha did not crumble and so had to be taken to the Kremlin while the 'worker-peasant government' alternative was being tried out.

Be it as it may, the six saddened but still adamant protagonists were bundled away unceremoniously to the airport and after a longish wait flown via East Germany and Poland to Western Ukraine in eviscerated transport planes. There were two stopovers on the way and Smrkovský has interesting things to say about them.[7] For two days they were held incommunicado, seemingly forgotten by the Kremlin and for all that the public knew may have been summarily executed right away. Smrkovský's posthumously published interview[8] describes the ordeal vividly.

Back in Czechoslovakia the Soviet plans, whatever they were, began to go wrong. The reformist majority of the party refused to vacate the positions they had attained during the Prague Spring even under the dual pressure of Soviet military presence and the knowledge that their top people had been abducted. The pro-Moscow faction showed pitiful half-heartedness, inefficiency and lack of nimbleness. In reality they did nothing of substance, except staff a propaganda radio station in East Germany, a silhouetted television screen from the Soviet Embassy in Prague, and a pro-invasion newspaper distributed by Soviet soldiers and burned on the spot by the public. All three activities were worthless to the point of being counter-productive. An indecisive meeting of some central committee members, as if half-prepared to start buttressing orthodox positions inside the party, petered out without result, in spite of the presence of several high-ranking Soviet officers.

Prague Castle, with President Svoboda inside, was surrounded by troops, but messengers could get through and some telephones worked. The fact that Svoboda was not taken out of circulation together with Dubček, although he had become almost as symbolic to the liberalisation course as the party's First Secretary, must be significant. If we discount the proposition that Moscow simply felt respect for old age and the history of a veteran war hero, the only explanation is that there was a design in which Svoboda was to play a part. In view of his stature, it could not have been a minor role. Asked to authorise or even create a non-Dubček government, he is reputed to have said a firm no, even if the invitation came from Russia with love, conveyed by Ambassador Chervonenko, with Indra and Pavlovský probably at his side. But Svoboda did not refuse to talk to the Russians and volunteered to travel to Moscow, with a team of his choosing, to negotiate a way out of the situation as head of state, not as a prisoner in the castle of Czech sovereigns. He probably insisted already then, on 21 or 22 August, on Dubček's presence at the Moscow talks. If Smrkovský's timing is right, Dubček was allowed to telephone Černik in the afternoon of 22 August (they were kept in separate houses in Subcarpathian Ruthenia) to tell him that they were being summoned to Moscow.[9]

One wonders whether the suggestion of a Moscow trip really came from Svoboda or was indicated to him as something the Russians wanted him to put forward. But he did turn down the offer of becoming a king-maker on the spot and that was probably felt as a set-back. Svoboda, whose war-time association with the KGB was subsequently rumoured, was certainly an erratic character, no matter how firm and principle-minded he may have regarded himself. Bred on the ideas of Masaryk's democracy and in an uncomplicated military vein, he had managed to be loyal to Beneš and helpful to the communists at the same time from 1939 to 1948. Then he appeared to have put his money squarely on the risen star of the Gottwald regime, only to be thrown overboard with offensive contempt in 1951. His fall was admittedly cushioned enough in comparison with others to permit his return from the cold at Khrushchev's beckoning, but while he may have recovered his medals he did not climb any political ladders. Until, that is, the lot of the innovative Prague Spring leadership fell on the old veteran when their search committee combed the thin lines of potential successors to Antonín Novotný. He had just the right amount of everything in his past, what was publicly known of it; communist, yes, but not unduly so. The public loved him; he enjoyed late-age spotlights and committed himself to Dubček's cause to the hilt. After wartime distinction and February 1948, when he cast his dice with a communist six on each surface, the real moment of truth came in those crucial days of August 1968. By refusing to play Moscow's game with Indra, he put Brezhnev's original plan in jeopardy. By offering to go to Moscow and talk, he left the door more than slightly open. By accepting Brezhnev's alternative solution, with only slight re-servations, he almost completed his own transition from the reformist to the counter-reformist camp, but he did so gradually, not with the umseemly haste which Brezhnev may have expected.

Svoboda was not the only one who refused to play ball initially; practically the whole of the Czechoslovak Communist Party did the same. Another miscalculation? The extraordinary congress was too near—it was to be held on 9 September—not to tempt people who could summon the delegates to convene it ahead of time. It was the self-evident thing to do, and so the congress met under the protective wing of workers in a Prague factory on 22 August, with 1192 delegates out of 1543 present.[10]

The government held meetings denouncing aggression under the chairmanship of a lady minister, Mrs B. Machačová-Dostálová, who lived down the onus of orthodoxy in this one sweep but rejoined the loyal flock not much later. The National Assembly whose makeshift conference hall was encircled by Soviet troops sat for an uninterrupted seven days, producing resolution after resolution against the invasion and demonstrating constitutional continuity with the Prague Spring course. The Foreign Ministry fired off repeated protest notes to Warsaw Pact embassies and the Foreign Minister spoke in the same vein in the Security Council, having travelled to New York from his holiday in Yugoslavia.

Not even in the provinces did any anti-Dubček platform arise from among the party or local government ranks. Such bulwarks of simple pro-Soviet orthodoxy as the People's Militia, the party's own private army, while perhaps more reticent than others, issued statements opposing the invasion and reiterating support to Dubček.[11] Party committees in the Ministry of National Defence and the Ministry of the Interior expressed solidarity with the kidnapped leaders and pledged support to 'legal' organs of the party and the state.

In the case of the Ministry of the Interior, especially its secret police administration, the situation was, however, far from unequivocal. The public expression of disapproval of the invasion issued from the Ministry blanketed an obvious conflict between traditional policemen of the Stalinist variety, some of whom had been retired earlier in 1968 but now returned to their place of work, and the new and mostly young cadres brought into the service by Minister Josef Pavel, a firm supporter of Dubček. Pavel had of course little time in the short months of the Spring to rebuild a service which by the nature of things had been staffed for years with handpicked and ardent promoters of orthodoxy. A man who almost certainly was privy to the invasion secret before 20 August, Deputy Minister Viliam Šalgovič, headed the secret service and was dismissed as such only on 24 August. (In a twist of piquancy, typical of the past decade of Czechoslovak politics, the government meeting which fired Šalgovič was presided over by L. Štrougal, now Prime Minister, then deputising for Černík.) With his trusted underlings, Šalgovič selected the group of pro-Moscow

24

officers who arrested Dubček and his colleagues 'in the name of the revolutionary government led by comrade Indra'. The publicised statement condemning the invasion on behalf of the Ministry of the Interior did however express the true feelings of a number of persons in the Ministry and probably the majority of uniformed police.

Thus the only open endorsement enjoyed by the occupiers came from their own propagandists. No Czechoslovak party, state or public organisation went on record to join them. As if to ram the point home, a number of the pro-Moscow bigwigs felt it later necessary, or were told to do so, to proclaim publicly that they had not had a hand in the preparation of the invasion. Some formulations were, however, ambiguous: they simply declared that they were not traitors and had done nothing dishonest.

On the surface, then, the facade of party unity was complete. No one had any illusions about the allegiance to reformist policies of men like Bilak, Kolder, Švestka, Indra, Kapek and Šalgovič, and dissention of some sections of the coercive machinery of state from the general consensus was well known and accepted as a fact of life. But there was a great deal of idealism and euphoria about the total unanimity of the party. To imagine that unity of this breadth would survive for long in a party riddled with political opportunism and deeply inculcated ideological tenets was illusory.

Activity of the mass media during the invasion week deserves special mention although it is well known. Spectacular in the sense of providing the political currents and undercurrents with a public image, the work of Czechoslovak journalists in the press, radio and television was not only politically courageous and unequivocal, but also good journalism. Dogmatic critics have denounced this activity as something which the alleged counter-revolutionaries prepared in advance with the assistance and indeed under the command of imperialist 'centres'. It was also said to be anti-socialist because the newsmen usurped for themselves the roles of policy givers and executors, something which constitutionally forms the prerogative of the party and the state. The first accusation is nonsensical and anyone who was only slightly connected with the operation knows that what enabled the journalists to behave as they did were dedication, improvisation, ingenuity, lapses by the occupation forces and above all the sense of having a totally committed audience. On the second score, the fluidity of the situation obviously called for a certain measure of devolution of decision-making, but one would be hard put to discover in the mass of printed and broadcast material really important political instructions which were not just conveyed through the media either as a result of their being the official political line of the Prague Spring leadership or at the direct request of such organs of party and state which continued to exist, including the party central committee, and even the party congress, the government of the day which never resigned, and the parliament which was in session. There were no other bodies to exercise jurisdiction over the media.

A detailed survey of materials published in the Czechoslovak media in the invasion week was carried out by a group of students at the Institut für Zeitungswissenschaft at the University of Munich.[12] They found that all the material could be divided into two approximately equal parts of 'mediated' and 'original' contributions. Most comment fell in the first group and was contributed by people who were not journalists, while the second group, originating among the journalists themselves, showed a clear preponderance of straight news over comment. In fact, the journalists were contributing less comment, analysis etc. than they would normally be required to do. There was no shortage of pundits outside the journalists' ranks and it simply will not do to lay blame at the newsmen's door for pursuing their profession. To say that the journalists ruled the country for a week, as the 'normalisers' often asserted, is simply not true.

By the nature of things, journalism is an intellectual preoccupation and the majority of non-journalist contributors always derive from the intellectual classes. The Czechoslovak media did, however, pay a great deal of attention to other sections of the community, especially the workers, both during the Prague Spring and in the invasion week. Conversely it was the workers who in many instances gave shelter and assistance to journalists driven out of their natural habitats by the invaders. This interaction was in accordance with the thrust of the Prague Spring.

The invaders had to import their own publicity. At 5.20 a.m. on 21 August, even before the occupation of the country had been completed, a radio station calling itself *Vltava* began to broadcast from Dresden in broken Czech and Slovak. (My own recollection is that the voices of the first announcers sounded suspiciously like a caricature of the Sudeten German accent which had become part of rather unpleasant Czech folklore.) A day later two other stations, probably of the same provenance, came on the air, styling themselves *Záře* (Glow) and *Dělnický hlas republiky* (Workers' Voice of the Republic). An improvised television transmitter was installed in the premises of the Soviet Embassy in Prague, but first programmes showed only silhouettes of news readers, or carried their voice over still pictures of beauty spots, presumably lest they were exposed to public anger. Finally, on 30 August, foreign troops began to distribute a Czech-language news sheet called *Zprávy*, printed outside Czechoslovakia. The battle between the legal press and the imported one was uneven; if anything, the occupiers' media influenced public opinion in the opposite direction from the one for which they had been intended. They also virtually abdicated the role of providers of news, and purveyed mostly comment in the usual language of hack writers.[13] Professionally, *Zprávy* was inferior even to the clandestinely manufactured press of the pro-Dubček orientation, and abounded in Soviet-type clichés, some arising from hasty translation. One or two issues of a pro-Soviet paper calling itself *Rudé právo*, like the main party organ, were printed at an unknown place and in a small number of copies.

The existence of anti-occupation media with their two-way link with legitimate party organs and a massive audience, caused constant headache and irritation to the invaders because, as the Soviet leaders kept emphasising to their captive Czechoslovak counterparts, it represented an obstacle to ending the confrontation swiftly. They knew that once they became full masters in the country, the usual centralised network of controlled press would have to be restored, but in the conditions of the day they were helpless.

Neither could they do much about the popular outburst of anger short of ordering their soldiers to shoot into the crowds. Anyone who saw the multitudes demonstrating their disapproval, but also going about their own business or simply strolling with curious eyes around rows of Soviet tanks and troop carriers with soldiers armed to the teeth, will know that a few selective bloodbaths would have had the deterrent effect which the Soviets hoped to produce without them. But mayhem there was not, even if threats involving hecatombs of corpses allegedly came down from Brezhnev's lips more than once during the Moscow talks. Short of the curfew hours, the public had the right of way in the streets of Prague except where the physical presence of armour made passage impossible. General and complete opposition of the population could thus be demonstrated beyond reasonable doubt. Western journalists and tourists were in the country in large numbers and broadcasts by Czechoslovak radio and even television were regularly monitored abroad. It seemed impossible for Moscow to continue with its story of a mere 40,000 counter-revolutionaries crouching in dark corners while welcoming parties of innumerable internationalists conveyed gratitude to their armour-clad class brothers. More importantly, the political settlement which they were seeking would have to take into account the barrier of rejection, and the hand of the Czechoslovak leaders was bound to be strengthened by the near-absolute endorsement which they were getting.

So that was why a change in the original scenario was made. Smrkovský noted that the first decent and civilised meal which he and Černík were served in their captivity on Soviet territory materialised at lunchtime on 22 August, including a bottle of wine. Did it signify that their status changed back from counter-revolutionary criminals to that of constitutional representatives of an ostensibly friendly country? Later that day Dubček called Černík who told Smrkovský: 'Sasha spoke to Brezhnev; he is to go to Moscow and told me that someone else was to go with him, so I will join him'.[14] Thirty-six hours after the invasion Brezhnev was changing his tactics and offering meat, wine and a clean shirt to his prisoners. The change was gradual: Smrkovský, more objectionable to the Kremlin, was left lingering in the Carpathians for another twenty-four hours.

A number of writers have interpreted this change as a political failure of the invasion and a victory of the Czechoslovak people. A more cautious judgement may be advisable.

That the political plans of the Kremlin suffered a setback there is no doubt. Nevertheless, once frustrated, the Soviet leaders adapted themselves to the new conditions with speed and determination, without giving up more than an inch. Instead of betting on Indra and company, Moscow decided to turn Dubček and his reformist colleagues into the executors of an anti-reformist will.

Public opinion in Czechoslovakia had become extremely agitated about the fate of their six leaders, to the point where their personal fate acquired the proportion of a cardinal issue that could make or break progress towards 'peaceful' settlement. The Dubček men became symbols of liberalisation: with them, there would be freedom, without them, slavery. To return freedom incarnate to the people meant defusing an explosive situation. Otherwise things might really get out of hand and bloodshed might no longer be avoided.

This solution, as against the Indra variety, could have been mooted in the Soviet party praesidium even before the invasion, and perhaps kept in mind as an exigency, so suddenly did it become acceptable to the Soviet leadership. But even if it had not been contemplated in advance, its adoption on 22–23 August betrayed a stroke of genius. The Soviets had nothing to lose, except a little bit of face and a little time. Let the reformers clear up their own mess!

IN MOSCOW WITHOUT LOVE

One version of the Soviet plan was thus being given up, but the objectives stayed on the table. The Moscow 'negotiations' from 23 to 26 August reflected the situation. When put on paper, Soviet demands appeared unacceptable to the Dubček camp, but in the end they succeeded in changing them but a little, and even then only their verbal form rather than substance.

Brezhnev saw to it that the ranks of 'negotiators' were diluted on the Czechoslovak side: altogether some twenty people were brought in, many of them ardent supporters of the Russian line, others awakening to the harsh facts of life and opting for collaboration as the only course that could keep them in power which they had attained only during 1968, and yet others customarily bowing to Soviet attitudes.

Neither were the negotiations regular in form; groups of people got together to discuss things, but never talked to others; there was no regular agenda and timetable, people seemed to come and go at will, and Dubček himself was sick most of the time, lying in bed in one of the Kremlin's rooms, a broken man who moreover hurt himself when fainting in a bathroom.

The convinced reformers may have thought that the 'negotiations' concerned the survival of the Czech and Slovak nations, but in fact— and a sad fact it was—they only concerned their own survival in positions of quasi-power for the ensuing eight months. Ponomarev shrugged his shoulders when Smrkovský complained about the harshness of the Protocol: 'If you don't sign now, you will sign in a week's time. If not in a week, then in two weeks, and if not in two weeks, then in a month.'[15] He could have added that if five or six refused to sign at all, another ten or twelve would. Svoboda, Husák and probably Černík would have signed, not to mention Indra, Bilak, Kolder, Švestka, Rigo, Sádovský, Lenárt, Barbírek, Piller, Jakeš, Dzúr, Kučera and Koucký. As it turned out, all of them signed, including Dubček, Smrkovský, Šimon, Špaček and Mlynář. The only *refusenik* was František Kriegel, a physician, chairman of the National Front, member of the party praesidium, fighter in the International Brigades in Spain, lifelong communist—and the only Jew among them.

The others had to put their foot down somewhere, so they successfully opposed Soviet intentions not to allow Kriegel to return home with the rest of them. He was kept in a Kremlin police cell during the negotiations and was only allowed to see the others when the communiqué and Protocol were ready for signature. He sat down, put his glasses on, calmly read the documents, pushed them aside, said he would not sign, and was led away. But Brezhnev let him go in the end.

The two documents adopted in Moscow reflected Soviet aims as regards 'normalisation' of conditions in Czechoslovakia, and the willingness of the Czechoslovak leaders, albeit obtained under duress, to assist in the attainment of these aims. The communiqué which was made public on 27 August reiterated the validity of the Čierna and Bratislava resolutions and contained a strong pledge by the Czechoslovak side to take 'immediate measures' in the interests of socialism and the leading role of the communist party, and to strengthen ties with the USSR and other bloc countries. On its part the Soviet Union promised to collaborate with the Czechoslovak authorities in this direction, not to allow its troops to interfere in the internal matters of Czechoslovakia, and to withdraw them when the situation was normalised.

To preclude a repetition of the post-Čierna problems which arose partly from the differing interpretations which the two sides attached to concepts like 'interest of socialism' and 'immediate measures', a Protocol was appended to the communiqué, but not published. Its text has however become available in the West.[16] It contained 15 points of which the first expressed, in somewhat hazy form, what was to become known a month later as the Brezhnev Doctrine of Limited Sovereignty. Both parties pledged themselves to wage 'an implacable struggle against counter-revolutionary forces which is an international obligation common to all socialist countries'. Then, in fairly rapid succession and with the bare minimum of ideological jargon, there followed undertakings which the Czechoslovaks took upon themselves. In their entirety they represented the Soviet concept of 'normalisation' at this particular stage. The so-called 14th congress, held on 22 August in a Prague factory, would be declared invalid; all those in the way of a strengthening of the party's leading role would be dismissed from office; the information media would be put under party control; the social democratic party would not be permitted to function; the Warsaw Pact troops would eventually be withdrawn but in the meantime their stay would be coordinated with the Czechoslovak Army; measures in the media would be taken to preclude conflict between the troops and the population; pro-Soviet party officials would not be victimised; economic negotiations would start about more intense cooperation; the Warsaw Pact and other joint anti-imperialist ventures would be cemented; joint foreign policy would be pursued; the 'Czechoslovak Question' would not be pursued by Czechoslovakia in the United Nations; changes in some posts would be effected, including an examination of the activity of Czechoslovak ministers who were abroad during the invasion and reinforcements for the Ministry of the Interior; there would be further bilateral meetings in the near future; all contacts between the two parties after 20 August, including the Moscow talks themselves, would be kept strictly confidential; fraternal ties for eternity would be pursued.

However abhorrent the Protocol must have looked to the moderate reformers (there is no doubt that Smrkovský was sincere when writing about it in his 'memoir') and still more to their radical colleagues and the public at large (which however knew about it only from hearsay), it still represented only a kind of minimum programme for the immediately ensuing period. Worse was to come. The Protocol was probably not much different from a programme which Indra's 'worker-peasant government' would have been enjoined to accomplish, had it been set up. From this angle, the change from Indra back to Dubček looks a mere hiccup in Soviet plans, not derailing the overall designs.

Dubček's own feelings and thoughts were for several days heavily influenced by the shock he had suffered. His broadcast to the nation in the afternoon of Tuesday, 27 August, was still coloured by this emotional attitude and only during discussions with the praesidium and the central committee members elected at the clandestine party congress did he gradually recover composure and began to put together the outline of a policy to be pursued in the difficult times lying ahead. Eventually a concept did emerge from consultations between him and others, and by the end of the month it was coherent enough to be presented to a central committee meeting on 31 August. In the meantime some pressing changes of office-bearers were effected and a compromise solution found whereby 80 central committee members elected at the Vysočany congress would be coopted to the pre-invasion central committee.

In brief, the new line consisted of an attempted combination of negative action, such as was demanded in the Moscow Protocol against reforms and reformers that were unacceptable, with a positive development of those Prague Spring features which were not covered by the Protocol. Among the latter, Dubček pinned hopes above all on the continuation of the economic reform, changes connected with the federalisation of the country, cautious promotion of diversity inside the party, and a consultative relationship between the party and other segments of the public, such as the intellectual associations and emergent interest groups. Rehabilitation of victims of pre-1968 judicial malpractices would also go on. All this would have to be done under communist tutelage which the public would have to accept as a *sine qua non*. Innovation and initiative from outside the party would have to be curbed or, better said, chanelled through the party. It was not such a bad plan, and it did not go contrary to the script of the Protocol. What was not expressly forbidden in the Protocol was to be considered a legitimate pursuit. At a confidential meeting of staff in the central committee secretariat on 5 September, Dubček said: 'I am in a determined mood. We must believe in the victory of truth and common sense. We must feel ourselves as the proletarians who have nothing to lose except their fetters'.[17]

There were two mighty obstacles in the way on which the plan eventually faltered. The public was unwilling to put up with what they considered capitulation before an unjust *diktat*, and they would go on pressing the leadership for a vigorous continuation of some of the Prague Spring practices that were bound to be seen as contravening the Protocol. And the party, while still preserving a semblance of unity, had already been divided at the top between a faction which accepted not only the script but also the spirit of the Moscow Protocol, and the group around Dubček. The invasion and the Protocol gave a tremendous boost to the conservative faction. Both groups were in coalition, and the post-invasion power centre became much more of a battleground than it was previously. At the same time Moscow had propelled itself back into the position of a recognised supreme arbiter and day-by-day supervisor of Czechoslovak politics, a place from which it was being pushed out in the reformist period.

Few things are new under the sun. Moscow had already once before exercised decisive influence over an enforced coalition in Czechoslovakia, from 1945 to February 1948. In the end, Moscow's side inflicted a dramatic defeat on its partners and acceded to undivided power. Communism hates genuine coalitions; they are cumbersome and troublesome. Dubček and his friends were dreaming an impossible dream if they thought that they could go on governing in tandem with the Bilaks of the day. They could not win, and one suspects that at least some of them knew it deep in their hearts. One thing was not yet certain in these early days: who will be the new Gottwald to lead the true believers into battle that will consign Dubček and the entire Prague Spring to oblivion? Indra lost the first bid, and losers do not become pretenders again, but of course other candidates were vying for the honour. Not that the name was important, but a Gottwald there had to be.

WORLD REACTION

The non-communist world reacted to the invasion in a predictable way: the Soviet Union was verbally censured in the United Nations, some contacts already agreed or about to be finalised were cancelled or delayed and the protagonists of the game of detente sat back during the inevitable pause to contemplate the steps the would seek to take once the 'normal' pace of international relations was resumed. This is not a cynical or reproachful statement: nothing else could happen, and few Czechoslovaks, certainly not the reformers, expected that the West would do more than castigate the Soviet action. In his interview almost ten years later, Jiři Hájek, the then Foreign Minister, said: 'We did not expect the Western powers to act differently from how they actually acted. I had had a talk with Henry Kissinger in Marienbad in April 1968. He then confirmed that the existing division of the world was regarded by both sides as an element of stability based on peaceful coexistence. And that every disruption of the equilibrium would have to lead to unfathomable consequences'.[18]

The State Department denied that Soviet intervention in Czechoslovakia had been made possible through a tacit understanding between the two superpowers about 'spheres of influence' by stating that the United States had never negotiated any such division with anyone, and this was correct inasmuch as no written agreement to this effect existed. Everyone knew, however, that there were 'hot areas' on both sides of the East-West divide which the opposite power considered off limits for itself. The British Prime Minister (Harold Wilson) said that the invasion, which he condemned forthrightly, should not lead to a return to the 'frozen immobilism' of the cold war, and this was of course an equally logical thing to say, considering that the frozen immobilism of the East European *status quo* under *any* international climate was any way irreversible.

And yet, there were two aspects of the Soviet action against Czechoslovakia which influenced the Western world. It probably contributed to Richard Nixon's victory over Hubert Humphrey in the American presidential election of 5 November 1968, even if this factor has been progressively more and more overlooked by historians. No one can say whether a quarter million more voters would not have opted for Humphrey (considered 'softer' than Nixon) without the tangible expression of Soviet threat to democracy and freedom still fresh in their minds. (Nixon's majority was just under half a million.) But a possibility that they would have done so cannot be denied. So, in the quirky way in which history sometimes operates, America could have been spared Nixon. Secondly, the Western public made another

33

substantial step towards shedding illusions about the Soviet Union as being just another great power. The ideological attractiveness of the Soviet system to all but the already convinced followers was reduced to nil. But the Soviet Union could not have cared much about losing a little more of the moral credit which had been waning anyway. It may have even believed, not incorrectly, that future friendly deals between East and West, once detente got going again, would again encourage public respect.

Repercussions of the armed suppression of reformism in the communist movement have been discussed often and thoroughly.[19] Many Czechoslovak reformers drew encouragement from the belief that Soviet pressure on the Prague Spring would remain relatively moderate because of the impact which overt interference would produce in the international communist ranks. Moscow could not afford, so people in Czechoslovakia reasoned, another Hungary. This was a mistaken belief from the start, even if we accept Moscow's preference for a non-military solution. Soviet leaders made little secret from early on that on their list of priorities the preservation of a status quo in Eastern Europe figured firmly above their interest in Western communism.

Gomulka allegedly told the Czechoslovak leaders in Dresden as early as the end of March 1968 that 'socialism in Western Europe is frozen for at least fifty years—and so we are not interested in it, our interest lies in buttressing our Western frontiers, in consolidating our power where we hold it'.[20]

The Poles were also reputed to have held the same line when representatives of a number of communist parties met for consultations in Budapest at the end of September 1968. A confidential report by the Czechoslovak delegation (led by Lenárt) submitted for internal use on return, noted that some 18 parties among those present were critical of the invasion. The Poles allegedly told them: 'If you don't want to go along, don't! There may be only forty or fifty of us left, but at least we will be united'.[21]

Before the invasion Western communist attitudes to the reform process in Czechoslovakia ranged from utter condemnation to warm verbal support. But the process of differentiation was then only in the making; these were pre-Eurocommunist times. The act of invasion forced the parties to come into the open, and many did it gingerly. Others were ambivalent: on the one hand they criticised the invasion and on the other they stressed their solidarity with the USSR, the invader. Some of the parties actually split over the issue and in several of them the ideological division was later completed organisationally. Only a few came out forthrightly on the side of the Czechoslovak victims of aggression and stuck to their guns later. Even these, above all the Italians and the Spanish, did not choose to leave the Moscow-led movement on this occasion, but decided rather to work within it towards its transformation into a decentralised framework.

The maverick Spanish communist leader Santiago Carrillo wrote later in his *'Eurocommunism' and the State*:

> 'For us, for the Communist Party of Spain, the culminating point in winning our independence was the occupation of Czechoslovakia in 1968. ... Czechoslovakia was the straw which broke the camel's back and led our parties to say "No". That kind of "internationalism" had come to an end as far as were were concerned. ... True internationalism is and must be something else'.[22]

For a number of important Western communist parties life has indeed never been the same after 1968, and 'business as usual' with the Soviet Union has become either difficult or impossible to maintain.

On the other hand, it would be wrong to exaggerate the importance of the impact of the Prague Spring on a process which had been in train even before this. Czechoslovakia may have been the catalyst, but it was not the cause. Save for the verbal criticism and the reduction of the movement's propensity for joint statements, Moscow has not had to face any real difficulty in dealing with the Czechoslovak black sheep. The Kremlin strategists calculated their odds correctly. There was discomfiture and some loss of following but the movement survived. Above all, the Sino-Soviet cleavage remained manageable, despite the border flare-up in 1969. That event, surely, can be attributed to the Prague Spring only by a most oblique interpretation. China, while strongly condemning the invasion, could not possibly have come out totally on the defeated Czechoslovak reformers' side. Their ideological, political and economic tenets were even further removed from official Chinese dogmas than the Soviet theory and practice, especially at the height of the cultural revolution. And so it was left to Albania to make the most dramatic gesture of all. She withdrew from the Warsaw Pact, and got away with it, scot free. Unfortunately, as is so often the case with the Albanians, it did not matter. They had not been treated as members for quite some time anyway.

All this is not to say that the international dimension was irrelevant. In addition to serving as a touchstone and catalyst for the continuing process of diversification in the international movement, two other phenomena deserve attention: the reaching of maturity of dissent and opposition in the Soviet Union, and the conclusions which the Soviet leadership has drawn from the Czechoslovak experience for the building of a new Byzantium, as Alexander Yanov calls the entrenchment of Soviet power in areas it had already conquered.[23]

While dissenting views had been formulated by individuals in the USSR before 1968 and opposition to the regime on national and religious grounds had a long history, practically all students of the phenomenon agree that an important point in this development was reached in the same year which saw the brief flourishment and suppression of the Prague Spring, and that this coincidence is not entirely fortuitous. Soviet dissidents found the ideas of the Czecho-(slovak reformers capable of fertilising their own attitudes.[24] One of the results was the transition of Soviet *literary* samizdat to a more immediately *political* criticism. At the same time Soviet dissidents went over to the publication of regular, magazine-type materials.

In April 1968 the first issue of the *Chronicle of Current Events* saw the light of the day, a remarkable service continuing with interruptions until today, which reports infringements of human rights and of provisions embodied in Soviet constitutional and legal order by the authorities. Its main theme is the relationship between the party-state machinery and man as an individual, which of course was very much a preoccupation of Czechoslovak reformers, next to their search for economic and administrative efficiency.

Events related to the formation of a dissident community in the USSR played a role in the Czechoslovak reform movement prior to 1968 in three main instances, in connection with the *Doctor Zhivago* affair (Pasternak's Nobel Prize), the trial of Sinyavsky and Daniel, and Solzhenitsyn's letter on censorship which was read out at the Czech Writers' Congress in 1967. By 1968 Czechoslovak reformism had acquired a logic of its own, and its pace quickened as a result of the temporary alliance between critics outside and inside the political structure. Soviet dissent could not keep pace because such a confluence was missing in the USSR. Hence the greater impact of Czechoslovak developments on Soviet dissident thinking than *vice versa*.

Soviet official attitudes to the Prague Spring were the subject of several protests before the invasion, including Anatoly marchenko's Open Letter to the Czech newspapers *Rudé právo, Práce* and *Literární listy*, dated 22 July, in which he warned of the danger of intervention. In the period of heightened tension, the editors did not dare to publish it.

Protests against the invasion did not appear to be as rare as many later believed. The *Chronicle* recorded the slogan 'Czechs! We are your brothers!' which an unknown Estonian student wrote on the wall of a cinema in Tartu in the night of 21–22 August. At the same time a 20-year old man in Leningrad succeeded in painting the slogan 'Brezhnev out from Czechoslovakia!' on three of the four equestrian statues on Anichkov Bridge, which cost him five years in jail. And walls in Akademgorodok near Irkutsk were daubed with inscriptions 'Barbarians! Out of Czechoslovakia!' Leaflets against the invasion circulated in Moscow, Leningrad and the Baltic Republics. Mostly they were too short to examine the nature of Czechoslovak reforms and concentrated on the fact of intervention. One such proclamation, found in Moscow, asked of its Soviet readers: how would you feel if the Chinese occupied our country which *they* regard as revisionist? The protest demonstration of seven dissidents in the Red Square at noon on 25 August is well known.[25] In the space of five minutes, before they were seized, the demonstrators unfurled several placards, one of them saying 'For your and our freedom!', in the hope that the captive Czechoslovak delegation in the Kremlin would see them. Miss Gorbanevskaya later declared that the belief that the Czechs and Slovaks, when thinking of the Soviet people, will not see only the occupiers but the protesters as well, gave them strength and courage. Sentences meted out to the magnificent seven were drastic and included prison, banishment and enforced psychiatric treatment. The suicide of Jan Palach in January 1969 influenced a 21-year old research worker in Riga to attempt self-immolation by fire in April 1969 while holding high a banner with the words 'Freedom to Czechoslovakia!'. He was saved and later consigned to a psychiatric hospital.

The *Chronicle of Current Events* summed up the nature of Soviet samizdat related to the Czechoslovak events by saying that it generally considered the invasion a consequence of continuing restoration of Stalinism. The new Stalinists wanted to put an end to Czechoslovak reforms lest they served as a dangerous example of a combination of socialism and democracy. The occupiers did suffer a moral defeat, but the Soviet people, and especially the intelligentsia, bore collective responsibility for the aggressive act. The ranks of honest and thinking people in the USSR must be consolidated in opposition to the regime.[26]

Already during the Prague Spring the Soviet leadership evolved a theoretical justification for the pressure they were exerting on the Czechoslovak reformers. Although certainly not an innovation and still less a surprise, the newly used line of argument signified an open and emphatic departure from the formulation of intra-bloc relations as expressed in a Soviet declaration of 30 October 1956 in the middle of the Hungarian crisis, which of course was left to lapse almost immediately after it had been issued. The new stipulation seemed to prove right the critics of the art of dialectic who see it as a verbal exercise unrelated to reality. It can be summoned up as follows: socialism is not a state of affairs whose maintenance should be overlooked after only by the people of the country in which it has been achieved but rather by the whole of the Soviet bloc. While there is room for every country to *improve* socialism on its territory, it has no right to *change* it. Neither has it jurisdiction to decide whether socialism is or is not being changed. If the supranational organ, evidently the Kremlin, comes to the conclusion that such changes, or threats of changes, are in train, it is this superior body than can intervene even against the wish of the country involved.

This interpretation was expressed in the Warsaw Letter to the Czechoslovak leadership in July 1968, in the Bratislava joint declaration of early August, in the *Pravda* editorial of 22 August and then, in clearest form, in an article by S. Kovalev 'Sovereignty and the International Obligations of Socialist Countries' in *Pravda* of 26 September. Only then did it become known in the West as the Brezhnev Doctrine. The Soviet leader implicitly endorsed it in his speech at the Polish Party Congress in November 1968.[27]

Since then the Doctrine has entered the ideological arsenal of Soviet-type communism, was embodied in preambles and even substantive articles of newly concluded treaties between the socialist countries, became the subject of many 'scholarly' articles by East European ideologues, and has currently the validity of a dogma which cannot be questioned. Yugoslavia and Romania do not subscribe to it, and neither do the Eurocommunist parties, but it should be noted that one of the main features of the Doctrine right from the start is that approval of the countries concerned need not be forthcoming when joint action against such a country is being planned. Czechoslovakia did not adhere to the Doctrine before it was invaded. In fact, Kovalev's wording is typically vague to allow for the applicability of the Doctrine to just about any country, including possibly those where socialism has not yet become victorious. Kovalev wrote:

'World socialism as a social system is the common achievement of the working people of all countries, it is indivisible, and its defence is the common concern of all communists and all progressive people on earth, first and foremost the working people of the socialist countries'.[28]

And of course he had to bring in the class and non-class nature of international law, in a no less instructive manner. First he referred to a class society in which there can be no such thing as non-class law. As the societies of communist dominated countries in Eastern Europe claim to consist of 'non-antagonistic' classes, viz. workers, peasants and the working intelligentsia, and as intervention in Czechoslovakia was presumably not carried out at the behest of one of them against the other two, Kovalev must be talking about world-wide society, in fact the world at large. He continued:

'Laws and the norms of law are subordinated to the laws of the class struggle and the laws of social development. These laws are clearly formulated in the documents jointly adopted by the communist and workers' parties. The class approach to the matter cannot be discarded in the name of legalistic considerations'.[29]

All this is not to say that the Soviet Union is, or was at the time of the

Czechoslovak invasion, raring to unleash a class war in the defence of socialism outside the territorial confines of its present empire. The Brezhnev Doctrine does, however, leave open the ideological options of waging extra-legal operations in a period of detente which by definition calls for the signing of all kinds of peacefully sounding proclamations and agreements.

Above all, however, Moscow's free hand in its East European orbit was once again put beyond any doubt. Whereas Moscow may feel constrained in Eastern Europe by certain considerations, they are not the legal ones. Neither do the international obligations signed for example under the auspices of the United Nations extend to Eastern Europe. East European regimes, should any of them again reach the same reform-imbued stage as the Cechoslovaks did in 1968, would be well advised to put no trust in contractual obligations involving the USSR, or in other international documents, but rather seek to restrict Soviet action-readiness in another way. Yugoslavia and Romania did precisely that in the crucial months of August and September 1968: they declared publicly and emphatically that intervention against them would be resisted with arms, and they facilitated such resistance by adopting appropriate legal and military measures. Alternatively, an East European regime dedicated to change can limit reforms to a level which Moscow is prepared to classify as perfection of socialism, not its systemic transformation. This is what the Hungarians have done, and the Poles after Gomulka have attempted to do.

THE PROS, THE CONS AND THE ULTRAS

Moscow knew that with the reformers at least nominally back in the leading posts it would have to expose the Czechoslovaks to sustained, heavy and specific pressure to get things going its way. At the same time, military presence would have to be made less conspicuous in order not to antagonise the public still further and to allow the leadership room for the pursuit of counter-reformist manoeuvres.

The troops were soon drawn back a little, out of the main streets and some towns, into interim camps and Czechoslovak army compounds. The non-Soviet troops were permitted to go home, and the overall numbers were gradually run down from the estimated half a million to 60,000, possibly 70,000. Nevertheless, the low profile could not be too low, lest the menace appeared bearable, and so the total remaining strength was not made public and a treaty on troops stationing was solemnly signed on 16 October in Prague in the presence of Alexei Kosygin. Four Czech deputies voted against, 10 abstained and 50 were absent from the Assembly on ratification day. Soviet military presence was still termed 'temporary' but promises of withdrawal and conditions for it were mentioned less and less. In most people's minds deployment of a foreign armed contingent became a fact of life, one obvious price the country was paying for its liberal euphoria. A permanent line of liaison between Czechoslovak authorities and the foreign troops structure of command was established at all levels, giving the Soviet military easy access to the Czechoslovak officials and virtually the right to discuss all matters with them, especially those concerning law and order—a primary concern in the still tense days of the last months of 1968.

Moscow's political supervision in the wake of the return of the Czechoslovak leadership from Moscow was effected through a variety of channels.

The usual inter-party communication system was restored both in the form of direct telephone and telex links, which were kept busy, and through the Soviet Embassy in Prague. Soviet diplomatic missions in East European countries are structured so as to correspond to the governmental organisation of the host country; this makes possible contacts outside the Foreign Office between individual ministries and the corresponding sections of the Embassy. It was these direct links that became reactivated in September 1968.

Leading party and government officials were being frequently summoned to Moscow to submit progress reports and to listen to instructions. This applied to the top levels of both the party and the state *apparatus* but did not, at least at first, extend down to regional or

40

district levels. A survey of the most important visits reveals that Prime Minister Černík was in Moscow on his own in September and again in October; Dubček, Černík and Husák went there at the beginning of October; Dubček met Brezhnev in Warsaw in mid-November (this meeting was not officially confirmed); Czechoslovak economic officials visited Moscow in November; M. Jakeš, the diehard chairman of the Czechoslovak Party Control and Auditing Commission, travelled to the Soviet capital in December; Dubček, Svoboda, Černík, Husák and Štrougal were summoned to meet Soviet leaders in Kiev on 7–8 December (the delegation did not include Smrkovský, then still chairman of the National Assembly, who was disliked by Moscow more than others); the new Interior Minister, J. Pelnář, went to Moscow in mid-December; a party delegation under J. Hetteš followed suit in January; a spate of visitors including E. Erban (National Front), J. Marko (Foreign Minister), M. Dzúr (Defence Minister) and J. Kempný (Czech Lands Prime Minister) arrived in Moscow at various dates during February; V. Bilak was there in march (having previously met with Soviet officials at international conferences in Budapest and also in East Berlin); Černík and two other economic ministers made the pilgrimage in March; and so did A. Indra. Also in March, Dubček, Svoboda, Černík, Dzúr and Marko attended a Warsaw Pact top-level meeting in Budapest. This was indeed saturation travel, testifying to the high level of determination on the Soviet side to keep a close watch on Prague.

Soviet Deputy Foreign Minister V. Kuznetsov was assigned a special long-term mission in Czechoslovakia as a plenipotentiary of the Soviet leadership, endowed with considerable powers and with direct access to the Soviet Embassy's line to the Kremlin. He began his roving presence on 6 September by calling on President Svoboda. Subsequently he paid visits to all Czechoslovak leaders, explaining to each of them individually what Moscow's position and expectations were. He talked to the following: Dubček and Černík (7 September), Husák (9 September), Smrkovský (11 September), Prague Mayor L. Černý (12 September), Černík again (14 September), Císař (18 September), Erban (21 September), Dubček again (23 September), Jakeš and Štrougal (24 September), Dubček once again (23 October), Indra and Bilak (24 October), Černík, Štrougal and Plenář (25 October), Svoboda and Husák (27 October), and Poláček (21 November). Kuznetsov eventually left on 3 December but came back with K. F. Katushev, then a Soviet Party Secretary, on 27 December, and stayed until 10 January. Another high-level round of supervision then occurred from 27 February to 13 March 1969 under the leadership of A. Pelshe, a member of the Soviet Party praesidium. Thus for most of the time during Dubček's post-invasion tenure Moscow had a high-ranking man on the spot.

Unofficial and consequently unpublicised contacts between Moscow and its orthodox supporters in Czechoslovakia must have been strengthened as well. In the nature of things it is impossible to document them, except the presence of high-ranking Soviet military officers at meetings of the several extremist pro-Soviet groups which began to come into the open again.

Economic ties with the Soviet Union had evolved since 1948 to the point where Czechoslovak survival depended both on Soviet supplies, especially of fuels and raw material, and Soviet and East European purchases of Czechoslovak manufactured goods. In 1968 over two-thirds of Czechoslovakia's foreign trade was realised with the communist countries. Needless to say, just a mention of a possible economic divorce, on the lines of Soviet breaks with China and Albania in the early 1960s, must have sent a chill down the Czechoslovak leaders' spines. We do not know whether the argument was actually raised at all during 1968 or indeed after the invasion. Economic talks did follow shortly after the intervention, but by then the essential issue of political control over the deviant country had been resolved in Soviet favour and the threat of economic strangulation would not seem to be necessary.

More likely, and that is what can be gleaned from the sparing communiqués published at the end of such talks, the military and political weight now wielded by Moscow was used to tighten the economic bear-hug further. The integration process within Comecon, limping badly before then, gained an added impetus and multilateral directives for it were eventually adopted in Bucharest in 1971.

Czechoslovak economic leaders had been mooting the possibility of a hard currency loan during the Prague Spring, although not much was done in the way of concrete explorations. They had loyally approached the USSR first, but in view of the uncertainty of Czechoslovak developments in its eyes, Moscow preferred to remain tightfisted. In the period immediately following the invasion, a financial transaction of this nature is unlikely to have been the order of the day. It is known that the Dubček leadership, once restored to formal position of authority, was bracing itself to raise the question of Soviet compensation for damage caused by the military operations and, for want of information, we can only assume that some kind of an arrangement was arrived at later, within the overall economic package, devised to help overcome the disruptive effect of the invasion and its aftermath. In the meantime Moscow probably preferred a continuation of previously agreed economic relations without much change. It was, nevertheless, publicly acclaimed that the Soviet Union would deliver 300,000 tonnes of grain to Czechoslovakia in 1969 over and above the 1968 figure, but in fact the overall Czechoslovak imports of wheat in 1969 decreased by some 150,000 tonnes, and 117,000 tonnes less wheat was imported from Russia. Admittedly, the import of Soviet rye for fodder increased by 79,000 tonnes and of maize by 93,000 tonnes.[30]

Taken together, Soviet domination over the policy of the Czechoslovak leadership increased dramatically as a result of the intervention, regardless of the partial setback which made the Kremlin change its choice of domestic agents earmarked to carry out their designs. The manoeuvering room of the Dubček leadership was reduced dangerously close to none at all.

At the same time, internal opposition to reformism became considerably stronger. Factionalism has always been a feature of the Czechoslovak Communist Party and of course it did not cease to exist during the reformist upsurge in the first eight months of 1968. The common front that forced A. Novotný's abdication and brought the reform programme into the open was divided into a 'diehard' (pro-Moscow, conservative) faction and the reformers, themselves not quite united as to the degree of readiness to pursue radical objectives. Now, after the invasion, the Moscow Protocol expressly forbade victimisation of the conservatives and Dubček tried to manoeuvre by shifting some of them further away from the centre of power while assigning them to lucrative positions. But despite appearances to the contrary, their star was once again rising and no relegation to ambassadorial or provincial posts could alter the fact that they were cutting more ice with the Kremlin, collectively and individually, than the reformers.

Simultaneously, a number of reformers were already turning their coats and the contours of a new coalition between traditional and converted pro-Muscovites were becoming visible. Not all of the diehards were of course of equal value to Moscow and it was quite prepared to consign some lightweights or embarrassments to comfortable oblivion or at least to playing second fiddle. But whatever the intricacies, the specific weight of conservatism inside the leading circles of the Czechoslovak Communist Party grew considerably.

Another group of hardliners emerged at the extreme left of the political spectrum of those days. These were the people who had felt most comfortable in the early days of Novotný's rule, the 1950s men, Stalinists of the traditional hue, with anti-semitic views and dead-set against all and every relaxation of the iron grip which the party imposed on the country as a result of the takeover in February 1948. A roll call was never held, and they had to operate in the political twilight even before the Prague Spring, but one would not be far off the mark in estimating their strength at several thousand in the whole country. They were mostly but not solely aged men, veteran members of the party, not holding any really important offices, except perhaps in the Czechoslovak-Soviet Friendship Union and of course behind the well-insulated doors of the secret police offices. Most lived and drew their pensions in Prague, but also in regions which had traditionally been strongholds of backwood communism, like North Bohemia and North Moravia, and elsewhere in the provinces and in Slovakia. They were the writers of anonymous threats to the intellectuals during the Prague Spring, and they extended a few fraternal hands to the invading troops. To distinguish them from their more sophisticated class brethern who occupied leading posts by the grace of Moscow, contemporary Czechoslovak sources called them ultra-conservatives, or 'ultras' for short.

As if Dubček did not have enough on his mind, the ultras chose to step out into the open, encouraged by the propitious post-invasion atmosphere. Their first important meeting was held in the Čechie Hall in Prague-Liben on 9 October 1968 from 7 to 10 p.m., in the presence of some 300–500 persons, including several Soviet officers and a correspondent of *Sovetskaya Rossiya*. Some information on that meeting, which otherwise was kept very hush-hush, later leaked to the reform-minded press which had not yet been completely 'normalised', but a fuller report and the complete text of the main resolution exist in typewritten form.[31] The praesidium of the meeting included A. Kapek, a secretary of the central committee and evidently a liaison man with the conservatives in the Moscow-tolerated post-invasion leadership.

The proceedings of the meeting make a sordid reading and the importance of the episode does not warrant detailed examination. Suffice to say that the ultras concentrated on three things. First, they stressed their own traditional and unswerving observance of Marxism-Leninism. It was they who had always best expressed communist policies in the Czechoslovak context. Secondly, they put forward a conspiracy theory according to which the entire revisionist sequence in the country, from the early 1960s, had been the outcome of imperialist planning to which the various liberalisers and reformers inside the country were a party. Their aim was to undo the great communist victory of 1948 and to throw Czechoslovakia back into the embrace of capitalism. Thirdly, and logically, they called for radical and wide-ranging punitive action against the culprits, whoever they may be, but above all the intellectuals, journalists and waverers in the top echelons of the party, in order to stop the rot at long last and reintroduce 'sound' conditions for practising genuine, Soviet-style socialism.

The Čechie initiative could not be wholly accommodated in the 'normalisation' scheme because Moscow saw its impracticality. A Soviet colonel Korolenko who addressed the ultras towards the end of their deliberations in the Čechie Hall declared, 'We will always be with you, that is why we are here. We have come to give assistance to true communists'. Yet the ultras could not be acknowledged by Moscow as the *only* true communists worthy of being given control over Czechoslovakia. For one thing, they were just a few and they were mostly old. And if *they* were to receive the Soviet stamp of approval, others would not be able to receive it, including Husák and Štrougal and Kempný and many others who Moscow correctly assessed as being able and willing to run the country with equal loyalty but also at least with a modicum of competence required by Czechoslovakia's position as an industrial entity in the outer reaches of the Soviet orbit in Europe. The Čechie ultras could possibly have administered a concentration camp and even for that they would have needed Soviet military support. In the long run a Czechoslovakia of this complexion would have become a permanent liability. Neither would the ultras be able to deliver the consumer goods and food which had to be provided for the pacification of the Czechoslovak population in the wake of the eruptive experience. Their Marxism was good enough for newspaper editorials and political indictments, but it had a lower pragmatic content than Moscow required of its client states.

Nonetheless, the candle of the ultras was kept flickering as a reminder that if worst came to the worst there was yet another line of orthodoxy to which the recalcitrant Czechoslovaks could be pushed.

There followed other 'ultra' meetings and demonstrations. On 7 November, when Dubček went to lay a wreath at the Soviet soldiers' cemetery to mark the anniversary of the October Revolution, he was shouted and hissed at. The large Prague hall *Lucerna* was the scene of fervent pro-Soviet demonstrations on 10 November; another gathering was held in the Čechie Hall on 22 January and yet another in the Military Academy on 17 March.

In March 1969 the constituent meeting of an ultra-conservatively orientated group of young people was held in a hotel in Prague, behind closed doors and strictly by invitation. They called themselves the Lenin Youth Union. According to reports, attendance was under 100 and comprised youngish officers of the police and the army as well as a dozen or so children of conservative party functionaries.

That was about as much as the ultras undertook while Dubček was still nominally head of the party. In the conditions of the day he was unable to prevent the ultra-left opposition from achieving a certain measure of institutionalisation. The fact that no more than a few incidents occurred, more in the nature of a nuisance than the birth of a genuine political movement, must have been due to the reluctance of the 'established' conservatives to join forces with the ultra faction, as much as to Moscow's decision not to render the *enragés* a helping hand. The ultras did not let up, however, and provoked another conflict, with the Husák leadership, in the latter part of 1969 and in 1970. More about that will be said later.

On the other side, the pincer movement of attitudes to 'post-invasion reality' which almost surrounded the Dubček group and severely curtailed its freedom of action, had its radical, anti-Soviet wing. Although the exact terms of the Moscow Protocol were not made public, except to the inner-most party circles, the public sensed 'betrayal' and 'capitulation'. Just as the pro-Soviet forces on the left advocated a range of solutions from moderate to instransigent counter-reformation, the committed reformers 'on the right' continued to press Dubček for a more determined stand against Moscow even now.

It may be safely assumed that the majority of the public still felt confidence in Dubček and his policy line, even if the feeling of frustration and fear for the future became more widely spread. One of the opinion polls (which until April 1969 were still freely held on sound sociological principles under the auspices of the Public Opinion Research Institute) put to a representative sample of people the following question in the middle of September 1968: 'Do you still support the endeavours of the Czechoslovak Communist Party to continue implementing the Action Programme [of the Prague Spring]?' The answers, in per cent, were: Yes, 94·6; No, 0·6; Don't know, 4·8.[32] At the same time people were asked to express their measure of confidence in the four protagonists of reformism (who by then had not yet been associated in the public eye with Husák), i.e. Svoboda, Dubček, Černík and Smrkovský. They were fully endorsed by 97·8, 97·2, 90·4 and 90·1 per cent of the respondents.[33] And as late as mid-March 1969, the list of 'most trusted' personalities derived from a survey of public opinion included at the top five places persons of a distinctly reform-orientated reputation: Svoboda (88 per cent), Dubček (76), Smrkovský (56), Černík (39) and Císař (20). Husák came out seventh countrywide, with eight per cent, and fifth in Slovakia (24 per cent). Only two per cent of Czech respondents trusted him.[34]

The importance of such surveys must not be exaggerated, and they do not explain everything. Even those who might already have doubts about some aspects of the post-invasion course as pursued by the leadership, still with Dubček at the head, would have felt that to give a firm endorsement when approached by a pollster and to suppress the feeling of unease was the right thing to do in the context of the time. There were other opinion polls which reflected misgivings, for example a mid-September survey in Slovakia revealed that nearly 40 per cent of respondents feared 'that there will be an attempt to reconstruct pre-January [i.e. pre-reformist] conditions'.[35]

Among the dedicated reformers in the party there was a relatively small, even if intellectually strong, group of those who believed that the Moscow Protocol should not have been signed in the first place. Kriegel's refusal to append his signature even at a possible risk to his personal safety was an example. Smrkovský himself had grave doubts as he revealed in his posthumously published recollections, but in the end he decided that even the limited scope of action was worth preserving. It may be unfair to the people involved but the classic dilemma of collaborationists probably applied to their mental processes: if I am not going to do it, someone much worse than I will.

Once signed, the Protocol could have been rejected as invalid after Dubček's group return from Moscow. Several members of the reformist alliance argued that the Moscow talks had been held under duress and their outcome anyway required ratification by such bodies as the party central committee and the National Assembly. Should such a ratification not be forthcoming, and it was quite possible that the two assemblies could be persuaded to deny it if Dubček and his colleagues threw their weight behind a rejectionist approach, the Czechoslovak authorities could notify the Kremlin that a new set of solutions, more satisfactory to Czechoslovakia, would have to be sought. This could be done in a dignified and non-antagonistic fashion. In the end the proposition to repudiate the Moscow Protocol was turned down.

It is difficult to imagine how rejectionism could have worked in the way its proponents hoped it could. The group who signed the Protocol was a heterogeneous one and included a majority of politicians with decidedly weaker reformist dedication than that of Dubček and Smrkovský, if any at all. The withdrawal of some signatures, but retention of others, would be useless, and it would only accelerate the differentiation process in the leadership which had already started. A non-ratification, while not impossible, would have taken at least a few days to prepare before an appropriate formula was devised and submitted. Surely the Soviets would have intervened to stop it from happening.

Anyway, which central committee would be asked to disavow the Protocol? The 'progressive' one, elected at the extraordinary 14th congress in Vysočany, which the Russians did not recognise and which was in the meantime promptly disowned by the Slovak section of the party at Husák's prodding on the very day of his return from Moscow? Or the old one, elected at the 13th congress in 1966 and containing a majority of potential collaborators? The latter was unacceptable to the reformers and doubtful as an instrument of anti-Soviet defiance, whereas the former was paralysed by Husák's action. Thus the Dubček line prevailed, even though it was not really his but Moscow's.

Another kind of opposition to the Moscow solution manifested itself in the traditional East European manner: tens of thousands of people voted with their feet and, either having lost hope or simply seizing the opportunity, emigrated to the West. Many were on foreign holiday when the troops came and chose not to return. Others went hastily and for good straight away, remembering the terror of the 1950s. There were an estimated 80,000 former political prisoners in Czechoslovakia in 1968 and their past experience was too horrible for them to contemplate a possible repetition. (This is not to say that all of them emigrated.) Yet others chose to mark time outside the country just in case, and they absented themselves temporarily, an easy thing to do because the frontiers remained virtually open. Most authorities bent over backwards to accommodate requests for passports and border guards turned a blind eye to incomplete documents of outgoing travellers or even shook their hands and wished them well. (Soviet troops, as mentioned earlier, did not go right up to the Czechoslovak frontiers with West Germany and Austria.) The Ministry of the Interior announced in May 1969, after Husák's accession to power, that 40,000 were abroad 'illegally', but the total figure eventually rose much higher. In the meantime the situation was fluid, people were coming and going, and even if some restrictions were imposed in November 1968, departure remained possible virtually until 9 October 1969 when the iron curtain fell in place once again.

Several high-ranking functionaries, reformers by persuasion, found themselves abroad at the time of the invasion. Ota Šik, Jiří Hájek, František Vlasák and Štefan Gašparík, all members of the government, were in Yugoslavia and talked to Yugoslav leaders before eventually returning home. Foreign Minister Hájek went to address the United Nations Security Council first, and Šik in the end, after a return visit to Prague, chose to stay away permanently. They, and others of lesser rank, who travelled abroad during the first week or so, must have mooted the idea of founding an emigre political centre of resistance, or an organisation, perhaps even a communist party in exile, but the idea was abandoned and allegiance was given to Dubček once again. The notion of a defiant party in exile surfaced again after Husák's takeover, when the numbers and contours of the emigre community became more clearly defined, but it was again rejected as impractical.

Thus the pressure to which Dubček's team was exposed on the part of the emigrating multitudes did not consist of the preaching of a more radical alternative than he was offering at home but was rather a psychological one, an expression of regretful lack of confidence, a state of mind of a large group of his compatriots over whom he could not hold sway. You go on trying, they seemed to be saying to him, we wish you all the luck and will keep our fingers crossed, possibly even help you from the outside if we can, but unfortunately we can no longer believe that you will succeed. Svoboda, Dubček, Smrkovský, Černík and others stated on repeated occasions that personal safety of Czechoslovak citizens was foremost on their minds and appealed to the emigres, many as yet undecided whether to stay out or return, to come back. These were not reproachful exhortations and even less so angry orders, but rather gentle proddings, lacking conviction and hence also the persuasive force which only an impossible turn of events inside Czechoslovakia could carry.

The intellectual community accepted the Moscow Protocol unwillingly and with a measure of defiant determination to carry on regardless. Writers restated their support for Prague Spring reforms without compromise, and journalists only reluctantly acknowledged the need for restraint but said they would fight for every inch of the ground which the leadership was asking them to surrender. Scholars and scientists proclaimed once again their dedication to free critical thought as an inalienable precondition of the survival of their professions. Students were among the most adamant opponents of a slide-back into pre-reform practices. They saw an alliance between radical intellectuals and workers as the possible backbone of resistance and stepped up their efforts in this direction. Delegations between factories and schools were exchanged. When university students staged a three-day sit-in strike in mid-November in support of the Prague Spring course, workers sent their best wishes and food. In December several written cooperation agreements between the students' union in the Czech Lands and various trade unions were concluded, pledging both parties to defend the achievements of the pre-invasion political course. Most of the trade unions which were at first rather slow in making use of the semi-independent status opened for them by the Prague Spring, expressed hope that they would be able to stand on their own feet even after the invasion. The formative stage of the enterprise councils as organs of employees' self-management was taken further and elections of a number of councils took place. Economists met to issue a proclamation defending the principles of a full-blooded economic reform.

The message could not have been lost on Moscow: the Czechoslovak public was extremely unwilling to submit to more than just the most formal aspects of the Moscow Protocol, and they were taking seriously above all the Kremlin's solemn protestations, never meant in earnest, that post-January policies could continue and that the troops were not in the country to interfere with internal matters. This was of course not how the Soviets wished the Protocol to be read and understood.

THE CIRCLE THAT WOULD NOT SQUARE

The fragile boat laden with 'the Dubček compromise' found itself floating between the Scylla and the Charybdis of two conflicting interpretations of a navigational chart which it did not want to use in the first place, with the crew divided and the winds singularly inauspicious. Dubček simply could not satisfy Moscow and his nation at the same time. But he gave it a valiant try.

Three commandments of the Protocol stood out as having primary importance in Moscow's eyes: removal of the most objectionable reformers, muzzling of the media, and discontinuation of the most sacrilegious reform processes.

We do not really know (until Mlynář tells us in his new book) how many reformers were pilloried by name during the Moscow talks, but if there was a black list, or if it emerged later, for example during the Kuznetsov mission, Dubček certainly succeeded in pruning it down to just a few names. František Kriegel was dropped from the party praesidium and as chairman of the National Front. Čestmír Císař and Zdeněk Mlynář ceased to be party secretaries, though Císař was tolerated for quite some time in fairly high positions and then as chairman of the newly formed Czech National Council, and Mlynář even became a member of the praesidium before resigning from political life on 17 November. Josef Pavel had to go as Minister of the Interior, and Jiří Hájek as Foreign Minister. And the two directors of Prague Radio and Czechoslovak Television, Zdeněk Hejzlar and Jiří Pelikán, were unacceptable. That was practically all until April 1969, even though the overall impression was of widespread and frequent shifting of people from one post to another.

This was partly the result of a musical chairs nature of the exercise but above all of two other kinds of changes of office which Dubček linked with the removal of progressives. The first of these was the co-optation into the leading bodies of a number of *other* progressives, voted into office by the clandestine Vysočany congress. This congress re-elected only 25 of the incumbent 108 central committee members and added 119 new ones. By 31 August the original 108 had become fewer due to previous resignations, and the remaining 104 or so were re-confirmed tacitly, while 80 newcomers and seven former candidate members were added by way of co-optation. Simultaneously, the composition of the party praesidium was changed beyond recognition, with five of the eleven dropped (Kriegel and four hardliners: Švestka, Kolder, Rigo and Kapek) and 11 new ones added, so that the number became an unwieldy 21 plus three candidate (non-voting) members. Later, in November, a smaller nucleus of eight was constituted under the name Executive Committee of the praesidium, comprising Černík, Dubček, Erban, Husák, Sádovský, Smrkovský, Svoboda and Štrougal. The idea of a large praesidium was abandoned at the April 1969 central committee session where Husák replaced Dubček as first secretary.

Secondly, the impression of a sweeping turnover of officials was strengthened by the release of a number of conservatives and their replacement by the followers of reform, without the former being actually pensioned off. Among people in the top party circles, Antonín Kapek alone announced his withdrawal from political activity on 29 August, only to pop up at the Čechie Hall meeting of the ultras on 9 October and to stage a fairly swift comeback thereafter. Oldřich Švestka was succeeded as editor of *Rudé právo* by Jiří Sekera on 23 August (formally on 31 August), but got instead the editorship of *Tribuna*, a newly formed party weekly for the Czech Lands, which eventually became the mouthpiece of diehard conservatism. Viliam Šalgovič was dismissed as head of the Secret Police, fell into Soviet-shielded obscurity and re-emerged in Slovak party circles later in 1969. He eventually ended up as president of the Slovak National Council. Miroslav Sulek was pushed into a diplomatic career after his replacement as director of the Czechoslovak Press Agency by Jiří Suk on 28 August. The one change that really seemed to matter in those chaotic days was Husák's appointment as First Party Secretary in Slovakia in succession to Vasil Bilak, a man whose name became the epitome of pro-Soviet diehard and cynical conservatism. Not that Bilak was sent packing; he remained a party praesidium member, though not a member of the narrower Executive Committee, and in April 1969 he easily transferred into Husák's praesidium. Animosity between Bilak and Husák was public knowledge but before long the two men were enthroned side by side in the governor's seat as the most powerful figures in the country, and they were to spend many happy years in fraternal embrace.

All in all, 'progressives' still heavily outnumbered 'conservatives' just about everywhere. Some students of the period concluded that there was not really that much difference between pre-August and post-August reformism. It should be said that the outward insignificance of cadre changes is misleading. The diehard group was preserved in good shape by the Protocol which devoted a special article to their rescue from political ostracism. Several of the reformers opted for an anti-reformist course dictated by Moscow, for example President Svoboda and Prime Minister Černík. Husák came strongly to the fore and caught Brezhnev's eye. Within hours of his return from Moscow he took impressive command of the Slovak Party Central Committee and made it reverse its decision of support for the clandestine Vysočany congress, which was as good as saying to

Brezhnev that 'normalisation' *à la carte* could be accomplished, and that he was the man who can do it. After Šimon and Špaček were pushed out of the central policy-making caucus, only Dubček and Smrkovský among the heavyweights could be taken for granted as determined and unswerving proponents of the reformist course, but both were bound by their signatures on the Protocol, something that honest men feel strongly about even in the company of chickens and wolves. (If pressed hard to make a distinction between the two, which one is not, a conjecture as to Moscow's prime shooting target at that time could be put forward.) The deduction is that Smrkovský and Dubček, in that order, were earmarked for elimination from the leadership as the greatest obstacles to a progress of 'normalisation' along the desirable lines.

Smrkovský was deliberately not invited by the Russians to Kiev on 7–8 December and shortly afterwards he was not made chairman of the Federal Assembly, something everyone expected to happen. Come April 1969 and he was dropped from the party praesidium. It took a while longer to displace Dubček but he did lose the first secretary's mantle in April and what followed was more an awkward and embarrassing *chute irrésistible* than just a fade-out.

A similar picture emerges when the fate of the reformist plans is examined. Bravely, many were being continued, none more vehemently than the federalisation of the country, which in practical terms meant the building up of two sub-systemic bureaucratic hierarchies in the Czech Lands and in Slovakia. The Slovak Communist Party Central Committee made it known in emphatic terms as soon after the invasion as 5 September that no delays in the federalisation plans on account of the other momentous events would be tolerated. And so, with a mass of problems generated by the military and political intervention of a superior power, the time and energy of the Czechoslovak leadership and virtually all sections of the political structure had to be lavishly expended on hammering out an effective division of a country where the cry for unity was heard and understood by many as the cry for survival.

The opportunity was evidently too precious to be missed and 28 October 1968, the 50th anniversary of the birth of independent Czechoslovakia, was too good a date not to be aimed at. Anyway, it had all been agreed before the invasion, had it not? Or most of it. And was not one of the cardinal reforms thus being put on the statute book? So everyone went through the motions: the government approved the drafts of the Federalisation and Nationalities Bills on 1 October, the National Assembly enacted them as constitutional laws on 27 October and Svoboda signed them in Bratislava on 30 October. As of 1 January 1969 Czechoslovakia became a federative country with three governments instead of one, and two parliamentary chambers, the House of the People and the House of the Nations, comprising the Federal Assembly. (Elections did not take place until the autumn of 1971; in the meantime seats were distributed administratively.) In addition there were separate parliaments for each of the constitutent republics, the Czech and the Slovak National Councils. Suddenly Slovakia had thousands of new posts to fill. The one among them which Husák energetically claimed for a Slovak was the chairmanship of the Federal Assembly which many thought should go to Smrkovský, hitherto speaker of the one and only National Assembly. Husák's argument had federative logic to support it: of the four top posts in the country, two were held by Czechs (Svoboda as President and Černík as Federal Prime Minister), but only one by a Slovak (Dubček as First Party Secretary). Smrkovský at the head of the federal parliament would upset parity.

The move caused a crisis, so many people and organisations protested against what they saw as further erosion of the 'progressive' ranks. Large trade unions threatened to strike should Smrkovský be by-passed. The affair showed clearly for the first time after the invasion how strong the pressure Moscow and the domestic conservatives in the leadership could exert. Smrkovský himself was persuaded to broadcast to the nation to stress how entitled the Slovaks were to get the post. And so it went to Peter Colotka, a mildly progressive person then, but above all a lacklustre Slovak politician who has lasted in the 'normalised' establishment to this very day, more recently as Slovak Prime Minister. No one went on strike, but people grumbled—an increasingly frequent public reaction to an outrage. (As at the time of writing, there are Czechs at the head of the Federal Assembly and the Federal Government, while one Slovak, Husák himself, combines the remaining two posts of President and party leader in one pair of hands.)

Why did the Russians allow federalisation to happen? It was not politically dangerous, it kept people busy, it took their minds off more objectionable designs, and it made at least some of them happy. Federal arrangements are largely a matter of form which can be filled with a democratic or an authoritarian content. Russia has had a quasi-federation since 1918 and as the Soviet Union since 1922. At the central committee meeting in November 1968 a Bureau for the Direction of Party Work in the Czech Lands was set up preliminary to the constitution of a proper Communist Party of the Czech Lands, such as the Slovaks had had for decades. In the end a Czech Communist Party has never been established.

The process of rehabilitating before courts of justice the victims of judicial persecution in the early years of communism in Czechoslovakia also continued. New judges to sit on rehabilitation benches were sworn in on 17 September, and on 12 December there even began in

Příbram a trial of seven former secret police officers accused of torturing and murdering political prisoners in 1949. (It was never to be brought to an end.) In another move, the administration of penitentiaries was transferred from the Ministry of the Interior to the Ministry of Justice in mid-December. Court rulings clearing people of past accusations still received publicity and could not but inject into the public the feeling that not all was lost. People did fear for their personal safety during and after the invasion and their *present* worries were being at least partly allayed by the knowledge that *past* injustices were being defiantly put right. It is not known whether the question of rehabilitations was specifically raised in Moscow. The Warsaw Letter of July 1968 stated on behalf of the five countries which eventually attacked Czechoslovakia: 'We do not stand before you as yesterday's men whose intention it is to prevent you from remedying mistakes and shortcomings, including violation of socialist legality, which happened in the past'.[36] But this point was not mentioned in the Protocol. When Kuznetsov talked to Smrkovský on 11 September about the whole range of subjects in which the Soviet approach to 'normalisation' differed from the Czechoslovak, he alluded to rehabilitations only obliquely in connection with publicity which the press was giving to 'the party's former methods which could be exploited by anti-socialist elements'.[37]

We cannot say whether absence of direct Soviet ruling on the matter was a loophole to which the Czechoslovaks became readily alert and decided to forge ahead under the assumption that what was not expressly prohibited was permitted, or whether the feeling of false comfort encouraged by the moral, but formal, return to the past was tacitly and knowingly tolerated by Moscow as a relatively harmless and even useful exercise. Husák was to put an end to it anyway.

Some organisational developments, begun as part of the monopoly-breaking processes initiated during the Prague Spring, went on, for example in the youth movement, with the consolidation and legal approval of sectional organisations of young people. The roof-structure which would preserve at least a semblance of centralised unity, was, however, also strengthened. All non-governmental organisations were in fact getting ready to adapt themselves to the new federative conditions with the pattern of two national hierarchies and one federal structure on most drawing boards. The National Assembly passed the new National Front law on 13 September, not as strikingly reformist as envisaged, but still with leeway for a less dictatorial relationship between the communist party and the other institutional members, but effectively ruling out new organisations outside the framework.

The theme of economic reform was reverted to, mainly in connection with the drafting of an innovative Enterprise Bill according to which the entrepreneurial powers of economic units would be significantly enhanced. And the politically delicate question of workers' self-management remained on the books. The government did recommend on 24 October that creation of new councils ought to be suspended, but the contrary appeared to happen. Most of the councils in fact came into existence after the invasion for two reasons.

Firstly, the self-management initiative in Czechoslovakia did not burst out into the open suddenly, and the councils did not emerge spontaneously as organs of working class power. A successful, if fitful, effort had been made in the latter part of the Prague Spring to coordinate workers' participation in enterprise decision-making with the general thrust of the economic reform in the direction of market socialism. The powers of enterprise councils and the method of their election were subjected to a thorough discussion, and it was not intended to hurry things up. For example, in the large Škoda Works in Pilsen the process began in early June, the statute of the council and the election procedure were first debated and then adopted on 30 July and, as time was allowed for everyone to get acquainted with the candidates, the election itself did not take place until 26 September. (Of 107 persons standing for election, 29 were returned: two thirds of both figures being communists.) A conference of some of the largest councils which had already been constituted took place in Pilsen on 9–10 January 1969.

Secondly, in hoping that the shattering of reformist aspirations by external interference could be arrested or at least minimised, a number of reformers gave added importance to the idea of self-management. Sufficient socialist radicalism had penetrated a part of the reformist community and such allies of theirs as a section of the students, to make them conceive of the workers' councils as the potential backbone of resistance. An article headline in *Listy* of 20 February 1969 called for 'All Power to the Workers' Councils!' The situation seemed to some people reminiscent of the one which the soviets in Russia faced in February 1917. But it was not to be. In their Czechoslovak variety the enterprise organs of workers' participation had been designed and created for a different purpose, much more modest from the point of view of revolutionary struggle, and much more geared to practical matters connected with running of the enterprise economy. The Škoda council consisted of six manual workers, seventeen technicians and four 'candidates of sciences', with two places reserved for supplying enterprises and customers.[38]

Why did the Russians tolerate even a diluted self-management movement which has always been and still is anathema to them wherever it appears? The answer probably is that they correctly assessed the possibility of truly revolutionary resistance based on the councils, or on their alliance with radical intellectuals, as extremely remote. The self-managing component of the Czechoslovak reform movement was in any case brought to an unceremonious and fairly abrupt end in the summer of 1969 under Husák's supervision.

Plans for a democratisation of the party—another crucial component of reformism—had to be given up almost immediately. As a result of the Moscow Protocol, the clandestine congress was consigned to oblivion. By the same token, the ascendance of progressive people within the party was slowed down and eventually halted. Moscow may have asked for public condemnation of the congress, but Dubček hoped to get away without a verbal renunciation. Even so, the congress became a "non-thing", as if it never happened. The holding of the constituent Czech Lands party congress as a launching board for a separate Czech Communist Party was also postponed indefinitely.

The new party statutes, published in draft form on 10 August, met with the same fate as the congress at which they were to be adopted. Abandonment of the statutes represented more than just a formality, in view of the revolutionary democratising tendencies which they could have introduced into the party.

It is impossible to overemphasise the significance of the virtual ending of reforms in the party. They had been conceived, rightly or wrongly, as the alpha and omega of the reform process. A democratised party, albeit still the leading force and possibly still the only real political party, was meant to preside benignly over social changes and eventually over the new model of socialism that would emerge as their result. Party reforms were absolutely essential for the success of reforms in all other departments. No benign party, no reforms and no new model of socialism.

Moreover, the split occasioned by the appointment of Husák as First Party Secretary in Slovakia soon proved to be a threat to reformism inside the party as a whole. the Slovak organs of the party became an instrument of 'normalisation' in Husák's hands, even though their nominal membership still included a number of reformers. As an example we can refer to a brief typewritten summary of the meeting of the Czechoslovak party praesidium on 3–4 January 1969 which discussed Smrkovský's candidature for the post of Federal Assembly chairman. Smrkovský himself told the Slovak members to realise that the Czech public viewed the Slovak Communist Party as a Soviet pressure group. Husák reacted by bluntly saying that if the Czech pro-Smrkovský campaign were to continue, he would start a Slovak counter-campaign. It was Husák's draft statement on the issue which was eventually adopted, with alterations, as the praesidium's resolution. The meeting was also symptomatic of the growing differences among the members of the praesidium. Svoboda sided with Husák and allegedly said that should Smrkovský be elected under public pressure, he, Svoboda, would immediately tender his resignation. Černík added that as Prime Minister he would not hesitate to order coercive suppression of public demonstrations in Smrkovský's favour.

Heavy inroads were made into the mass media. Offices and committees for press and information were set up soon after the return of the leaders from Moscow and plenipotentiaries for radio and television were appointed to replace the reform-minded incumbents. The law discontinuing censorship was rescinded on 13 September. Several Western journalists were expelled from the country. Two periodicals were suspended at the beginning of November and two more in early April 1969. Editors were summoned several times and warned not to permit any criticism of the Warsaw Pact countries, the occupation armies and the basic ideological tenets of Marxism. For a few months the party leadership sought to keep the lid on the media without resorting to straightforward pre-publication censorship. It should be said that this was an impossible situation on both sides. What the Russians wanted, and the growing front of pro-Soviet party and state leaders was pressing for, could not be delivered by persuasion and appeal only. The public had been outraged and at least wanted to talk, write, read and hear about it. The word had become one of the few weapons left to them, and no appeals could persuade those wielding it that it should be surrendered because 'realism' so demanded. It would have to be silenced in another way.

The praesidium formed a four-man group on 7 January to supervise the media in cooperation with the press department of the central committee and the new Office for Press and Information (acrostically dubbed 'Oppression'). Pre-publication censorship was still shunned but the new group was given a list of eighteen instructions which represented a considerable tightening of the screws. Some of the more important ones, according to an unpublished source obtained privately, were as follows: public statements by leading officials must no longer be spontaneous and improvised but prepared in writing and adapted for publication or broadcasting; every day an assessment of public reaction to such statements must be made; Press Agency releases must accurately reflect party policy and intentions; all political and news broadcasts, sound and television, must be 'under control'; certain named periodicals (and one daily paper) must submit their editorial plans for advance approval; proportion of items originating from the socialist countries must be 'substantially increased', as must be the number of items criticising the West; party and state leaders must not be 'attacked'; a weekly meeting of all chief editors must be held to evaluate their work; and work of several named journalists must be examined. (A hint was dropped that at least one of them should be told to write on other than domestic political topics.)

The leadership also put an early end to two organisations which Moscow and the conservatives regarded specially dangerous, the Club of Committed Non-Party People (KAN) and the Club of Former Political Prisoners (K 231). Dubček himself called them anti-socialist and the ban was made easier by their statutes not having been previously endorsed by the Ministry of the Interior as required by law. A somewhat similar fate befell the maverick trade union organisation entitled Federation of Engine Crews which was denied recognition. It had sought to establish itself during the reformist period because of non-confidence in the official railwaymen's union. The embryonic Social Democratic Party had not filed a request for official endorsement of statutes, although a preparatory committee existed and had conducted negotiations with communist leaders before the invasion. Now the committee was simply given to understand that there was no question of any further activity being tolerated. The Students' Union was internally divided with regard to the question whether to affiliate to the National Front, the only legal way an organisation of this nature could function. (Many jurists questioned the legality of the stipulation that National Front membership was a proviso for tolerated existence, but the time when legal niceties could be debated had passed.) The Society for Human Rights was a special case in that it had applied for endorsement and was given it. It was even permitted to hold a conference on the protection of human rights on 4–5 December and was only disbanded after Husák's accession to power.

Restrictive measures in the field of public organisations did not lead to the desired pacification. The genie of defiance was out of the bottle and it was proving difficult to force it back. 'Normalisation' was not proceeding according to Moscow's plans and timetables, and Moscow was getting impatient. Tension was specially highlighted in situations of critical magnitude of which several occurred during the eight post-invasion months. Not all were equally explosive and they had different causes, but just one common denominator. Public demonstrations of anti-Soviet feelings on 28 October (Czechoslovak National Day) and 7 November (October Revolution anniversary) were the first, followed by the student strike from 18–20 November, the Smrkovský affair in December-January, the self-immolation of Jan Palach and his funeral in the second half of January, and finally the street demonstrations in celebration of two Czechoslovak ice-hockey victories over the Soviet Union on 21 and 28 march. As Moscow saw it, in all these instances the Dubček leadership failed to act firmly and decisively as required by the Moscow Protocol.

Jan Palach, a twenty-year old student of the Faculty of Philosophy of Charles University, poured petrol over himself in Wenceslas Square on 16 January 1969, died of his wounds on 19 January and was buried on 25 January. His funeral, which the government decided to leave to the students to organise and supervise, turned into an impressive and moving statement of public will to stand up against the *diktat* of 'normality'. Although an estimated 100,000 people marched in the procession and at least twice as many watched from the pavements, the demonstration passed without incident. The nation was shocked and aggrieved. More self-immolations followed in the capital and the provinces, some prompted perhaps by less directly political reasons. On 25 February another student, Jan Zajíc, burned himself to death, also in Wenceslas Square. He belonged to the same group as Palach, according to student sources.

Jan Palach's farewell note indicates that protest suicides were not the policy of the Students' Union, but of a much smaller group, while the formulations in the note were almost certainly his own. The note warned that further suicides would be committed if three demands (two of them numbered in the note) were not met within five days: abolition of censorship; a ban on the distribution of the pro-invasion broadsheet *Zprávy*; and proclamation of a general strike unlimited in time. With all respect for the supreme sacrifice of the author, none of the three was attainable. A postscript added somewhat incomprehendingly that Czechoslovakia had gained room in international politics after August and that this should be made use of. Public reaction rightly took note of the more general meaning of Palach's self-sacrifice as a double-pronged appeal to the leadership to stand firm and to the population to do more than it had done so far. A student leader who spent hours with Palach before he died reported that Palach believed in his act having achieved its purpose. 'But it would be better if nobody repeated it. Lives should be spared for other purposes. We are involved in a great struggle today'.[39]

Husák, who was more and more clearly emerging as Moscow's ideal candidate for the post of a strongman and must have been acting in conjunction with the Soviet leaders or reading their minds well, summed up the need for a different kind of policy than the Dubček group was offering at a confidential meeting of army officers on 5 February 1969 (at which notes were taken privately and survived). He was reported to have said that the battle cannot remain a battle of words only. The sooner the leadership puts an end to political conflicts, the better. Time must not be wasted on disputations with the Hochmans (a journalist) and the Šiks (an economist), or else the leaders will be seen as incapable of leading. There exist handfuls of political tricksters and adventurers who want to turn Czechoslovakia into an anti-socialist shooting range [!]. What a section of the press, radio and television dares to do today has no match anywhere in the world. The problem is not that the enemy is strong, but that the leadership is inconsistent. Political life in Czechoslovakia resembles the manners of a pack of barking dogs. Discipline must be enforced. There has been enough discussion and imploring. What is needed is the adoption of energetic and democratic [!] measures. The removal of several scores or hundreds of people from public life will be the most democratic and humane solution from the point of view of the fourteen million citizens. (Then he allegedly corrected himself: he did not have physical elimination in mind.) The government must govern well and vigorously. What is needed is a prophylactic, hygienic surgery.

When exactly Moscow chose Husák as Dubček's successor is of course impossible to say. It could not have been in Moscow during the dramatic 'negotiations' in August 1968. At that time he was a relative newcomer to the top team (a Deputy Prime Minister from April 1968), heavily committed to the reformist cause (judging by his public pronouncements right up to invasion day), and probably slightly suspect because of his incarceration for 'bourgeois nationalism' in the 1950s and long years in the wilderness afterwards. But it is likely that he caught Brezhnev's eye already then by the amount of pragmatism which he was able to generate on the spot, when faced with the overwhelming odds of a military intervention. His swift and skilful handling of the Slovak party virtually hours after returning home must have scored in his favour. When Dubček and company talked, Husák acted. As late as November 1968, at the Central Committee meeting, he still gave support to Dubček's policy of 'normalisation' conceived as an operation to salvage the gist of the reform, but he already remained sufficiently vague to permit a different interpretation. Hejzlar says that Husák's gradual dissociation from the Dubček line began after his return from a Moscow visit on which he accompanied Dubček and Černík on 3–4 October. Brezhnev dressed the Czechoslovak leaders down for continuing non-observance of just about every stipulation of the Protocol—and Husák realised that pussy-footing had no more chance of succeeding as a political programme. He allegedly confided to an acquaintance: 'We came, we saw, we lost'.[40]

I think that Moscow decided to give Husák a chance to prove himself further when evaluating the results of Kuznetsov's mission. The Soviet Deputy Foreign Minister, who allegedly had a vast apparatus of aides and evaluators with him, returned home on 3 December and four days later Dubček, Svoboda, Černík, Husák and Štrougal went 'hunting wild boars' with the Soviet leaders near Kiev. Štrougal later told Smrkovský that there was a great deal of debating between individuals rather than in plenary sessions and that at the end of it all Brezhnev stated: 'And we note that the post of Federal Assembly chairman will go to a Slovak'.[41] This topic had apparently not been discussed at a formal meeting at all. This might have been the testing bit. Either Husák came forward with the idea of using the

Slovak issue to dump the awkward Smrkovský, or Brezhnev put it to him and he accepted. After killing off the clandestine party congress, he now engineered Smrkovský's demotion, both feats by employing arguments with nationalist undertones. Having thus proven himself, he became a serious contender.

Among the others, Štrougal's star was rising fast too; from Minister of Agriculture and then of the Interior under Novotný (after the fall of Barák in 1961) to Deputy Prime Minister during the Prague Spring and party praesidium member and secretary from September 1968. He turned his coat no less promptly than Husák and may have lost the race to the very top only because he did not wield power over, and command loyalty from, any particular section of the party as Husák did in Slovakia. In November 1968 Štrougal was made chief of the Party Bureau for the Czech Lands but this was an artificial body, albeit powerful in terms of control over purges, and Moscow probably knew already that a fully-fledged party organisation for the Czech Lands would not be permitted.

Svoboda could not have been considered seriously as any more than a welcome figurehead, lending his reputation to the team of a stronger man. He was 73 years old. Černík might have had some qualities speaking in his favour but his ties with the Dubček line and his share of the 1968 limelight were probably just a little too much to win him Moscow's full trust. It is said that when Dubček realised that he would have to go, he suggested Černík as his successor but by then (around 10 April 1969) the idea got a cool reception.

None of the true diehards was really suitable either because of the amount of animosity they provoked in the public and even among people then still occupying influential party posts or because they were relative lightweights, unknown and fumbling.

That there was determination on the Soviet side to bring to an end its temporary pact with Dubček can be little doubt. The normalisation strategy as understood by Dubček was becoming dangerous and there was a chance that it could make things even more awkward for Moscow. Dubček hoped to push through the convocation of a Czech Party Congress to elect counterpart organs to the Slovak section of the Party. In view of the discrepancy in membership (Czech communists heavily outnumbered Slovaks) and the fact that delegates to the congress had been elected when reformism was in its prime, such a congress would be little different from the clandestine gathering in Vysočany on 22 August and the elected committees were likely to comprise a majority of obstreperous 'progressives'. A general election was also overdue and even a mildly democratised electoral procedure would strengthen reformist positions. Hejzlar also mentions Dubček's intention to release a somewhat subdued version of a report on political trials in the 1950s, prepared during the Prague Spring, which he now kept in his private safe.[42] The Enterprise Bill, a linchpin of continued economic reformism, was also ready for enactment. And finally, Moscow could not enjoy the prospect of Dubček's presence at the forthcoming international communist conference in Moscow. (It was eventually attended in June by Husák, while Bilak acted as chief Czechoslovak delegate at the preparatory talks.)

On the other hand, Dubček was not entirely in breach of contract. He blunted the edge of popular determination to the point where further direct resistance to 'normalisation' became much more difficult in April 1969 than it was in August and September 1968. But he was unable and unwilling to run the reformist movement into the ground totally. The time had come when the Moor had to go. His exit could be engineered more safely in the Spring of 1969 than seven months ago, above all because a powerful dogmatic front had emerged and taken shape, far stronger than the isolated Bilaks and Indras were last August. The ground had been paved and even the choice of a new leader had been made.

Before the mantle was placed on his shoulders, the ice-hockey episode occurred, one of those curious developments which litter history books as if to prove that nothing is silly enough to be unimportant if the powerful of the day so decree. It happened as follows.

At the world championships in Stockholm the Czechoslovak side beat the Russians, their arch rivals, on 21 March 1969 and there was great jubilation in the streets all over Czechoslovakia, obviously amplified by the game's projection into politics. Ice hockey is dear to Czechoslovak hearts almost as much as football, and the year divides equally and easily into a football summer and an ice-hockey winter. The combination of sporting and political excitement led to many an anti-Soviet slogan being shouted, inscribed on makeshift banners or chalked on walls. But on the whole it was fun, betraying the cloven hoof of unholy joy. A private informant recalls that there was no foreboding in top party circles. The return game, a true finale of the tournament, was scheduled a week hence, for 28 March.

It is possible to argue that preventive measures against a repetition of the demonstrations ought to have been taken before the second game and that the public ought to have been alerted to the danger of a Soviet clamp-down as a response to any large-scale presence of crowds in the streets which under the circumstances was bound to have an anti-Soviet edge. If the Soviets wished to take the 'normalisation' process one step further by removing Dubček, it was best done in reply to a demonstrable failure of the incumbents to keep peace and order. There had been rumours, even before the first match, of the Russians getting ready to take advantage of the forthcoming May Day celebration when large crowds could be expected to get out of hand. A 'second military intervention' was feared and spoken about. But perhaps no one anticipated a second victory over the Soviets in a row. It was later suggested, without much evidence, that expensive equipment and furniture were removed from the Aeroflot office in Wenceslas Square and a heap of paving stones deposited in front of it, without visible signs of any repair being planned, a day or two *before* the second match. I have even heard people say that when the first stones were eventually thrown and the first matches lit, the perpetrators looked suspiciously like plainclothesmen. It is a dubious proposition, but not entirely inconceivable. Anyway, a gamble it must have been because not even the Russians could know in advance that their players would lose in Stockholm once again. Had they won, there would have been no demonstration. Unless of course they were ordered to lose. Be it as it may, the Czechoslovaks scored four goals against the Russians' three and the nation exploded with triumphant and somewhat malicious joy again. Thousands and hundreds of thousands flooded the streets throughout the country in spite of the late hour (it was an evening game) and in the confusion the Aeroflot office in Wenceslas Square was ransacked and set on fire. Demonstrations occurred in a number of provincial cities as well.

The government apologised, condemned the demonstration (which was in the end dispersed by riot police with some but not excessive violence), and sat back, hoping for the best, notably that the Russians would take it in their stride. Svoboda, Dubček and Černík even went to West Bohemia to inspect frontier guards troops. Two days passed and then things began to move. Marshal Grechko flew in, unannounced, to a military compound near Prague, to a welcome by several Czechoslovak generals loyal to Moscow, and Deputy Foreign Minister A. Semenov arrived in Prague, both on 31 March. The note which they handed to Svoboda, Dubček and Černík the following day spelled disaster.

It began with the matter-of-fact statement that the Czechoslovak organs did not know how to govern the country. Counter-revolution was rampant again, more so than before last August. The Moscow Protocol was being seriously breached. Even members of the Czechoslovak leadership were interested in fermenting anti-Sovietism. Either order would be imposed at once through police action, preliminary censorship and cessation of polemics about the leading role of the party, *or* a request would be addressed to the Warsaw Pact to help impose order, *or* if nothing was done the Warsaw Pact countries would intervene once again of their own will and as they deemed fit. The note also demanded greater freedom of manoeuvre for Soviet troops inside Czechoslovakia.

Grechko added that appropriate orders had already been issued to his soldiers to open fire if further street demonstrations occurred.

63

It was rumoured in Prague, then and later, that a group of pro-Soviet generals in the high echelons of the Czechoslovak army intended to take advantage of the situation to carry out a 'generals' coup' and install a military government. A memorandum and a plan of action were allegedly prepared along these lines and presented to Grechko for endorsement. After consulting Moscow, he quashed the initiative. Once again, if this is true, Moscow opted for a political solution, knowing that a generals' government would be extremely unpopular even in some hardline quarters, let alone among the population. They could have installed military rule of their own, had they wanted to do so, at the time of the invasion. A Czechoslovak variety, which would have anyway had to rely on the Soviet military machinery, was no better. There is of course in the Soviet army a special service trained to provide military government for an occupied country ('enemy occupied territory' and 'liberated allied territory') but it does not seem to have been introduced into Czechoslovakia. Without it, a purely military chain of command over essentially civilian affairs was a fiction. The Soviets were said to have established 35 places of command for the conduct of their own military affairs in Czechoslovakia (more were to be set up after the ice-hockey riots), much too small a number for overall administration.

Nevertheless, military pressure on the Czechoslovak leadership was obviously an important part of the political offensive which the Soviets stepped up in the first fortnight of April. Not only were Grechko and Maerov, then in command of Soviet troops in the country, active companions of Deputy Foreign Minister Semenov, and not only were Soviet troops placed on alert with new tough orders, but most probably new contingents were brought into the country, a movement over which the Czechoslovaks no longer had real jurisdiction, and troops in East Germany were on the move. A large-scale military exercise, code-named *Vesna*, was announced on 31 March (eventually held in May) and smaller manoeuvres by Soviet troops took place in the first week of April and then again from 14–16 April.

The Czechoslovak leadership is said privately to have commented bitterly on the military element in Soviet pressure which they saw as violating the Moscow agreement on non-interference by the troops in internal Czechoslovak matters. Even Husák was allegedly not happy, but he and Štrougal soon were visited separately by Semenov and Maerov and it was probably during these visits on 3 and 4 April that impending personnel changes in the Czechoslovak party praesidium were finalised. Formally the reshuffle was approved by the central committee on 17 April.

As a result of this change a new power-political arrangement at the top of the Czechoslovak Communist Party came into being which has remained in existence to this day. In essence it consisted of the establishment of an alliance between the new tandem of Husák and Štrougal (both formerly of a moderate reformist reputation, now also called 'centrists' or 'realists') and the old diehard and pro-Moscow faction led by Bilak (which had always been considered conservative, but not extremist or 'ultra'). The immediate victims were Dubček, who ceased to be First Secretary but for the time being remained in the praesidium, and Smrkovský, who was dropped even from that august body. At the same time the anomaly of a large party praesidium was ended and a tighter eleven-member organ created. The quintessential nature of the April 1969 change did not, of course, preclude a ripple effect in other central and territorial links of the party and state mechanism. On the contrary, it signalled further changes, and they were to become the content of Husák's first 'normalisation' phase.

Part Two

Expurgation and consolidation

April 1969–May 1971

THE PARTY IN THE PURGATORY

The policy shift

When Gustav Husák made his concluding remarks at the central committee session on 17 April and again when he delivered the main report to the ensuing central committee meeting on 29 May, he repeatedly referred to the November 1968 central committee resolution. With his two speeches, these three documents provided a framework for party policy after the change in leadership. By invoking a resolution which had been adopted when Dubček and Smrkovský were still in charge, however restrictive the circumstances may have been, the new First Secretary put emphasis on continuity. Neither he nor Moscow evidently wished to give the impression that an entirely new policy content was being injected into the consolidation framework. Policy was not to change, or so they were saying, but the approach to its implementation was.

References were made to other party documents and periods. The Novotný regime remained a target of criticism, although gradually and subtly the critical edge was directed towards its alleged inability to control 'liberalisation', not its conservatism. Husák even harked back to the period which affected him personally: if only Novotný had de-Stalinised the party in 1956 as the Soviet comrades had done, the future could have been different. Thus the deposition of Novotný in January 1968 and the party's embarkation on a new course were still regarded 'necessary and inevitable'. (A lip service to January is being paid to this day, albeit only sporadically and without any obvious connection with real political processes: witness the party statement on the tenth anniversary of the events in January 1978.[1])

The Action Programme of April 1968 began to fare somewhat worse relatively soon. It was said to have contained some 'correct' precepts but because it was adopted hurriedly and under intellectual pressure, the party would now, in the middle of 1969, be better served by the November 1968 resolution than by it.

The continuity was not entirely fraudulent, and of course it was tactically opportune because of the nervous disposition of the public and indeed large portions of the party apparatus. Brezhnev himself had endorsed the November resolution when Dubček presented it to him in Warsaw where the Soviet leader was attending the Polish party congress, before it was actually promulgated in Prague. It seems quite possible that the new Czechoslovak leader received a Soviet instruction which initially was not more complicated than 'act on the November resolution, but make it work'.

Apart from changes in occasional formulations, the main difference in policy content between November 1968 and May 1969 was in the replacement of the section on 'creative Marxism-Leninism, science and arts' in the November resolution by a section on 'reinforcing the functions of the socialist state as an organ of the working class and the working people' in Husák's May speech.

The Committees and the Apparats

In a reshuffle arising from Husák's ascendance to the top post, Dubček became chairman of the Federal Assembly, Sádovský Slovak First Secretary and Colotka Slovak Prime Minister, but apart from showing that Dubček's slide into disfavour would happen in stages rather than abruptly, these transfers altered nothing in the political complexion of the new regime or the balance of power within it. Further changes in the leading posts were obviously not far away, and the first one occured only two days after the April session when the progressive J. Sekera was replaced as *Rudé právo* editor-in-chief by the hardliner Miroslav Moc.

The May meeting of the central committee expelled F. Kriegel from the party and five other prominent reformers from the central committee. With one possible exception, the six secretaries appointed on 2–3 June were all followers of Husák or worse. The hub of the central party apparatus thus came under conservative control, an important development in a hierarchically organised institution where observance of centrally issued directives has become second nature to officials of a lower status. On the same two days in early June Husák himself supervised the first of several purges which were to befall the Municipal Party Committee in Prague: the chief secretary B. Šimon was replaced by O. Matějka. The Prague party organisation had grown in stature during the Prague Spring and became instrumental as the host of the clandestine congress at the time of the invasion. Pro-Moscow 'realists' later called it the mainstay of the 'second centre' in the party, a condemnatory designation which was used in 1952 by Gottwald when indicating Rudolf Slánský. By definition the communist party can have only one centre-point, and Husák diligently set out to ensure that he provided its focus. More resignations were reported from the Prague municipal committee on 24 September. In the meantime turnover in cadres began in the regional party committees in the Czech Lands.

Then the turn came of the central committee itself, the congruence of whose composition with the party policy of the day had been disturbed at the beginning of 1968 and never quite restored. At first it was considered over-conservative when the party under Dubček was pressing for progressive reforms. The 14th congress was to put things right, but the congress could only meet in abnormal conditions and the central committee elected by it was vetoed by Moscow virtually the next day. A compromise of sorts was reached at the end of August with the co-optation of eighty newcomers into the pre-Vysočany central committee. A head count then became difficult if not impossible because there had been individual resignations and one expulsion (Novotný) even during the Prague Spring. The old rules of secrecy also began to operate shortly after April 1969, so that no one really knew how many members there were, which ones were absent and why, and who voted for and against what.

It should be said that the Czechoslovak Communist Party has always been more secretive about such rudimentary statistics as membership and social composition than the Soviet Communist Party.[2] Without a claim to full accuracy, after April 1969 the incumbent central committee, having lost 19 members (ousted and resigned) and gained six by co-optation at its session in May, consisted of some 170 full members, in addition to alternate, non-voting members, of whom about two-thirds had been elected (and hand picked) under Novotný in 1966 and one-third could be termed 'progressive'. But even the pre-1968 survivors included many who had played the Dubček game. No wonder that the screening out of unwilling 'normalisers' took long, and it was not before the 14th congress in 1971 that a satisfactory composition was achieved.

Thus in September 1969 there were 19 ousters and eight co-optations, in January 1970 twenty dismissals or resignations and eight co-optations, and in June 1970 twelve losses and seven gains. Finally, at the 14th congress in May 1971, a 115 strong new central committee was elected which consisted of 61 survivors and 54 newcomers.

This may look like a dreary recitation of figures which, however, shows that the leadership sought to re-shape the constitutionally supreme organ of the party between congresses in a way which contravened the party constitution. Co-optations, strictly speaking, should be made only from among the alternate members and, according to amendments passed only in May 1971, should not exceed ten per cent of the total membership of the committee. It also exemplified the way in which a handful of real party leaders can manipulate the ostensibly superior body which elected them. Also concealed behind the statistics are the changing personal fortunes of a number of individuals who had perhaps thought, on being elected to the central committee, that they had made it, only to find themselves smitten by upheavals such as the party had not known since the 'bolshevisation' years of 1928 and 1929 when Gottwald was getting to power.

Some intriguing patterns emerge, illustrative of why regime stability is so dear to the communist power elite's heart. The Vysočany congress retained only 25 central committee members elected at the 13th congress in 1966. The 14th congress in 1971, interestingly, also kept only 26 of those first entering the central committee in 1966, except of course that they were mostly different people from those who made it at Vysočany. The reduction to virtually the same number, albeit accidental, is uncanny. An evergreen medal should surely be awarded to the two persons who managed to get themselves elected successively at the 13th, the Vysočany and the 14th congresses: Peter Colotka and Kliment Neoveský, both Slovaks, the former a party official who served Novotný, Dubček and Husák equally well in high positions, and the latter a technician in the West Slovak Oil Enterprise, otherwise undistinguished. Only nine of central committee members elected at Vysočany and 34 of those comprising the committee as of its session on 31 August 1968 made it into the 'normalised' body in May 1971.

The most momentous of the central committee sessions after April was held in September 1969. It seems that it was at first intended to be a 'self-critical' meeting at which Dubček, Smrkovský and other hitherto recalcitrant reformers would admit their sins and give public endorsement to the leadership of the day. This would not save them politically, although the impact of the purge on them might be cushioned off a little more then it eventually was, but a seal of approval from the popular Men of the Spring would have had considerable significance for Gustav Husák and Leonid Brezhnev in terms of pacifying the irritated population. In the end the reformers refused to play ball and delivered defiant speeches restating their interpretations of the Prague Spring, the invasion and the subsequent return of career-conscious functionaries to an orthodox course.[3] The step-by-step demotion and removal of reformers continued: Prchlík, Slavík and Černý were expelled from the party; Smrkovský, Hübl, Mlynář and Hájek from the central committee, and Dubček from the praesidium. Several were 'permitted' to resign and those still holding non-party posts (in the Federal Assembly) were 'recommended' for dismissal from them. Non-conformist speeches were not published in the Czechoslovak press, which was a pity; this meeting of the central committee was to remain for a long time the last one at which a clash of views on issues that mattered was tolerated. Thereafter the good old times of unanimity returned.

A word or two on the nature of central committee sessions between the invasion and the 14th congress. Until the end of 1969 they were almost wholly introverted, i.e. concerned with reversing the effects of the reforms inside the party, mainly by way of changing the cadres. Starting in 1970, economic matters began to be discussed but purges still figured more prominently on the agenda. The economic items had an air of formality around them, such as the presentation of outlines for the fifth five-year plan in December 1970 which anyway was approved only in mid-1971. And of course there was a gala session on 7 May 1970 to mark the 25th anniversary of the end of the war and liberation by the Soviet army. In 1971 the main preoccupation was with the 14th congress and the general election.

Not that the party praesidium remained stable once Husák and Štrougal ensconsed themselves in it. Dubček lost his seat in September 1969 and was replaced by J. Kempný. (Dubček was subsequently named ambassador to Turkey, recalled from there and expelled from the party in June 1970.) Černík, Poláček and Sádovský were dropped in January 1970 while A. Kapek, J. Korčák and J. Lenárt got in. (Černík had to surrender federal premiership to Štrougal, was recalled from his ministerial post in June 1970 and expelled from the party in December of the same year.) J. Piller was 'permitted' to resign from the praesidium in February 1971 and A. Indra was appointed in his place. Finally, at the first post-congress session on 29 May 1971, K. Hoffmann was taken in.

A comparison of the praesidia at three crucial points, the night of the invasion, the start of real normalisation in April 1969, and the completed build-up of cadres in May 1971, shows that Bilak alone provided continuity, though other full members had been candidates for membership previously, and Svoboda would have done, except that under reformist conditions it was considered advisable to leave the President of the Republic out of the top party body, perhaps to enhance his formal independence and seniority. Four of the team elected at the 14th congress in 1971 were traditional opponents of reformism (Bilak, Hoffmann, Indra and Kapek), two were complete newcomers to the top, with technocratic reputations (Kempný and Korčák), three changed sides without having overcommitted themselves in 1968 (Colotka, Lenárt and Štrougal), and two would have passed as dedicated advocates of reform in Prague Spring conditions (Svoboda and Husák). Bilak, Hoffmann, Indra, Kapek, Lenárt and Štrougal could also be considered as forming a bridge with the pre-reformist past, and it was perhaps not accidental that this section of the praesidium was in a majority.

Two of the three 'candidate members' of the praesidium (non-voting but privy to practically all secrets and present at all meetings) from the time of the invasion were converted to full members as of 1971 (Kapek and Lenárt), whereas the remaining one, B. Šimon, staked his political health on Dubček and as leader of the powerful Prague organisation of the party followed Dubček into the political cold.

Central committee secretaries are leading functionaries, some of them members of the praesidium and all members of the secretariat (which however has also members that are not styled 'secretaries'), who have direct responsibilities over the various sections in the top office of the party and are in charge of vertical lines of command stretching down to local branches via regions and districts. There were six secretaries in August 1968 and seven in May 1971, Alois Indra being the only one to hold the post on both dates. Of the remaining five who were secretaries in 1968, Dubček and Císař did not survive because of reformism, even if Císař tried hard and stayed on for quite some time. Kolder and Sádovský were dropped after some initial service to Husák in the second round of the purges, Kolder presumably for alcoholism and Sádovský because his behaviour on invasion night became a drawback as revenge-taking became commoner. (According to an eye-witness report he 'expressed full solidarity' with the statement condemning the entry of troops.) Lenárt, together with Indra, was a 'normaliser' in 1971, both advanced to membership of the praesidium, but Lenárt did not retain a secretary's job. New secretaries in May 1971, in addition to Husák and Indra, were V. Bilak, J. Fojtík, M. Hruškovič, J. Kempný and O. Švestka.

After the successful seizure of the praesidium in April 1969, 'normalisation' in the way of removal of reformers proceeded apace in regional, district and local party branches, and somewhat less avidly in Slovakia. Nine regional and 59 district chief secretaries of the party were removed, and more than one-third of functionaries elected to various central, regional and district committees either had to resign or were expelled from party ranks.[4]

Jozef Lenárt explained the less drastic purge in Slovakia by the fact that a truly Marxist-Leninist group had been in existence in the Slovak party's leadership, headed by Vasil Bilak, all through the Prague Spring, countering the worst excesses of reformism. Leading men of Slovak culture were also opposed to counter-revolution, unlike their Czech colleagues. Slovakia had undergone far-reaching social changes in the socialist period of its history and its population's level of socialist awareness was high. In addition, many people remembered the joint battles which Slovak partisans and Soviet soldiers had waged against the Nazis during the Slovak National Rising in 1944. Finally, the process of federalisation 'pushed aside those questions which the right-wing was raising, notably the so-called democratisation'. Nonetheless, as Lenárt did not forget to add (and as others have stressed as well), 'a dangerous counter-revolutionary situation was gradually taking shape in Slovakia too'.[5]

Parallel to their dismissal from party posts, leading communist reformers were being purged from responsible positions in governmental and important public organisations. Unlike in 1968, the ostensibly non-communist sections of the country's political structure and infrastructure once again came to be regarded as extensions of the

party's institutional empire and as instruments of the party's governance over society, for the staffing of which with trusted followers the
party was responsible. Husák and other ideologists made this clear
when stressing right from the start that it was the party who delegated
people to work in the government, the parliament, the trade unions
and the other social organisations. They were servants of the party, not
of their respective constituencies (although even a mildly skilful
dialectician would have no difficulty in explaining that there was
compatibility, not divergence, between the two). If the party decided
that they must go, go they must. Intra-party purge was thus
inextricably linked to the exercise of the party's leading role over non-
party institutions.

It would seem that from April to September 1969 most enforced
changes concerned party organisations, whereas after the September
session of the central committee the waves of expurgation spread wider
and wider. No particular pattern in the purges is discernible except
that some bodies were affected several times, which must mean that the
purge criteria were progressively tightened. Many of those who
exchanged the reformist policy for an anti-reformist one with ease
after Husák's new course was proclaimed, prematurely sighed with
relief when the first round of purge was over; they were hit six months
or a year later.

To exemplify the process of purgation: the Federal Assembly
underwent substantial changes in October and December 1969, in
July 1970 and in March 1971; the Czech National Council in
November and December 1969, December 1970, January and March
1971; the Slovak National Council in December 1969, April 1970 and
January 1971; the Federal Government in September 1969, January
and June 1970 and January 1971; the federal Trades Union Council in
February and June 1970 and March 1971; the Youth Union (under its
various titles as it was undergoing a process of recentralisation) in
September and November 1969, April, October and November 1970,
and June 1971.

A certain amount of purging had to be done even in the police and
the army. The leadership of the Ministry of the Interior under
Dubček's nominee Josef Pavel showed a determined tendency in 1968
to discontinue some lines of activity altogether (domestic surveillance
of dissidents), to drop certain practices (both in the sense of using
spying equipment and certain forms of surveillance as well as during
interrogation), and to put some order into the remaining pursuits. The
overall impression was that Pavel sought to divest the ministry of its
sinister and dreaded reputation as the iron-gloved guardian of
ideological orthodoxy. Pavel's time turned out to be short, however,
and his efforts were anyway impeded by the entrenched conservatives
of whom there must have been more in his ministry than in all the

others put together. Shortly after the invasion Pavel had to go; this the Russians are said to have demanded in Moscow as an absolute *sine qua non* of any further discussions. His first successor, J. Pelnář, a typical compromise appointment of the time, soon made way for a far more diehard trio when the government was federalised and the Ministry of the Interior happened to be one of those which existed at both federal and the two national levels. The Czech Minister of the Interior, J. Grösser, even belonged to the 'ultra' dogmatic faction and had to go when he allegedly became implicated in an anti-Husák plot in October 1970. Before then he could however report to the central committee in June 1970 that the 'right-wingers in the Ministry' who had allegedly ceased to wage battle on the 'internal bases of the enemy and against ideological subversion' were discharged and things were being put right once again. This, he warned, would be a long drawn-out process because in some fields the system had been completely exposed to the enemy and there were even cases of 'open betrayal'. (Obviously a reference to several defections of fairly high-class security agents and officials.) Nonetheless, the Minister assured the central committee that those sections of his office which were designed to combat anti-socialist forces had been politically consolidated to the point where no one would be allowed to disrupt the honest work of the citizens.[6]

Relying on unofficial information where official publicity remained scant throughout the period of 'normalisation', it can be deduced that the shake-up in the armed forces was even more profound. (Military intelligence and counter-intelligence may have been an exception. Private sources suggest that people there were rather reshuffled than altogether removed.) Of the 80 per cent commissioned and non-commissioned officers who had been party members, one-fifth are said to have been expelled or struck off the party lists (some 11,000 persons), and about half of those so affected had to leave the army altogether, the others being transferred to positions without real importance. Of 136 generals (in August 1968), at least 20 were expelled from the army and degraded. These included V. Prchlík, former chief of the Army Political Administration, K. Peprný, former Deputy Minister and commander of the Border Guards, A Procházka, J. Kamenický, commander of Anti-Aircraft Defence, J. Štika, chief of staff under Kamenický, J. Frýbert, head of the Political Adminis- tration of the Western Military Sector, Dr Engel, head of the Central Military Hospital, and others.[7]

Even the party's private army, the People's Militia, had to undergo 'a process of differentiation and consolidation' between August 1968 and the end of 1970. According to a high officer in the Militia, the wavering people, fellow travellers and dissenters were purged, and the overall numbers declined (by an unspecified number).[8]

The recruitment of new loyal members of the officers' corps appeared to run into problems, not the least of them being reluctance of potential recruits. An *Obrana lidu* writer complained that this contrasted unfavourably with the USSR and East Germany where young people themselves called at recruitment centres and asked to be sent to military schools. In Czechoslovakia the army and career officers in particular stood low on the social status scale as a result of right-wing attacks, theories of neutrality and propaganda about the peace-loving nature of American and West German imperialists. Voices were even heard questioning the need for an army at all. In the USSR every school has a special room or at least a corner of a room dedicated to military traditions and every child knows and respects war heroes, whereas in Czechoslovakia this thing is almost non-existent.[9] Eventually a longer-term solution was found in the setting up from the 1971–72 school-year of a new type of officer training centre for young apprentices with an appropriate political and moral profile and full physical capability. In two years, the trainees would receive 'normal' secondary education (which otherwise takes three or even four years) and adequate military instruction to be immediately commissioned at junior lieutenant level. In return for the two-year course (all expenses paid), the recruits had to sign for six additional years of military service.[10] A pay-rise for national servicemen came into force in June 1971. Volunteers with secondary or higher education were being attracted to a commission by cash bonuses and the allotment of a flat on signing. Housing was and still is a most precious commodity.

Simultaneously purges were unleashed and continued unabated in the third most important governing apparatus, next to the party and the police, the national committees which in Czechoslovakia (as in the other communist countries) constitute a centralised instrument of state power extending right down to small communities. The elements of genuine local government in their activity began dwindling away once again. And of course loyal communists were being mobilised to prepare for takeovers in state institutions which operated in the intellectual fields. A trustworthy president of the Academy of Sciences was appointed in October 1969.

How was the removal of overcommitted reformers and persons unwilling to play the new game accomplished? From the information available we can reconstruct the expurgation process in general contours.

First, the 'hard core' (or 'sound core') of 'communist internationalists' had to be identified in every organisation.

Then the 'normalisation' platform as formulated in documents sent to the organisation from the central organs of the party (which had already gone over to the new policy) was presented to a membership meeting for discussion.

The 'sound core' comrades would see to it that the general postulates of the platform were transposed into conditions pertinent to the organisation (committee, etc.) in question, for example by exposing officers or members who had been eager in implementing reformist policies, acted against the invasion or harboured views no longer advocated by the party.

Where the strength of the local diehards was suspected to be insufficient to carry the day, comrades from higher party bodies were delegated to preside over the proceedings.

A vote was eventually arranged on a resolution supporting the Husák leadership and condemning reformism in general and its local variety in particular. If the organisation in question had passed statements in 1968, before and during the invasion, which did not correspond to the new policy (nearly all of them did not), a recantation was called for. The party praesidium set an example by revoking its reply to the Warsaw Pact warning letter of July 1968 and its condemnatory resolution of 21 August 1968 at the central committee session of September 1969 which also renounced the Vysočany congress fully and publicly.

By the same token, the party gradually came over to calling the invasion 'an act of internationalist assistance' or 'fraternal assistance'. (Husák himself used the latter term for the first time on 29 August 1969, but Sádovský appears to have beaten him to the tape first on 4 and then 28 August.)

As a result of the debate and the vote (or in some cases before the vote), functionaries associated too closely with the Prague Spring and those reluctant to support 'normalisation' to the hilt (not always necessarily the same people) were either allowed to resign if the measure of their guilt was not seen excessive, or were 'relieved' or 'dismissed'. The semantics mattered to an extent; resignation signalled the possibility of a transfer to another, inferior but still comfortable position whereas dismissal more often than not led to blacklisting and relegation to manual jobs.

Several institutions were considered infested with reformism beyond repair and were disbanded, e.g. the party committees for universities, the departments of Marxism-Leninism at universities, the Military Political Academy in Prague, the party committees in Prague Radio and in Czechoslovak Airlines, and some institutes of the Academy of Sciences. Neither was any attempt made to take over such organisations as the Society for Human Rights (suspended by the Ministry of the Interior on 28 May 1969), the Students' Union (statutes rejected on 20 June 1969), the Ostrava and Prague branches of the Journalists' Union (disbanded on 5 and 8 September 1969 respectively), and the art unions.

Things were then fairly rapidly beginning to take shape in the scheme which Moscow designed for them, and the familiar features of authoritarianism became clearly visible.

The Membership

Bowing a collective head to superior institutions is a time-honoured practice in authoritarian societies. Indeed, it has happened so often that many individual members of such institutions are insensitive to it. Under the cloak of enforced unity the communist societies of Eastern Europe have managed to conceal a growing diversity of opinions, many impotent but, at auspicious times, some of them not insignificant. Czechoslovakia went through such a patch in the 1960s when far-reaching reform plans were hatched behind a facade of ostentatious uniformity. Many a Western observer was deceived by the apparent calm on the surface and then surprised by the vigour of the Prague Spring. Many reformers, especially those in the second line, not exposed to Moscow's watchful eye (or so they believed), hoped that a period of hibernation in the wake of the invasion was not without promise for the future. If only they could stay put, hiding behind formal manifestations of unity, the time would again come for a rebirth of change-seeking within the party. The trouble was that Husák knew that much too.

Having commanded obedience in the decisive institutions, and committees, he initiated a personal purge with the express aim of putting every single member of the party and employee of the state on the rack. Where the institutional conscience (if there is such a thing) can possibly be burdened with a false proclamation of loyalty without great harm being done to the immunised individual consciences of the men who comprise the institution, an individual pledge can be clad in fewer layers of protective or self-apologetic make-believe. Not that people under communism are not used to signing their names under all sorts of avowals, in order to save their skins, and many would no doubt disown Sasha Dubček three times without blinking in the forthcoming purge again. But the openness of the Prague Spring was so great that the prosecutors would have no difficulty in seeing through the mimicry. An individual purge would crown the Husák leadership's effort in a manner from which there was no escape.

Much would of course depend on how strict the criteria and their application would be. Party purges are not new in the history of communism although one would be hard put to compare the Husák purge with anything short of the Chinese cultural revolution. Both the party, then about 1,650,000 strong *and* the state and public organisation employees and members were to be screened. Even if we leave out manual workers who traditionally, as Marx opined, had nothing to lose but their chains, the total number scheduled for screening would amount to some five million or one-half of the adult population, each with his own little Damocles' sword over the head. If the purge were to be benevolent, a kind of public relations exercise where a few Christians are thrown to the lions but the religion is permitted to go on, well, perhaps not all was lost yet. Some people were incorrigible optimists. If, however, ...

Before the purge there were signs pointing both ways. To quote from the horse's mouth, Gustav Husák said at the May 1969 central committee meeting: 'This political battle will on the one hand require a Leninist principle-mindedness and on the other great sensitivity in relation to party members and citizens as well as patience in explaining, arguing and winning people over'.[11]

One has the feeling, and a feeling it must remain in the absence of hard information, when reading Husák's speeches and articles from the period between the summer of 1969 and January 1970, when the purge was being prepared, that the tendency which he represented in the party leadership aimed at a middle-of-the-road purge, neither too hard nor too lenient. As he put it: '. . . we should not lose honest people, but we must not retain enemies in the party'.[12] And his strong words about those who had chosen reformism at the cost of Marxism-Leninism were accompanied by a special warning against the staging of a witch-hunt on the intelligentsia. In September 1969 he said: 'We are not butchers. Our party is not a slaughterhouse. . . . The party politics are not executed with sabres. Education is not a matter of scything people down, of vengeance, revenge or settling of personal accounts.'[13] Especially he singled out teachers, technicians and even cultural workers and scholars as deserving a sensitive treatment during the purge.

'People have to be fought for, won over, not just mechanically condemned, labelled or even cast aside. There were many mistaken people in this field [cultural intelligentsia and scientists]. And to mistaken people, as we have already said, we must extend a helping hand . . . so that we do not exclude them or drive them away from a positive road. In questions of principle we shall make no compromise, but a principled attitude need not mean rudeness and it does not mean that we should approach people with an axe in hand when all they need is a kind word.'[14]

It was in this connection, at the January 1970 meeting of the central committee, when the purge was just about to start, when the Kadarian echo resounded in Husák's words:

'He who does not go against us, is our potential ally. He is not an enemy, he must be striven for, he must be won over'.[15]

Nonetheless, Husák's philosophy of the purge was difficult to reconcile with the more detailed instructions about how the purge interviews should actually be conducted and which answers every party member was required to answer. The selection of screening commissions was also important. There may have been a 'moderate' philosophy, but the practical framework was positively intransigent.

The party purge was conceived as a series of individual interviews of every member before a screening commission. Eventually there were 70,217 such screening groups comprising 235,270 interviewers, many of them veteran party members.[16] Over 1·5 million members were interviewed (an estimated 150,000 who had left the party on their own accord between January 1968 and January 1970 were of course not subjected to the procedure and automatically considered lost). This means that there was one interviewer for every 6·37 members and that every screening group processed 21·36 members, including themselves. (In fact lower screening commissions were interviewed by higher ones.) The going was tough in most places and the average length of an interview would seem to be one hour. Some were even longer, while others lasted barely a minute, such as the one that became part of the purge folklore: Enters a member, places his party card in front of the chairman of the screening commission and says, 'to put it bluntly, the so-called fraternal assistance was an invasion and the Russians are scoundrels, good-bye'.

The commissions had a list of composite questions (fourteen, some sources say) which together comprised a minute guideline to a full life story of every member from January 1968 to the present and his future undertakings. All questions but the last two had the character of attitude probing against a checklist of events, e.g. what was your attitude and your behaviour *vis-à-vis* the Action Programme, the 2000 Words Manifesto, the Čierna and Bratislava talks, the entry of Warsaw Pact troops, the death of Jan Palach, the ice-hockey riots, the replacement of Husák for Dubček, etc. The last two questions required of the member to say what specific work he was doing at the moment to help promote 'normalisation' and what did he intend to do in future to enhance the party's leading role at his place of work and in his domicile.

Purge questions in non-party organisations, such as the National Committees, the trade unions, the youth union, were formulated similarly but not with the same thoroughness.

In many enterprises and offices (all of which are of course in Czechoslovakia state-owned in the last instance and therefore staffed with employees of the state who were all required to submit to the purge) people were handed out questionnaires which were later evaluated by purge commissions. Here there were only nine questions, relatively simple. Some had a general character: 'What is your opinion of the changes effected in January 1968?' Or 'How did you accept the change in the party leadership in April 1969 and the subsequent May measures aiming at consolidation?' Others were more specific: 'What public activity did you evolve and which public functions did you hold in 1968, in 1969 and now?'

The outcome of purges outside the party was directly dependent in each individual case on whether the person in question was a party member and whether he had been cleared in the party purge or not. (Many people, members of the party and, say, three other organisations, had to go through the purge procedure in each of them *and* at their place of work.) Of the permutations, one can say (without statistical information to prove the point) that a party member cleared by a party screening commission was virtually certain to be cleared in his enterprise or institution, although in some cases zealous informers in non-party organisations implicated people who managed to pass through the party sieve unscathed. A party member not cleared in the party purge, on the other hand, was virtually certain to suffer as a job holder. The size of his punishment would depend on whether he had been just 'struck off the party roster' or 'expelled'. A person handing in his or her party card or not bothering to turn up at the purge interview was considered expelled. No one can simply dis-join the communist party. A 'striking off' designated a lesser offence and a lesser penalty, for example demotion to lower paid or menial position. Straight expulsion signified utter condemnation and was as a rule accompanied by dismissal from work and blacklisting. Only very menial, manual jobs were open to the expellees and they had to be such as not to give the victim opportunity to mix with people easily, for fear of spreading discontent.

Husák's putative moderateness at the beginning of the purges did not only come into conflict with the technical instructions on how the purge should be conducted of which he must have been aware and which went down to the screening commissions from the central committee secretariat. Circumstantial evidence suggests that advocates of an even more diehard course in the party leadership, probably in conjunction with the diehards in some regions and districts, pushed for maximum severity right from the start—and eventually prevailed. Alois Indra and Vasil Bilak were reputed to have insisted on reducing the party to half its numerical strength and even more. Indra's statement was quoted around Prague: 'So what if there are only 400,000 card-carrying communists left in Czechoslovakia?'

The purge criteria were tightened even further some three months after the operation began, in April 1970, at a national conference of regional and district secretaries of the party. *Rudé právo* reported:

'It has been established that the principled Marxist-Leninist compliance with the envisaged aims of the interviews, i.e. the purge of the
party ranks of right-wing opportunist elements, impassive members
and others who do not belong to the party, is being jeopardised by
conciliatory and unprincipled attitudes. At all levels purposeful efforts
must be made to win over communist workers for the policies of the
party so that the working-class nature of the party is strongly enhanced.
The national conference has unanimously agreed that during the next
stage of the process whereby party cards are being replaced by new ones,
a decisive turning point should be achieved towards a more energetic
struggle against conciliation and lack of principle which threaten to
leave the Czechoslovak Communist Party unpurged of all the right-
wing opportunists, revisionists, various career-seekers and passive
members'.[17]

The prevalence of the radical line in relation to the purge can
perhaps be explained as the outcome of a rapprochement between the
diehard faction in the leadership (Bilak, Indra) and the neo-Stalinist
'ultras' who again came into prominence. It is also worth noting that
the rehabilitations of political prisoners from the early years of
Czechoslovak communism also stopped at about the same time, by
decision of the National Front of 7 April 1970. The Rehabilitation
Law of 1968 was then amended on 8 July.

It is not easy to draw a clear line between the attitudes of individual
personalities who represented the three tendencies in the party and
were all now riding the post-invasion crest of orthodoxy. Husák's
stand only looked 'moderate' if compared with the ultra-diehard
demands, while in comparison with the attitudes of the reformers, and
indeed his own of less than two years ago, he was a manifest
reactionary. There was a certain amount of crossing the lines between
the factions until the overall political structure stabilised in the middle
1970s. Some people were also more true to their original loyalties than
others and covered little political ground travelling from one faction to
another. Vasil Bilak, for example, never really departed from his firm
orthodox beliefs and policies to the left of Husák, but whatever
sympathies he may have felt for the 'true levellers' in the ultra-left
faction, he was too much of a shrewd politician ever to join them.
Antonín Kapek, on the other hand, seemed to have crisscrossed the
division several times before finally striking root in the Bilak camp.
Lubomír Štrougal, who once helped Novotný to arrest Rudolf Barák,
the man whose post as Minister of the Interior he thereby acquired,
threw in his lot with the cautious section of Dubček's supporters in
1968 and even signed an anti-Soviet statement in the invasion days,
only to show such goodwill for 'normalisation' of the Soviet type that
he rose meteorically at Husák's side, acquiring at the same time the

reputation of a hardliner. More recently he is being credited with representing the rational, technocratic trend in opposition to the continued ideological war in which Bilak and company revel.

Be that as it may, the tussle between the ultras and the conservative camp with its 'moderate' and hardline wings flared up after the September 1969 central committee plenum and took the form of thinly disguised polemics in the press, various shifting of officials in which all sides appeared to score victories and suffer defeats, and finally a kind of truce resting on compromise. The circumstantial evidence and a mass of rumour would seem to suggest that on balance the orthodox conservatives prevailed over the extremists in that the latter had to wind down their two organisations, the Left Front and the Lenin Union of Youth, which were merged into the mainstream institutional frameworks of the Socialist Academy and the Socialist Union of Youth. (The Left Front had its statutes legalised on 9 July 1969 and was wound up on 26 February 1971. The Lenin Union of Youth held its constituent meeting on 7 March 1969 and was disbanded on 23 April 1970 in Slovakia and on 11 September 1970 in the Czech Lands, both dates coinciding with impending national constituent conferences of SSM—Socialist Youth Union.) Insofar as staffing of responsible positions was concerned, the ultras ended up as losers as well. Their followers had to vacate the positions of the Czech Minister of the Interior (J. Grösser, 23 October 1970), the liaison officer with Soviet troops (O. Rytíř, 27 October 1970) and the Czech Minister of Education (J. Hrbek, 8 July 1971), to name but a few. On the other hand, the man who was often tipped as the ultras' envoy in the party's innermost sanctum, Antonín Kapek, became chief secretary of the important Prague organisation of the party on 16 December 1969 and is a praesidium member to this day. In the most recent unofficial reports from Prague, early in 1978, he is still said to be a contender for ultimate power and a hardliner to boot. Viliam Šalgovič, erstwhile secret service chief, banished to Budapest after the invasion as a military attaché, staged a gradual comeback to become chairman of the Slovak Communist Party's Control and Auditing Commission and in 1975 member of the Slovak party praesidium and chairman of the Slovak National Council. Although they may have been re-admitted to top places on Husák's terms, there can be little doubt that they strengthened the hardline tendency once ensconsed there.

It would therefore seem that the ultras were organisationally dispersed but they did score important victories in the sense of helping to bring about several policy decisions which shaped the course of 'normalisation'. The severity of the purges was a manifest example of the strength of their influence.

If the purge of the party and the other institutions of the state and the infrastructure was conducted leniently, more change-orientated people would have remained in positions of influence to enable the crystallisation of a moderate conservative regime which would preserve some reforms even under the overall umbrella of ideological orthodoxy. Kadarisation would have been possible. The economic reform could have continued, Hungarian fashion, without the self-managing element. A more open relationship between the top of the party and its lower structures, between the party and the rest of the population, and between the party and its potential consultants (scientists, scholars) could have been maintained. The cultural disaster could have been avoided. Demoralisation based on fear could have been averted, and links with the non-communist world could have been restored on a livelier and more beneficial basis than eventually happened. It would still be a tutelary society, but the road to modernisation and cultural satisfaction would have remained open. Furthermore, and perhaps even more importantly, the political actors of Czechoslovakia would not have been divided into the three large groups which comprise the political scene now: the fanatic elite, the cynical servants and the aggrieved oppositionists. After the trauma of invasion, reconciliation was still possible. Not however with some one million victims of extremist intransigence emerging as the product of a savage purge conducted on the lines of an ideological vendetta. If there ever was a moment when Gustav Husák should have put his foot down, then the purge of 1970 was it. No matter his turning of the coat at the moment of the invasion, no matter his replacing Alexander Dubček, no matter his kowtowing to the almighty Soviet Union. He could have kept all those and much more. But when it came to perpetuating a split in the society which he was about to govern and to closing the avenue leading to a morally defensible regime, he should have known better. Fatalists will of course say that he could not have done otherwise since adaptation to pressure is the stuff he is made of, in spite of appearances to the contrary. Pity.

It looks as if the party leadership was unable to agree on what set of statistics on the purge to present to the public, or perhaps the confusion is in fact obfuscation. Three different results of the purge have been made public: by Husák in December 1970, by Balik in September 1975, and be Jakeš at the 15th congress in April 1976. Not only do they not tally, but each is camouflaged in its own way.

Husák told a plenary session of the central committee[18] that 'over 1·5 million' members were interviewed and that the new party card was denied to 326,817 or 21·67 per cent. (This would give the base figure of 1,508,154.) With the departure of members on their own will, the party was said to have lost 473,731 members or 28 per cent as against membership figures on 1 January 1968. (That membership must accordingly have been 1,691,896.) The number of those expelled in the course of the interviews was 67,147 whereas 259,670 were crossed off the register of members. If only the loss of membership during the purge was taken into account, the percentage of those expelled as against those struck off would be 20·5 and 79·5. But there would still remain 146,914 persons who were not in the party at the end of the purge but had been there on 1 January 1968, and presumably on the eve of the invasion, because membership was not thought to go down during the Prague Spring. If we assume that Husák did not include loss of members due to deaths in the party's ranks, the overall picture in terms of the two categories of persons who were victimised more severely because they were either expelled or quit, and those whose punishment was less because they were only struck off the roster would be 214,061 in the former and 259,670 in the latter, or 45·2 and 54·8 per cent.

The second set of figures comes from Vasil Bilak's interview in the American communist *Daily World* (as reported in *Rudé právo* from which the information is taken).[19] He said that 70,934 persons were expelled and 390,817 deleted from the party's register, a total of 461,751. Bilak further volunteered the information that of those who lodged an appeal one-fifth had it 'considered favourably' (presumably being reinstated in the party) and that 30 per cent of those failing to pass the sieve lost their jobs as a result. This would indicate victimisation for political reasons in 138,525 cases. Bilak's figures are however suspect. On the one hand they are substantially higher than Husák's (by 3,787 expelled and 131,147 struck-off), which could indicate that the purge was still in progress when Husák reported to the central committee in December 1970 although it had officially terminated by then. At the same time, Bilak talked to the American newspaper after the appeals against expulsions had been dealt with (during 1971 and 1972), so that his figures should have really been smaller than Husák's in view of at least some dismissals being revoked.

Neither Husák nor Jakeš (chairman of the Control and Auditing Commission) gave any statistics at the 14th party congress in May 1971, at least not in the materials that were included in the published protocol. Jakeš did mention some figures concerning appeals but made it clear that handling of appeals was still going on.

Jakeš returned to the statistical riddle at the 15th congress in April 1976. (Husák did not, although he spoke about the party's attitude to those who had lost membership in 1970.) He first stressed that appeals had been treated with severity and then said that a total of 64,926 of 'those whose membership had been ended' filed an appeal which represented 18·3 per cent of all, 7·9 per cent of those struck off and 65·2 per cent of those expelled. If 64,926 equals 18·3 per cent, then 100 per cent equals 354,787 which is more than Husák had said by 27,920 and fewer than Bilak had said by 106,964. Jakeš also gave a lie to Bilak in regard to the number of revoked purge decisions on appeal which Bilak put at 'one-fifth'. Jakeš stated authoritatively that original decisions were changed in only 10·1 per cent of appeal cases which moreover included only 3,913 reinstatements and 2,623 cases where 'expulsion' was requalified as 'deletion from roster'. (Jakeš is also unreliable: if 3,913 and 2,623 equals 10·1 per cent, then 100 per cent equals 64,713, not 64,926, but this discrepancy is minor.)[20]

Whichever set of final figures one believes, the discrepancies are not such as to prevent the drawing of conclusions. First of all, close on half a million members of the party became non-members because of disagreement with the 'normalisation' and all its implications. They joined the not insignificant number of people who had been for one reason or another driven out of the Czechoslovak Communist Party before.

There had been four 'proper' purges since 1945, one each in Slovakia and the Czech Lands on separate dates in 1946 and 1946–47, and two in the whole country in 1948–49 and again in 1950, producing a total of almost 600,000 expellees and otherwise ousted members. To this figure must be added another 300,000 who departed either of their own will or were chucked out without undergoing the screening interviews from 1948 to 1950.[21] Most previous expellees had been discarded on grounds of passivity and failure to discharge the duties of a party member which put them in the same large category as the victims of the 1970 purge, though not necessarily in the same league as active seekers of social reform. Allowing for the death rate, the combined numbers of erstwhile card-carrying communists were by the end of the 1970 expurgation not much less than the actual numerical strength of the existing 'official' communist party. An alternative communist party was thus in existence, unorganised and dispersed, but bound together by opposition to the precepts which sustained the official party in power. If by an act of God the official party suddenly disappeared, another one would be available immediately to fill in the vacuum, and it would most probably do so in a reformist spirit.

Secondly, this large constituency of ex-communists could not, however, be expected to act in unison. Many of its members had left the party in disgust and disenchantment and no longer felt any kinship with communism, however democratic it might pretend or aspire to be. This was true probably of a large majority of the earlier victims who had quit in the 1950s, but also of a sizeable proportion of the new constituency of expellees. The tendency of former believers to turn away from communism has been very strong in Czechoslovakia, and the traumatic events of 1968 could not but accelerate the process still further. On the other hand, the 'unofficial party' did include a large nucleus of dedicated reformers, freshly aggrieved, who had no wish to lay down arms as yet. We can only surmise what their strength might have been at the turn of 1970–71 and my estimate is as good or as bad as the non-statistical information available permits. There probably was a quarter of a million people who would there and then be willing to do something by way of non-violent resistance in order to change the course of 'normalisation'. In addition a number of waverers might be swayed to join such an effort if the chance of success was more than nil.

Thirdly, the official, purged party still remained a large organisation, almost certainly larger than the advocates of a drastic cleansing operation wanted it to be. It numbered some 1,200,000 persons which meant that every eighth or ninth adult citizen of the country still carried a party card with the seal of official approval, testifying that he had now been 'normalised'. By the same token, this large body must have carried a lot of dead wood. Jakeš said so at the 14th congress in May 1971: 'The Party still has a contingent of passive members, a fact to which we must not be reconciled'.[22] The Czechoslovak Communist Party has always been known for the size of its inactive component, due perhaps as much to the methods of recruitment after February 1948 (at one time the membership stood over 2·5 million in an adult population of under 10 million) as to the traditional streak of Czech nature along the lines 'if you can't beat them, join them', also otherwise known as the survival-in-comfort syndrome. At a time when the sword of punishment for dissent hung threateningly over every member's head, the percentage of submissive ones must have been greater than in more leisurely periods. The hangers-on, the careerists and the cowards did not disappear simply because circumstances had called for a major weeding-out operation. Nonetheless, there was a difference against the early 1960s in that the non-orthodox constituency inside the party no longer included reform-orientated activists. The people who did remain in the party may not have been all enthusiastic about communist ideals and methods but neither were they ex-believers wishing to exculpate the sins they had committed in the early days of communist government, socialist-inclined revisionists, proponents of efficiency at the expense of ideology or all-round pragmatic reformers.

Instead, and that is our fourth conclusion, the sway was now held by a hard-core of orthodox fanatics, veterans, people with single-track minds, cynics and calculating politicos. It is easier to estimate their strength because we know how many were hand-picked to man the screening commissions in the 1970 purge: 235,270. The Prague Spring reformers were often asking themselves before the invasion how many genuine and active opponents of the reform plans they would have to contend with, and the consensus seemed to be that there were probably around 400,000 of them. The opinion polls of that period showed a variation in the number of opponents of the reform programme or of the Dubček leadership from two per cent of the sample who 'strongly disapproved' to nine per cent who 'rather disapproved', which would indicate absolute figures between 200,000 and 900,000 if the total adult population is taken as being ten million. The strength of the 'disapproving' constituency was probably some-what eroded by the military intervention; many people are known to have lost the last vestiges of faith in August 1968. On the other hand, as the post-invasion political course unfolded and acquired the basic features of permanence in the eyes of the public, a movement back to orthodox precepts inevitably occurred. How much of it was prompted by sheer opportunism and how much was due to a miraculous rebirth of hardline dedication is impossible to say. Be that as it may, the post-purge Communist Party of Czechoslovakia consisted of a hard-core of anything between a quarter and a half-million persons, a somewhat more aloof group of those willing to pay unto Caesar what he exacted from them and make the appropriate noises while doing so, and an outer circle of tacit survivors going through the motions and hoping that pussy-footing would be an acceptable form of collaboration. The hard core would no longer have to compete with active reformers for domination in the party and over their dormant partners. With the might of the state behind them, they scaled the commanding heights and made them unassailable to others.

EXPIATION ON COMMAND

Organisations

It can be argued that in a Soviet-style communist country political infrastructure does not exist. The structure has swallowed it. There are no non-governmental organisations in the real sense of the word. All organisations that do exist have their place cut out for them within the overall hierarchy of political influence, authority and control. They are 'transmission belts'. This is true even of essentially non-political institutions, such as for example in the fields of science and culture, which the party wishes to use as instruments of governance over their respective constituencies and which their members—at auspicious times—wish to make to play a political role or at least convey a message to the holders of power and to the population at large. The disappearance of a political infrastructure was one of the features of Soviet-type communism which the Prague Spring reformers desired to put right. Had they had their way, the subordination of every political (or potentially political) organisation to the centre of power would cease or at least be relaxed, and a certain amount of uncontrolled political life would be tolerated. The concept and the plans for its implementation were not finalised and the reformers did not all see eye to eye as to what should be done and how. But the move towards a certain amount of independence was unmistakable in typically 'state' institutions, such as the parliament, the government itself and the national committees; in the sphere of state-owned economy, such as in industrial enterprises; in state-directed economy, such as in agricultural cooperatives; in the traditional 'transmission belt' organisations, such as the trade unions, the youth union, the women's union; in state-supervised research and educational sectors, such as the Academy of Sciences, the universities and the rest of the schooling system; and in state-influenced interest organisations, such as the artists' union (writers, fine artists, film and television artists, theatre artists, composers, performing artists, architects).

The normalisers' considered the independence of the infrastructure dangerous and *prima facie* evidence that things were getting out of control. The leading role of the party had been eroded and must be restored. After repairing itself in the purges, the party must set out vigorously to repair everyone else.

The party in a communist state, apart from governing through the power structure of organisations under its control (including what should be the infrastructure), exercises its power also in a more direct way through the coercive apparatus of the state. The party and the state are intertwined and the one embraces the other, so that in the

90

sociological sense they are one, and it does not matter which denotation we use. This apparatus includes the police, the military, the judiciary and the legal system, as well as the private army which in Czechoslovakia is called the People's Militia and was 80,000 men strong.[23]

It was absolutely vital, and an emphatic condition imposed on the 'normalisers' by the Moscow Protocol that the coercive mechanisms should be brought into line, purged and put to work. A police force of which only a few score people in the secret service department show willingness to act on behalf of the Soviet Union while the uniformed police stand by and even join the crowds that celebrate an ice-hockey victory over the mighty Soviet side, is not worth a penny. It must be seen to work, to disperse crowds, to track down and arrest political culprits, to maintain law and order as the party desires them to be maintained. An army that refuses to have truck with their Soviet brothers deployed next door and achieves lousy or indifferent results in joint military exercises is no good either. Moreover, the army is not politically neutral or scheduled for external confrontation only; it must be seen to conduct class-conscious action inside the country as well, hip to hip with the police which chases away counter-revolutionary demonstrators. A legal system that gets entangled in federalisation and even rehabilitation of former political prisoners while neglecting its class mission, must obviously be turned back to the tasks which it had been ordained to pursue in the first place, notably repression of inimical elements. For too long a time no piece of repressive legislation had been passed and implemented in Czechoslovakia. A People's Militia that only writes letters of solidarity to the Soviet Union (thankfully accepted as they are) but has to hide away in a disused hangar when it wants to hold a meeting because the reformist leadership fears unfavourable public relation, must come into the open if it is not to lose credibility as the proletariat's armed fist.

Finally, the party exercises its influence, asserts its authority and buttresses its control through the communications media and in order to be able to do all that, it must have power over them. Revisionist and counter-revolutionary media are obviously anathema, but neither are meek and passive media any good. Here the target is not to browbeat into passivity as may be sufficient with a certain percentage of party members and the majority of the non-party public. The press, radio and television must become keen, enthusiastic and uncompromising advocates of 'normalisation' and beyond. Theirs is the treble task of all ideologies: to legitimate, to mobilise and to anesthetise.[24]

The Husák leadership encountered little difficulty in returning the legislative and executive branches of government under party suzerainty. The National Assembly's back was broken when it was first marshalled to ratify the treaty on the stationing of Soviet troops in Czechoslovakia and then, not much later, when the party enforced its will during the federalisation stage on who should be Federal Assembly chairman. All will to resist the hard line seems to have wilted in a body whose members spent seven uncomfortable nights and days during the invasion week in a continuous session, in defiance of the occupiers. The takeover was effected only partly through a reshuffle of those who presided over the Assembly, its praesidium and committees. The sheer weight of party pressure which had been the parliament's way of life before the Prague Spring prevailed fairly easily. It should not be forgotten that the members had been elected in June 1964 and had to legislate themselves into prolonged tenure of office to preserve a semblance of legality. This was also the case with the Slovak National Council. The Czech National Council—or parliament for the Czech Lands—was not elected at all, but selected. As the selection occurred in conditions of general reformism (in July 1968), its composition showed a greater proportion of reformers and the change of personnel had to be more extensive. On the whole, however, manipulation of cadres was all that Husák needed to secure obedience in all the three representative bodies.

The same was true about the government, only more so, because no one proposed even to question the right of the party praesidium to reign supreme over the executive branch of the state. Once the party praesidium came into the hands of the 'normalisers', the government's doing the same was a foregone conclusion.

Local government, the National Committees, were purged on the same lines, without any particular defiant stand on the record. From incomplete data half-way through the purge process, it transpires that just under 10 per cent of members at all levels were being replaced by more trusted persons. In the Czech Lands 2,798 had been recalled and 9,923 had resigned out of 147,409 by April 1970.[25] This suggests a lesser intensity of the purge when compared with the party's 28 per cent.

The trade unions threatened to be a problem but in the end turned out not to offer more resistance than some heavy arm-twisting could not overcome. Separate congresses of the Czech and Slovak trade union organisations in January 1969 revealed the extent of the different approaches to the situation in the two parts of the country. Where the Czech unionists made further verbal avowals of 'democracy, truth, humanism and freedom', their Slovak brothers met in a subdued atmosphere and did not allow the ill-winds from the outside to ruffle their feathers. The 7th Czechoslovak Trades Union Congress in March of the same year heard defiant yet confused words from the chairman, K. Poláček, and the mixture of defiance and confusion reflected fairly accurately the split personality of the times or, as the apt saying goes, the attitude of someone who would like to keep the cake after having eaten it:

'The basic attitude of the trade unions towards the party [i.e. as its ally] cannot immobilise the independent approach of the trade unions, restrict their own views, or even push them back to a secondary role as mere executors of party decisions. In future we will press our point of view . . . but it will never be our wish to stand in opposition to the Communist Party of Czechoslovakia'.[26]

And 85 per cent of the sitting members failed to get re-elected to the Executive Committee of the TUC. Less than two months later Poláček and his even more reform-committed comrades had a good opportunity to choose between trade union independence and party supremacy of the old style. Many chose the latter and those that did not had to go. Poláček who sought to repent and eat his words lasted only until January 1970; the leading reformer in the trade unions of the Czech Lands, Rudolf Pacovský, lasted until May 1970. During the purges, the trade unions differed from the party in that people were not being expelled (only in the campaign against Charter 77 was the ultimate ignominy of denying trade union membership to dissenters decreed over several individuals; otherwise just about everyone is a member), but the turnover of functionaries stood at about 20 per cent.

The question why the trade union movement failed to strike against 'normalisation' when it said it would, and why it submitted to the axe without putting up a fight, is not difficult to answer. It was not really a workers' movement, but an essentially bureaucratic organisation into which the successive regimes breathed only as much life as they wanted. The link between the shop floor and the office holders and policy formulators was, to say the least, tenuous—in many instances non-existent—and this state of affairs only began to be repaired during the Prague Spring. Indigenous worker functionaries were few and far between. The system had been positively ill suited to breed them for twenty years. Even the best-intentioned reformers belonged to the social group of trade union bureaucracy, connected through many visible and invisible threads to the power structure of an authoritarian mono-party society. When it came to the crunch and they were to choose between a firmly given party order and a rank-and-file action, they opted for the former no matter how they felt about it. Not that the grassroots were raring to have a go. The rapport between them and the reform-orientated trade union leaders was not strong enough for the two sides to influence each other in the direction of anti-normalisation protest on the lines of typical working-class action.

The recentralisation of the youth movement was also accomplished without major setbacks, except the refusal of a number of student leaders and their constituency to be bulldozed into submission. Their newspaper *Studentské listy* was banned on 6 May 1969 and their statutes rejected by the Ministry of the Interior on 20 June 1969. Promptly a loyal student union was founded (on 25 June) consisting at first mainly of young officers from military colleges. In November they began publishing their own newspaper (called *Předvoj*). The youth movement had disintegrated in the course of the Prague Spring but total independence of its sectional parts was even against the reform leaders' intentions. They knew that the Russians were viewing it with suspicion. A loose federation of all the existing organisations was on the drawing board when the invasion came. With the advent of Czech-Slovak federation the recentralisation process became even more complex, not to mention the fact that some organisations had not yet quite constituted themselves while already facing the certainty of losing their independence again. For example, the Boy Scouts' Central Council only came into being on 16 November 1969. The 'progressive' leaders of the provisional federated council of youth and children associations were duly replaced by 'normalisers' in September 1969, but for a while it looked as if a conglomerate of semi-autonomous organisations would be allowed to exist. The logic of 'normalisation' turned out to be stronger in the end and from early 1970 preparations were under way to re-establish a united and uniform organisation with the three-cornered top layer that had by then become typical, viz. a Czech, a Slovak and a Federal Central Committee. By the autumn of 1970 constituent congresses of a new Socialist Youth Union absorbed all quasi-autonomous organisations, including the new union of students. The Youth Union membership at that time (300,000 state-wide, including 80,000 in Slovakia[27]) was three times lower than that of the pre-reformist Youth Union in its heyday. It soon began to grow, however, although a purge was inaugurated in February 1971, barely three months after the constituent congress. Termed 'exchange of membership cards' and thus likened to previous year's process of expurgation in the party, it had all the markings of a campaign masterminded by the diehards, if not the ultras. The Union's paper admitted: 'Many think that this action is but a continuation of the interviews and screenings in the party and the issuance of new Youth Union cards is dependent on whether the members' parents were or were not purged from the communist party'.[28] The tough line was eventually toned down and the Union permitted to acquire the character so well known from the past, of an organisation which alone affords the young people to engage in some of their pastimes in exchange for a modicum of public profession of fealty, and a necessary springboard for those who wish to prove their commitment in order to gain access to higher education.

Scholarship and Education

The takeover of other organisations lying within easy jurisdiction of the party and the state, such as the research institutes, was largely accomplished through replacement of 'unreliable' leaders by trusted ones, as already mentioned earlier. Where the measure of reformist guilt was too high or the loyal executors of the party's new will were too thin on the ground or altogether absent, reorganisations, mergers and dispersals were ordered. Thus for example the separate institutes of the Academy of Sciences for philosophy, sociology and theory of science became just one. This new institute took over only a small minority of the 'leading cadres' and about half of the rank-and-file researchers from its three predecessors.[29] Altogether 523 institutes were checked and purged, and forty of them were either disbanded or merged.[30] Appropriations for academic institutions were cut back, e.g. the Institute of State and Law was getting 20 per cent less money because 'a changed cadre situation' so warranted.[31]

The percentage of dismissals was staggering and even those who passed the multiple screening as party members, trade unionists, state employees and scientists were relegated to positions without influence and in constant fear of a future round of axe-falling, unless they were willing to engage in public protestations of activism and ideological orthodoxy. A politically passive or indifferent scientist and scholar, even in fields miles remote from contemporary social sciences, became a creature of the past, exposed to vilification and constant inroads on his conscience.

The onslaught on social sciences was of such scope and intensity that it cannot be briefly described in the context of a study which traces the political contours of 'normalisation'.[32] It was accomplished promptly and brutally, using shortcut unceremonious methods, not by gradual strengthening of the orthodox line in competition with the alleged revisionists. The latter were simply and swiftly eliminated from the scene with no regard for the vacuum which had thus arisen. Their publications were withdrawn from circulation regardless of the subject, and of course they were not allowed to publish anything new. More than that, it was forbidden to quote from their previously published works except when derogatory pamphlets were written, (even this hatchet job was entrusted to specially authorised luminaries), and their names could not appear in surveys, dictionaries, anthologies etc. Security of tenure for those that were allowed to remain in institutes of the Academy of Sciences decreased with the introduction of short-term employment contracts and as a result of hawk-eyed supervision by informers. The new watch-dog director of the Nuclear Research Institute went on public record with a remark which became part of the academic folklore in Prague: 'I would chuck out even Einstein if his political views were not in order!'[33]

The field of education in general, and the universities in particular, reflected the endeavour of the post-reformist party leadership for an ideological return to old practices as much as their concern lest the schools again produce change-orientated and hence reliable intellectuals. It also saw the application of the entire scale of 'normalisation' methods, from the enforced provision of diehard leadership through large-scale personnel changes and purges, return to class-based practices of the early communist days (selection of entrants on political criteria, special training for handpicked young people without secondary education, and censoring of textbooks), introduction of a surfeit of ideology into even improbable subjects in the centrally controlled curricula, strengthening of polytechnical aspects at the expense of pure and social sciences, and elaboration of far-reaching reforms modelled on Soviet practice (reduction of primary education etc.).

The initial stage of 'normalisation' in this field is connected with the appointment of Jaromír Hrbek as Czech Minister of Education on 27 August 1969. This was in itself a notable attempt to integrate a well-known member of the extremist 'ultra' faction into mainstream politics and as such viewed by the left wing as a probing stone of how far to the left the Husák leadership would veer. In the end Hrbek became an embarrassment and was dismissed less than two years later, on 8 July 1971, not before he inaugurated a tough course which has never been really abandoned although some of his methods were. Hrbek was a veteran party member, a professor of neurology by profession and training, one of the rare breed of truly dogmatic and Soviet-orientated left wing of Czech intelligentsia of pre-war vintage. (He was born in 1914.) Hrbek opened his ministerial career with a witch-hunt designed to uncover and eliminate 'progressives' at first in his ministry, then in the universities and finally in secondary schools. There is little doubt that he would have come round to kindergartens if his time had not run out. As it turned out he will be remembered above all for the loyalty questionnaires which he distributed among university staffs and as the merciless ouster of teachers and students.

Hrbek's questionnaire of 16 September 1969 was in fact a circular letter to rectors and deans asking them to produce a detailed report on the behaviour of their staffs and students at various critical moments in recent history. Individual members of staff were to be ordered to submit a written self-critical statement and the entire dossier was to reach the Minister by 12 October. An accompanying separate letter decreed immediate cessation of the publication of student newspapers and broadsheets.

An amendment of the University Act in December 1969 reinforced ministerial powers over institutes of higher education, both in the appointment of professors and functionaries and in day-to-day administration and supervision. An end was thus put to the slender offshoots of academic autonomy which had its origin even before the Prague Spring.

A shameless and overt ideologisation of all education was being enforced and the universities were singled out for special treatment. In a sweeping gesture, the Departments of Marxism-Leninism were abolished and replaced by Institutes in which only 35 per cent of members of the Departments were retained.[34] Departments of Marxism-Leninism had a history of deviation from official dogma and policy even before the Prague Spring, and were in the process of evolving into research and teaching centres of 'social and political sciences'. Now the trend was reversed, many members dismissed, a tighter structure set up, and because not enough able personnel was available, reliable party veterans from outside the academic world were invited to teach Marxism to students. Later Soviet and East German lecturers came to help out. (Marxism is an obligatory subject for *all* students.) A proponent of the ideological offensive in education said: 'For twenty-five years we have been overburdening the socialist educational system with scientific knowledge while under-estimating its party-mindedness. We have believed that our schools will be the more socialist the more scientific knowledge they absorb. Now we have learned that there is no science without communist party-mindedness. As Lunacharsky said, education will be the most objective and the most scientific if it becomes the most communist'.[35]

Some specialisations in social sciences and arts were closed down for the academic year 1971–72, including geography, philosophy, political economy, political science, world literature and others. Admission was made specially difficult for children from intellectual families and well nigh impossible for children of parents who had been stripped of party membership and/or public office. Working-class children who could prove political loyalty or at least absence of disloyalty in their families had their entry facilitated by a points system which gave them automatic credit to the extent of one-fifth of the maximum number of points achievable. Preparations were started for special one-year training of selected workers without secondary education to enable them entry into universities. (The first of such courses was opened in the 1973–74 year.)

Even access to secondary education became more difficult for children from proscribed families as numbers of those admitted were cut. In February 1970 the headmasters were served with an instruction obliging them to set up special evaluation commissions at all nine-year elementary and junior secondary schools which would consider each prospective candidate for entry into the senior sections of secondary schools (at the age of 15) individually. Among the criteria for admission, 'the family's attitude to political interest of the state' was to be taken into account.[36]

More than one-third of teachers who had been members of the communist party were purged and most of them lost their jobs as teachers. *Učitelské noviny* wrote that it was the duty of the educational authorities to ensure that only teachers who brought up the children in a socialist spirit could stay in the profession.[37] The same source reported the following removal of functionaries from the teachers' union: 42 per cent from the central committee and the central auditing commission, 48·6 per cent from regional committees, 60 per cent of chairmen of district committees and 43·8 per cent of members of such committees, and 22·5 per cent of chairmen and 15·05 per cent of members of basic committees.[38] Textbooks, notably of civics and history, were withheld because of political objections, and deletions by way of crossing out or even tearing out pages had to be done in other books by children themselves under the teachers' supervision according to central directives.

J. Hrbek reported on the results of educational purges in July 1970 but his figures look improbably low when compared to first-hand experience of dissident sources. The purge anyway continued after his article had been written. He said that of the 16,000 university teachers 332 emigrated, 154 were dismissed and 134 forced to retire. Of the 587 members of the Departments of Marxism-Leninism in the Czech Lands only 286 were admitted to the new Institutes. Of the 140,000 students (the actual figures being 100,000 regular daytime, 37,000 extra-mural and 3,000 foreign), 1,036 emigrated, 66 were expelled for repeated participation in anti-state activities (39 in the Czech Lands and 27 in Slovakia), and 199 were disciplined (103 and 96). Of the more than 200,000 teachers and instructors at elementary, secondary and vocational schools, 734 emigrated and 7 were dismissed from educational services. Of the 20,206 educational functionaries (administrators), 383 were recalled from their posts.[39]

A month after Hrbek was forced to leave the ministerial post because of his implication in the anti-Husák 'ultra' plot, a Teachers' Working Statute was published which had been prepared under his guidance. It contained an oath of allegiance which all teachers would be required to take. As a kind of Hrbek's testament it is worth quoting at some length:

'I swear that I shall always work for the interest of the working class and implement the policy of the Czechoslovak Communist Party .... I shall teach [the children] respect for the working class and the Czechoslovak Communist Party. I shall educate them in the spirit of the Marxist-Leninist *Weltanschauung*. I pledge to develop internationalist sentiments in the young people and to cement their friendship with the socialist countries and especially the Soviet Union. . . .I am aware of the consequences which would transpire for me from a failure to stand by this oath.'[40]

It was also under Hrbek that the foundations for a number of educational reforms were laid, most of them designed to stress uniformity and ideological control. Some of Hrbek's precepts were eventually not implemented to the full but they should be quoted here to illustrate the scope and depth of the counter-reformatory effort to which the Czechoslovak educational system was exposed in 1970. The professed aim of the changes was to restitute the principle of 'a united socialist school' (comprehensive) which had been infringed by the reformers in 1968. Streaming in any grade up to the ninth should be abolished because it discriminates against workers' and peasants' children. Extra-curricular group activities should be expanded in order to build up a day-long educational process under which children would be kept within the school's influence mornings and afternoons. Mandatory school-time should be reduced to obtain time for non-teaching pursuits by cutting the duration of a class to 40 minutes. Elementary education should be reduced from five to four years following 'supreme satisfaction' with the then recent arrangement of the same kind in the USSR. And class justice should be attained by ensuring progress of children from working class and farmers' families to secondary and tertiary educational cycles in proportion to their percentage in the social composition of the population. This aim should be achieved through supplementary tuition and a class-based admissions system.[41]

As it turned out, Hrbek also laid the foundation of an immoral practice of corruption, previously little known in Czechoslovak education. In order to get their children through the various committees, screenings, evaluations and examinations, many parents were prepared to offer bribes and many educational administrators were prepared to accept them. Not much has changed since Hrbek left, except that some of his cruder practices have been refined. The 'points system' of admissions was replaced by 'comprehensive evaluation' where hypothetical points still can be scored on account of political involvement and the parents' behaviour. The dismissed professors were not allowed to return. The ideological inculcation continues.

The Media

The importance which Moscow and its agents in Czechoslovakia attached to full party control over the mass media at all stages of the 'normalisation' process has already been emphasised. Husák was quite clear and explicit on this score from the start of his tenure. He told the central committee in May 1969 in his inimitable way that no more discussions were really needed any more as to how to bring the media to heel, action was now called for:

> 'I will tell you what we have been telling each other a hundred times, namely that if the party does not secure for itself a decisive ideological control over the radio, television and the press, it will be unable to fulfil its role in this state. . . . We must make personnel changes or some other changes.[?] There is no other way. People can say a hundred times that freedom of communications is being curtailed. I know those theories, I have debated them I don't know how often . . . An absolutely anarchic interpretation of freedom, non-class, non-Marxist. As if we lived somewhere on the Moon'.[42]

Husák's Dr Hyde, Vasil Bilak, colourfully conjured up a vision of blood-thirsty mass media under reformism when he addressed a district meeting of communists in Prešov in July 1969:

> 'The television, radio and newspapers could have easily made other exhortations [during the Prague Spring], for example "Kill the communists! Kill them because they are an encumbrance and stand in the way of the building of some kind of a socialism without communism!" . . . Maybe fifty thousand and maybe a hundred thousand communists and other honest people could have been murdered. . . . Mountains of corpses . . .'[43]

There were two reasons then for seizing control over the media: because the one-party system so commanded and because they became counter-revolutionary in 1968. The whole gamut of instruments and methods available to the new leadership was applied to the purpose: new staffing in party-supervised media, censorship, closure of newspapers by governmental decree, dispersal of defiant party branches in editorial offices, disbandment of sections of the Journalists' Union and takeover of the Union's central committee by a handful of trusted lieutenants, and even some arrests. But more than suppression was necessary. Whereas few people will notice in the short run that a research institute has been closed down and no more books on the philosophy of man are being published, radio and television must go on broadcasting and at least some newspapers must reach the stalls every day. Hence the need for a positive aspect in the anti-reformist drive against the media. A hard core of journalists must be identified and deployed simultaneously with the ouster of the unreliables. Then new people must be attracted to the profession from other fields, even if they are novices and lick their fingers when turning news sheets in front of a television camera or read CDU/CSU as CDU *over* CSU. And both the old trustees and the tyros must be tempted and rewarded by lucrative salaries and specially high fees.

The question of financial inducement underwent a two-stage

development. At first it was simply a matter of *ad hoc* granting of high fees to authors of political articles and programmes, often with minimum accounting formalities. People were known to come to Prague Radio with a ten-minute text in their pocket and a party recommendation in their hand, read the former out before the microphone, descend two flights of stairs, collect a fat envelope at the cashier's office and walk out. Some order was introduced with a new salary tariff for journalists as from 1 January 1971 but the political background was no less blatant. An official of the 'normalised' Journalists' Union explained that the new scales were meant to 'support by material incentives the political commitment of journalists in the decisive mass information media and to enable their editors-in-chief to grant clear salary advantages to those newsmen who commit themselves on behalf of the politics of the party'.[44] The idea of the new scales was to fix basic pay according to the political importance of the medium and of the man concerned. The latter's editor-in-chief was also given the discretion to award a 'personal salary' to specially committed journalists which could be up to 50 per cent higher than the upper limit of his basic salary. Of the three kinds of bonuses payable on top of whatever was applicable (again on the chief editor's decision), two had political overtones: rewards for successful performance of duties and rewards for writing *engagé* materials. There is no doubt that a system of this kind was effective and that it considerably strengthened the chief editor's control over what was written and how it was written.

On 17 May 1969, a month to the day after Husák replaced Dubček, a group of newsmen committed themselves publicly to the pursuance of 'normalisation' under Husák's leadership and proclaimed their obedience to the revived tenets of communist ideology. Others gradually joined them. On 2 September the first issue of a loyal 'weekly for politics and culture', *Tvorba*, appeared, thus giving the new leadership a second weekly paper, next to *Tribuna* which had been in existence under hardline editorship from the beginning of the year. The Journalists' Union was put under new management in September and then purged in December. From its 4,000 members about a half were dismissed. All through this time newspapers and periodicals were being banned. Special training courses for newcomers were organised, mainly of three-months' duration, and so-called workers' correspondents were mobilised. (These are people who write letters and even articles and poems for the press by invitation or on their party branch's commission.) Censorship was of course reintroduced immediately after the invasion but remained ineffective. For a few months after Husák's takeover pre-emptive blue-pencilling was tough in non-party publications, although it was said that sufficiently loyal cadres had been found to edit out objectionable matter from party papers without the restoration of formal censorship structures. In September 1969, according to Husák himself, the same kind of self-effacing editorial action was allowed in all media.[45]

A system whereby loyalty and activism is ensured without a special group of people censoring texts before they are printed or broadcast, can only operate when no newspaper (radio, television programme) is allowed to be run by potentially untrustworthy people. Given the fear of consequences, even just one person of authority in the editorial office is sufficient to prevent slip-ups or defiance. The greater the number of loyal activists in proportion to the reluctant collaborators, the more aggressive a tone can be adopted. In an authoritarian state a good deal of materials arrive from the power-wielding offices of the party and the government, which are either simply reprinted at length or only marginally adapted. No additional knowledge is needed, and indeed desired, to append a comment; it can be put together from the text of the original document by means of simple re-phrasing. Add to it the issue of general and specific directives to which the chief editors are regularly exposed, and the clearance of an overwhelming proportion of foreign and domestic news through the one and only official press agency—and the system is evidently workable. In conditions such as prevailed in Czechoslovakia after April 1969 there was no will left to break through the imposed constraints on the part of those who survived in the editorial offices after the purges. Grading of the press into the more and the less important helped as well. Some things were still being published in 1970 in the 'entertainment' and provincial press or the specialised journals with long production deadlines that were obviously not to the full liking of the new holders of power, but they did not matter. Complete control was gradually imposed on them too.

Culture

The Prague Spring had been to a considerable extent a cultural event whether we understand culture as the refinement of human thought, emotion and behaviour or in the more limited sense of literature and the arts. In both instances men and their society began to depart from the precepts of communism as preached and practised in the Soviet orbit. Their strivings found expression both in the appearance of actual products of culture, such as books, films, radio and television programmes, work of fine arts and the accompanying cultural theory and criticism, as well as in the divorce of many cultural institutions and associations from the mono-organisational pattern of the communist system. Associations of writers and other artists, originally created to transmit policy from the power centre into the respective fields of cultural life, claimed and achieved a considerable amount of independence.

The post-reformist leadership could reverse the first trend—production of works of literature and art not subservient to ideology—with relative ease by cutting off the technical outlets, such as publishing houses, film studios and the media, from the actual 'producers' of culture. Once these facilities were taken over by the new regime, an order prohibiting the publication of books, making of films, etc., by identified deviationists could be and was issued. It took the form of several successive blacklists, naming the culprits or their works or both. Blanket censorship directives were also issued.[46] One should note that censoring in this direct manner extended beyond the ranks of non-conformist Czechoslovak nationals; the blacklists included names and works by objectionable foreign writers as well. Managements of theatres were also compelled to banish plays by undesirable authors or with undesirable content, and things went as far as textual adjustments in classical plays where it was thought (rightly) that the audience might relate speech from the stage to histrionics in outside reality.

Some of the stories which leaked out are too strikingly illustrative to be missed. The hardline manager of the National Theatre in Prague issued the following order before the start of the 1970–71 season: (1) Before the first reading rehearsal the actors will be instructed as to the one and only correct ideological interpretation of the play. (2) A delegate from the party central committee will follow every new staging from the first rehearsal to the premiere. (3) A special party central committee commission will see every new play ten days before the first night to rule whether to go ahead with the premiere or not. (4) Deletions will be made in Brecht's *Mother Courage*, Anouilh's *Becket* and Fry's *The Lady Is Not for Burning*. (5) Rehearsals of Griboedov's *Woe from Wit (Chatsky)* will be discontinued as the play could be interpreted provocatively in the given Czechoslovak context.

The deletions in *Mother Courage* concerned, for example, the scene in which the chief character, a Protestant, describes how she tricked her way through an interrogation session supervised by Catholics, a possible allusion to the purge interviews. Within the scope of two seasons, new original plays by domestic authors were driven out of the country's theatres, the main film studios at Barrandov ceased making 'new wave' films whose producers were forced out into the cold, and publishing of new belles-lettres virtually came to a complete halt.

It proved somewhat more difficult to take over the 'creative unions'. In most of them the majority of members refused to be bulldozed into submission and to repudiate their loyalty to the reformist leaders simply because they had been chucked out of the party. The creative unions were practically the only link in the non-governmental

infrastructure which had played a political role during the Prague
Spring and now refused to surrender it when the winds changed. The
composers' union, something of an exception, bowed to pressure first.
On 24 November 1969 it accepted resignations of the majority of its
central committee and renounced its reform-imbued resolutions of
1968. It did not save the union from the fate which was eventually
meted out to all of them. They were officially declared disbanded in the
course of 1970 because a 'peaceful takeover' by a 'sound core' of
committed normalisers could not be accomplished. A letter from the
chairman of the Czech Writers' Union, the poet Jaroslav Seifert,
addressed to the National Front praesidium on 29 September 1970,
can be quoted as an illustration of the resistance:

'...only a democratic organisation is worthy of being a respectable
representative of artists in a socialist society. It belongs to the
inalienable principles that the leadership of such an organisation must
not be imposed on it, but elected by its membership.... The committee
[of the Writers' Union] expresses its regret that it has not been given the
opportunity to implement the programme of a consolidation which
would not be just a facade but real accomplishment based on the will of
the overwhelming majority of the members. Thus another long and
unrepeatable period in the life of the Czech Writers' organisation
becomes history. And history is the teacher of life, the light of truth and
the witness of time'.[47]

In Slovakia the cultural offensive of the 'normalisers' had a less
vehement pace, mainly because the Slovak *national* programme
provided a wider base for the formation of a new platform. Fewer
people were forced to resign and fewer were pushed out into cultural
banishment. In the end, however, some two dozen prominent writers
could not have their works published. They were enumerated in a
speech which their colleague, Mrs Hana Ponická, wished to deliver at
the Slovak Writers' Congress in March 1977 but was prevented from
doing so and lost her membership of the Union and publication
possibilities in return.[48] Only the Slovak Union of Film and Television Artists was liquidated *in toto* while transition to new leadership
and policy in the other unions was accomplished comparatively
smoothly. For example, the Slovak Writers' Committee met on 15
December 1969, re-appraised some of its former decisions and
'expressed its sincere and honourable interest in maintaining its
existing positive relations with the leadership of the party'.[49] Even the
journalists' union in Slovakia survived without too much damage to
the membership base. Slovak cultural 'normalisation' was presided
over by Miroslav Válek, Minister of Culture in the new Slovak
government.

Válek's counterpart in the Czech Lands, Miroslav Brůžek, a

104

conservative of the Husák hue, finally completed the destruction of the creative unions' independence and succeeded in identifying and prodding into action a sufficient number of people to start new associations. In order to do that he had, however, to turn to the not insignificant number of 'cultural officials' (rather than the artists themselves). These are the people who staff the large number of cultural offices in local government at all levels, in central institutions, in the 'mass organisation' (such as the trade unions) and even in enterprises. They would normally look after entertainment for the employees, hire halls and performing ensembles, buy tickets wholesale at a discount, organise lectures and fancy-dress balls, release funds for library acquisitions, arrange transport for trips to theatres and collective outings, and pursue a myriad other useful, if essentially bureaucratic, activities. As employees of the state and free of the intellectual torments that plague creative artists, they were much more susceptible to pressure, persuasion and financial lure. Joining them was a smallish contingent of real artists, veterans of pre-war communist culture, people implicated in the cultural witch-hunts of the 1950s, compulsive yet unrequited manufacturers of unprintable prose and poetry, tired authors of historical novels who could not face ostracism, hacks in anyone's employ, lovers of money, and a few genuine believers in the party as it now was. Under Brůžek's tutelage this assortment of administrators, pen-pushers, fanatics and weary men produced a loyalist statement in November 1969, accepted from the government assets confiscated from the 'revisionist' unions during 1970, and eventually set themselves up as preparatory committees of new unions in December 1970, having their officially drawn statutes promptly endorsed by the Ministry of the Interior. The Soviet Ambassador sent them his well-publicised best wishes. At that time there were to be four unions consisting of 27 writers, 25 composers, 42 dramatic artists (incorporating both theatrical, film and television people), and 33 fine artists. Publicists, musicologists, critics and art theorists were included.[50] (For comparison, in 1967 the Czech Writers' Union had 299 members, 87 candidates for membership and 158 members in its translators' section.) Membership of the new unions grew thereafter and by the time the unions took enough hold to constitute themselves properly at inaugural congresses in 1972 it reached approximately one-quarter of their pre-invasion strength.

What neither Brůžek nor the new unions could deliver were committed and loyal works of art. Books were still being published, but mostly re-editions of classics, translations and the two time-honoured genres of escapists everywhere—detective stories and historical novels. (Cookery books also became plentiful, to the point where the officials complained.) Films were still being shown, but mostly foreign ones (with quite a large number of imports from the

West, presumably to keep the public happy and bring money into the treasury's coffers) or newly made non-political comedies. Theatres were still playing, but mostly classics, Russian and otherwise. Art was still being exhibited (though much less spontaneously than before), but mostly in the realist and monumental compartments. Needless to say, the organisational measures were accompanied by the imposition of strict ideological criteria whereby art in all its forms was to return into the mould of socialist realism and to the role of a didactic and militant instrument in the hands of the party.

Religion
Extension of decreed 'normalcy' to religion was a natural corollary of the process in the other cultural sectors. Unlike the case in Poland, communist governments in Czechoslovakia have not had to contend with a strong Catholic Church as an alternative ideological centre exercising active influence on large segments of the population. Even in Slovakia coexistence between religion and communism has had a subdued rather than intensive character, at least since the first years after the communist takeover when the power of the church was broken by force. A collaborative strand among the clergy before 1968 found expression in the so-called Peace Movement of Catholic Clergy which disintegrated under the impact of the Prague Spring. At that time an organisation entitled Council Renewal came into life to act as the clerical partner to a much more tolerant and understanding party and government. As a 'normalisation' writer put it, atheism had been neglected by the revisionists and even totally abandoned for the sake of so-called positive humanism. Struggle against religious ideology was replaced by a dialogue between the Marxists and the Christians, often understood not as a battle of ideas but as conciliation. Now the active atheistic stuggle must be resumed.[51]

First forays after Husák's 'normalisation' course was inaugurated were launched against 'Zionism', although the Jewish dimension had been brought into focus even earlier. It was rumoured that Dubček had in fact been earmarked to be put on trial as leader not only of an anti-socialist but also a pro-Zionist conspiracy before the Soviets changed the scenario and let him run the sinking ship for another seven months. (František Kriegel was to provide the connection with 'world Zionism'; Brezhnev allegedly referred to him as 'that Yid from Galicia'.) Now the Zionist plot was dusted again in December 1969 and conveniently linked to the pro-Israel stand of many of the reformist writers in 1967, especially since several of those who were Jewish chose to emigrate. A high official in the party central committee publicly denounced Zionism as one of the spearheads of counter-

106

revolution in Czechoslovakia and singled out for condemnation the alleged attempt of the Zionists to seduce a section of the younger Jewish generation for anti-state and anti-socialist activities.[52]

In reality, as a result of the Nazi occupation and through successive waves of emigration, the Jewish community in post-war Czechoslovakia has long been but a shadow of its once proud past. By the time of the onset of 'normalisation', some eight thousand Jews, mostly elderly and ailing, have been leading a quiet and unassuming existence, the highlights of which consisted in helping to preserve monuments of the past and cemeteries. There was no bridgehead for Zionism or militant Judaism in Czechoslovakia, no matter how they might try to intervene from the outside.

Militant atheism got under way during 1970 and soon became regularised as an indivisible part of escalated ideological propaganda and a tough stand on the part of the government towards the practical aspects of church-state relations. Since the great anti-religious campaigns of the early 1950s the state of affairs which developed in Czechoslovakia became anomalous. The state took it upon itself to pay all priests' salaries, to enable religious instruction of children in state-owned schools outside normal teaching hours (which unlike the case in the Soviet Union is legally possible, albeit with difficulty and risk), and to look after religious premises and monuments. This has always been represented as giving the government super-arbitrary powers in deciding about what the churches as a whole and each priest as an individual could or could not do. The Church and the state were not separated; the former was in a bear-hug of the latter. A special governmental Office for Church Affairs was in existence which, while admittedly not prescribing action in matters of dogma or faith, assumed almost a national papal role in just about everything else that concerned the inner life of the church and its proselytising function. Matters like retirement age of priests, filling in of vacant offices from the parish level to the archbishoprics, signing of loyalty oaths by all priests, numbers of students and curricula at colleges of theology, all could not be decided without government's approval. The Office for Church Affairs, a kind of collective Henry VIII, partnered the Vatican in inter-state negotiations, and if the Holy See wanted to communicate with its priests in Czechoslovakia in any other but the narrowest matters of liturgy and dogma, it had to go through this Office.

In the reform period a great deal of relaxation came about, not the least because of a change in the directorship of the Office and of course as a consequence of the more enlightened and benign approach of the Dubček leadership to religious matters. Now the old head of the Office was back (Karel Hrůza), the Council Renewal was abolished and a new pro-regime clerical association was in the making. (It was set up in August 1971 in the two national republics, and in November of the same year as a federal body under the name *Pacem in Terris.*) All 'normalised' party and state organisations were obligated to re-activate preaching of atheism. Rehabilitations of priests sentenced to enormous prison terms in the 1950s were gradually stopped. Only one of the fourteen Catholic dioceses in the country had a resident bishop in the middle of 1972. Premature pensioning off of parish priests was threatened. *Katolické noviny* said that with many priests dying of heart failures and apoplectic strokes, there soon would be only five priests in every district and even this proportion would go on getting worse.[53] Several students were expelled from the Bratislava Theological Faculty in March 1972 because they or their parents allegedly 'engaged in inimical activities' in 1968, and applicants for study at the two Catholic Faculties of Theology (Litoměřice and Bratislava) were being weeded out to just over 50 per cent in Litoměřice and under 40 per cent in Bratislava in the 1971–72 school year.[54] A third faculty, in Olomouc, re-opened during the Prague Spring, was gradually phased out again.

The one and only Greek Catholic (Uniate) diocese of Prešov in East Slovakia came into existence in 1968, the church having been banned in 1950. Its property was then transferred to the Russian Orthodox Church. Twenty years later, during the Prague Spring, many Uniates proclaimed their old faith again, seized back their churches and even chased out Orthodox priests. At that time the Church was estimated to comprise 150,000 believers. In 1970 the authorities complained that Uniate believers were still able to persuade building firms to construct new churches without National Committee approval and that building materials were somehow obtained without a permit. 'An end must be put to this practice'.[55] The last resident bishop of the Uniate Byzantine rite, Pavel Gojdič, died in a state prison in 1960 where he was serving a life sentence imposed in 1950. In 1969 Vasil Hopko was appointed an ordinary in charge of the Prešov diocese. He was old and of ill health and died in July 1976. The existence of the Uniate church has been grudgingly tolerated until the present (it is illegal in Soviet Ukraine) and it even can publish a monthly news-sheet called *Slovo*.

There is one Old Catholic diocese in Varnsdorf without a bishop. (Augustin Podolák was removed from office in 1971.) The church also re-activated itself in 1968 and established ties with a protestant church.

Apart from general ideological attacks, the protestant churches (evangelical) did not appear to be the object of as much harassment in this period as the Catholics. The *numerus clausus* at their seminaries however continued to apply, and a number of their members, including some ministers, established contacts with socialist ex-reformers who were now being forced into active opposition.

The party propagandists complained that only one-fifth of secondary students were leaving school with religious convictions fully quashed. Modernisation of religious philosophy, especially in the protestant churches, which transferred religious motivation from the intellectual into the existential sphere, had deformed and confused the young people's *Weltanschauung*. Also attractive were new 'recruitment methods' of some churches which now included jazz, pop-style rites and sport.[56] They may have had a point there as witnessed by a report from a missionary meeting of young members of the Baptist Unity of Brethren in Prague on 20–22 November 1970, at which evangelical sessions were supplemented with music, singing, poetry reading and personal testimonies. At the beginning of 1970 the Unity had set up a choir of boys and girls who now performed for the first time in uniforms (pale blue for the girls and dark suits with white rollneck pullovers for the boys). The choir numbered eighty and they sang to the accompaniment of a piano, electric guitars and drums. Some young people present at the gathering declared for the first time that Christ was their saviour and they resolved to live as he preached.[57] This state of affairs would obviously not be allowed to go on for long. Consolidation was the programme, but not of the churches.

Coercion

It has already been said that Moscow put repeated emphasis in all its dealings with Dubček and then Husák on the reinvigoration of the so-called 'power functions' of the state, i.e. the coercive machinery which they saw undermined and under-used during the reformist period. This the Husák leadership set out to put right in four ways: by establishing its control through cadre changes and purges in the main armed forces, by engaging them firmly and publicly in confrontation with large numbers of the population on the first anniversary of the Warsaw Pact invasion, by adopting a series of repressive amendments to coercive legislation and by staging a series of political trials on a selective basis.

It is not possible to identify accurately the causes of the street battles that raged in Prague from 19 to 21 August 1969 because the information is simply not here. Some indications are, however, obvious. The public was embittered and the first anniversary must have offered itself as an occasion to vent pent-up frustrations. On the other hand, warnings from the authorities that peace and quiet would be maintained resolutely started to be issued early (a trade union appeal to this effect was published on 7 August) and multiplied as the day drew nearer, suggesting that perhaps an encounter was sought to prove the point. That point could have only been the capability of the new leadership to suppress a riot with its own means, rather than with the help of Soviet troops, who were of course standing by. Was this not what Brezhnev had reproached Dubček for failing to do? Dubček could not or would not, but Husák would. What better way of proving oneself? This is admittedly a speculation, but it falls in line with the pattern of things as they were emerging in the 'normalisation' process.

Some anonymous information has filtered through from the party and state circles which by then had not yet been completely rid of people willing to talk to their former reformist colleagues. This information (available in type-written form) pointed to large-scale preparations on the part of the party apparatus and the coercive services for the anniversary day. People's Militia was put on red alert from 18 August. Factories were patrolled and machinery checked for malfunctions that could be interpreted as sabotage. Many radio and television employees were sent on special leave and only a trusted skeleton staff had access to buildings, and to the actual broadcasting facilities. All programmes were taped in triplicate in case a saboteur turned off the 'on the air' switch. Frontier guards were moved to Prague to patrol post offices, the radio building, the telephone exchange and other premises. Two tank divisions were brought in to control access roads to the capital. Armoured troop carriers had water cannons and special tear gas throwing equipment mounted on them. According to sources in the party secretariat, the leaders expected subversive action above all in the media (e.g. sabotage in the radio building and in printing houses), and possibly in factories. Illegal news sheets were predicted and even 'black' (pirate) radio stations were feared.

In fact, the only clandestine leaflet circulating before the anniversary appealed to the public to take passive action, such as boycotting public transport and wearing a black or a tricolor in the lapel. But people did go out into the streets and the demonstration was massive, prolonged and mainly staged by workers and young people. Prague and Brno turned into battlefields, but demonstrations also occurred in 31 towns. Police, soldiers, the People's Militia and secret servicemen were fighting tens and possibly a hundred thousand demonstrators. It was reported from knowledgeable sources that rank-and-file soldiers and police had not been issued live ammunition (lest it fell into wrong hands?) but officers and secret servicemen had, and they used it. Two people are said to have died in Prague and three in Brno, all from among the demonstrators. (A confidential telex message from the party praesidium to regions and districts, dated 22 August 1969, hitherto not published, gives the names of the Prague victims as F. Kohout, aged 18, and V. Hrubý, aged 19.) Four members of the People's Militia and 'many members of the police and the army' suffered injuries. In Slovakia 'the situation is on the whole calm', according to the telex.

The party praesidium also noted that professions of loyalty to the party had begun to arrive as a result of a previous day's telex message which had asked for them to be arranged. (This message is available only in summary form.) Both messages say that it was the demonstrators who used firearms, even submachine guns, and that no shots were fired by the police and the army. (But no firearms appear to have been seized.) Foreigners were allegedly among the hundreds who were arrested, especially West Germans. Barricades were being built and attempts made to set cars and even a restaurant on fire. Shop windows were smashed. The first telex sees a parallel with street demonstrations in Paris in 1968, while the second likens the Prague events to anarchic action in West Germany, especially in that 'small mobile groups of 500–2500 people were milling about'. Counter-revolutionary aims were allegedly evident from the chanting of slogans which denigrated the party and the USSR.

The end of it all was inevitable. Non-shooting guardians of order vanquished shooting demonstrators even though heavily outnumbered. It was not necessary to call on Soviet comrades to render yet another act of fraternal assistance. The party proved to be strong again.

Emergency repressive legislation was hastily passed on 22 August as Law No. 99/1969 'on temporary provisions necessary to protect and strengthen public order'. It was to expire on 31 December 1969 but some of its stipulations were then taken over into Law No. 148/1969, which together with other subsequent legislation tightened the legal system with permanent effect. This concerned sentencing a person to banishment from a named place and liability to severe punishment for such petty offences as failure to comply with a properly served demand to preserve public order, participation in an act that constitutes a breach of public order, refusal to fulfil duties deriving from a labour contract (strike?) and breach of duty. New offences were formulated in December 1969, such as exporting and importing printed material, including manuscripts, films and records, which might damage the state's interest, obtaining travel documents under false pretences or on incomplete information, and illegal exporting of personal documents. The Labour Code was simultaneously amended by the inclusion of a new provision according to which an employee could be dismissed 'if his activities violate socialist social order, and he thus cannot be trusted . . . to perform his present duties'. (This formulation was taken over literally from the emergency legislation of 22 August.) Other amendments restricted the jurisdiction hitherto belonging to the trade unions, including the authorisation of the government to suspend 'for some categories of workers' the legal provision under which they could be dismissed only with the agreement of the appropriate trade union committee.[58]

Lively legislative activity during 1970 and 1971 followed in the

Table 1. Political and related offences 1966–1971

Year	Source	Against the Republic	Assault on public figure	Misdemeanours	Petty offences
1966	Yearbook 1969	2,615 (84)	4,908 (130)	—	2,618 (—)
1967	Yearbook 1969	2,512 (79)	4,148 (93)	—	2,700 (—)
	1970	2,512 (79)	4,148 (93)	—	2,700 (—)
1968	Yearbook 1969	946 (25)	2,296 (63)	—	1,201 (—)
	1970	946 (25)	2,296 (63)	—	1,201 (—)
	1971	111 (2)	2,296 (63)	—	1,201 (X)
1969	Yearbook 1970	1,524 (143)	4,055 (160)	—	959 (—)
	1971	942 (66)	4,058 (160)	—	959 (X)
	1972	942 (66)	4,058 (160)	—	959 (X)
1970	Yearbook 1971	1,576 (128)	5,872 (242)	28,718 (3,812)	288 (X)
	1972	1,576 (128)	5,872 (242)	28,718 (3,812)	288 (X)
1971	Yearbook 1972	861 (54)	5,214 (106)	47,795 (6,582)	— (—)

footsteps of the emergency measures and included purging of judges, the ending of rehabilitations of former political prisoners, improved conditions for the police, the granting of greater powers over law and order to the federal (as against national) Ministry of the Interior, and others.

It is not easy to establish how many people were tried and sentenced for political offences and misdemeanours in this period, if only because of statistical incomparability. Discrepancies between data in subsequent issues of the official *Statistical Yearbook* are considerable. Table No. 1 reveals their extent and the general trend. (The years 1966 and 1967 were included for comparison with pre-reformist practices.) Three categories of offence are juxtaposed:

(1) Offences against Part I of the Criminal Code entitled 'Offences against the Republic'; these are the most explicitly *political* offences, but may not include sentences under Article 109 for 'illegal departure from the republic'.

(2) Offences under Articles 153–156 qualified as 'assaults on organs of state, organs of a social organisation and public officials'; these will include a number of non-political offences arising, say, from drunken brawls with the police or outbursts of anger over National Committee rulings.

(3) Petty offences and misdemeanours which will include a large number of non-political acts, presumably a majority, but to which were added in December 1969 some lighter cases relating to breach of public order, such as are committed during political demonstrations. Figures in brackets give the numbers of adolescents, under the age of 18, sentenced on the same charges.

Fewer people were tried and sentenced for political reasons in 1968 than in previous years. As a certain number of those actually put on trial in 1968 would have been arrested in 1967, before the Prague Spring, and the Amnesty of May 1968 further reduced the numbers of those actually sent to jail (although sentenced), the reformist regime can demonstrably be seen as either being more lenient towards offenders of this kind or as having fewer political offences committed against itself. Political prosecution picked up again in 1969 and continued at a fairly high level in 1970, although the pre-1968 level was not reached (except in the number of juveniles) in convictions of offenders 'against the republic'. We have, however, no means of knowing how many people were ordered to jail for ostensibly non-political offences under other headings of the Criminal Code while in fact motivated by political reasons; requalification of political offences as non-political has been reported by dissidents in later years of the 'normalised' regime.

Fewer people assaulted public figures in 1968 or were prosecuted on this charge, but in 1969 the pre-reformist level was almost reached and in 1970 and 1971 substantially surpassed, testifying perhaps to an increased level of direct confrontation between forces of the state and the public. The number of persons convicted of 'petty offences' continued to decline throughout the period but due to requalification of some acts this trend cannot be interpreted in the context of political crime. When the category of 'misdemeanours' was introduced in December 1969, and several commonplace 'political' offences entailed in it, the number of people prosecuted on such charges soared. It is perhaps in this more 'lenient' form of prosecution that the real scope of judicial conflict between the state and the public was best reflected. In the public mind, 'liberalisation' under Novotný, leading on to the Prague Spring, was seen as less oppressive than 'normalisation' under Husák, regardless of the lesser number of convictions on 'crimes against the republic'. Things were getting worse, not better. Hence the widespread fear that the dreaded 1950s would soon descend on the nation again.

Husák himself went repeatedly on record to deny that the early practices of Czechoslovak communism would be reintroduced. At that time he had been a victim himself, having spent nine years in prison, and people accepted his credibility on that score. As he was giving his assurances, Husák must have been aware that fear of the re-enactment of the 1950s could play into his hands as much, if not more, as the belief that he would not allow it to happen. For, notwithstanding solemn affirmations and good intentions, 'normalisation' has inculcated fear into Czechoslovak society. People had again started to be afraid of things which they gradually stopped being afraid of during the 1960s, and especially in the first eight months of 1968. Now you could again be demoted and transferred to a menial job for saying something to which the party objected and which an informer would pass on. Your children could be prevented from pursuing an education and a career of their own choice. You could be taken to task for reading certain books by certain authors, or for listening to foreign radio stations. You knew that the powers of the secret police were waxing rather than waning, and that you could become an object of their attention. If by disclaiming a return to the 1950s the new leaders meant that in-fighting among communists would not lead to one faction chopping off the heads of another faction, that was fine and no doubt a step forward, and this may have been what the 1950s boiled down to in Husák's mind. For the population at large the objectionable features of that period were, however, wider, and in the feverish counter-reformation from 1969 to 1971 they saw the contours of the past filling in threateningly.

The question of whether the leading proponents of the reform course should be put on trial as part of the 'normalisation' process must have cropped up in the new leadership on several occasions, and was probably put forward as a serious and deliberate proposition by the 'intrasigent' group. Husák is said to have belonged to those opposing such a step. A few quotations will illustrate the evolution of his ideas or, perhaps, the development of his tactical arsenal.

On election as First Party Secretary in April 1969 he said on television:

> 'It is first of all Western propaganda which spreads the rumour about us returning to the old times or, as some even say, the 1950s. I can assure you all that the party leadership ... has no such aims now and will not have them in future. Neither I personally nor any other person in the party leadership would approve of such a thing'.[59]

On the same day he told the central committee:

> 'People ask whether we will have a police state. Even one comrade here asks whether we will not have political trials again. . . . On behalf of all the leadership I can say that we will observe legality in this country very strictly and that we will protect the rights of the people very strictly. But we will also very strictly watch over the observance of laws. . . . Comrades, this does not mean, however, that we will endlessly tolerate certain things where laws are infringed and where objective [sic!] state organs have investigated the case. . . . A government party which cannot put legal coercive means to use, is a weak party and condemns itself'.[60]

At the September 1969 meeting of the central committee he said:

> 'He who is not willing to take advice and keeps putting his hand into the fire, must expect to get burned. . . . He who violates the laws of our state must expect to bear the legal consequences of his action'.[61]

So, the tenor was that there would be no return to the political trials of the 1950s, but those who infringed the law would be prosecuted. The 'observance of laws' assurance was phoney in a state where the party leadership determines what is to become law. Soviet-type communism has long operated the theory of 'pure law' which itself is of pre- and non-communist origin. Leonard Schapiro expressed the nucleus of the theory thus:

> 'Where there is a state there is a legal order: and the legal order is the state in action. State and law are therefore one; and it follows that every state is necessarily a *Rechtsstaat*. . . . In fact neither Hitler nor Stalin found that law was much of an obstacle to his plans in view of the ease with which each of them could enact new laws or amend existing laws at will . . .'[62]

Suffice to introduce a law that 'whoever publicly defames a state belonging to the world socialist system or its leading representative shall be punished by imprisonment for a term of up to two years' (section 104 of the Czechoslovak Criminal Code) and it becomes a breach of the law to say that the USSR invaded Czechoslovakia because the official ruling is that the entry of troops in August 1968 was an act of 'fraternal assistance'. No more than the use of one word instead of another can cost a man two years in jail. And of course so much depends on interpretation. What constitutes 'defamation', 'subversion', 'damaging the interest' is subject to pronouncements by the party leaders. In a sense, everything can be illegal. The 'pure theory of law' as applied by communist states, far from making the state automatically into a lawful state, makes relations between the state and its citizens arbitrary and volatile. Neither the law nor its interpretation by jurists and judges, but the leadership's expediency governs the legal system.[63]

Thus the question of whether to hold political trials or not had practically no relation to either the existence of suitable legal grounds for them, or indeed to the fact whether infractions had actually been committed. Much rather, the leadership deliberated (or so we assume) whether it would be advantageous to stage such trials and who should be the defendants. Now we are not talking about demonstrators arrested in August 1969 whose fate would not be debated by the bigwigs; they would have to face the music and they did, hundreds of them. Where the praesidium's discussion of legality would affect them was only in the severity of sentences, another area of the penal procedure under communism which usually depends on the general thrust of party policy of the day. The question that the praesidium was really mulling over was that of the protagonists of reform, well-known names, whose indictment and condemnation would echo outside the courtroom walls.

The advocates and the opponents of such trials were in protracted conflict. It was even rumoured at one time that internment camps for anything up to 2,000 people were being prepared, with Husák insisting that the conditions in them must be better than the ones he experienced in the 1950s. In the end, probably sometime between the August demonstrations of 1969 and the end of the year, they resolved on a compromise. Yes, some political trials would be staged, but the key men of the Prague Spring would not be put in the dock. Only lesser known figures would be tried and detained, people from the most exposed fields of political science, culture, the media and the younger generation. In addition, a certain number of equally selective trials would be held in those regions where the authorities feel that the level of intimidation requires a boost. It was hoped that this procedure would have the requisite punitive and intimidatory effect.

Thus there was political prosecution resulting from the infiltration and arrest of 19 young people in the so-called Movement of Revolutionary Youth or the Revolutionary Socialist Party. They were detained in November–December 1969 but put on trial only in March 1971, their sentences ranging from one to four years. Three signatories of the so-called Ten Point Manifesto, in fact a petition sent to the authorities on the first anniversary of the invasion, were detained without a trial for a year.[64] They were eventually not tried in this connection at all but were later convicted on other charges; their long detention was, however, widely known and served essentially the same deterrent purpose as a trial would. Vladimír Škutina, a well-known television personality, writer and journalist, was arrested in September 1969 and sentenced at the beginning of 1971 to two years' incarceration plus another two years at an additional trial on 1 July 1971. Bohumír Kuba, a secondary school teacher in North Moravia, was arrested in August 1968 and sentenced in May–June 1971 to three years' imprisonment. Luděk Pachman, the journalist and international grandmaster of chess, arrested in August 1969, was released, re-arrested and eventually sentenced in May 1972 to two years. General Vaclav Prchlík was sentenced in March 1971 to three years (reduced on appeal to 22 months). Jiří Lederer, a journalist, arrested in January 1970 was sentenced to two years, later re-arrested and his most recent conviction was in October 1977. Ota Filip, a novelist, arrested in August 1969, was sentenced in February 1970 to 18 months' imprisonment. In addition there were several espionage trials with high sentences and such improbable information about the indictment that the substantiation of the charges must remain suspect. It seemed that conversations with foreign diplomats and journalists were involved.

For example, a journalist got ten years for allegedly telling American diplomats and Western newsmen about the content of coded orders from the Ministry of Defence, movement and deployment of Soviet troops in Czechoslovakia, negotiations held by the Czechoslovak Foreign Minister abroad, military exercises, scheduled discussions in the party central committee, changes in party and state organs before they actually occurred, secret speeches by party leaders, attitudes held by officials at a ministry, rumours about conflicts between party leaders, conferences of cultural unions, statements by right-wing personalities, numbers of employees at central offices 'and many other things'.[65] The mélange of utterly innocuous items of legitimate interest to every journalist (and member of the public, for that matter) with sinister-sounding intelligence activities makes the entire case look distinctly wobbly.

Also before the courts were people who distributed leaflets, those who had enabled the functioning of a broadcasting service during the invasion week (for example by lending technical assistance or the use of premises), and others.

117

Already at this stage the substantiation of prison sentences revealed a predominance of diehard political phraseology which made full use, often beyond a tolerable limit, of the elastic wordings of laws. Disagreement with the official policy line and its criticism was shamelessly presented as a legally sound cause of prosecution and incarceration.

Thus General Prchlík was accused that at a conference on 15 July 1968 (even the date gives a lie to Husák's claim that no one will be tried for views expressed before the invasion) he 'criticised organs [*sic*!] and their activity in an impermissible form, and adduced information which he must have known would aggravate not only the already acute internal political situation but above all the friendly relations with the USSR'.[66] Bohumír Kuba was sent to jail because he 'made light of Czechoslovak developments after 1948 by one-sidedly generalising certain mistakes and shortcomings, by attacking and offending social-ist principles of the building of socialism [*sic*!], especially the status of the communist party in society . . . and because by attacking alliance with the USSR and insulting leading representatives of the country and the party he made more difficult the ongoing process of con-solidation in our society'.[67] The New Left group of Petr Uhl received prison sentences because they 'compiled and duplicated various printed matter and leaflets whose content could [*sic*!] arouse disagree-ment with and resistance to the socialist social order and impede the communist party's endeavour to consolidate political and economic conditions'.[68]

To bring some kind of an order into the confused situation is impossible. There were fairly large-scale arrests in connection with the anniversary riots and other causes at the end of 1969 and people were held in detention throughout 1970 only to be sentenced in the first months of 1971, when the campaign leading to the 14th party congress started. Some cases revealed lack of purpose, as if the authorities did not know what to do, witness releases and re-arrests. Some people were jailed for acts committed before the invasion (Lederer, Kuba, Prchlík), while others had their pre- and post-invasion activities wrapped together in the verdict. A continuing conflict about the line to be taken can serve as an explanation. Even with this confusion, political incarceration once again began to be applied for intimidatory reasons.

THE FEDERAL EBB AND FLOW

Tightening of political control from one centre could not remain without effect on the federalisation arrangements which were enacted in October 1968 and came in force on 1 January 1969. For such a major constitutional change, the drafting of the legislation had been completed rather hastily and, in its final stages, under the impact of momentous external circumstances. An *idée fixe*, sound at the core, justifiable on moral grounds and probably workable under normal conditions, was translated into constitutional reality for political reasons and in a half-baked form. It would almost certainly have had to be amended even if no 'normalisation' followed. As it was, the recentralisation that occurred in 1970 was prompted by considerations of the incongruence between a federative arrangement, albeit incomplete, and the aims of central and unitary political control stretching from the Kremlin through the Prague leadership down to the last organ of party-state power in towns and villages.

The intention to federalise the party had to go first. Obviously a Czech Lands party congress could not have been allowed to convene when the 14th state-wide congress was postponed until after the situation was 'normal'. Instead, the Czech Lands party bureau was created to simulate Czech national representation in the party, but it was placed under conservative leadership and given a press organ (*Tribuna*) under hardline editorship (O. Švestka) to nip in the bud the possibility that it would become the stronghold of 'progressives'. For a short time after his access to full power, Husák may have believed that federalisation of the party would be possible within a conservative, 'normalised' framework. Or else he was deliberately deceiving the public in his radio and television address of 30 April 1969 when he envisaged the holding of all three party congresses, the federal, the Czech and the Slovak in the first half of 1970.[69] The dating, incidentally, indicates that he might still have had an idea about the party purges which differed from the actual conduct of the campaign. Then something or someone changed his mind fairly rapidly because at the end of May 1969, addressing the central committee, he gave warning of a completely different role of the party and added in the same breath:

> 'The federal system must not weaken the unity of our state and neither must it weaken inevitable central control in the spirit of the federalisation law.... The party is not federalised, on the contrary it is a unitary body and we [meaning the praesidium or the central committee] are responsible for the work of communists in all departments, both federal and national'.[70]

The very title under which his winding-up speech at the September 1969 session of the central committee was published makes the same point: 'One party, one policy, one leadership, one discipline'.[71]

In January 1970 he could not be more specific:

> 'As a unifying and integrating force the Czechoslovak Communist Party must play an important role—as a unitary party led by a united central committee, with a united programme and objective. Certain elements of federalisation have got into the party, with the national elements, the Czech bureau and the Slovak central committee playing their part vis-à-vis the old leadership. These questions too will have to be put in order in new conditions; the various controlling elements in our party will have to be harmonised with the uniform principles of our programme but also specifically, in action, as this will enhance the strength of the whole of the party considerably'.[72]

By that time Štrougal became Federal Prime Minister, other Czech bureau members were being gradually shifted to other posts and not replaced, and the bureau practically disappeared from the public eye. Eventually it was unceremoniously buried at the 14th congress in May 1971, without as much as a public obituary. The amended party statutes simply failed to mention its existence. It had been; it was no more.

The dismantling of the federation on state lines required slightly more regard for public relations because many Slovaks believed that an age-long national objective had been attained precisely thanks to Husák's principled stand both in the face of the Czechs and the Russians. That is why the removal of the content and the preservation of the form was chosen.

Already in September 1969 the integrative function of the federal government became enhanced when the Czech and Slovak Prime Ministers became Federal Deputy Prime Ministers, subordinate to the Federal Prime Minister, while retaining their national offices. In January 1970 this was followed by the abolition of the offices of state secretaries in federal ministries. (They were meant to be held by Slovaks where the federal minister was a Czech, and vice versa.) Then the admittedly clumsy two national citizenships (Czech or Slovak) gradually gave way to the previous practice of a single Czechoslovak citizenship. Economic arguments in favour of recentralising such areas of national jurisdiction as planning, finance, labour, social welfare and construction developed during 1970, and finally—in December 1970—the constitutional law on the federation was amended, with effect from 1 January 1971, giving the federal government the power to overrule laws passed by national governments, and to federal ministries decision-making powers on matters previously subject to joint jurisdiction between them and national ministries. The country's economy was now proclaimed to be a 'united' one. (Originally each of the two nations was said to be 'economically autonomous' while the overall Czechoslovak economy remained 'integrated'—an impossible proposition in the first place.) Existing federal 'committees' for prices, technical development, investment, industry and posts and communications were transformed into federal ministries and accorded full supremacy over their national counterparts.[73]

The episode concerning Regional National Committees was symptomatic of the zig-zagged path of Slovak fortunes in the federalisation saga. These committees, the largest territorial administrative units in the country since 1949, are directly linked to governmental power in Prague and fall under the jurisdiction of the Ministry of the Interior. (Local government in Soviet-type societies serves at once local interests and as transmission channel for central directives, though more the latter than the former.) The Slovak National Council decided to abolish the three such units in Slovakia (West, Central and East) in July 1969 with the aim of eliminating an unnecessary bureaucratic link and at the same time weakening Prague suzerainty over local administration in Slovakia. Henceforth the Slovak government in Bratislava would directly supervise the lower-level District National Committees whose ties with Prague were much less. Bratislava would then be able to aggregate and meet Slovak local interests in a much fuller way and its hand in representing and promoting such interests *vis-à-vis* the federal authorities would also be strengthened. But the regional structure of the communist party remained in existence, although the regional party committees in Slovakia suddenly had no state-line counterparts to deal with. The Regional National Committees were re-established on 3 December 1970 in conjunction with the other re-centralising legislation.

If there was resentment on the Slovak side, it was not permitted to come to the surface. The fact of a large bureaucratic apparatus in Bratislava remained unchanged (in reality it probably contracted a little, but as it was still only in the building-up stage the growth of staffs in the national organs that did remain in existence soon compensated numerically for the lost jobs), and what in fact gained in importance immediately and over the next few years was a steady flow of Slovak administrators to federal offices in Prague. One cannot avoid concluding that the attractiveness of positions in Prague was meant to compensate the Slovaks for factual loss of power in Bratislava.

The effect of federalisation on the growth of bureaucracy can be measured fairly accurately both in the Czech Lands and in Slovakia, as shown in Table 2. How many of the so-called 'non-productive' employees in Prague were Slovak is difficult to ascertain. From successive statistical yearbooks it appears that the peak in Slovak residence in the Czech Lands occurred in 1968 (369,000) and 1969

Table 2. Number of administrative employees 1968–1973

000's	1968	1969	1970	1971	1972	1973
Czech Lands						
Employees in non-productive sectors	1,054	1,098	1,112	1,129	1,126	1,132
including: employees in administration and judicature	80	81	85	97	97	96
Slovakia						
Employees in non-productive sectors	386	406	421	434	457	468
including: employees in administration and judicature	31	37	36	37	41	44

Source: Statistická ročenka 1973, p. 115–6, and *1975*, p. 134–5.

(377,000), but then declined to 309,000 in 1970; is not given for 1971; and went up again to 334,000 in 1972. Most were residents of long standing, in agricultural and borderland areas. In 1971 only 13,775 Slovaks were registered as permanently residing in Prague.[74] But of course you can keep your 'permanent' domicile registration while working elsewhere.[75]

R. W. Dean, whose thorough and thoughtful account of the first three years of federalisation it is difficult to surpass in a brief summary, concludes that in terms of the actual distribution of power the Slovaks have once again found themselves unable to define and control their own interests. One would wish to add that they could project at least some of their newly attained influence through positions of authority in the federal organs of the party and the state. Dean sees four points in which federalisation remained meaningful even after the December 1970 emasculation: in the Slovak public mind it took hold as a moral and psychological victory; it provided institutional conduits through which the Slovaks could secure a bigger share of the economic pie than they would in pre-1968 conditions; deference to Slovak sensitivities persists in the party and federal government; and in the given context recentralisation is conducive to greater rationality and efficiency both in economic management and in administrative procedures.[76]

Czechoslovak economic and political life was once again directed from Prague, with greater Slovak participation and with residual powers over Slovakia vested in a Slovak party-governmental set-up. The Slovaks may not have gained as much as they wanted, but the Czechs lost more than they thought.

ECONOMIC INVERSION

As with other aspects of the situation in which the logic of central-isation mingled with ideological tenets and perhaps even a little genuine exigency, the real nature of the economic problem facing the 'normalisers' is well camouflaged. Much of what they said about the country's economy was confused by non-economic consideration. With the pouring out of the political bathwater, the economic baby was suffering damage.

As the Hungarian case was proving, a market-orientated economic reform *per se* is not *casus belli* for the Kremlin, provided the accompanying political safeguards are considered adequate. Post-invasion and post-Dubček Czechoslovakia, in a state of political and ideological tumult, was of course different from circumspect Hungary twelve years after *its* anti-communist experiment. Moreover, apart from the normalisers' attitudes being blurred by suspicion that *every* reform was by definition sacrilegious and therefore must go, the causes and effects of the military intervention became hopelessly in-termingled in their minds. Which economic problems of the middle of 1969 were caused by the incipient reformist plans and which trans-pired from the disruption occasioned by massive military intervention—this they were never able or willing to recognise and acknowledge. They found it certainly more expedient to rage against the reformers for having caused just about every economic sin in the book.

The alleged sins were legion; the main ones included the desire to transform 'socialist ownership' into 'group ownership', the doing away with central planning in exchange for 'the blind rule of the market', the introduction of workers' councils as a counterpoint to the party's leading role in the economy, the unleashing of inflationary pressures through both wages, prices and the opening of Czechoslovak economy to the West, and the promotion of private enterprise.

The question of ownership and planning had to do with that principle of the economic reform which envisaged the efficiency criteria to be determined through the market participation of individual enterprises, still state-owned, rather than by central plan-ners. In order to behave adequately, the enterprises were to be given far greater amount of independence. As all employees of such a enterprise, from management to workers, would derive benefit or bear the consequence of a loss, it was thought right that all of them should be able to exercise entrepreneurial influence on their enterprise's action. Hence the idea of 'workers' councils' as partners of the management, with powers over the decisions affecting the performance and prospects of the enterprise. The state plan would still have remained in existence as a framework for market relations ('commodity-monetary relations') and to control those lines of socio-economic activity which a market cannot regulate adequately, e.g. long-term trends of development, ecological problems and the social effects of economic processes.

In the emotional language of the 'normalisers' this theoretical construction acquired a much more lurid dimension:

> 'In economic theory and practice the reformers were gradually preparing and implementing a transformation of socialist economy into a system which was meant to deprive the working class and all the working people of all the revolutionary attainments and of their fundamental political and economic security. The bloc of right-wing opportunist and anti-socialist forces expected the step-by-step worsening of the economic situation to create spontaneous discontent among the working people which it would then take advantage of to fight socialist power. As the most manifest expression of such endeavour, our economy ceased being controlled through a national economic plan. The enforcement of a market economic model gravely disrupted the proportions of the creation and distribution of sources as envisaged by the fourth five-year plan. In this way our economy found itself in a state of crisis'.[77]

Practically none of it was true, and much of it was childish, but the underlying thrust of the attack on the economic reform was unmistakable. The concept of enterprise autonomy in a market would have to go, and fairly quickly it did go. Further discussion of the Enterprise Bill was halted as early as 29 April 1969. Not much later, in May 1969, self-management was rejected, although formal disbandment of the workers' councils did not follow until later. (The Škoda Enterprise Council was disbanded on 11 November 1969.) In June 1969 the federal government 'revoked its decision of 1968–69 on the creation of enterprise councils'. Soon afterwards, in July 1969, it was announced that the state plan for 1970 would be once again binding in all its stipulations.

Thus, almost at a stroke, the pillars of economic reform were knocked down; without them there would obviously be no reform of the kind planned during the Prague Spring. Some economists believed that the return would be no further back than to the January 1965 postulates of a reform, adopted still under Novotný and then circumscribed in the course of the three remaining years of his rule. This was a half-baked compromise which would still accord some importance to efficiency criteria in enterprises albeit under close, constant and politically based supervision from the state planning office. This in fact turned out to be the case, but with alterations. The system that emerged in the post-reformist period remained under central command, but the detailed quantitative planning of the early Stalinist times was not resorted to. Even so, the 1968 reform was dead, while it slowly unfolded in neighbouring Hungary, with increasingly better results.

The leadership also applied itself diligently and energetically to the more immediate practical situation. Control over prices (which never got out of hand contrary to the smear campaign against the reformers) was re-asserted, frugality measures announced, new investments suspended and a complete price freeze announced as from 1 January 1970. The leading role of the party in the economic sector was loudly reasserted in January 1970 in a document which obliged party organs and indeed all members to get involved in the supervision of economic functionaries at all levels. This mobilisation of the party apparatus was obviously intended to counter that principle of reform which suggested that economy would best work if left alone, tied to the policies of the party and the state by no more than the general perspectives of the development of society. The plan for 1970 was fixed at a rather modest level, almost equal to the 1969 growth targets. Special emphasis was put on developing consumer goods production, construction materials (especially for housing), machinery for export and electric power. The overall level of investment was reduced. The slack discipline of the workforce was countered by an amendment of the Labour Code.[78] It authorised tougher penalties for persons and enterprises not discharging their duties properly. Work started on the formulation of the fifth five-year plan for the period from 1971 to 1975.

The effectiveness of the practical measures, ostensibly promulgated to overcome disruption caused during the Prague Spring, is difficult to prove on the basis of available statistical evidence. What can be concluded is that Czechoslovak economy under the short impact of an economic reform did not work worse than before 1968, and that in the post-reformist period it did not start working worse than during the Prague Spring. In other words, Czechoslovakia has experienced a steady economic growth from 1966 (or 1967) to 1978, perhaps not buoyant and confident, but more than satisfactory in East European conditions. This development was assisted by agricultural success. The years 1968–69 mark no substantial deviation from the trend. If anything, they showed an improvement in the standard of living of the population, a development confirmed by people who spent the Prague Spring months in the country. They will also testify to a manifestation which statistics cannot well reveal, notably an improvement in the variety and quality of goods in the shops.

The price explosion also appears to be something of a myth when subjected to scrutiny. (This was one of the main accusations against the reformers.) Wholesale prices in industry hardly moved from 1 January to 30 August 1968, and in fact remained remarkably steady afterwards. During the Prague Spring proper they increased by 0·27 per cent.[79] Retail prices in 1968 were 1·3 per cent higher than on 1 January 1967 and raised the cost of living in non-farmer households by 1·2 per cent.[80]

Wages on the other hand did grow faster than before: the average monthly wage increased from Kčs 1,618 in 1967 to Kčs 1,750 in 1968, i.e. by 8·1 per cent, whereas from 1966 to 1967 it grew only by 5·5 per cent.[81] This trend was indeed arrested by central action by the Husák leadership and subsequent growth was much slower: 3 per cent in 1970 and 3·7 per cent in 1971. The rationale in the 1968 jump did not lie so much in deliberate wrecking designs or in succumbing to spontaneous pressure by the workforce, as asserted later, but in realisation that some outlet had to be opened to a workforce which had been held at tight rein for too long. It was hoped that higher purchasing power would boost industrial growth by creating demand for the more sophisticated durable commodities which had been in short supply.

The panicky and venomous attacks on the economic reform on the part of the 'normalisers' were perhaps mainly prompted by the fear that neither consumers' expectations nor the purchasing power newly created in 1968 could be met by an economy which was being administratively reverted to its pre-reformist stage. People with money in their pockets strolling past shopwindows with few goods in them were unlikely to take kindly to all the other aspects of 'normalisation'. The new regime was afraid that it would be unable to deliver the goods which the economic reformers had promised.

That is also why the Czech leaders and economic experts travelled to Moscow again and again for assistance. The time-honoured practice in the Soviet bloc, whenever a member finds himself exposed to real or potential public discontent based on economic grievance, has been to ask the others for help. East Germany had been the recipient of such assistance for quite some time, until it evolved into a strong industrial nation, and so was Cuba. Hungary had to be injected in this way in 1956–57 and so had Poland. Now Czechoslovakia's turn seemed to arrive.

The question of bloc aid after the invasion has been much discussed in the West, never conclusively and often misleadingly. People simply took for granted that there was aid and reports in Western newspapers seemed to confirm it. How else could the trauma of foreign intervention and the subsequent re-Stalinisation be overcome and how else could the Czechoslovak economy be restored to the impressive strength it was to reveal in the 1970s? In reality, things were not that simple.

There was almost certainly no aid in the sense that it is normally understood, i.e. as unreturnable gift of money, goods or services. As for cash loans, we cannot be certain because the East European countries, with the exception of Yugoslavia, do not publish their balance of payments. Private sources have persistently reported that the Czechoslovak leaders' repeated requests for a Soviet loan, part in dollars, part in rubles, were always turned down. The one official reference to a Soviet loan in freely convertible currency comes from the Slovak weekly *Nové Slovo* of 27 November 1975. According to it the loan was granted 'in the years 1968–69' and its specific purpose was to purchase consumer goods in the West. The size was not mentioned. A Western speculative report spoke much earlier of $20 million, and other wild guesses went as high as $1,000 million. Official statistics do not bear out a large grant. There was certainly no sign of spectacular Czechoslovak buying in the Western markets in 1969 or 1970 either of consumer goods or modern technology. (Some loans were negotiated for specific purposes later through Comecon banks, but only after the critical period was over and the economy was booming again.) In proportion to its potential, Czechoslovakia has in fact remained the most reticent of all the bloc countries in acquiring Western machinery to this day.

So, no gift, and at the most a small short-term loan to liven up Christmas 1969. Obviously Moscow must have thought Czechoslovakia's economy strong enough to weather the storm largely on its own, or may have been so outraged by the reformist excesses and confident of its grip on the country that it decided to make it go without direct aid even at the cost of a drop in the standard of living. There still remained one or two other possibilities of making life easier for the Husák leadership. About the first we can only speculate: financial commitments of Czechoslovakia to Soviet or Comecon or Warsaw Pact programmes, including military ones, might have been cut back. The second is more evident: contractual trade deliveries from Czechoslovakia to the bloc countries were left to go slow while credit was being extended for stepped-up supplies in the opposite direction.

In September 1970 the Federal Minister of Foreign Trade, A Barčák, wrote that the 'slight surplus' in Czechoslovak trade with the bloc, which by the end of 1967 had stood at 1,700 million crowns, had been drained away and transformed into a deficit of some 3,000 millions by the end of 1969. He warned that things were going too far and that energetic remedial measures must now be taken. Imports must be allowed in only sparingly and they must concentrate on what was needed most, viz. electric power, coal, meat, etc. Czechoslovakia's partners had shown full understanding for the problems of consolidation, the Minister continued, but they could not be expected to tolerate non-fulfilment of agreed quotas indefinitely. Moreover, the quality of Czechoslovak exports was not good either. It was a matter of honour and communist responsibility to comply with the contractual commitments.[82]

This ministerial warning was somewhat at variance with an item in the same newspaper just a week later which stated that all industries had fulfilled their export quotas to the socialist countries in the first half of 1970, except power generation and engineering.[83] It was explained three months later when Czechoslovak manufacturers were told that Soviet markets posed a more serious challenge to them now in terms of quality because of higher expectations and competition from capitalist firms. This particular article went on to say that there had been a large decline in Czechoslovak deliveries to the USSR although they had been contracted for. The balance of payments (i.e. not just the trade balance) still showed a considerable deficit in Czechoslovakia's disfavour. The volume of unfulfilled deliveries had grown from 31 million *rubles* in the first quarter of 1968 to the peak of 85·5 millions in the third quarter of 1969. (This is not borne out by statistics which showed Czechoslovakia running a surplus in the *trade* balance with the USSR to the order of 78 million *crowns* in the first three months of 1968, unless the deliveries referred to concerned officially unrecorded items, such as arms.)[84] From the fourth quarter of 1969 the deficit was said to have begun to decline (in fact it continued in October and November, while picking up suddenly and dramatically in December to the point where the whole of 1969 ended with Czechoslovakia exporting more than importing). The article also listed five types of equipment which Czechoslovakia was delivering below the agreed quotas: rolling mills, textile machinery, amonia-producing equipment, china and ceramics-producing equipment, and equipment for the Volga Car Factory.[85]

A month-by-month breakdown of the Czechoslovak trade balance overall, with the Comecon countries (including the USSR), and with the Soviet Union separately is given in Tables 3, 4 and 5.[86]

The tables allow us to make the following conclusions. In the eight months of the Prague Spring, from January to August 1968, Czechoslovakia had a favourable trade balance overall and with Comecon as a whole, though it cannot be said how this reflected fulfilment of trade agreements. From the Soviet Union Czechoslovakia imported more than it exported to it, to the value of Kčs 196 million. (Of which 125 million was incurred in August, the invasion month.) Even so, both imports from and exports to the USSR grew steadily from 1967 to 1971. From September 1968 to April 1969 (Dubček's 'period of grace') Czechoslovakia scored the following results: a 32 million overall deficit, a 1,252 million deficit with Comecon, and a 45 million surplus with the USSR. Whoever was going to be hurt by the economic consequences of the invasion, it was not going to be the Soviet Union, even if all contractual deliveries were obviously not being fulfilled. The main 'sufferers'—apart from the Czechoslovaks who were not getting anything free of charge—were the other

Table 3. Total balance of trade 1967–1971 (million Kčs)

Month	1967	1968	1969	1970	1971
January	+ 278	+ 143	+ 160	+ 70	+ 334
February	+ 233	+ 350	+ 124	+ 115	+ 205
March	+ 212	+ 297	− 97	+ 76	+ 492
April	+ 202	+ 177	+ 47	− 15	+ 293
May	+ 298	+ 27	− 55	+ 106	+ 205
June	+ 389	+ 48	+ 203	+ 417	+ 545
July	+ 127	+ 93	+ 126	+ 55	+ 5
August	+ 113	− 305	− 281	+ 97	+ 6
September	+ 130	+ 242	+ 169	+ 663	+ 818
October	+ 118	− 14	− 37	+ 83	− 9
November	+ 264	− 48	− 27	+ 359	+ 232
December	+ 35	− 446	+ 475	− 132	− 624
Annual total	+ 1326	− 517	+ 182	+ 700	+ 1225

Source : Statistické přehledy, various issues.

130

Table 4. Balance of trade with Comecon countries 1967–1971 (million Kčs)

Month	1967	1968	1969	1970	1971
January	+ 157	+ 116	+ 103	− 96	+ 90
February	+ 230	+ 232	− 22	− 68	+ 79
March	+ 233	+ 91	− 210	+ 51	+ 329
April	+ 148	+ 127	− 22	− 78	+ 183
May	+ 248	− 58	− 109	− 12	+ 137
June	+ 181	− 144	− 139	+ 224	+ 237
July	− 16	− 49	− 95	− 122	− 134
August	− 30	− 311	− 382	+ 28	− 71
September	− 129	− 140	− 193	+ 332	+ 232
October	− 71	− 162	− 271	− 77	− 59
November	− 23	− 283	− 266	+ 274	+ 65
December	− 414	− 516	+ 398	+ 312	− 134
Annual total	+ 470	− 1065	− 1060	+ 688	+ 869

Source : *Statistické p̌ehledy,* various issues.

Table 5. Balance of trade with the USSR 1967–1971 (million Kčs)

Month	1967	1968	1969	1970	1971
January	− 10	− 27	− 6	−151	− 84
February	+ 60	+ 41	+ 9	+ 4	− 4
March	+ 80	+ 64	− 13	− 46	+118
April	+ 75	+ 1	+ 36	− 93	+ 25
May	+138	− 43	− 48	− 29	− 15
June	+ 78	−113	+ 32	+ 66	+ 50
July	+ 5	+ 7	− 1	− 94	−105
August	− 41	−125	−200	+ 65	− 45
September	− 45	+ 25	− 44	+184	+ 97
October	− 85	− 41	− 20	− 60	−120
November	− 18	+ 1	− 77	+ 93	− 78
December	−134	+ 34	+459	+190	− 61
Annual total	+ 85	−203	+139	+ 92	−251

Source: Statistické přehledy, various issues.

Comecon countries in Europe. Be it as it may, the economic problems connected with foreign trade occurred only *after* the invasion and as a result of the disruption which it caused in actual production and by making the workers unwilling to fulfil Soviet orders. *Post hoc ergo propter hoc* for once did apply.

To find out which of the other Comecon partners had to make do, for a change, with the role of Czechoslovakia's creditor, I have examined exports and imports between each of them and Czechoslovakia from May 1969 to September 1970 when it can be assumed their temporary disadvantage was to the loyal Mr Husák's advantage. (We are of course operating with a concept peculiar to the command economies of Eastern Europe and their international trade linkage. In the West every country rejoices over flourishing exports and declining imports. Not so in the Comecon where Czechoslovakia and East Germany are considered the bloc's workshops, duty bound to export more than they import from the other partners.) It transpires that 'normalising' Czechoslovakia incurred a deficit with five out of the six, the exception being Poland. In descending order the deficits (May 1969–September 1970) were as follows: with East Germany Kčs 365 million, with Hungary 215 million, with Bulgaria 165 million, with Romania 142 million and with the Soviet Union 92 million. The surplus with Poland was 71 million.[87]

Towards the end of 1970 Czechoslovak trade balance with the Comecon and the USSR was getting massively better so that the calendar year ended with overall Comecon deficit *vis-à-vis* Czechoslovakia of Kčs 688 million. In 1971 this even increased to 869 million, as Czechoslovakia was beginning to step up her exports in repayment of earlier imports. The Soviet Union enjoyed receiving more goods from Czechoslovakia than it sent there already in 1969 (by 139 million). Then, in 1971, especially the latter half of the year, probably in connection with the building of a gas pipeline traversing Czechoslovakia from East to West (or deliveries of new military hardware?), Soviet exports to Czechoslovakia soared to a calendar year surplus (for the Soviets) of Kčs 251 million. In 1972 and 1973 Czechoslovakia had again a favourable balance both with the USSR separately and the Comecon as a whole. In 1974 there was a surplus with the USSR but a deficit with the Comecon. If anything, the oscillation proves that Comecon assistance to Husák was nothing extraordinary.

Not that everything is clear. An article about something else, dated October 1971, casually mentioned that Czechoslovakia's 'foreign debt' in 1970 was 6,204 million crowns.[88] The term 'debt' is normally not used in such context in official sources, and of course there is no statistical evidence. Just a reminder that trade balances will not tell a statistical mole what he is not allowed to learn from unpublished sources.

An anonymous Prague dissident source suggested that Czechoslovakia had been allowed to contribute less to Warsaw Pact expenditure on armaments for a few years, that she could temporarily reduce her aid to such developing countries as Cuba, Vietnam and the Arab states, that Comecon countries were repaying debts and credits outstanding since the second half of the 1950s, and that domestic investment outlays were cut.[89] Except the last item, these suggestions cannot be verified against available statistical data, but may of course well be true.

The Husák leadership went undoubtedly through a tough patch, but one has the feeling that in the long perspective it was not more than an economic hiccup. Three things helped the new leaders survive with flying colours: the Czechoslovak economy was strong, the agricultural results were good, and the workers were not Polish. By the middle of 1971 things seemed to be settling down. Everything began to have that *déjà vu* look: a surfeit of ideology, a hardline leadership, and just enough consumer goods and food to keep the public pacified, if grumbling. All set to stage a party congress to draw up the balance sheet, cross the t's and dot the i's.

CONGRESS OF VICTORS

As the Year of the Great Purge was coming to an end, it became clear that the party was still not fully united. Active reformers may have been driven out from its ranks and from the positions they held in governmental and other organisations, but attitudes to potential reformism still divided the conservative coalition in power. It was not a great divide, but rather a Czechoslovak replica of the 'hawks' and 'doves' bifurcation within the ruling political élite. The Husák group was publicly indicating that, thank God, the purge was over and the process of consolidation only required a few formal finishing touches to be completed. The Bilak group, on the other hand, was exhorting to further vigilance and a kind of permanent war on real and potential deviationists. In this the intransigents had the support of the 'ultra' dogmatists.

Husák carried the day in the party praesidium when the formal announcement on the end of the purge was formulated in September 1970. Its emphasis was on winding up the emergency forms of party life and on progress towards regular and positive methods without further ado.[90] Husák himself anticipated this line in a speech in Slovakia by saying that emergency political measures had been temporary and inevitable. He added that they had been implemented in a humane way; in many other countries there would have been bloodshed. Having overcome the critical period, the leadership now intended to resume normal life and normal forms of socialist democracy again.[91] The Prime Minister, L. Štrougal, even went as far as admitting that the purge had had its defects and stated that the time had come to re-start systematic and planned work in all fields. The detrimental policies of recent years (meaning the Prague Spring) had been masterminded by a relatively small group of people. Now everyone would once again be invited to cooperate, including those who had to leave the party because of their mistakes and past attitudes.[92] Another official added: 'We are now glad that the purge is over'.[93]

These 'moderate' vioces were occasionally directed against the advocates of continual class war, without however specifying who they were:

> 'Some people are impatient. They . . . refuse to see things soberly and all but condemn moderation (which is necessary if consolidation is to succeed) as a retreat from Marxist positions. . . . The party will never promote destructive criticism. . . . Therefore it cannot listen to those who sit on the fence, mark time and do nothing but preach that things

should be done in this or that way, without themselves positively contributing to this work'.[94]

The implication was, as also stressed by Štrougal in the speech cited above, that the leaders had a country to administer, with its manifold economic and social problems, and could not make it into a permanent ideological battlefield. J. Fojtík, a central committee secretary, pursued the same line. According to him only the competent party leaders were entitled to judge people's qualities and past behaviour, not groups of people who bypass responsible resolutions adopted by the authorities.[95]

The pragmatists appeared wary lest their sorties against the hard line be interpreted 'as an admission that the previous policy failed'. A writer in *Obrana lidu* suggested that the defeat of the right wing had been completed and the party purified. The leadership had never intended to prolong the emergency situation indefinitely. Now it offered a hand to everybody, except the enemies.[96]

It has been said earlier that the plotting of the 'ultras' was thwarted while some of their political dicta were allowed to influence the official attitude to the purge and its tightening in April 1970. By September 1970 a number of extreme left-wingers had been removed from positions of influence, and the cautions against unabating radicalism might be seen as no more than a culmination of the process. In reality a new leftist front was emerging, this time connected with speculations that Husák's patron in Moscow, L. Brezhnev, would either resign or be forced out of office before or during the impending 24th congress of the Soviet Communist Party. Much of the information on background politicking is hopelessly inadequate and perhaps even garbled in transmission through unofficial channels. What is available suggests that the then Czechoslovak Ambassador in Moscow, Bohuš Chňoupek (who eventually became Foreign Minister and joined the Husák camp), passed signals about alleged prospects of a hawkish victory in the Soviet capital to the hardliners in the Czechoslovak leadership who opposed Husák's 'conciliatory' post-purge policy, above all Bilak in Bratislava and Kapek in Prague. The plan which they purportedly hatched was not unlike the one which Husák himself (and others before him) used in his offensive against the Vysočany congress and Smrkovský's candidature for chairmanship of the Federal Assembly. The hardliners intended to engineer a further round of personnel changes in the Slovak Party central committee to gain an upper hand for their supporters there and then take off from the Bratislava springboard to enforce a similar change in Prague. Coinciding with the envisaged anti-Brezhnev developments in Moscow, the Slovak party congress in the spring of 1971, scheduled to take place before the state-wide 14th congress, would provide them with the institutional pre-requisites. Husák himself would then be removed at the 14th congress. The Slovak stage of the operation was considered a relatively safe bet because the Slovak party was thought to be in a situation, under Vasil Bilak, amenable to such a 'correction of the course'. As for the Czech Lands, the 'ultras' who had been dispersed but not eliminated after Husák secured for himself Brezhnev's approval to strip them of influential positions, were to supply the 'second-rank support' while a few waverers in the top leadership would cross over to join Bilak, Kapek and Indra, seeing that this was the way the wind was blowing.

At the December 1970 plenum of the central committee both factions stated their case in relation to the purge. The hardliners took advantage of the presentation to the central committee of a document drawing conclusions from the 'reformist crisis' to raise once again the thesis according to which the Soviet Union had saved Czechoslovakia from counter-revolution in response to a written invitation from loyal internationalists in the Czechoslovak party. Two formulations were used: either 'a group of high party and state officials' or 'thousands of true communists' had allegedly sent a call for help to the Kremlin. This was not just an attempt to vindicate the original justification thesis used by the Soviets at the time of the invasion. At this stage it had a distinctly anti-Husák flavour. Bilak, Indra, Kapek, Chňoupek and others had directly or obliquely identified themselves as being members of the 'group' or the 'thousands' who had recognised the revisionist danger in time and acted in a truly communist way. Husák was not in that number. Was it right that someone like him, who only belatedly joined the pro-Soviet camp, should now be at the helm? The implication was clear even if unsaid, but a compromise patched up the differences once again. The document adopted for public consumption under the title 'Lessons from the Crisis Development in Party and Society since the 13th Party Congress' used the less pungent phrase of 'thousands of communists'. The actual wording was as follows:

> 'Thousands of communists, individual citizens and teams of working people, representatives of all layers of the population and various organisations, including members of the Czechoslovak and Slovak Communist Party Central Committee, the Czechoslovak government and deputies in the National Assembly and the Slovak National Council, aware of their class, national and international responsibility for the fate of socialism in Czechoslovakia, were avidly seeking a way out of the oppressive critical situation. [This part could be said to include the Husák group.] As the right wing of the party refused to take the requisite measures which would frustrate a counter-revolutionary coup and ward off a civil war, they began to address themselves to the leaderships of the fraternal parties and the governments of our allies

with the request that they render internationalist assistance to the Czechoslovak people in defence of socialism at this historic moment.' [This was a watered-down section from which reference to the 'writing of letters'—*litera scripta manet*—was left out. Who knows what Husák *et al.* did behind the scene? Maybe they also 'addressed themselves to the leaderships of the fraternal parties', unless of course a post-Brezhnev Soviet leader declared that Husák had *not* done so.][97]

In its other passages, the 'Lessons' were not unfavourable to Husák and, while the door did stay open for a possible U-turn in his fortunes, the document reflected a predominance of his policy line. It was of course utterly negative as far as reformism was concerned and gave a seal of approval to the post-April 1969 witch-hunts, but this was to be expected in an ideological package of this kind. The Husák interpretation could also be seen from the document's acceptance of the deposition of Novotný as a necessary thing, although his sins now included excessive toleration of liberal tendencies which led to the Prague Spring. Neither did Husák give way to those who were calling for a critical re-examination of at least some postulates of the 13th party congress in 1966, for example the economic reform and the setting up of a commission to study possible political changes in the societal structure of the country. A party congress, Husák opined righteously, is the supreme organ of the party and it can be adjudged only by another congress, not the central committee.

The December 1970 plenum also passed a statement on 'topical questions of party unity', another sign that Husák was holding out against the advocates of another split and a further shift in the leadership towards the left. The thrust of the statement would, however, point to another compromise where the organisational changes propounded by the diehards were rejected but their hawkish policy line accepted. The newly endorsed unity of the party appeared to be directed more towards a prolonged combat of the right wing than to constructive work for modernisation. Husák was unable to induce the central committee to re-adopt the old party dictum about the need to 'fight on two fronts—against the right and the left wings', if he ever wanted this to be stipulated, although some in his camp did. The danger from the right (reformism) remained the focal point of attention. The only oblique hint that sectarians and dogmatists, who traditionally comprise the left-wing bogey, might also be at work, can be deduced from the use of the adjective 'main' in association with the word 'danger', implying that there was also a lesser peril, albeit not quite defined and certainly not identified.

A hardline reading of the 'main danger' tenet was supplied by the Bratislava *Pravda*:

'The fact that the right wing continues to represent the main political danger [means] that it is impossible to permit a relaxation of the revolutionary principled approach. It is therefore necessary to reject the advice of some people that all should be forgiven and forgotten. People can forgive one another much, and forget a great deal, but the communist party and society must not and cannot forget'.[98]

The December plenum thus marked a small step forward in making the Husák line stick but did not quite preclude continued left-wing onslaught on his positions. According to confidential information relating to February 1971, the possibility of unseating Husák through Slovak pressure and in conjunction with changes in the Kremlin was being pursued further. (Coming from a private source, the information has to be taken with a pinch of salt as to its accuracy in detail, but it cannot be dismissed as entirely fabricated.) Bohuš Chňoupek met a few of his friends in Bratislava in February 1971 and is said to have told them:

'It is not true that the situation in Slovakia differs in substance from that in the Czech Lands. The only difference is that whereas in the Czech Lands counter-revolution came into the open under straight right-wing slogans, it was more disguised in Slovakia. It followed a predominantly Trotskyite [sic!] platform which combined right-wing, sectarian and nationalist attitudes. The time is now approaching when this platform must be unmasked and with it Husák as its chief protagonist'.

Roughly at the same time, in February 1971, Antonín Kapek held a secret meeting with his trustees in the ČKD Locomotive Works in Prague, to whom he confided that 'we must be ready for various changes. It may happen that the Soviet Party Central Committee elected at the forthcoming 24th congress will not put up Comrade Brezhnev as a candidate for First Secretaryship. And we must take into consideration that Prague will not be under fire from Moscow but from Bratislava because the Slovak party congress will be held prior to our 14th congress. Consolidation is not yet completed. It is being impeded by the hesitant attitudes in the leadership of some comrades, such as Husák and Svoboda'.

We have the advantage of looking back at these wrangles from the distance of seven years and of course we know that the charting of an extremist course at the turn of 1970–71 did not lead to the desired replacement of one team of 'normalisers' for another. Perhaps it was not all that clear when it actually was to happen, but one has the distinct feeling that the plotters (if that is indeed what they were) engaged in a great deal of wishful thinking. There probably was background disputation in the Soviet leadership about the budding detente course which Brezhnev was pressing through, but the Kremlin was likely to bet on a pragmatic workhorse of the Husák type rather than on the visceral ideologists, even if—or precisely because—Husák had a reformist blot on his fairly recent record. The conspirators may have also expected too much from Vasil Bilak, in a sense the pivotal figure in their designs. From his attitudes and action since the inauguration of the new leadership in April 1969 we know that he has always pressed for hardline solutions and thus constantly weighted the whole leadership towards the left, but at the same time he always stopped short of committing himself irrevocably to anything else but the left margin of the mainstream position. He may be the bad man of the Husák team, but he has so far refrained from rocking the boat too dangerously.

Be it as it may, Husák manoeuvred through the muddy waters without losing his position and without giving up the notion that 'we have passed through a certain stage, we have shed some of our worries and now we face new opportunities to develop fully the democratic character of socialist democracy in a Marxist-Leninist sense of the word'.[99]

A tall order, but it did coincide with Mr Brezhnev's belief in what was right for Czechoslovakia at this time. Husák seemed rather well suited to steer the new Czechoslovak leadership into the international communist movement without provoking the Italians too much. He even went to Romania in March 1971 to help breach Ceauşescu's initial aversion. In fact, Husák travelled widely as the new leader, engaging in intra-bloc pomp and circumstance with a little personal diplomacy on the side. In 1969 he left the country no fewer than twelve times and five of the twelve trips were to the USSR (plus two to East Germany, Poland and Hungary each, and one to Sofia), and eight times in 1970 (four times to the USSR, twice to East Germany and twice to Hungary). In 1971, before the 14th congress in May, he managed to go twice to Moscow, and to Bulgaria and Romania. Over the same period of two years he received in Czechoslovakia the Soviet leader once (plus a visit by Podgorny in November 1970, rumoured to have been undertaken in order to persuade President Svoboda not to resign as this could be interpreted as non-confidence in Husák and a boost to the 'ultras'), Zhivkov twice, Gomulka twice and Gierek once, Kádár twice and Ulbricht once. Thus Husák diligently projected himself, no doubt under Brezhnev's protective wing, as a statesman of stature throughout Eastern Europe. The new treaty with the USSR which was signed in May 1970 incorporated the so-called Brezhnev Doctrine and Husák's party became the foremost exponent of tighter integration within the Soviet orbit in Eastern Europe. Having used the police and the army against demonstrators on the first anniversary of the invasion in August 1969, Husák proved a winner in the pacification campaign as well. In spite of sporadic attempts, the second anniversary in 1970 passed without incident. During the riots on the Polish coast in

December 1970 and subsequently until March 1971, Husák was said to agree unreservedly with the use of Czechoslovak troops should a military intervention prove necessary. A red alert was rumoured to have been declared in the Czechoslovak armed forces on 9 March and a certain number of reservists were called up on 19 March. In short, Husák could do anything that a leftist opponent of his would do, only better.

When the 14th party congress convened on 25 May 1971, Husák could mount the rostrum with fair confidence alongside the leaders of the five Warsaw Pact countries which invaded Czechoslovakia 33 months ago, except that two of them had in the meantime given way rather unwillingly to new men. The presence of Brezhnev, Kádár, Zhivkov, Gierek and Honecker had an importance which could not be lost on friend and foe alike. That was what really mattered about this congress, together with the outline of economic policy in the fifth five-year plan. With the highest authority in the communist movement behind him, Husák had arrived. The degree to which his own ideas were changed in the process of expurgation and consolidation can be the subject of debate. If, as we suspect, he opposed his potential rivals in the dogmatic camp but did not hesitate to accept their counsel and present it as his own, he had a distinguished precedent for such action. In the second half of the 1920s Stalin waged a war on the Left Opposition, vanquished it and proceeded to implement the policies they had advocated against him. These policies were now being confirmed and the congress resolution associated Husák's name with them: 'The congress notes that a serious crisis in the party and in society has been overcome on the basis of a policy pursued by the party central committee headed by comrade Gustav Husák'.[100] January 1968 still remained 'an expression of necessity', but was said to have failed to provide a clear-cut class framework for further development. Counter-revolution and imperialist intervention threatened the country, and the congress gave 'sincere gratitude' to the Warsaw Pact countries for 'understanding the justified fears of Czechoslovak communists and socialistically thinking citizens about the fate of socialism, and for having complied with their appeals for assistance'.[101] With the ascendance of Husák pre-requisites for overall consolidation were created which the congress appreciated highly. The purge of the party had been necessary and correct; the congress would not allow anyone to cast doubts on its results. Finally the congress got near to saying, though it did not say it unequivocally, that things were normal once again: 'The consolidation of the party and of the society makes it possible for us to devote all our strength in the forthcoming period to a further reinforcement and development of a socialist society'.[102]

But Husák did not have it all his way. In any case, after all the

141

compromises he had made, what was his way? The resolution of the congress once again left sufficient elbow-room to those who would wish to continue the class war. While proclaiming that the party had reclaimed its own revolutionary vigour and achieved ideological unity and capacity for action, it also contained the following passage:

'Right-wing opportunism and revisionism is the main danger which we must combat. The politically defeated rightists are adapting their tactics to new conditions, they seek to influence the minds of some people and to take advantage of our mistakes and the objectively arising difficulties. They denigrate the results of honest work and by slanders, rumours and provocation they endeavour to distract our attention from urgent social tasks. We have paid dearly for a conciliatory attitude to right-wing tendencies in the party and their proponents. *Never again must we give them the slightest opportunity to assert themselves.* To complete the defeat of the right wing in the ideological sphere is an extraordinarily important duty of the party in the present stage'.[103] [Emphasis added.]

So what was it to be? The entire party's attention 'to speedy creative solution of emergent problems of the present time and to the finding of optimal roads towards further multi-sided development of the socialist society as the main and decisive objective of the party's work'[104] or the further taking of revenge? The resolution of the 14th congress suggested that both could and should be done simultaneously. The italicised sentence in the longer quotation above is Vasil Bilak's; people have heard him use it on other occasions before and since the congress. Brezhnev's choice was a duumvirate after all, with honours and eulogies going to Husák and the duty to sharpen his policies to Bilak. By its dual nature, the resolution of the congress presaged further victimisation, discrimination, police rule, blackmail and blacklisting as the permanent feature of the times to come, next to and often overshadowing all the pragmatic and positive activities required of a party which has taken it upon itself to preside over the modernisation of a complex society.

Perhaps it did not have to be so. The congress could have been a good opportunity to call it a day and to start seeking the advice and consent of even the defeated reformers. Instead it was decided to follow the vanquished enemy in hot pursuit. This action was bound to cause reaction.

Part Three
Trials, errors and feats

1971–1976

OPPOSITION ATTEMPTS TO ORGANISE

'Normalisation' in Czechoslovakia can be defined as restoration of authoritarianism in conditions of a post-interventionist lack of indigenous legitimacy, carried out under the close supervision of a dominant foreign power which retains the prerogative of supreme arbitration and interpretation but which prefers to work through its domestic agents. It had two principal aims: to remove reformism as a political force, and to legitimate a new regime resting on old pre-reformist principles. In the period described so far, the first of these aims had high priority. Towards its attainment, two simultaneous processes were pursued with determination. The population at large was intimidated into acceptance of imposed rules, and both real and potential opposition was pushed out from positions of influence, authority and control. The 14th party congress in May 1971 was to mark a watershed, following which the second—legitimating—objective would become the order of the day, with emphasis shifting towards ideological education and the pursuance of a high level of consumerism and conservative tranquility.

Three factors caused the first period to extend beyond the intended time-limit: (a) the hardline faction in the Czechoslovak party pressed for the prolongation of counter-reformatory struggle, (b) the 'moderate' faction was not strong or determined enough to withstand this pressure, and (c) the Soviet leadership failed to uphold the 'moderates' in this clash of intentions as its sole trusted agent.

The resulting state of affairs can be described as a mixture of ideological and rational elements in a one-party state, itself a common feature of all Soviet-type societies, which however distinguished itself in Czechoslovakia by a specially high level of the former and a permanently subordinate position of the latter. In other words, where the interests of continued class warfare against the defeated reformers and of rationality in political and economic governance came into conflict, real or imagined, the guardians of ideological purity invariably triumphed.

Regardless of the ethical issues involved, this was an obnoxious political course to take for a country which among the Soviet client states in Eastern Europe was the best suited to meet the modernisation challenges of the latter part of the 20th century. In April 1969 there was sufficient recognition in the constituency of people who had launched the Prague Spring, as well as among the population at large, that the experiment in bold systemic innovation had been defeated, that the geopolitical circumstances militated against its continuation in the same form and to the same extent, and that a much more modest *modus vivendi* for the future would have to be found in conjunction with the Soviet leadership and those conservative forces in the country whose departure from power had been demanded during the Prague Spring. A compromise in the form of a social contract between Moscow, local conservatives and the defeated reformers, while certainly not popular, was possible, and Gustav Husák could have been almost the ideal person to preside over it.

Even after the unnecessarily vicious purges of 1970 there was still time to embark on a cooperative course, although the room for compromise had become smaller. In all institutions which together comprise the political structure and infrastructure of a one-party state, including the communist party, there were still people able to provide enlightened even though authoritarian guidance, provided that they received a go-ahead from the power centre for cooperation with the immensely talented, skilful, educated and keen people who had been stripped of political office. Even the half-million strong expulsion from the communist party need not have mattered so much, provided that the ex-communists were allowed to supply their expertise to the new office holders. It was a narrower path than the one which had been open before the purges, but it could be walked provided there was acumen, foresight and determination on the part of the new rulers, including Moscow. It was not to be.

For the sake of revenge and the irrational fear expressed allegedly by Vasil Bilak in the laconic sentence 'if they ever get to the top again we will hang', Czechoslovakia had to sacrifice the modernisation requirements which even the communist regimes came to recognise as indispensible for the attainment of technical rationality and economic efficiency. Dogmatic constraints were once again imposed on such vital lines of activity as research, flow of information, planning, administration, selection and training of cadres, consultation between political leadership and experts, and even élite security under the rule of law. 'Normalisation' has set the clock back. Its impact in non-technical and non-economic fields has been even greater and for a precariously long time the country was tottering on the brink of a cultural disaster. The effect of restituted ideological coercion has all but wiped out participation, political awareness, cultural creativity, research in social sciences, and morality. Without them, consumerism (the foundations of which were only being laid at the time of the 14th party congress) was to amplify the traits which threaten every society and none more than the one which works on command, notably selfishness, career-seeking, corruption, economic larceny, escapism and dipsomania.

Sensing the danger, many people in the ex-reformist camp (and with them non-communists and even non-socialists who had believed in the promise of the Prague Spring) were searching for the best way of resisting 'normalisation' conceived in this way. The Dubček alternative of co-governing the country with the conservatives, both hardline and 'moderate', failed under the combined attack of Moscow and its partners, while the public was much too discomposed to be helpful by way of patience, calm and self-denial. Almost immediately after the stipulations of the Moscow Protocol became known (or suspected), a more radical form of opposition began to manifest itself among students, some workers and trade union functionaries and the intellectuals who disbelieved in the lop-sided coalition to which the Dubček wing was a party. It remained largely non-institutionalised and found expression in protest and defiance. The only effort to put a backbone into anti-normalisation resistance can be seen in the 'Student-Worker Coordinating Committees' which concluded cooperation agreements between branches of the Students' Union and a number of trade unions, and in the founding of the clandestine 'Movement of Revolutionary Youth', later renamed the 'Revolutionary Socialist Party', which was already mentioned as the first group to stand trial in the spring of 1971.

Some existing organisations, especially in the fields of journalism and culture, also became focal points of disagreement but not to the point of setting up fully fledged oppositional outfits. This was true about some branches of the Journalists' Union, the Czech Writers' Union, the Union of Film and Television Artists, the Society for the Protection of Human Rights and the Coordinating Committee of Creative Unions. Other organisations which had emerged during the Prague Spring subjected themselves to the discipline which the Dubček team was forced to impose on them without much demur and with no provision for continued clandestine existence. This applies to the Association of Former Political Prisoners (K 231), the Club of Committed Non-Party People (KAN) and the preparatory committees of the Social Democratic Party. For 'counter-revolutionary' organisations, as they were dubbed, they thus behaved with remarkable meekness and self-discipline. Perhaps it would be best to say that they recognised the overwhelming odds they were facing. It is anyway not easy to engage in underground activities in a country like Czechoslovakia where everybody knows everybody, the supervisory powers of the authorities are well developed and nearly all-embracing, and people have anyway come out into the open with their views during the Prague Spring so that to identify potential oppositionists is easy.

The mainstream of resistance to 'normalisation' has comprised the reform communists who believed in changing society peacefully and gradually. A good number among them were prepared to accept Husák as a man of the same ilk. He had personal friends among them and it is known that during the fortnight preceding Dubček's deposition he spoke to many privately, assuring them that a slow, cautious, circumspect reformism would continue. He behaved almost like a candidate canvassing among members of the electoral college. And he got their votes at the central committee session on 17 April 1969. The central committee then still consisted of just over 100 members elected in 1966 and around 80 members coopted at the end of August 1968 mainly from among the 'progressives'. Husák is said to have been endorsed as First Party Secretary by 177 votes against 5, though this has not been announced officially.

The scope and speed with which Husák began to purge the high bodies of the party and the government and the other drastic actions he took, for example in the mass media field, shocked his reformist supporters into realising that private political promises would not be kept. The oppositional constituency began to take shape and first ideas about an oppositional programme began to be mooted. The formative stage of a democratic-socialist opposition to the objectives and methods of 'normalisation' can be pinpointed from April 1969 to the Spring of 1970.

Czechoslovak ex-reformers do not wish to be called dissidents. They argue that while the majority of the Czechoslovak population may also be inactive under the impact of 'normalisation' and withdrawn into their private cocoons as their Russian counterparts are, they most certainly disagree with the political philosophy and practice of their present rulers. In 1968 they were given a chance to say so openly and they did do that unmistakably. An overwhelming majority of the Czechoslovaks are dissidents or, so the ex-reformers argue, it is the leadership that dissents from the political culture of the nation.

Anti-normalisation opposition in Czechoslovakia introduces strain, division and contest into political life, and in this way influences political processes and decisions. It is more than dissent; it is dissent translated into action.

The first oppositional document which did precisely that after Husák's seizure of power was the so-called Ten Points Manifesto of 21 August 1969. (It has also been referred to as the Manifesto of the Ten because of the number of signatures under it.) Two of the signatories had been political functionaries (R. Battěk, a member of the Czech National Council, and J. Wagner, deputy chairman of the Council of Youth Organisations), four journalists (K. Kyncl, M. Lakatoš who was a jurist by profession and ex-member of the Institute of State and Law, V. Nepraš and L. Pachman, the chess grandmaster), two writers (V. Havel, the playright, and L. Vaculík), one political scientist (L. Kohout) and one historian (J. Tesař).[1]

The Manifesto had the form of a petition to the Federal Assembly, the Czech National Council, the Federal Government, the Czech Lands Government and the Communist Party Central Committee.

(Petition right is guaranteed in Article 29 of the Constitution.)

The Ten Points have a preamble in which 'normalisation' is contrasted unfavourably with the Prague Spring. Point One rejects the military intervention. Point Two rejects retreats before threats and foreign interference after April 1969, notably the purges. Censorship is rejected in Point Three. Point Four expresses anxiety about possible infractions of the legal order by the 'normalisers'. It also includes an expression of early concern for human rights: 'We regard the banning of the Society for Human Rights as an ill omen. We wish to see an early ratification and implementation of the international pacts on civil, economic, social and cultural rights'. Point Five rejects the role of the communist party as a power wielding organisation superior to assemblies elected by general vote. Concern about the effect of 'normalisation' on the economy is expressed in Point Six, especially in that the purposefulness of the economic reform has been replaced by a return to irresponsible and wasteful practices. Point Seven disagrees with the postponement of elections and calls for a democratic electoral law. 'We repudiate in advance elections which would be similar to those held previously, and we shall take no part in them'. Satisfaction with Czech-Slovak federalisation is expressed in Point Eight; it should not remain formal. Point Nine reiterates the right of citizens to disagree with their government. Until this right is adequately guaranteed the signatories will resist in a lawful way 'all that is contrary to reason, human conscience and our convictions'. More particularly, they will ignore 'office holders who would have to be dismissed under normal conditions'. Point Ten states that 'negation is not our purpose'; the signatories are in favour of all citizens working well, improving their lot and preserving their philosophy of life.

The Manifesto ended with a passage that was to become standard for many future unofficial documents, namely a disclaimer of anti-state, anti-party, anti-socialist or anti-soviet intentions. The demurrer did not help much. Battěk, Tesař and Pachman were promptly arrested and detained for over a year. Others were interrogated at length. Charges were prepared against all ten and they were even told when to appear before a court, but the trial was continually postponed and then never held. Nonetheless, Nepraš, Pachman and Tesař were arrested later and indicted on other political charges.

The Ten Points were attacked from the other side as well, by the New Left among Prague students. The only critical comment available castigates the Manifesto as 'an avid lamentation, full of pathetic moralism and the typical naiveté of a victim which brings law and good manners to the robbers' notice, hoping (my God!) that it will be enough to defend oneself'.[2]

The New Left group led by Peter Uhl was active at the time of the Ten Point Manifesto. One of its members, the West German left-

149

winger Miss Sibylle Plogstedt, later described their activity. At first they studied the writings of old bolsheviks and Western Marxists, they made propaganda at universities, translated and published texts, and debated. All this until July 1969 when 'the whole group left for West Berlin to hold discussions with radical leftist groups in Germany and West Europe'.[3] Then they projected the results of their study on to an analysis of Czechoslovakia 'in a socialist perspective' and worked out statutes for a clandestine organisation which, however, was not a centralised one and could be easily infiltrated by a police informer. In December 1969 they were all picked up by the police.

The Ten Points were not an exemplary programme of political opposition, but they were not meant to be that. The petition contained some ideas which were subsequently taken over by others, but its authors had no intention to build up a clandestine group with a programme of action. These were the groping months, when many things were not clear. The purge had not yet been announced, although it was known that *some kind* of a purge was coming. The petition was in fact written before the police, the military and the Militia were sent out to stage a show of force in a number of Czech cities. Dubček was still a member of the party praesidium. All told, the Ten Points were a courageous statement of defiance on the part of ten individuals, a kind of personal articles of faith nailed on Husák's door.

The illusion that some kind of opposition could be conducted from within the party even under Husák was dying every day. The influence of those who were still tolerated diminished rapidly, not to mention their authority over nominal subordinates. Their channels of communication, horizontal and vertical, were blocked. The more radical ones were being discarded from the party and often from their jobs. Suddenly they faced unknown problems and anxieties: how to find other jobs, how to get used to manual or dreary clerical labour, how to ensure a reasonable well-being of their families, how to get hold of information which came naturally to them while they were still in office, how to cease being a member of the élite in terms of access to power, information and even money. What is called in Eastern Europe 'existential worries', that is the everyday concern for material standard of living, began to be felt by large numbers of people who had been used to better times. The reform communists were reliving the experience of the masses of non-communists who had been deprived of their jobs and material standards after February 1948. In fact they were luckier: fewer were being thrown into jail. To say all this is not to detract from the worthiness of the cause or the personal courage of these people. They could save themselves by turning their coats. Many did that, and it would be unjust to say 'serves you right' to those who did not.

The notion that the course of 'normalisation' could be effectively softened from inside the Establishment perished. The logic of authoritarian regimes requires that there is no opposition.

> 'Since all opposition is potentially dangerous, no distinction can be made between acceptable and unacceptable opposition, between loyal and disloyal opposition, between opposition that is protected and opposition that must be repressed. Yet if all oppositions are treated as dangerous and subjected to repression, opposition that would be loyal if it were tolerated becomes disloyal because it is not tolerated. Since all opposition is likely to be disloyal, all opposition must be repressed'.[4]

The purges of the first half of 1970 further stunned the ex-reformers and dashed their hopes that a party base would still be available to resist the progress of orthodoxy. Henceforth any opposition would have to come from outside the party. This was no great discovery although to some reformers it may have come as a painful revelation. The change-orientated cadres, committed to a programme of reforms, were transplanted into a non-party milieu against their will but by a superior force. From now on they had three options: they could recant and keep professing loyalty to the new masters loud enough and long enough to earn re-admission, or they could shut up and look for the most comfortable non-political niche they would be allowed to occupy, or they could re-adjust their attitudes and action so as to fit the new situation and oppose the party—their party—from the outside.

It is to their credit that many chose the last alternative. In the course of 1970 an oppositional front began to crystallise in which ex-communists formed the mainstream. They were not alone in the cold, others had been there for long, the 'total' or 'integral' opponents of communism who had accepted the Prague Spring somewhat bemused by the sight of communists quarrelling with each other but in good faith because they mostly understood that this was their chance as well and God knows maybe the only one.

Propagandists of 'normalisation' went to some pains to uncover the social roots of the Prague Spring in the participation and indeed a kind of *eminence grise* role of the remnants of the exploiting classes defeated in 1948. Pains they were, in view of the twenty years that had elapsed between the two momentous events. In the document on 'Lessons from the Crisis' these anti-communist tendencies were identified as 'a gradually widening stream ... of petty bourgeois elements and representatives of defeated bourgeoisie' and as 'political forces from the ranks of former small bourgeoisie which until that time tottered on the periphery of socialist society'.[5] A more detailed and sinister interpretation was propounded in the press. Something called 'concealed class composition of society' was invented. According to it about 300,000 members of the bourgeoisie 'including children from these families' were said to be still alive in 1968–69, embracing just under 100,000 former business men, estate holders, industrialists and 'other owners of capital'. To them must be added 'their helpers', i.e. exponents of bourgeois political parties, the press, the bourgeois state apparatus and some civil servants. Furthermore there was a great deal of petty bourgeoisie, some 380,000 of them, mainly small farmers in Slovak mountains. And finally, some 2.5 million members of former petty bourgeois families who 'survived in the socialist sector to which they had been transferred'.[6] Thus was conjured up the spectre of some 3.5 million people 'class-connected' with the capitalist order. One-fourth of the total population or every third adult became suspect once again—without actually having to set a foot wrong.

It would therefore seem surprising that in reality only a compara-tively small number of people who had not been members of the communist party joined the active opponents of 'normalisation' and that indeed the edge of the purges and victimisation campaigns was directed above all against ex-communists. Non-party people who were not prepared to oppose 'normalisation' publicly even gained a curious advantage in that they could hope to gain promotion to the jobs vacated by forcibly removed ex-reformers.

Neither did any of the opposition platforms reveal features which one normally associates with 'bourgeois' and even 'capitalist' political planks. Not one agricultural cooperative dissolved itself during the Prague Spring and return of land into private ownership did not figure in reform or oppositional programmes, giving the lie to the doctrinal incorporation of small farmers in the 'petty bourgeois' category. No equivalent of Russian 'Slavophile', 'nationalist' and 'orthodox' dissent has manifested itself in Czechoslovakia. Pan-Slavism of all varieties, including the one artificially revived by the communists, had been dead for a long time. It was anyway only meaningful in Bohemian 19th century history and even then it was more tenuous than many assumed. Nationalism in the Czech context is distinctly liberal, and there is precious little anti-semitism. (Slovakia is somewhat different in this respect. Nationalism had been reactionary in the Second World War, and sporadic anti-semitic slogans were privately reported to have been seen on walls in Bratislava after the invasion. Some harking back to the 'independent' Slovak State cannot be excluded. But all this is contrary to the official presentation of Slovakia as generally more consolidated and ready for 'normalcy' than the Czech Lands.) The pre-war First Republic is a democratic term of reference. There are no pro-Habsburg monarchists. The Catholic Church has not played an aggressive political role for a long time (again except in Slovakia), and has been preoccupied with shielding the little that was left to it by successive communist governments. The individual Catholics who joined the opposition community are almost invariably the product of the Second Vatican Council, and the communist advocates of a dialogue with religion (much maligned by the 'normalisers') have impeccable reformist and democratic credentials. Members of the protestant churches, including a few clergymen, declared themselves in favour of socialism based on humanism. A Black Hundred does not exist.

The liberal non-communist intelligentsia accepted readily, immediately and without reservation that the predicament which the nation faced in the form of 'normalisation' called for a unity of basic frameworks. 'Socialism with a human face' was such a framework which they were prepared to call their own, even if under different circumstances their beliefs, goals and methods could set them apart from the socialists and ex-communists.

The emergent oppositional spectrum included, as already mentioned, young people who had reached the age of political participation shortly before or during the Prague Spring. Some had been members of the party, but a majority had not. They included the 'radical radicals', socialists of a leftist but non-communist variety, akin to their New Left counterparts in the West, deceptively clear in their minds as to what a new society should look like and biased towards revolutionary methods of achieving their ideals. The Czechoslovak context moderated their theoretical fervour. They did look for inspiration and with sympathy towards the neo-Marxists of France and West Germany, but of course 'normalisation' was a coercive measure such as the Western democratic governments could never apply. Its all-embracing scope and the ability to manipulate people's lives from the centre put an effective curb on such weapons of neo-leftism as street demonstrations, open preaching of a new revolution, advocacy of Marxism of a non-Soviet kind, and terrorism. They must have also sensed that the Czechoslovak public had been through such an intensive indoctrination course in communism since February 1948 that they were more reluctant than people elsewhere to have a second bite at the cherry. Neither were the Czechoslovak workers prepared to join a leftist adventure.

This is not to minimise the determination and acumen of radical groups in the younger generation. They were mostly willing to cooperate with the oppositional mainstream. They were active and bristling with ideas. They were instrumental in providing many a liaison without which no clandestine work is possible. Most were students but as 'normalisation' proceeded, their ranks included more and more young workers and employees, if only because universities barred non-conformists from admission and they themselves were unwilling to put on a protective mimicry. They brought into the opposition emphasis on systemic alternatives and courage to engage in activities which for many ex-communists were difficult to imagine in view of the cushy existence they had led and the propensity for intra-party intrigue which they had acquired but now could no longer practise.

The largest segment of the opposition consisted of ex-communists. Every stratum of society was represented, but the intelligentsia still predominated. Writers and scholars, with a good sprinkling of former party officials, were the most numerous. Even during the Prague Spring there evolved a division in the reformist ranks between 'moderates' and 'radicals'. Now all were ousted from office, expelled from the party and often without a job. The cautious-radical division became anachronistic: all were in the wilderness. But of course political habits die hard, especially those nurtured for many years and fired by remnants of youthful dedication to a cause that is believed to change the world irreversibly for the better. Nevertheless, as time went by, the cautious 'insiders' (those who worked for reform from within the party apparatus) realised that they would have to give up the hope that the run of things could be changed by working with the Husák party, while the 'radicals' became more and more adapted to non-radical alternatives, seeing that popular action, that *sine qua non* of any truly radical attack on the regime, was becoming less and less possible. Thus there occurred a certain meeting of minds, a mental adjustment in both groups to the fact that Soviet-style communism in Czechoslovakia would have to be opposed from the outside but not by direct attack. By the same token, its criticism could and should be far more radical than an inside operation permitted and a number of shibboleths would have to be looked at anew.

The one concept which the ex-communist constituency preserved as a basic framework of reference was that of socialism in its Prague Spring form. They were prepared to correct or make bolder a number of premises on which the reform movement was born, and they were even ready to admit mistakes and errors of judgement which they themselves had made. Not all of them were united in how to evaluate the experience of the first eight months of 1968. Some thought that the Prague Spring had not gone far enough promptly enough, while others believed that greater circumspection would have made a difference. Some were even willing to accept that elements of Soviet criticism of the Prague Spring had not been entirely without substance. On the whole, however, the consensus remained that socialism with a human face was the right objective. The Prague Spring remained for them morally right, economically necessary and politically sound. In it Czechoslovakia had produced its form of Eurocommunism.

The emphasis of this oppositional group was on criticising the violence which 'normalisation' was doing to the cause of socialism, pointing out the damage which it was at the same time inflicting on the international communist movement, emphasising that it was also causing irreparable harm to the good feelings of the Czechs and

Slovaks towards the Soviet Union, and re-asserting the programmes of the Prague Spring.

The ex-communists had no one social stratum to turn to as their natural ally. The ties between intellectuals and workers, often invoked and emphatically proclaimed as a desideratum, never really came to a truly meaningful fruition. Good personal relations were mostly established between reformers who began to wear a cloth cap as a result of the purge and the 'traditional' workers, but on the whole there was little dynamite under the shop floor. The Czechoslovak workers did not become political as a result of the Prague Spring or the invasion, and the overall economic success of the 'normalisation' years removed material grievance as a source of political discontent. All accounts of the real mood in factories speak about widespread grumbling and the usual anger over chaos in production, corruption and incompetence of newly imposed managers, but there is no sign of a boiling point being reached. If anything, the prevailing trend has been towards indifference, private preoccupation and further corruption. The farmers had no grievance of the kind that would induce them to act politically. Even in the white-collar sector, the embryonic group of independently thinking managers had its life cut short by the discontinuation of the economic reform, and the technical and research staffs were cowed into submission.

The question then was what to do. According to a well-informed source[7] a number of people removed from public life were meeting during 1970 to find a way. Some were pessimistic: nothing could be done in the party any longer, and to organise a socialist opposition outside the party was equally impossible. Neither international nor national conditions were ripe. One must sit back and wait for reformist tendencies to re-assert themselves among the members who remained in the party. When this happens, the ex-communists will come to their assistance and offer advice, drawing on their Prague Spring experience. Others were on the contrary proposing to set up an illegal communist party from among the expellees, with its own theory, programme and clandestine organisational principles. Parallel to the officially 'normalised' party, the new organisation should seek to integrate itself into the international communist movement. For a time this idea appeared attractive to a number of people but in the end the disadvantages were seen to outweigh the temptation. The very word 'communist', to which many clung even after the recent events, had to be recognised as so hopelessly discredited that it would make communication between the illegal party and the 'masses' virtually impossible. The police would keep an easy check on the leaders because they were so well known. And the international communist movement was still under Moscow's tutelage to a degree which made the recognition of the new 'party' highly unlikely. Eventually, instead of doing nothing or establishing a closely-knit illegal body, the ex-communists decided to set in motion a broadly based socialist movement, dissentiating from the official policies and in opposition to them. They themselves would become the movement's 'intellectual leading centre' which would take it upon itself to work out a profession of faith and a programme of action.

On 28 October 1970 the 'Socialist Movement of Czechoslovak Citizens' issued its first manifesto. The day marked the 52nd anniversary of the foundation of independent Czechoslovakia in 1918 and was chosen to demonstrate the combination of national and socialist aspirations of the new political actor. The Manifesto was a restatement of beliefs as they had been formulated in 1968.

> 'Our struggle is political and positive. Neither violent terror nor sabotage are our methods. . . . We know what we want: a socialist political system in which political and non-political organisations will be partners, public and enterprise self-management, institutionally guaranteed control over power, and basic freedoms, including freedom of religion, as they were formulated among others in the Declaration of Human Rights which even this state has ratified.'[8]

The authors of the Manifesto asked the readers not to shut themselves off from fellow citizens, not to succumb to cynicism and help victims of oppression. The ideas of the Prague Spring should go on being debated. A new action programme will be worked out.

Soon the Movement received an injection of hope when strikes on the Baltic coast led to the fall of the Polish leader Wladyslaw Gomulka, known as an ardent critic of Dubček and advocate of intervention in Czechoslovakia. A proclamation was issued on 21 December 1970 expressing solidarity with the Polish workers, identifying their struggle as part of the general movement to which the Prague Spring had also made a contribution and acknowledging that the participation of Polish troops in the occupation of Czechoslovakia two years earlier had been contrary to the will of the Polish people.

Then came the Short Action Programme of the Socialist Movement of Czechoslovak Citizens, published in January-February 1971 as an underground text of some 8,000 words. The aims of the Prague Spring were again re-affirmed but the authors stated their readiness to take note of post-1968 development, including the progress of 'normali-sation', the Polish events and the progress of reformist ideas in West European communist parties.

The Movement itself was conceived in the programme as a kind of communist-socialist party in the underground but without the tight organisational and ideological discipline normally associated with communist oppositions in countries where the legal existence of the party is banned. The authors drew their inspiration from the arsenal of Marxist experience but excluded the Leninist dimension. Thus the Movement was said to aspire to become 'a new political vanguard of socialism'. It would consist of four layers: the membership base, estimated at several hundred thousand people (presumably the 'party of the expelled'); the 'leading political stratum' of several tens of thousands (presumably the local 'functionaries' or trustees); then the 'initiatory groups' (i.e. those that have already shown some initiative) comprising several thousand people (presumably district and regional officers); and at the very top a 'centre', also called the 'vanguard of the vanguard'. As most of the Movement's activity—at least according to the programme—would consist of compilation, copying and distribution of various materials, the tasks assigned to the Movement's branches at the various levels were defined only in terms of ideological freedom which they would be allowed to exercise. Samizdat and materials obtained from abroad would be put into circulation by the 'initiatory groups' at will. (No special activity in this respect was earmarked for the 'leading political stratum' and the 'membership base'.) What the programme called 'longer documents of all kinds' would however be subjected to the jurisdiction of the 'centre'. The programme stated: 'The content should be regularly assessed and checked to ensure that all programmatic, theoretical, analytical and polemical activity is closely linked to the needs of the movement'.[9]

The programme contained the following objectives: interests of the working people against the bureaucrats should be advocated and promoted outside and inside legal organisations, including the official communist party; close bonds should be forged between the workers and the technicians (a warning was made not to consider the technical intelligentsia simply as bureaucrats); the farmers' right to be treated on equal terms with the rest of the population should be pursued and democratic elements introduced into the management of agricultural cooperatives; an alliance of all social groups in the younger generation should be promoted; and the government's influence on white-collar workers should be resisted.

Finally, in the brief international section of the programme, a disguised warning was given against too close a cooperation with Czechoslovak emigres who were not of socialist persuasion, 'which should not mean mutual isolation'. Ties with 'the European Left' ought to be established and recognition of 'communist opposition' in Czechoslovakia on the part of West European communists should be won. 'Careful consideration needs to be given to the complex of Chinese and Sino-Soviet questions'. (The exact meaning of this cryptic sentence is not clear.)

The programme represented a last-ditch effort by reform communists to oppose their former fellow party members, now in power, by traditional communist means, influenced by the philosophy of the

Prague Spring. Unfortunately, democratic doctrines, even such a limited one as the Prague Spring, offer little assistance to clandestine activists. Underground opposition to communism either has to be 'communist' and illegal to the hilt, including strict hierarchy and discipline, or is has to cease being communist and rest on different premises, such as a human rights movement. The content of the platform of the Socialist Movement was nebulous and general to the point of abstraction, and the numerical estimates of the supporting base were over-optimistic. To use communist parlance, in 1970–71 the revolutionary tide was ebbing away. The time had come to signal retreat, cut one's losses and concentrate on protecting sectional interests of the various groups affected by the purges, in cooperation with willing supporters in the population at large. An overall, quasi-party programme had become outdated. The only blanket demand on which people from most social strata could agree was the return of civil rights to the estimated one million persons affected by the purges.

From what happened later, when the leaders of the Socialist Movement were interrogated and put on trial, we know that the police had no great difficulty in finding out who was who and who did what in the Movement. All the same, the government did not strike for another nine months—not until the Movement issued an Appeal to the citizens in connection with the general election set for November 1971.

The party leadership conceived of the election as a massive public endorsement of the consolidation process. New electoral laws were promulgated in July to supersede an act of 1967 which was memorable in that it was passed but never used. Single-candidate seats would be voted for, and the public was not given a choice but simply the right to cross out or not to cross out the name of the official candidate on the ballot paper. As there had to be several different kinds of con-stituencies (for the Federal Assembly's two chambers, the Czech and Slovak National Council and the various National Committees), each voter received a plethora of tickets and names which somewhat obscured the fact that no one was contesting anyone. Nomination of candidates (formally through the National Front) was firmly in the hands of the party. All trusted party members were once again mobilised to engaged in a propaganda campaign and pairs of 'agitators' were visiting each household to talk to people, invite them to pre-election meetings, and elicit their views about the state of the country. Dossiers were then compiled or amended in district party branches about individual voters. Nothing was left to chance. Perhaps by oversight or because the safeguards were considered adequate, the new electoral law included a provision that voting was the citizen's right not his duty.

The Socialist Movement of the Czechoslovak Citizens took the opportunity to issue a leaflet which circulated between September and

November 1971. Husák himself allegedly said that 100,000 copies were printed illegally. Some were seized by the police. The appeal warned the voters that the elections would be rigged. The Movement learned that the party leadership had already decided what the percentage of affirmative votes would be, and that district electoral commissions would be issued with the results in their particular constituencies beforehand. The commissions would, however, be required to report to the party and government the real results confidentially, including abstentions and deletions, and some citizens might therefore want to let the leadership know at least in this way what they thought of it all. The Movement would not presume to tell the voters how they should vote, but it would like to point out that those wishing to register their disapproval of 'normalisation' could either abstain from the ballot altogether, since voting was not a legally enforceable duty, or go behind the screen in the ballot room because even the number of people who did so would be reported, or cross out the whole name of the official candidate completely and thoroughly. (Deletion would have to be adequate because the commissions were advised to count partly or casually crossed out names as an 'aye'.) It was also possible to leave in the names of candidates to local national committees while scoring out those nominated to the higher bodies. Alternatively the voters may decide to replace the entire official ballot paper with another one, compiled privately, or with a slip of paper saying some such thing like 'January, not August!'

Officially the election results could not have been better. In the country as a whole 99·45 per cent of registered voters took part in the ballot and 'yes' votes for National Front candidates ranged from 99·77 per cent in District National Committee elections to 99·94 per cent in election to the Slovak National Council. Almost immediately the problem arose of how to explain the near unanimity while not slackening the class war against an enemy who was still being portrayed in the media as rough, tough and dangerous. *Rudé právo* wrote rather feebly that many dissidents had cast their votes for the National Front because they were afraid of being morally excluded from the 'collective'.[10] Another interpretation was that the hostile campaign of the right-wingers failed and so they turned out in force in the polling stations to camouflage their failure.[11] A more intricate explanation has to be summarised at greater length. According to it the election victory of such magnitude did not mean that all believers in socialism were Marxists [!]. Neither did it signify that the defeat of the right-wingers had been completed. Even some leading dissenters cast their votes for the National Front, but their political turnabout does not constitute an ideological change of heart. In fact it was a tactical manoeuvre of a sly politician who otherwise had spurious designs. The party had no illusion since it knew that 99 per cent of votes did not represent 99 per cent of conscientious Marxist-Leninists-Internationalists.[12]

With that problem explained away, it was seen all right to mention *en passant* that one candidate in a Slovak local national committee constituency had not been returned.

The opposition had no means of measuring to what extent its leaflets were effective, but some high party dignitaries who were still not adverse to leaking a secret or two let it be known that 'in large towns' some 10 per cent of people did not vote and of those who did, between 10 and 25 per cent crossed out official names. One must wonder why the central engineering of election results, if it in fact existed, did not aim at a plausible figure in the first place. If 90 per cent were said to have voted for the regime, surely an impressive achievement a mere three years after practically the entire nation opposed the policies that were now being pursued, the results would have been regarded credible by many people in Czechoslovakia and abroad.

Be it as it may, the election tolled a bell for the Socialist Movement of Czechoslovak Citizens. In December 1971 and January 1972 about 200 people were arrested and then, during the summer holiday period, from 17 July to 11 August 1972, ten political trials were held which resulted in 47 persons being sentenced to a total of 118 years in prison. The 'vanguard of the vanguard' was put out of circulation at a stroke.

When the arrests were first announced, the accusations were of manufacture and distribution of anti-state leaflets, setting up of illegal anti-state groups determined to disrupt peace and order and even to conduct organised struggle against socialism. The culprits were said to have been in contact with emigre and other foreign enemy centres, and foreign nationals had taken part in this culpable activity. (This was an important indication of the nature of the trial scenario as it was being prepared in January 1972.)[13]

With the usual shroud of secrecy descending on decision-making at the highest level and especially on operations involving the secret police, it is not easy to reconstruct the reasoning behind the arrests and subsequent trials. We can only piece together inadequate information and allow ourselves some speculation.

The arrests and the staging of political trials were the logical consequence of the tough 'normalisation' course adopted earlier, when the purges were being prepared towards the end of 1969. For the leadership, no matter how divided it might have been, it would be illogical to purge the party of all reformists and at the same time let a quasi-party of the self-same reformists carry out its activities in opposition. Such an arrangement goes against the grain of an authoritarian regime. No faction among the power holders of the day, no matter how 'moderate' it might be, could tolerate a reformist opposition, and there was not likely to be any disagreement on this point.

But disagreement there probably was about the way in which to put an end to organised oppositional activities. Husák probably meant it when he went on record in the early days of his tenure to say that there would not be any political prosecution, except of course that he had a condition: provided there was no opposition to his leadership. What he really intended to achieve was a return to the good old days *after* the Stalinist policies towards dissenters had been relinquished and *before* reformism got under way. A kind of 'no opposition, no prosecution' limbo. This was the quintessence of his private promise to ex-reformers in April 1969. He spelled it out more clearly in another private pronouncement in September 1969, when he succeeded in decisively shifting the balance of power in the party central committee in his favour: 'And don't you think that you will engineer another January against me!' He was of course referring to the overthrow of Novotný in January 1968 as a result of a gradual growth of reform orientation prior to the Prague Spring.

He knew (or so I believe) that outbursts of discontent, anger and defiance would necessarily occur for some time after the traumatic experience of the invasion, and was probably willing to quell them without resorting to large-scale direct police action. This explains the haphazard pattern of arrests and trials until the 14th party congress in 1971, and the fact that a number of the detainees were simply held in isolation without being brought before the court. He hoped that the fervour of the resisters would spend itself as political 'normalisation' progressed and that the deterrent effect would be achieved by the few inconclusive incarcerations. He also successfully defended against the hardliners his opposition to judicial prosecution of the top leaders of the Prague Spring, men like Dubček, Černík, Šimon, Špaček, Smrkovský and even Kriegel. Finally, he is most probably the man to whom credit is due for withstanding Soviet pressure (if there was such a thing) to allow arrests to be made directly by the Soviet occupation authorities, be it the army or the KGB. His record in this respect is therefore not entirely negative.

Nevertheless, because of the coalition with the hardliners which he was either pressed into or could not avoid (or accepted willingly?), and as a result of ultra-dogmatic pressure from outside this coalition, he had to compromise on each of these points. The coercive apparatus had to be applied on a large scale to demonstrate its regained strength during the anniversary riots in August 1969. Some trials had to be held to punish rebellious intellectuals, especially journalists. General Prchlík had to be tried for his 1968 views on the Warsaw Pact and the Czechoslovak-Soviet relations. (It has been rumoured that the Russians insisted on trying Prchlík themselves, but eventually agreed to the case being put before a Czech court.) And more leeway was probably given to the police than Husák liked.

Above all, the creation of a category of second-class citizens from half a million reformist party members and an equally large constituency of their relatives, friends and other victims, produced a breeding ground for oppositional activity which would have to go counter Husák's intention to eschew political prosecution. Developments acquired a logic of their own, but he has to carry a large part of the blame for steering them onto a collision course. It is no use to say 'if you do not oppose me there will be no trials' and at the same time do all sorts of things (or allow them to be done) to push a massive number of people into a situation in which they have to fight back.

Husák probably sought to resist the logic of the development for a while longer. The police knew about the Socialist Movement when it issued the 28 October Manifesto in 1970, if not before, and had a fairly full dossier on its leading members since that time. No action was taken on the issue of the Short Action Programme at the beginning of 1971 and for ten months afterwards. From private sources we know that at least from the summer of 1971 the secret police were working on a court case whose outlines were gradually defined with more precision until the early months of 1972 when it was presented to the party leadership for endorsement. After the election appeal of the opposition Husák lost out to the diehards. The Short Action Programme had been a declaration of intent, but the election leaflet was an appeal to action, something that he had been declaring a culpable offence from the start.

It should be understood that we are trying to explain this development within the terms of reference of an authoritarian system, not a democratic one. Of course the opposition should have had freedom to criticise 'normalisation', adopt its own programme and put up its own candidates in the general election, or at least tell people not to vote, as the constitution and the valid electoral law entitled them to do, but this is not how politics operate in a mono-party state and it is futile simply to go on restating the fundamental differences between the two systems.

The police, the Soviet 'advisers' and the hardline faction in the leadership believed that the time had come for the staging of a large show trial. They may not have had much confidence in the 'show' aspect of it, which presupposes confessions and self-accusations of the defendants, but they rather counted on the trial becoming a 'show of strength'. The leaders of the Socialist Movement of Czechoslovak Citizens would be for the purpose of the trial grouped together with some other well-known names of non-socialists, with post-invasion emigres (to be tried *in absentia*) and with a few foreign nationals whose participation would 'prove' the Movement's links mainly with Israel but also with the Berlinguer wing in the Italian communist leadership.

(The possibility of a British link was also being studied.) The Italian connection was to be provided through the personal acquaintance of Jiří Pelikán, a leading Czechoslovak emigre and publisher from 1971 of a bi-monthly journal called *Listy*, and Enrico Berlinguer's brother Giovanni. The police hoped to apprehend a suitable Italian communist who would be accused of acting as a courier between Milan Hübl, one of the leaders of the Socialist Movement in Prague, and Jiří Pelikán in Rome. A journalist, Valerio Ochetto, was in fact arrested at Prague airport on 5 January 1972 but expelled after six weeks of interrogation on 17 February without a trial. A *Rudé právo* statement did say that he confessed to carrying two envelopes from Pelikán to Prague and another two envelopes back to Rome (the name of his Prague contact was not given at that time)[14], but it seems that Ochetto, a Catholic, was mistaken for another person of the same name and would not be able to provide the requisite Eurocommunist dimension.[15] Two more attempts were made with different people (Ferdi Zibar and Dimitri Volcic), but by then the Eurocommunist side of the case had run into trouble and was eventually not followed. One cannot imagine a decision for or against the implication of a Western communist party having been made without consultation with Moscow. It might have even proved embarrassing because as Pelikán notes, Milan Hübl had been 'an old friend of Husák's who under the rule of Novotný and with Husák's approval had maintained contact with a number of communist parties in the West, notably with the Italian Communist Party'.[16]

The effort to 'de-stabilise' Berlinguer before his election as secretary-general of the Italian Communist Party at its 13th congress in Milan in March 1972 was dropped. No similar designs on the French Communist Party leadership were noted. There had been signs in 1969 and 1970 that the French communists, while maintaining their negative attitude to the invasion itself, would be willing to repair the bridges singed in 1968 and acknowledge Husák's 'normalisation' as an acceptable fact of life. A notable example came to light in connection with the conflict that ended in the expulsion of Roger Garaudy from the French party. Towards the end of November 1969 a delegate of the French Communist Party on a visit to Prague (E. Fajon) handed over to Husák the transcript of a conversation which Waldeck-Rochet had had with Dubček in Prague on 19 July 1968 on the French communist leader's return from a mission in Moscow during which he sought to avert military intervention by the USSR. The minutes had been taken for the French party by Jean Kanapa and apparently contained some strong words by Dubček about the Soviet leadership. Alois Indra noted in a radio speech on 13 January 1970 that no record of this conversation had been preserved in Czechoslovak files and the French minutes obviously contributed to the denunciation of Dubček which was then being prepared.[17] A French politburo member (R. Leroy) visited Czechoslovakia in February 1972, after the arrests, and obtained Husák's specific assurance that 'there will be... no trials, no arrests on the grounds of opinion'.[18] There the matter rested until after the trials when the French Communist Party interceded in Prague again and has adopted a more critical posture *vis-à-vis* the Husák regime ever since.

With the Italians on the other hand, and some others (the Spanish and Australian Communist Parties, for example), the altercations have never ended since the damning of the invasion. The Italian communists were willing to give room in their manifold publications to the defeated Czechoslovak reformers and to publish open criticism of the 'normalisation' of their own. In September 1971 the communist-controlled *Giorni Vie Nuove* carried an interview which Josef Smrkovský gave to a member of the Italian Communist Party central committee member David Lajolo, an outspoken protest of a man who by then was moving around only with difficulty, on crutches.[19] And the speech which the Italian delegate to the 14th party congress in Prague was not allowed to deliver was published in Italy. (A number of Western communist parties chose not to send delegations to the 14th congress at all, either because of their continuing opposition to the after-effects of the invasion or because they had been told to censor their speeches by the Czechs. They included the communist parties from Australia, Britain and Spain.)

Even then, with the Italian allusion deleted from the indictment, Husák is said to have wavered, and with him the members of his faction who constituted a slight majority in the party praesidium. (Svoboda, Colotka, Kempný, Korčák and Štrougal as against Bilak, Hoffmann, Indra and Kapek, with Lenárt somewhere in the middle.) They were seeking to find a way in which the leaders of the opposition, now in jail, could be effectively and publicly silenced without actually being ordered to prison. In the end no such solution was identified and the pressure in favour of a trial was anyway too strong. Husák however managed to persuade his opponents and Moscow not to insist on one large trial of a 'conspiratorial anti-party and anti-state centre' which smacked too much of the 1950s, but rather to hold a series of smaller trials, stretched out over a period of time. One of the arguments, allegedly, was that the deterrent effect of several successive trials would be as great, if not greater, as that of one big show. In the end there were several trials but one announcement in the press.

The charges were also adjusted downward so as to exclude heavy sentences applicable to, for example, cases of espionage. (President Svoboda even pardoned ten young people from Brno before the trials began to cut down the number of defendants and to exclude young people whose sentencing might enrage the students.) It is rumoured that Husák wanted even lighter sentences but eventually had to agree to go for the middle range. He then made another gesture designed to dissociate him personally from the trials. It was decided to hold the trials in the summer when people are on holiday and students are dispersed. This made it possible for Husák to absent himself from Czechoslovakia for his usual holiday in the Crimea from 15 July to 5 August. During that time responsibility for security matters, normally the prerogative of the First Secretary, was transferred temporarily to Vasil Bilak. This caused some commotion in the leadership (if one is to believe unofficial sources), even among the members of the Husák group, and the last of the trials (with J. Šabata in Brno) was allegedly deliberately drawn out and a hastily arranged meeting of the praesidium held immediately on Husák's return to decide what sentence ought to be imposed, thus implicating the party leader more directly.

A dissident source reported from Prague that pressure for a sweeping action against the opposition had acquired the dimension of a small 'colonels' revolt' at a police *aktiv* in June 1972 where thinly veiled demands were allegedly made to put some members of the *present* party leadership in the dock with the members of the Socialist Movement. Interrogators apparently told the detained oppositionists as early as January that they were determined to uncover a conspiracy at the top. 'We know about enemies who occupy the uppermost positions in the party'. Husák, Štrougal and Indra went to the police meeting in June and explained that political and international connotations had to be taken into account when staging trials and that the whole affair was anyway being run by the party, not the police. Husák is reported to have said: 'This is not Latin America or Greece and we will not have the colonels rule over us!'[20]

Five of the ten trials were held in Prague, four in Brno and one in Bratislava. Among the 47 defendants, a one-year suspended sentence 'was not imposed' on a woman who had fallen seriously ill. Of the remaining 46, thirteen sentences were suspended or on probation ('trial period'). The other thirty-three ranged from nine months to six and a half years. Six defendants, those that received the heaviest sentences, were by implication considered ringleaders: Dr Milan Hübl, an historian, formerly Rector of the Political Party School and a member of the party central committee (six and a half years); Dr Jaroslav Šabata, a psychologist, formerly secretary of the South Moravian Regional Party Committee and a member of the central committee (six and a half years); Dr Jan Tesař, an historian and one of the authors of the Ten Points Manifesto of October 1969 (six years); Jiří Müller, a former leader of the Czech Students' Union and probably the only one who was beaten up badly by the police during interrogations, although all were exposed to severe psychological pressure and acute physical discomfort (five and a half years); Dr

Milan Šilhan, a medical doctor and former secretary of the (non-communist) Socialist Party in Brno (five years); and Antonín Rusek, an economist and former member of the Czech National Council (five years). A heavy sentence of four years in jail was also meted out to Mrs Vlastimila Tesařová, a lecturer in Marxism-Leninism at the Medical Faculty in Brno. In addition to Šilhan there were several other non-communists in the group, including a protestant pastor and an historian-philosopher with religious leanings. The Slovak trial was that of Professor Ladislav Kalina, head of the Film Department at the Bratislava Academy of Drama and a writer. He received a two years' sentence. Unconfirmed reports suggested that an anti-Zionist trial had at first been contemplated in Bratislava. Jaroslav Šabata's two sons and a daughter were also jailed for terms from two to three-and-a-half years.

The Italian connection was raised but not reported during the trial of Milan Hübl. His contact with Pelikán in Rome was said to have been Ferdinando Zibar, a correspondent of *l'Unità* expelled from Prague in February 1972. Hübl admitted sending materials to Italy but said they were of communist content and intended for the leaders of the Italian Communist Party. The line was not pursued.

According to the indictments and Czechoslovak press reports, the Czech groups were variously found guilty of creating an illegal organisation, formulating a programme of hostile action, holding conspirational meetings, writing and disseminating hostile printed matter and maintaining contacts with emigres. They were said to have acted out of hostility to communism, socialism and the republic and their long-term aim was to bring about a removal of the incumbent regime. The fact that all defendants proclaimed themselves to be convinced socialists found reflection in a *Rudé právo* report which said that 'the means they used' were not serious enough to cause grave threat to, or to destroy, the socialist foundations of the state.[21] The Slovak trial of Dr Kalina was described as having been a case of sedition. It is not clear whether he was connected with the Socialist Movement as the press report said that 'up to October 1970' (i.e. before the first proclamation was issued by the Movement) he had possessed and distributed various materials, including tape recordings and written matter, of a seditious anti-state nature. In conjunction with several foreign nationals he was preparing to publish in the West a satirical book which grossly slandered the Czechoslovak state system and its alliance with the Soviet Union.[22] It thus seems that the timing of his trial to coincide with the Prague and Brno proceedings against the Socialist Movement may have been just a matter of convenience.

Gustav Husák commented publicly on the trials in a speech in Bratislava on 26 August 1972 when opening a new bridge over the Danube. He said that neither the trials themselves nor the protest campaign in the West, which he called Goebbels-like, had disconcerted the Czechoslovak people. The subversive elements had been isolated and stripped of influence. Anyway, strict fairness of legal procedure had been observed and the organs of state had received explicit instructions not to infringe human rights and freedoms. The defendants had been publicly and privately warned beforehand. Only when they declined to cease breaking the law were the organs of state compelled to discharge their duty and punish them. Husák at the same time said he was sorry that even some leaders of 'progressive forces' in the West should show surprising indifference when faced with objective information about Czechoslovakia and should join the ranks of bourgeois slanderers instead. This did not contribute to the class struggle.[23]

Condemnation of the trials in the West was indeed massive and many communist parties and individual personalities expressed themselves openly. It is believed that complaints about the trials were also raised through international communist party channels and that the presence of Czechoslovak official delegates abroad (such as Vasil Bilak's at a conference on Vietnam in Paris) was taken advantage of to send direct communications to the Husák leadership. For the Eurocommunist parties the Czechoslovak political trials of 1972 marked another step on their road to independence. There was some reluctance at first to go the whole way. For example, the French communist politburo issued a carefully worded statement at the end of July (while more trials were still to come) which recognised that a socialist regime had the right 'in principle' to protect itself against 'activities hostile to socialism' but suggested that the current political prosecution in Czechoslovakia did not seem to be in the same category.[24]

Generally speaking, the Western communist parties realised that a trick was being played in Prague where dissent and opposition which in Italy and France would be considered normal (or so the parties in question were beginning to say) was interpreted as law-breaking and anti-socialism. A *Morning Star* editorial summed up this matter of principle as follows:

> 'A further argument used in the Czechoslovak press is that the accused have not been tried for their political convictions, which they are entitled to hold, but for turning their "hostile and subversive opinions" into deeds and concrete acts. Socialist democracy, however, cannot be limited to the right merely to hold views on the development of socialism; it must embrace the right to express them'.[25]

A Belgian communist theoretician reflected the emerging Eurocommunist concern for the effect which 'normalisation' Prague-style was having on the domestic policies of communist parties in the West:

'To our potential allies in the struggle against capitalism, we wish to confirm that our public disapproval of the [Prague] trials implies the profound conviction that the realisation of socialism in our country must pass through the enlargement of individual rights and liberties, an enlargement which will make possible collective structures based on the interests of the great majority of the population'.[26]

The trials of the summer of 1972 decapitated the main opposition group, consisting of a coalition of moderate and radical ex-communists and their non-communist allies. In one thing Husák was right: no one in Czechoslovakia outside the circle of immediate relatives and friends of the defendants moved a finger. The 'vanguard' of the opposition was unable to mobilise its active constituency, let alone the 'membership base'. It is easy to say why this was so, and the case has already been stated earlier. The effects of 'normalisation', that mixture of coercion and material comfort, were strong enough to lead people away from direct pursuit of something that had increasingly begun to be felt as a lost cause. Also, cleverly, it was the second line of Prague Spring personalities that went on trial, whom the public knew little or not at all. The population continued to retreat into private preoccupations and political passivity. The distance between the generals and the troops had widened, and quite a few of the generals were behind prison walls now.

In December 1972 an attempt was made by a number of Czech writers to offer Husák and his allies in the leadership an opportunity to take the steam out of the repressive drive. They signed a petition urging President Svoboda to grant an amnesty to political prisoners and, before it could take effect, to allow them to visit their families at Christmas time:

'Whatever views we, the undersigned, may hold about various fundamental and partial questions, we are agreed that benevolence toward political prisoners cannot diminish the authority and esteem of state power; on the contrary it can prove its humaneness. That is why we turn to you, Mr President, at the time of Christmas, understood in most countries of the world as a festival of humanity . . .'[27]

According to unconfirmed reports, relying on samizdat publication in Czechoslovakia, the idea of the petition had been inspired by the President's daughter, Mrs Zoja Klusáková, whose husband was to be appointed Czech Minister of Culture in May 1973. Klusáková allegedly told Jaroslav Seifert, the old poet and chairman of the now disbanded Writers' Union, that her father wished to retire in the near future and would like to leave on a note to remember.[28] Thirty-five writers signed the petition before five of the collectors of signatures were arrested and interrogated for several hours. More signatures were appended later. Some of the petitioners were members of the new, 'normalised' Writers' Union, but following an official outburst several (probably seven) withdrew. In the end 36 names apparently remained under the petition (an exact tally is impossible to make) which the chairman of the new Writers' Union said had been manufactured with the full connivance of foreign anti-communist centres and was imbued with 'inhuman hatred of socialism under the hypocritical guise of concern for man'.[29] Needless to say, neither a Christmas leave nor an amnesty were granted. When the presidential amnesty on the 25th anniversary of the communist takeover was announced in February 1973, it specifically excluded all those convicted on charges of subversion, endangering state secrets and harming state interests abroad. Another opportunity to soften the 'normalisation' course was passed over.

EMIGRATION

In the wake of Soviet invasion and in the last instance because of it, a large number of people left the country for the non-communist world. Both the Czech and Slovak nations have a long history of emigration, sorrowful and defiant, nostalgic and aggressive, political and based on material grievance. With the Czech inclination to take recourse to history in search for self-identification and the aptness to draw parallels where they exist only remotely, the post-1968 emigres could easily revoke the shining prefiguration of 17th century religious exiles, Protestants fleeing their country when it was seized for traditional Catholicism with outside help. Then they gave the world a great figure in the person of Johann Amos Comenius, the educational reformer and systemiser, a thinker of peace and freedom, to this day remembered and esteemed throughout the reaches of Western civilisation. The early exiles of the post-White Mountain battle had also militants in their midst, who joined the Protestant armies of the European North and even briefly came back to their own homeland in the hope—vain as it turned out—to recover it for toleration and progress from the Habsburg clutches. Masaryk, whose towering presence in Czech democratic thought even twenty years of communism could not eradicate, chose to engage the foreign rulers of his country in battle from abroad at the time of the First War and did he not win history's rare award by being allowed to return as the victor supreme? Tens of thousands fled before Hitler's occupation, including Masaryk's disciple Beneš, but also ordinary men and women whose crusade ended in the country's liberation. Admittedly, the one hundred thousand people who went to the West after the communist victory in February 1948 met with a less resounding success but did history not prove them right too? Did they not contribute to international and national scholarship, culture and science wherever they found new homes?

As with every tradition, the past dimensions that seem to bode well for the present or imbue the strivings of today with a morally commendable message from yesterday, tend to overshadow the less congenial developments which also comprise indivisible history. In particular the Slovaks had a history of emigration in which the economic factor predominated; they were leaving their homeland in large numbers in the 19th century, before the Great War and even in the inter-war period because of poverty and unemployment. Theirs was the star of a promise of better material conditions, perhaps with the family left behind hopeful of the emigre's return as a rich man. This time-honoured propellant of emigres the world over, no matter what the political complexion of their particular fatherland, played a

170

part in the complex motivational spectrum of the post-1968 emigration wave. Often not very knowledgeable of what to expect in the new environment, this was however a somewhat different breed of an emigre from the deliberate prospector for better living who fills consular offices of rich countries in the West and has all the colour brochures, job evaluation charts and attractive wage tariffs needed for a responsible decision. Nor was this of course the move of a tax-haven seeker.

The motives for emigration in most people consisted of three basic factors: disgust over the forcible termination of the reformist experiment, fear of the turn which future events in Czechoslovakia could take, and the vision of material betterment for themselves and their children. A great majority would probably fall into a category embracing all three motives, although obviously in individual cases any one motive could be found to carry more weight that the other two. The spectrum of the emigrational mainstream would range from the 'mostly political' to the 'mostly economic' groups. (No data has been collected.)

A small but not insignificant number were prompted by the dedication to a cause, mostly that of a democratic evolution in Czechoslovakia on socialist principles or otherwise, and they chose emigration either because it was foisted on them or because they saw it themselves as an important corner of the battlefield on which the struggle that had begun during the Prague Spring and earlier would continue.

As for the social composition, no surveys exist and the exiles themselves are wary of being polled because they suspect foul play or simply fear that results would fall into the hands of the Prague regime. Experience would suggest that the majority fall into the middle-class category, more specifically what is called in Eastern Europe 'employees' or 'white-collar workers'. But the number of manual workers, especially in the skilled categories, is not small either. If comparison with the overall social composition of the Czechoslovak population was possible, the new emigration would most probably reveal a larger proportion of 'intellectuals' or 'experts' (people with tertiary education or less but with considerable expertise in fields like science, technology, engineering, medicine, social sciences and arts and culture). Age composition is more difficult to assess, but the feeling is that it is heavily inclined towards the young and the lower half of the middle age groups. Many people went with small children. Czechs heavily outnumber Slovaks.

One point worthy of note, and directly relevant to our story, is that most people did not apparently opt for permanent emigration immediately after the invasion, although a number did. There was a great deal of wavering, marking time and waiting to see what would happen next. The relaxed Prague Spring rules on foreign travel remained in force until the autumn of 1969, technically restricted in the autumn of 1968 by the cancellation of permanent and multiple exit permits and some other measures, but in fact easy enough to allow procrastination. Thousands, including some prominent people, went out, returned for a while and left again, a practice which Husák criticised bitterly even before he had the power to do something about it. This is like a promenade, he said, implying that national borders should not be negotiated easily as a matter of course. Others kept their options open while staying out, which they could do because many of the exit permits affixed into their Czechoslovak passports had a year's validity. Thousands applied to Czechoslovak embassies for an extension of the 'legality' of their stay abroad and were granted it. The clampdown came in October 1969 when all exit permits to the West were declared invalid, the frontiers were closed, some unfortunates were even taken off international trains speeding westwards, and Czechoslovak consulates were only prepared to grant 15-day extensions to people to settle their affairs abroad before responding to the summons.

The wait-and-see tendency is borne out by statistics which, however inaccurate they may be in other respects, show that most would-be emigres actually departed from the country in 1969 but the final decision to stay abroad came in 1970. With evidence being not conclusive, I would surmise that most emigres had not made their choice so much because of the Warsaw Pact invasion as because of the turn that 'normalisation' took under the Husák leadership. If the impossible had happened and Dubček's rescue operation from August 1968 to April 1969 succeeded, even at the cost of a much limited reform in the presence of Soviet troops, a considerable section of the emigre community, then in the making, would have returned home or not left at all. Only after April 1969, in the remaining part of the year, under the impact of the sweeping changes in the leading bodies of the party and the state, the rank-and-file purges announced for 1970 and the re-ideologised content and tone of the Czechoslovak media, were the decisions to remain in exile made *en masse*. If this tentative deduction is true, the record of the Husák leadership has to include another notch in the minus column. It might have been possible to 'normalise' so as not to repel tens of thousands of skilled people. But then, as we said earlier, it might have been possible to strike a conciliatory Kádár-like note in regard to those who stayed at home anyway. Once again the argument returns to the working out of a pattern for the purges in 1970, wherein the intimidatory and vindictive content of the 'normalisation' policy was allowed to become super-incumbent on all other considerations. One is tempted to conclude that the discontinuation of the reform programme, though regrettable, was not the real *casus belli*. The vengeance taken on its advocates was.

The authorities took care not to divulge just how many people emigrated, and when they gave figures it was always with some qualification or they were so evidently wrong that they cannot be relied on. For example, the Ministry of the Interior said in May 1969 that some 40,000 had left the country after August 1968, but did not say how many had resolved not to come back. In any case, more were to follow. In February 1970 'preliminary figures' were quoted in the press to the effect that about 50,000 were abroad after August 1968, that over 500 made use of the presidential amnesty to return, and that some 22,000 had applied for extension of their exit permits.[30] The various official statistical serials have the disadvantage of not making clear whether they list only 'official' emigration, such as by members of the German ethnic community or Czech girls legally wedded to foreigners, or 'illegal' emigration as well. (Neither do the crime statistics say how many people have been sentenced for 'departing from the republic' without authority.) One useful piece of information is that some 31,000 ethnic Germans were permitted to leave from 1968–1970.[31] This figure tallies with annual reports of the West German Red Cross Society.[32] It does not follow from the division into 'official German emigration' and 'unofficial Czechoslovak emigration' that motivation applicable to ethnic Czechs or Slovaks was less true about their German compatriots.

A picture closer to the truth can be obtained if we compare population figures at the beginning and the end of each critical year against the natural increment data (difference between live births and deaths). This exercise produces figures given in Table 6. The presumed number of emigres over the four years, 171,376, is enormous even though it includes 31,000 ethnic Germans, and I am reluctant to accept it. There may be an explanation which this statistical exercise does not take into account and the available data do not reveal. (Internal migration between Czech Lands and Slovakia cannot, for example, be included in overall state-wide figures. The fact that separate Czech and Slovak data in the table add up to the country total indicates that internal migration has not been included.)

Those of the new emigres who took it upon themselves to stand up for the ideas of a democratically reformed communism chose not to form an organisation in exile, even though some advocated such a step at first. After much deliberation and soul-searching they remained unorganised but in touch and loosely associated through a bi-monthly periodical, *Listy*, published since 1971 in Rome under the editorship of Jiří Pelikán, director of Czechoslovak Television from 1963–1968 and a member of the National Assembly since 1948. *Listy* is published as 'an organ of the Czechoslovak Socialist Opposition' and has been following the same line as the Socialist Movement of Czechoslovak Citizens and, subsequently, the socialist dissenters and oppositionists

Table 6. Calculation of Number of Emigres 1968–1971

Year	Territory	Population 1 January	Natural increment	Population 31 December	Presumed emigrated
1968	Czechoslovakia	14,333,176*	60,536†	14,387,345*	6,367
	Czech Lands	9,866,006	22,242	9,886,686	1,562
	Slovakia	4,467,170	38,294	4,500,659	4,805
1969	Czechoslovakia	14,387,345	61,658†	14,443,029‡	5,974
	Czech Lands	9,886,686	22,512	9,906,474	2,724
	Slovakia	4,500,659	39,146	4,536,555	3,250
1970	Czechoslovakia	14,443,029	62,964†	14,349,557§	156,436
	Czech Lands	9,906,474	24,538	9,809,667	121,345
	Slovakia	4,536,555	38,426	4,539,890	35,091
1971	Czechoslovakia	14,349,557	72,011†	14,418,969§	2,599
	Czech Lands	9,809,667	31,805	9,843,962	+2,490
	Slovakia	4,539,890	40,206	4,575,007	5,089
1968–71	Czechoslovakia	14,333,176	257,169	14,418,969	171,376
	Czech Lands	9,866,006	101,097	9,843,962	123,141
	Slovakia	4,467,170	156,072	4,575,007	48,235

All references to *Statistical Yearbooks*:
* 1971 p. 101; † 1975 p. 108; ‡ 1972 p. 102; § 1975 p. 105.
Separate references to Czech Lands and Slovakia on same pages as Czechoslovak totals.

in Czechoslovakia. It has also accepted the Charter 77 line. The *Listy* group has no written programme of its own and its members cooperate with other emigres. *Listy* has close ties with a publishing house in Cologne, Germany, called *Index*, which has been producing books in Czech and Slovak by exiles and blacklisted domestic authors. The natural constituency in the West towards which members of the *Listy* group tend to address themselves is the European Left, socialists and communists of all colouring, except of course the pro-Moscow variety, especially the Eurocommunist circles in Italy, France, Spain, Britain, Belgium and elsewhere. The intellectual and ideological kinship is self-evident, and the joint legacy of the Prague Spring makes collaboration easy, notably in exchange of information, holding of conferences and seminars, contributing to the press etc. Circumspection and a certain aloofness on the part of the highest official circles in the West European communist parties derives from their continuing membership of the international communist movement. In January 1978 two members of the group (Pelikán and Mlynář) were received in Madrid by Santiago Carrillo. Also at about the same time the group elected a coordinating committee comprising Z. Hejzlar, Z. Mlynář, A. Müller and J. Pelikán.

Both Marxist and non-Marxist members of the new exile have become involved in Western academic world and in arts and culture. After some initial problems, which were however incomparably less severe than the difficulties faced by the 1948 emigration wave, they found positions of respectable influence in business, industry, technical services and science. In doing so, they were able to join many of their compatriots and their children who had left Czechoslovakia for political reasons twenty and more years earlier. Between them the successive emigration waves from Czechoslovakia constitute a large, intellectually strong diaspora which comprises a part of modern Czechoslovak civilisation, both in its contribution to the national cultures of the new homelands and in influencing developments in the 'old country'. Having been circumscribed at home, Czechoslovak culture became internationalised through its successive enforced expatriations.

Understandably there has been some recrimination and mistrust between the 1948 and 1968 emigres, the former feeling themselves to an extent the victims of the latter, and the latter, especially the reform communists among them, shedding only gradually their dislike for non-communist politicians of the *ancien regime*. At the same time there is contact, cooperation and cross-fertilisation. The older exile has kept alive such institutions as Pavel Tigrid's Paris-based Journal *Svědectví* (a quarterly of high calibre, which now however seems to come out only three times every year, or even twice), and the American-based Czechoslovak Society for Arts and Sciences with its quarterly journal

Proměny, edited by Jiří Škvor. Both have become mixing grounds for members of the two groups. The non-communist newcomers have provided another solid publishing outlet in the shape of *68 Publishers* in Toronto, led by the formidable and indomitable pair of writers, Zdena and Josef Škvorecký. Other publishing houses operate in Europe, also with a growing series of books to their credit. The research department of the Czechoslovak section in Radio Free Europe in Munich has achieved an unusually high standard of scholarly coverage, factual and analytical, of events in Czechoslovakia.[33]

The 'normalising' regime considers the emigres dangerous, and a scapegoat. In an instructive and wide-ranging book[34] a Czechoslovak specialist on combating emigre influences stresses that the enemy must be kept under constant observation and his arguments must be studied by the people at home. Two pages later he adds that it is not possible to let the enemy arguments circulate in Czechoslovakia because they can in no way contribute to the attainment of truth.

From private information it would seem that especially two lines of emigre activity are viewed with special hostility: contacts with, and possible influence on, West European communism, and the fact that emigre writers can communicate their insight and perception of East European reality to Western public opinion. Official attitude alternately and even concurrently presents the emigres as unimportant renegades who have reached the dustbin of history and as highly dangerous puppets of 'foreign inimical centres', which is a generic term apparently embracing intelligence agencies, academic institutions and interest associations, all masterminded and led by the hand by 'the imperialists'. Occasionally distinction is drawn between prominent emigres who are said to be doing well thanks to the dirty money they earn for their sinister services, and the poor seduced man-in-the-emigre-street who is either destitute or desperate or both. Amnesties have been proclaimed several times for the latter, but no announcement followed as to how many responded (except the early one mentioned above), giving rise to suspicion that probably only a few, otherwise there would have been jubilation. A private estimate is 'several thousands' in the course of ten years. In 1977 the government issued a decree whereby all the 'decent' emigres can regularise their status in relation to Czechoslovakia, provided they have not 'pursued an activity which is hostile to the Czechoslovak state or harms in any way the interest of the Czechoslovak Socialist Republic'[35]. This is further defined as meaning 'hostile pronouncements' in the media or at meetings, attendance at hostile gatherings and other denigration of the socialist order, Czechoslovakia's allies, Czechoslovak leaders etc. Compliance with the directive makes the emigre's relatives eligible to go and visit the stray sheep abroad, a privilege to be denied not only to the established villains but also to those who do not feel like paying the heavy fees chargeable on everything connected with the 're-gularisation'. All this two years after Helsinki and over a year after Czechoslovak ratification of the United Nations covenant on political and civil rights.

Like its 1948 predecessor, the post-August exile has remained a constant term of reference for the Czechoslovak regime, a bogey, a scapegoat, a target for cheap invective and a means to blackmail friends and relatives into submission. 'Contact with emigres' has become a standard charge in political trials and a *de facto* ground for indictment. Innumerable questionnaires and interviews associated with jobs held and applications for new ones feature a special inquisitorial rubric demanding of people to own up to kith and kin abroad. If they do, certain posts of influence, enumerated in the mysterious and all-pervasive party 'nomenclature lists', remain barred to them. Officials travelling abroad on business must include contact with emigres as a special item in the detailed reports which they are required to file in on return. A few police informers recruited or sent abroad returned home with pitiful but widely publicised horror stories about the gambols of emigre circles and the fat cheques they are getting from the CIA.

The general public, on the other hand, if the many personal stories and reports one has come across are anything to go by, does not seem to have fallen in for the crude game and feel no aversion to their ex-compatriots. There may be a trace of the primitive envy of the standard of living the emigres are suspected of having attained, but emigration is much too widespread a phenomenon for the people in Czechoslo-vakia not to realise that 'there's a cloud to every silver lining', to reverse a proverb. Some people are afraid lest an innocent postcard or letter, apprehended by the police, jeopardises their job prospects or their children's access to higher education; so most emigres can tell you about a message from home: do not write, it's dangerous. Correspondence with relatives is generally not stopped.

Emigre journals and books circulate and are being reproduced by typing and even in longhand in spite of police searches and the fact that possession of such material constitutes ground for prosecution. A good number of Czech and Slovak girls have been allowed to marry foreigners 'legally' and they come and go. Once again the Czechos-lovaks are avid listeners to foreign radio stations (according to estimates made by the stations themselves as well as by diplomats and journalists) in which emigre activities are reported. It has not been possible to lower an iron curtain again.

An anonymous writer from Prague had the following to say in 1973:

'People react to this abnormal state of affairs [surfeit of ideology] by showing apathy and disinterest in anything political to a degree which is

177

conspicuous. Nonetheless, even a person who is ostensibly interested in no more but the size of his pay packet and the earliest possible departure from work for a weekend holiday will show immense interest if you give him, say, Pelikán's *Listy* or Tigrid's *Svědectví* (provided he does not take you for a police informer). And when the self-same person discovers that books by Czechoslovak writers are being published abroad and that many daily newspapers published a proclamation on the situation in Czechoslovakia on the fourth anniversary of August 1968, he will react by saying something like this: "How splendid that at least somewhere else something is being done, that not all people are as silent as over here and that the achievements of 1968 have not been completely forgotten but persist at least in a certain form". And a feeling of satisfaction radiates from such a man, even though he himself belongs to the silent majority'.

The same writer continued:

'... Czechoslovak political exile, supported from home in an indirect way is the only possible spokesman of our nations. Figuratively speaking, the political and cultural life of our nations must acquire today the form of a modern diaspora, with all that this term entails in the cultural context. Saying that much, we at home are unfortunately aware of what it implies for us personally. And believe us, to become aware of it and to admit it is not easy . . . But having become aware of it, we must say it clearly and publicly in order to "give a mandate" to those outside and to make our political exile realise what is their obligation, and to act upon it.'[36]

POLITICS: BUSINESS AS USUAL

So the Establishment had its victory entered into the records of the 14th congress with the appropriate stamp of approval, and it then proved its strength once again by inflicting another defeat on the opposition in 1972. Now the time had surely come to engage diligently in positive, forward-looking activity in order to restore the country's potential of creative work for the benefit of all and sundry. This was indeed the professed intention of the leadership. Gustav Husák told a party *aktiv* as early as April 1971, on return from the 24th Soviet party congress, presumably with Moscow's approval for his objectives, that the country had been led out of a deep crisis into normalcy. From now on energy would be directed towards social, economic and political tasks of the future.[37]

Miloš Jakeš, the hardline chairman of the Central Control and Auditing Commission which acquired political weight at the time of the purges, respectfully and obliquely disagreed. According to him right-wing opportunism and revisionism remained the main danger and the new adaptation tactics of the right-wingers must continue to be combatted vigorously. New 'cadres' section and departments must be established at regional and district levels and new 'cadre lists' must be compiled. 'Today it is no longer tolerable that there be people in important social and economic functions who had to leave the party for their committed right-wing activity'.[38]

Husák had the list of priorities slanted somewhat differently. He told a pre-election audience that consolidation had been achieved and the country could now devote itself to the solution of problems which originated in pre-reform times and which the people wanted to remove in January 1968. These were problems of political and economic stagnation, still very much alive, and it was on them that the party would concentrate in a wiser and altogether better way now than during the Prague Spring.[39]

Looking back at the five-year period between the 14th and 15th party congresses, one cannot but acknowledge Mr Jakeš' success and Mr Husák's failure. Too much of the party's activity remained backward orientated, in constant search for deviation and heresy, and too little energy was directed towards the future. In the process the innovative spirit has died. The leadership has based its behaviour on ideological aggressiveness, police powers and a social contract between party and people whereby consumerism is exchanged for political compliance. It may be enough—as long as it all works. It may in fact be the optimal way in which the party can function without incurring the danger of change. It may be the adequate way of keeping a coalition of hardliners and not-so-tough conservatives in power without it being torn by factional strife. The Czechoslovak leadership went about securing the mainstays of such a state of affairs in a methodical way. First, the party itself had to be put in a better shape because even after the purges it was still suffering from several ills: it was passive, old and had few workers in its ranks.

Passivity in a party whose membership card is a passport to better jobs has always been a problem. Such a party is a far cry from the lean and hardened nucleus of militants battling for or in a revolution. Activity can be artificially whipped up on occasions, but not sustained. The safest way to make large masses of party members *do* something, as against just *be* in the party, has been found in the succession of campaigns *against* something or someone, most frequently an 'enemy', more rarely and less reliably, *for* something. Invariably the campaigns do not just happen, but are staged on command. A groundswell of activity is almost unknown in communist party history, although the membership masses do occasionally react vehemently at their leadership's bidding.

As it is not easy to go on inventing real issues around which massive action can be built up, especially if innovative change is feared and a recent experience with popular energy sends shivers down the spine of the commanders, they most frequently resort to pulling ideological triggers. Reason for action can also be found inside the party itself. The ultimate aim of inward-looking campaigns is ostensibly that of gearing the party to a better discharge of self-proclaimed roles *vis-à-vis* society as a whole. But the party is a large body of people, one-tenth of the adult population in the Czechoslovak case, and enough problems are generated inside it to justify maintenance operations for their own sake.

Passivity in the wake of the frenzy of the purges became the target of early criticism. As if weary people were settling down to routines from which the watchful leaders wanted to rouse them again and again. The measure of their success is difficult to assess, but complaints and exhortations continued unabated throughout the period under discussion. There were inherent contradictions. The active critics had been discarded and the timid and pliable ones retained, next to the fervid traditionalists. Every word of criticism had to be weighed carefully, and preferably not uttered at all, lest it was interpreted as reformist heresy. The only channel of 'involvement', 'commitment' or '*engagé* attitude' was alongside the activists' continuing witch-hunt on the deviationists, and many people were apparently not willing to break their backs in joining it, even if they themselves recanted their 1968 sins abjectly in order to pass through the sieve.

A Slovak voice deserves to be cited in this respect:

'After the interviews only those who had proved themselves in the years of crisis remained in the party. However, it is becoming manifest that a considerable number of comrades have not progressed since the interviews. Their political and ideological maturity has remained on a certain level, which does not correspond to the party's needs.'[40]

A loyal 'normaliser' complained in a letter to *Tribuna* that many comrades stayed away from the cinema in Lomnice nad Popelkou when politically committed Czech and Soviet films were shown in spite of having been personally invited. For the complainant this was 'sad and embarrassing'.[41] *Tribuna* became an outlet for many such reproaches. According to another, it was really astounding that some communists did not consider it necessary to join the Czechoslovak-Soviet Friendship Union. At a time when tens of thousands demonstrate in Paris against unemployment and intone the Internationale, when the world is shocked by Bloody Sunday in Londonderry, when Italian proletarians go on strike, when people die in Vietnam and when the entire progressive world struggles to keep Angela Davis alive, some members of the Czechoslovak Communist Party still fail to appreciate what kind of an honour it is to be a friend of the Soviet Union. The eyes of millions of suppressed workers all over the world are glued with hope to the Soviet Union. If our party members do not see it, what kind of political maturity have they attained?[42] What indeed.

Some comrades seemed even ashamed of being party members because they did not display flags in their windows on festive occasions and failed to turn up at collective undertakings organised by the party.[43]

Attendances at members' meetings were small, and party committees somehow failed to take the absentees to task. Many members showed little activity even if they came to a meeting. There were even such who had not spoken for a full year.[44] And in some five to ten per cent of party branches there were problems of non-payment of party dues or understatement of incomes from which the size of the contributions was calculated.[45]

The leadership sought to counter the trend in various ways. In January 1972 the party praesidium adopted a guideline to a new purging operation entitled 'complex evaluation of cadres in state and economic administration as well as members of the apparatuses of social organisations'. Most of those at whom the new onslaught was directed were party members, and even those who were not fell under the supervision of party bodies. In the framework of the 'complex [comprehensive] evaluation' to be conducted by party branches or specially set-up committees, the following criteria were to be applied to every 'cadre worker': total political commitment, active implementation of party decisions, enhancement of the party's leading role, active party-minded behaviour, winning over others for party policies, practical implementation of proletarian internationalism [*sic*!], personal involvement in combating bourgeois and petty-bourgeois ideologies; all these only to be followed by competence and efficiency at work, knowledge and skill, organisational qualities, moral and personal qualities and others in a similar vein. Every 'evaluation' was to end by the drawing up of specific conclusions indicating future career prospects of the person under review and suggesting what kind of indoctrination he or she should undergo.[46]

It was also decided that a 'comprehensive assessment' of this nature should be carried out regularly in two-year intervals, thus keeping the entire managerial class on its toes. Unfortunately we do not know how many demotions or promotions were effected in its wake, but private sources have indicated that much time and energy were expended on this watchdog operation in 1972 and then again 1974.[47] The effect in terms of intimidation and frustration was considerable. The leadership was, however, apparently satisfied because the second round of the campaign in 1974 was ushered in under the same politically biased criteria as the first, and the exercise was said to have an important part to play in the 'integrated system of personnel work'.

All the same, passivity did not disappear and lapses of discipline continued to occur. Again, we have no aggregated information to examine the detailed working of counter-campaigns. One example was cited somewhat more fully, even if without names. As in a hierarchically commanded party it is unlikely that there would be just one isolated case of a campaign promoted from the centre, it can be safely assumed that the single example reflects similar developments elsewhere. The North Bohemian Party Control Commission investigated questions of discipline in three districts, 21 basic branches, six factory organisations and three municipal organisation of the party from January 1972 to May 1973, and concluded that stricter observation of party rules was generally called for. Altogether 72 individual members were summoned to account for their behaviour, but 36 were let off with 'comradely criticism and reproach'. In 30 of the remaining 36 cases 'full disciplinary proceedings were instituted' and six persons had their party membership rescinded. Of all the 72 cases the most frequent infringement was non-attendance at meetings or educational courses and general passivity (47 persons), loss of membership card or stamps (eight), breach of labour discipline (six), moral lapses (four) and stealing of socialist property (one). (No reason stated in six cases.) In addition, the report said that 267 persons in the three districts had their membership annulled without prior disciplinary measures.[48]

Gradually a certain shift of emphasis in complaints about disciplinary infringements seems to have occurred, at least insofar as the 'leading cadres' were concerned, i.e. people in positions of authority rather than rank-and-file members. When the second round of the 'comprehensive assessment' was evaluated, the party still found one-quarter of its cadres wanting in terms of non-compliance with duties set for them in 1972. This was particularly true about unwillingness to partake of the party's educational schemes: only 12 per cent of the *nomenklatura* cadres who had been told to improve their political and professional qualifications actually did so. At the same time, moral and character evaluation revealed instances of 'ruthless striving for material advantage and self-idolatry' as well as of petty bourgeois way of life, plotting, protectionism and corruption.[49]

The efforts to stamp out indifference and disciplinary infractions were accompanied by a determined drive to bring new working-class and young members into the party. The decision to embark on an enlargement of the party almost immediately in the wake of a deliberate endeavour to reduce its membership must have been taken after profound debate in the leadership and with Moscow's blessing. Not so long ago the hardline faction had advocated a small party of committed activists and dedicated internationalists. They had regarded the party as too large, carrying the explosive cargo of revisionism in its roomy holds. Now the dead weight of passive members—after the purge—was being vehemently criticised, and yet a full-scale recruitment scheme got under way. The danger signals must have been very strong. Had the party stayed as it was after the 1970 purgation, possibly with only very restricted and selective admissions of new members, it would have continued to grow old. On 1 January 1971 the average age of a party member was 49. ('Fifty years after its foundation, a party of fifty-year-olds', as the saying went in Prague.) More importantly in my view the percentage of workers would have continued to decline. On 1 January 1971 workers formed only 26·1 per cent of members while another 18·7 per cent were retired workers.[50]

The leaders desperately wanted to prevent the party from being identified only with the non-worker population. The Polish workers' rebellion in December 1970 probably added weight to the argument that willy-nilly a recruitment campaign would have to be started. Moreover, in the wider context, the time had come for the party to start delivering the goodies. And since there were a number of vacancies to be filled after the demotions and dismissals of the reformers, such as only party members were able to fill according to the *nomenklatura* rules, what better way of showing the public that party membership does carry material advantage—without really saying so—than to open the party door again to the seekers of promotion?

Even if these rationalisations were persuasive enough to make the entire leadership support new recruitment, I still think that the campaign was a victory for the Husák group. The notion of a tight, militant party was being abandoned. Moreover, the initial keenness of the newcomers, if any, was likely to erode as they became established. Could a seed of future reformism have been planted in the recruitments that started in 1971?

Be that as it may, the 14th congress officially endorsed the recruitment campaign which was to concentrate on workers and the younger generation. A two-year 'candidacy', i.e. a trial period, abolished in 1966, was re-established for new entrants. The party secretariat worked out a detailed plan, assigning regions and districts the quotas they should aim at. It was not to be an entirely open-door policy for all and sundry, but rather a kind of recruitment by invitation. A Slovak poll, incompletely reported, suggested that 'over one-third' of new entrants had applied for membership themselves, while the rest had been asked to join.[51] Even with the campaign masterminded from the centre, its progress was uneven and the party press complained about a number of organisations not meeting their target figures.

I have attempted to trace the progress of recruitment in Table 7 from the scant data published haphazardly between the 14th and 15th party congresses, i.e. from May 1971 to April 1976. Of the two end figures, the first one—of May 1971—was only given as 'approximately 1,200,000' survivors of the purge, while the more recent one—of April 1976—was announced to be 1,382,860, comprising 333,952 new recruits. It follows that 151,092 persons ceased being party members in the five years between the two congresses. Some were undoubtedly expelled or 'struck off', as witnessed by the above reference to the North Bohemian discipline check, but we do not know how many. It would not have been an entirely insignificant number. The rest died. The mean deathrate in Czechoslovakia in those five years was 1,150 per 100,000, but this can hardly be taken as a yardstick, considering that the party had a higher proportion of old-age people. A considered guess, but no more than a guess, would probably put the number of deaths at 125,000 and other departures at over 25,000 in the course of the five years. More recently an exact membership figure as at 1 October 1977 appeared in the press. This has been added to the inter-congress pattern. From Table 7 we can extrapolate an approximate monthly intake of new members between the two congresses and until September 1977, assuming that none were recruited before the 14th congress, which is probably not true, and further assuming that our insertion of time points in two of the source references which were unclear is close to reality; both assumptions make Table 8 less accurate although still valid as an overview of the trend.

It would seem to transpire that a stocktaking of the recruitment was made at the end of 1973 and dissatisfaction expressed with its slow progress. Rudé právo reported a 'grave imbalance': in 1973 nearly 40

Table 7. Party recruitment 1971–1977

Period	Number of new recruits		Reference
1971			
first nine months of 1972	about	25,000	*Život strany*, 3/1972, p. 13
May 1971 to end of March 1973		42,237	*Rudé právo*, 16/11/72, p. 3
May 1971 to 30 June 1973	over	90,000	*Rudé právo*, 6/7/73, p. 3
May 1971 to end of 1973 (?)		107,145	*Život strany*, 22/1973, p. 11
May 1971 to 1 July 1974	nearly	124,000	*Rudé právo*, 26/1/74, p. 1
since May 1971		187,821	*Rudé právo*, 9/8/74, p. 2
May 1971 to 1 April 1975	over	230,000	*Rudé právo*, 5/3/75, p. 1
May 1971 to 1 April 1976		245,837	*Rudé právo*, 4/7/75, p. 1
April 1976 to 1 October 1977		333,952	Protocol of 15th congress, p. 71
		68,342	*Rudé právo*, 3/12/77, p. 2

Table 8. Monthly admissions to the party 1971–1977

Period	Number of Recruits		Average Monthly Intake
May 1971—December 1971	25,000		3,125
January 1972—September 1972	42,237		4,693
October 1972—March 1973	22,763		3,794
April 1973—June 1973	17,145		5,715
July 1973—December 1973	16,855		2,809
January 1974—July 1974	63,821		9,117
August 1974—January 1975	42,179		7,029
February 1975—March 1975	15,837		7,918
April 1975—March 1976	88,115		7,343
	Total	333,952	Average 5,727
April 1976—December 1976	11,579		1,287
January 1977—September 1977	56,763		6,307
	Total	402,294	Average 3,797 (since April 1976)

per cent of party branches, including some in important factories, failed to admit a single new candidate for membership.[52] And *Život strany* complained in November 1973 that there were still too many white-collar members as against manual workers. The journal cited Central Bohemia with its party stronghold in large industrial agglomerations as an illustration of the adverse ratio. In a coal-mine construction enterprise at Kladno every 35th worker and every fifth administrative employee were in the party. In 66 large enterprises taken together every ninth worker and every third employee were party members.[53] So instructions went down to step up the screening and selection of prospective party members, the branches complied and the monthly numbers jumped up. A lull in recruitment set in after the 15th congress, as if the party branches enjoyed a little respite, before the campaign was jerked into gear again in 1977.

In the absence of more than percentages and some approximate figures, often mentioned only in passing rather than in proper surveys, it is even more difficult to map out progress in the recruitment of workers. The greatest handicap is that we do not always know whether an official speaker is talking about currently practising workers or party members who 'originally' were workers but have long since occupied non-worker positions in party and state *apparatus*. Nevertheless, let us try. Assuming (as was stated officially) that 26·1 per cent of the 'approximately 1,200,000' members at the time of the 14th congress were real workers, further assuming that all of the 151,092 members who ceased to be members between the two congresses died, still further assuming that all of the deceased members were from among the original 1,200,000 (new recruits were mostly young), and finally assuming that the social background proportions of the overall membership applied to those who died, then the number of workers would have been further reduced by 39,435 (26·1 per cent of 151,092) and brought down to 273,765. It was then stated at the 15th congress that 62 per cent of the new recruits were workers: this would work out at 207,050 (of the total of new entrants of 333,952) and the party would thus have 480,815 workers in April 1976, or 34·8 per cent of the total membership of 1,382, 860. This would point to a considerable success of the recruitment campaign, even though it would not do more than bring the party back to where it was in 1958 when it had 34·9 per cent of workers in its ranks. (The percentage then improved a little before plummeting in the 1960s.)

Calculation with a still greater measure of inexactitude helps us to ascertain improvement in the average age of party members from the 49 years at the beginning of 1971. The assumptions here are that all the 151,092 'missing' members died and were primarily in the high age brackets, and that this natural improvement of the average age was offset by the natural aging of the remaining 1,048,908 members by five years. Of the 333,952 new recruits, 90 per cent are said to have been under 35 and 50 per cent under 25, i.e. from 18 to 25 (eighteen being the age on which new members can be admitted). It follows that the age composition of the membership intake was 166,976 of 18–25 years old, 133,581 of 25–35 years old, and 33,395 over 35 years old. We have no guide as to the average age within these groups and have to fix it arbitrarily at half-way between the lower and upper limits, i.e. at 21·5, 30 and 52·5, the last one being a crude middle point between 35 and 70. This would indicate 28 as the average age of the entrants and 43·9 as the average age of a party member as on 1 April 1976, or a reduction by some five years compared to 1971. In December 1977 Husák said that 'over 25 per cent' of the total party membership was now 'young', i.e. under 35.[54] He was relating figures valid as of 31 October 1977, and at that time the party had 1,450,000 members (an approximate figure because we do not know how many died or left between the 15th congress and October 1977); the 'young' members would appear to number 383,000.

A researcher cannot take pleasure in statistical conjecture of this kind. He is however forced to engage in it by the paucity of official information, a regrettable state of affairs, especially since no state secrets are involved and no imaginable harm can be caused to anyone or anything if the real figures were periodically disclosed. Whatever the circumstances, the Czechoslovak communist leadership can take pride in ameliorating the party's composition through a determined effort. As long as party statistics are not released regularly, the party administrators will, however, always be open to the suggestion that their books are being cooked.

To illustrate the strenuous way in which young people were being won over for party membership, we can adduce the experience of the district party committee in Prostějov (Moravia). They resolved to revive the 'tradition of communist families', in which membership of the party passes from generation to generation. In the spring of 1974 party officials compiled full lists of children over 18 in families in which one or both parents were members. They discovered that 1,453 children, aged 18–25, from such families were not themselves members. They counted among them 634 workers, 65 cooperative farmers, 118 clerks, 56 technical and economic employees, 29 teachers, 181 students, 92 apprentices and 278 others. The list was subdivided into territorial and enterprise lists which were then handed over to the appropriate party committees at lower level with the instruction that they should work on such young people. Then the district committee went a step further by compiling lists of youngsters aged 16–17 (192 of them) and 17–18 (325) from communist families and sent them to their parents' places of work and the children's schools (or other establishments), with covering letters notifying those whom it concerned that these young people ought to be groomed for future party member-ship.[55]

Unofficial information from Prague draws attention to another aspect of the membership problem: it is said that over a half of the 500,000-odd members who lost their party cards in 1969–1970 had been 'old' in the sense of having joined the party before it seized power in 1948. Only 25,000 people were alive in 1971 who had been party members before the war, and only 8,000 of them—so the anonymous source says—survived as party members after the 1970 purge. They included only 30 of the 500 surviving Czechoslovak members of the International Brigades in Spain.[56]

With its leading role firmly reasserted, the party was progressing from one congress to the next rather uneventfully. The central committee met more or less regularly. The frequency of meetings at four per annum was more or less followed, with additional gala sessions every five years (1970, 1975) to mark Liberation Day and with the party congress and the general elections consuming much of the business time in subsequent years (1971, 1976). The year 1974 was an exception, with only two central committee sessions, both devoted to the economy. From 1972 (after the purges, personnel changes, congress and elections), the agenda resumed its 'normal' pattern and included the economy, social policy, science, youth, ideology and foreign policy. In this scheme of things the last session every year is given over to a survey of economic results and the announcement of economic policy for the ensuing year. Every five years, the five-year plan is submitted. A central committee session is usually followed by campaigns on the particular theme which dominated the agenda, and all party and non-party bodies hold meetings to 'elaborate the topic for onward implementation'.

Over the nine years from 1969 to 1977 a rough count of items on the agenda of the central committee (as publicly announced, i.e. without any possible closed door sessions) reveals that party matters, such as personnel changes, purges, recruitment, etc. were discussed 22 times, economic matters (general, by branches, plans, budgets) 20 times, international issues (communist movement, foreign policy) four times, elections seven times, and ideology (including youth and education) twice.

From official descriptions of the meetings and the speeches de-livered at them both from the rostrum and from the floor it appears that from April 1969 the central committee has not been convened to solve any momentous questions which were not prepared for rubber-stamping by the praesidium and the secretariat. Decisions are being reached outside the central committee plenum and prior to its sessions which are then used as launching pads for policy drives and as electioneering forums.

FROM DUBČEK TO CHARTER 77

The duration of a central committee meeting has tended to get shorter over the years. Whereas in 1969 and 1970 only one meeting lasted just one day, and all the others two, three or even four days, in 1976 only one and in 1977 no meeting lasted two days or more.

Altogether, from 22 August 1968 to 1 December 1977, forty-six central committee meetings were held of which one lasted four days, two three days, seventeen two days, nineteen one day and seven were shorter than one day (gala meetings and constituent meetings of committees elected at congresses). If even gala and inaugural meetings are counted as full days, the central committee sat for a total of 70 days out of 3,417 between the above dates. The tally is somewhat disappointing for what passes as the supreme organ in the country between party congresses, but it is not surprising. (The two congresses between them lasted ten days and were equally, if not better, stage-managed as the central committee meetings.) With rare exceptions, a communist party of the Soviet type treats its central committee as an instrument of the praesidium and the secretariat, not as a policy-making body. Members of the central committee wield considerable power and influence *vis-à-vis* the party-political structure lower than the central committee, not in the committee itself or towards the praesidium and the secretariat.

The Central Control and Auditing Commission of the party gained importance under its hardline chairman Miloš Jakeš (until 1 December 1977 when he was promoted to candidate membership of the party praesidium and replaced in the Control Commission by his vice-chairman Miloslav Čapka), especially since 1970 when it was co-responsible for the conduct of the purge and the handling of appeals. Judging from Jakeš' obligatory reports at the two party congresses, the commission's remit is wide-ranging, particularly with regard to surveillance over the party apparatus and elected committees right down the line to the local branches. It follows party work systematically but also conducts 'raids' into selected regions, districts or organisations. It keeps an eye on the party's coffers, including membership fees. From Jakeš' pronouncements during the period under scrutiny it would seem that he aspired to participate in policy-making in addition to exercising his supervisory powers, but information is insufficient to pinpoint his specific involvements. The commission normally sits four times a year, but has an apparatus of full-time officials in the party secretariat. In 1971, when most appeals against expulsion were handled (though not all of them by the Central Commission: over a half were in the jurisdiction of lower commissions), the commission held eight meetings, five seminars of instruction for chairmen of regional control commissions and two for chairmen of district commissions. In 1972 there were six meetings.

Personal changes in the praesidium, secretariat and top places in the government and in Slovakia were few after the 14th congress. Observers have suggested that such a delicate balance of power was struck in the top layer of the pyramid that no one dared to interfere with it lest a change causes dangerous veering to one side or the other. A more pragmatic observation may be called for. While it is undoubtedly true that there have been and still are diverse opinions in the leadership, mainly but not solely along the dividing line between advocates of hard and not-so-hard policies, the leadership has over the years established a *modus vivendi* which suits all members. In other words, active Byzantine plotting of one person against another (or between groups) has probably diminished since 1971–72 to the point where stability matters more to every single member than the transfer of all power from right to left or the other way round. At the same time, as is habitual in the close quarters of every monopoly group, the step of every person is intensely watched by all the others, and should someone trespass the unwritten rules of conduct by going too far in his personal enhancement or by advocating a policy which deviates too much from the consensual inertia of the ruling coalition as a whole, such a person will be allowed to fall, with a push, by mutual agreement of the rest. In stability, interpreted as an absence of change, lies the security of the Czechoslovak power elite.

Tensions beneath the crust of unity are once again reported to be near boiling point since December 1977, with alleged mismanagement of the country's economy as the main bone of contention. A regional critic (Jaroslav Hejna, party secretary in South Bohemia) was dismissed and shipped off as ambassador to Bulgaria. Husák allegedly threatened to resign or actually resigned for three days or three hours and only withdrew his resignation on promise of obedience from the others. He purportedly forbids members of the leadership to travel to the provinces for fear of a plot being hatched, and prior consent for such travel must be given by the entire praesidium. These rumours were explicitly denied by Husák himself in a speech during the lacklustre celebrations of the February 1948 takeover, but his remarks were edited out from the printed version.

Several leading personalities nearly became a liability or embarrassment, such as Kapek for his association with the 'ultras' and even Bilak for his visceral sorties against heretical communist parties, East and West, which were leaked to the public. And several 'lobby groups' appeared cutting across the hard-soft divide, such as the reputed 'Czech nationalist' group of Indra and Kempný. The existence of such divergencies changes little in the overall assessment of the leadership as remarkably stable in the sense that for nine years it has always managed to reconcile its differences without dramatic showdowns, even if it meant a retreat of one group before another.

Two changes were occasioned by deaths of incumbents. Federal

Minister of the Interior Radko Kaska (and his Polish counterpart) died in a plane crash at Sczeczin in Poland on 28 February 1973. Rumour has it that he attended a meeting of Warsaw Pact ministers of the interior at which an international corps of riot police was to be established to be used against 'counter-revolutionaries' in various communist countries. This does not sound plausible if only because nothing has been heard about such a plan since then. The death of two of the participants would not have invalidated a plan of this nature for long. Also rumoured was an act of sabotage on the plane, as was Kaska's previous health trouble on account of having to cope with rebellious dogmatists in the ministry. (Kaska was a Husák man.) He was replaced by Jaromír Obzina, also a follower of the party's first secretary, whose last previous appointment was as head of the Education and Science Department in the central committee. It took a month to find a successor to Kaska, and it probably was significant that none of the deputy ministers was eventually chosen but a man without previous 'security' experience. Husák is said to have introduced Obzina to senior members of the ministry as a man who was not coming to pursue a new policy but to carry out the policy of the party.

When Jan Baryl died in November 1977 his place as alternate (candidate) member of the party praesidium was taken by Miloš Jakeš. Jakeš also became a secretary of the central committee and chairman of the commission for agriculture and food.

A spate of changes in 1975 did not have a common denominator. Viliam Šalgovič made it to the top in Slovakia by becoming a member of the Slovak party praesidium in June, then chairman of the Slovak National Council in July (when he relinquished his previous post of chairman of the Slovak Control and Auditing Commission) and a member of the Federal Assembly praesidium in October. Bilak was made a member of the last-named body in September. Vaclav Hůla became a member and Jan Baryl a candidate member of the party praesidium in July, both probably to strengthen the 'technocratic' element in that body, Hůla as chief planner and Baryl as the man in charge of agriculture. In September Oldřich Švestka returned to his pre-invasion function as editor-in-chief of *Rudé právo* (replacing Miroslav Moc who went as ambassador to Switzerland) and in October Švestka lost his post in the party secretariat in favour of Jaroslav Havlín who in turn was replaced as Czech Minister of Education by Milan Vondruška. This reshuffle is difficult to decipher but it most likely was less important than it looked at first.

The major change of 1975 and indeed of the entire period was the re-unification of the country's presidency and First Party Secretaryship, and the decision to entrust both offices to Husák. Svoboda was re-elected president on 22 March 1973 at the age of 77 and in frail health. Rumours about his intention to resign, or alternatively refusal to resign, were ripe before 1973 and gathered momentum in 1974. The first official announcement of his falling gravely ill came in April 1974 when Štrougal as Prime Minister began to deputise for him. It took over a year, until 29 May 1975, before the mantle definitely fell on Husák's shoulders.

In the last instance the thing that matters is whether the joint incumbent is or is not a dictator like Stalin was, or whether the two separate incumbents can peacefully cooperate with each other, always assuming that primacy—and pride of place—goes to the party boss. The presidency or the premiership can, but need not be used as a vehicle to provide a balance or a check on the party leader. In the Czechoslovak context, with the existence of a coalition of two cooperating factions in the party praesidium which do not quite see eye to eye but have learned to reconcile or hide their differences for everybody's benefit, the only real danger to the 'moderates' would arise from Husák's being manoeuvred into the presidential position while relinquishing his first secretaryship to a hardliner. The 'moderate' or 'centrist' conservative line would thus suffer a setback which Husák would be unable to resist from the subordinate position at Hradčany Castle. Husák might opt for this course if he chooses to end his political career as a venerable old statesman on the presidential throne without much influence but with some illusive prestige. He would then however be seen presiding over a country run on more dogmatic and diehard lines than he had been willing to allow.

There were other possible permutations and the Hradčanologists had a field day counting the pros and cons for each of them.[57] Some of the possibilities had inherent limitations, including the lack of charisma in the potential contenders, although of course just about any appointment to any of the top offices could be pushed through. Still, to have Bilak or Kapek or Hoffmann as president somehow did not sound right, and neither is there any evidence that this is what they wanted. The main contention must have been about the post of first party secretary and there the Kremlin's preference was for Husák. Andrei Kirilenko praised him a few weeks before the presidential change when he came to attend celebrations of the 30th anniversary of the end of the war at the head of a Soviet delegation. The accolade included all four kudos that had become customary, although the formulations occasionally differ: a loyal son, a patriot, an internationalist and an important functionary of the international communist movement. The die had thus been cast and once again the obvious choice was made. Husák's supremacy was confirmed and perhaps somewhat enhanced, but one should remember that the endorsement went not to a moderate who can stand up for moderation but rather to a reputed moderate who is known to give way to diehard pressure.

As this is being written, rumours seep out from Czechoslovakia about an impending separation of the two positions, not quite three years after they were reunited. Almost everything is possible in Eastern Europe. A good reason will no doubt be found to justify the undoing of a recent compact as indeed was made quite clear in 1975. When explaining the return of the joint holding of the two offices, Josef Kempný then stated that the joining or separation always depended on existing conditions and on how the party central committee thought the party and society would best operate. In 1975 the party was convinced that merging the two functions in Husák's pair of hands corresponded to the requirements of the day.[58]

One hitch had to be removed, notably the provision of Article 64 of the Constitutional Law No. 143 of 1968 which allowed only temporary deputising for an ill president, implying that election of a new one would have to wait until the incumbent's term of office ran out. It was rumoured that Svoboda, though ailing seriously, put down his foot and refused to clear the way by a resignation. (He is still alive in April 1978.) The constitutional hurdle and indeed the entire formal procedure was cleared expeditiously within less than four days. The party's decision to nominate Husák and to let him keep both posts was communicated to the public on Tuesday, 27 May. The National Front duly welcomed it with enthusiasm on Wednesday. The National Assembly made Husák president unanimously on Thursday. And the new president called on his predecessor on Friday. A picture of the two, shaking hands, appeared in Rudé právo on 31 May. Public acclaim started to pour in virtually hours after the announcement so that it was possible to conclude already on 28 May that 'the working people of the whole of our homeland appreciate the decision of the party central committee: they approve of it and give it full support'.[59] On the following day five large pictures of Husák were featured on page 3 of Rudé právo, each in the company of the leader of one of the five fraternal countries which had invaded Czechoslovakia less than seven years previously: Brezhnev, Zhivkov, Kádár, Honecker and Gierek.

The one process on which the in-fighting between hardliners and 'moderates' could be measured throughout the period between the 14th and 15th party congresses, was the leadership's policy towards the defeated reformers both in terms of a general attitude and as response to individual cases. In retrospect, the relationship between government and opposition centred around the issue of whether the ex-members of the party and other victims of the purges should or would be granted 'a small pardon', such as would enable them to resume practising the professions for which they had been educated while at the same time lifting the apartheid practices which made them and their families lead the lives of second-class citizens. All oppositionists seemed united in seeing the 'small pardon', even if a selective one, as the prerequisite of any further adjustment in the country's political and economic life.

There were signs that some kind of a relaxation was being planned or at least contemplated. Addressing the central committee meeting in October 1972, practically in the wake of the political trials of the summer of that year which decimated the leading circles of the Socialist Movement of Czechoslovak Citizens, Husák said that it took a long time to educate people and that impatience and haste were detrimental. He brought in Lenin who had stated that 'we have to work with people as they are'. People must be differentiated between, and approached sensitively. This was particularly applicable in the fields of science, the arts and culture. Not that some kind of general amnesty should be declared but the party must examine who could be won over and who could not, who was clearly an enemy and who was simply confused. Both right-wing liberalism and sectarian pseudo-radicalism must be eschewed.[60] These nice words, although it took over a fortnight to decide whether they should be published for public consumption, an almost sure sign that there was a difference of opinion, unfortunately remained largely on paper.

A series of amendments to various coercive laws was passed by the Federal Assembly on 25 April 1973 which among other things created a new offence defined as 'untrue reports on the international position and the foreign policy of Czechoslovakia'. It also legalised and simplified infringement of the secrecy of the mails by the police, introduced a stricter regime in prisons (e.g. a hunger strike would henceforth constitute a culpable offence to be rewarded with an additional sentence of imprisonment), introduced 'protective supervision' by the police over ex-convicts (including control over residence, employment and behaviour as well as such stipulations as free entry of police into an ex-convict's flat), promulgated stricter penalties for offences such as betrayal of state secrets and sustained absenteeism from work, simplified rules which restricted police and the judiciary in handling some offences, and instituted a novel measure *('trestní příkaz')* in that 'where evidence is clear' the judge is empowered to send a person to prison for up to two months without a hearing. (An appeal by the defendant would, however, make the hearing compulsory.)[61]

Even with the safeguard of these laws behind them, the party leaders somehow could not bring themselves to inaugurate a policy of reconciliation. Miloš Jakeš explained what selectivity of approach to the victims of the purges meant in his, and presumably other hardliners' view. He conceded that the past should not continue to weigh down the punished ones, but stressed that the bearers of right-wing ideas and organisers of reformist activity should go on being isolated. For them, apparently, the past was to remain a stigma. Only those who had been impassive and 'seduced' in 1968–69 could now hope for a better deal. Even they however had to comply with certain pre-conditions which he set out as admission that they had been guilty open and total self-criticism, profession of loyalty to the present party policy, and proof of expiation by work in social organisations and fringe functions at national committee level. He also hinted that they should be seen to educate their children 'in a positive fashion' and must stop looking at the party's attitude to them so far as some kind of victimisation.[62]

Compared to Husák's interpretation the Jakeš approach could hardly be regarded as acceptable by the victims of political persecution. A 'small pardon' ceased to have the nature of a pardon and became total capitulation and self-abasement. The bickering behind the scenes went on. A dissident source from Prague reported a leak from the party secretariat in the autumn of 1973 according to which a complicated charade was being worked out to categorise the purge victims into as many as eight groups depending on a host of criteria. These included length of party membership prior to expulsion, mode of departure from the party (expelled, struck off, quit), manner in which appeal was lodged (no appeal, meekly worded appeal, impudent appeal), and behaviour since expulsion. Thus, for example, a veteran party member who had been crossed off the party register (i.e. not expelled), filed a self-effacing appeal and showed loyalty ever since could now hope to have his party membership returned. Others would be allowed to submit application for a new admission. Yet others might not be recommended for entry into the party, but would be given their civil rights back, or such of them as existed. The last group, the eighth, would comprise those who must be left lingering in the limbo.[63]

Then came the year 1974 and with it not only a new purge of management and other prominent 'cadres', as described earlier, but also Alexander Dubček's two statements, the first ones after he had made his speech at the September 1969 session of the central committee. (It circulated in samizdat form, as did the 1974 ones.) The first of the two was a letter to the wife of Josef Smrkovský dated 18 January 1974. Smrkovský died on 14 January and the police intercepted and delayed the delivery of a telegram sent to Dubček so that he was unable to attend the funeral of his old friend. This angered him to the point where he decided to speak up at least in this way.[64] Then, on 28 October 1974, he broke silence again and mailed from his domicile in Bratislava a long letter to the Federal Assembly in Prague and a copy to the Slovak National Council. In the first part of this letter he listed in detail the surveillance and harassment to which he was being subjected in contravention of valid laws and in spite of his abstention from all oppositional activity. In doing so he identified himself with the main cause of complaint on behalf of the million or so compatriots who felt they had been made second-class citizens because of the views they held. When this letter reached the samizdat orbit (much later, in 1975), it was greeted with satisfaction by the public: 'Dubček has not recanted!' The second part of the letter is a scathing criticism of the official policy of 'normalisation', even though it bears signs of having been written by a man who stayed out of the mainstream of opposition as it formed itself chiefly in the Prague intellectual circles. Dubček wrote:

'In addition to protesting against what the Ministry of the Interior organs have been doing, I am writing here about some of my political thoughts and views. I have no opportunity to consult with anyone, and in the present atmosphere I do not even want to.... This letter should then be understood in the context of the times and arising from the situation which has prompted me to write it. More than at any time before I now understand that the system of personal power entails political, ideational, organisational, personnel and other mainly power-political measures and instruments. It is not enough to disagree verbally with such a concept: it has to be purposefully surmounted and circumscribed by legal norms, its restoration and perpetuation must be resisted, as we tried to do. Such a system is incompatible with Marxism-Leninism. It is not so much a question of which individuals translate this concept into reality (although that too is not negligible) under the guise of protection for orthodox Leninism which is allegedly threatened by various "innovators". Much rather it is a question of destroying theoretically, organisationally and politically the very quintessence of this ruling method, based as it is among other things on a manipulation of the masses and their subjection to obedience and discipline, ostensibly to save socialism. If this method, harmful to socialism, is not exposed (under the pretext that in doing so one would play into the hands of enemy propaganda), injurious adaptability and indifference will be promoted especially in the younger generation. The notion will be encouraged that to adapt oneself to unlawfulness brings personal benefit to one man at the expense of his fellow men, not infrequently his own friends and comrades. The idea that human rights must be actively protected and defended even under socialism, is fully justified.'[65]

According to Prague sources, the leadership was furious, including Husák, especially when Dubček's second letter received publicity in the Western press. This did not happen before mid-April 1975, more than five months after it had been written and posted, and only when the authorities to whom it was addressed failed to reply. In fact when the anti-revisionist campaign, featuring Dubček prominently as the main culprit, got under way again in December 1974[66], Western observers were perplexed and speculated as to what could have prompted the Prague leadership to arch its back again. Dubček's letter

197

to Mrs Smrkovský was known, it had been published in Italian communist papers early in the year, but his second letter was still a matter between him and the addressees. When Husák himself let fly on 16 April 1975, in a speech to the National Front, he made some telling remarks. Speaking in a manner which suggested a certain measure of improvisation, he felt injured by the failure of the opposition to acknowledge that they had been treated 'mildly' and wondered whether it had not been a mistake. Absence of mass arrests and executions was not a sign of the leadership's stupidity, and Husák warned the small groups 'around Smrkovský and Dubček' (Smrkovský had been dead since January 1974) that everything had its limits. If Dubček so wished, he could leave the country tomorrow and the Swedish Prime Minister, Mr Palme, who had shown concern, could have him as an instructor in 'democratic socialism'. 'Admittedly, I do not know what the Swedish people . . . would say to it if Dubček ruined their kingdom in the space of a few months as he did Czechoslovakia in 1968'. Should Dubček decide to stay in Czechoslovakia, he must respect the laws and take the consequences if he chooses to do otherwise![67]

A stream of readers' letters was paraded through the pages of the press condemning Dubček's letter to the Federal Assembly which of course they had not read. The late Josef Smrkovský got a rough ride at the same time because of his so-called memoirs, in fact a series of taped interviews with a friend, which were being published in the Italian newspaper *Giorni-Vie Nuove*. As if to underline Husák's 'argument', the Federal Minister of the Interior spoke a day later at a gala meeting of police officers and his speech was promptly featured in *Rudé právo*. He warned that an alliance between right-wingers, anti-socialists and imperialists was at large and spelled counter-revolutionary danger to the country. The police were and would be doing their utmost to suppress all unlawful activity of reactionary groups and individuals at home as well as imperialist intelligence from abroad. He added that Czechoslovak police was however different from capitalist police which repressed the entire working class, other strata and the people as a whole, whereas the Czech police was not an instrument of general oppression; it only acted against anti-socialist and criminal elements and political reactionaries.[68]

Not even then was the idea of 'a small pardon' quite abandoned, although it remained dormant for a good part of a year. In the meantime the police apparatus was being steadily strengthened through financially lucrative conditions for new recruits (it was rumoured that after a year's training a 19-year old policeman's pay packet was twice the size of a university graduate's first salary) and improvement of social facilities and fringe benefits (a new Police Law became effective on 1 July 1974). Anonymous sources from Prague estimated the strength of the Secret Police (STB) at 14,000 in the Czech Lands alone plus another 10,000 officers strategically deployed under cover as employees in various institutions, such as the ministries of foreign affairs and foreign trade and the export-import companies. Police officers provided information to party and state bodies on a host of subjects, and conveyed their own wishes and suggestions to them. Hundreds and thousands of people were being interrogated about all kinds of seemingly irrelevant and unrelated things. The 'people in the ghetto' (as the blacklisted victims of purges were called in Prague) were the direct responsibility of the police who maintained bulky dossiers and paid daily attention to what they were doing, how much they were earning, who they were consorting with and so on. Cases are known of plainclothes police officers arranging dismissals of people whose salaries were thought to grow too much or who came into contact with too many other, 'ordinary' citizens in the performance of their jobs. The selfsame officers would call on headmasters and deans to drop a hint about the undesirability of children from proscribed families getting too high on the educational ladder ('like father, like son, isn't it so, comrade dean?'). Passports, even for travel to socialist countries, were being gradually withdrawn from ex-reformers. They could not, of course, possess licences entitling them to hold guns and sporting rifles. Driving licences tended to be confiscated for the slightest of offences. People were being warned not to maintain any contact with their friends in the 'ghetto'. The misinformation department now and then issued fake letters. Anonymous telephone calls became more frequent. And specially heavy street shadowing was imposed on prominent dissenters now and then. (One of them counted three cars and six plainclothesmen following him when by chance Husák went by accompanied by only one extra car and three bodyguards.)[69]

It was rumoured that some of the leading exponents of reformism were visited by emissaries of the new regime at the turn of 1975 and that cooperation with the Husák leadership was suggested to them. They would even be allowed to re-emerge in important positions. The names mentioned in this respect were Oldřich Černík, Čestmír Císař, Bohumil Šimon, Josef Špaček and Martin Vaculík. This is impossible to verify and of course it cannot be deduced from the available information whether such approaches were just soundings or genuine offers of collaboration. What does seem clear is that the conditions laid down by the regime, if indeed all this is true, were more on Jakeš' terms, not Husák's, and included a full public recantation of their previous views and policies and a profession of loyalty to the new rulers. Whatever the real course of events, as of the time of writing, almost ten years after the Prague Spring, a great number of former communist officials have still remained out in the cold, partly because their successors have made a point of it to prevent their comeback but partly also because they refused to accept the humiliating conditions exacted by the 'normalisers'.

So when it came to the 15th congress of the party in 1976, the 'small pardon' was whittled down to one short paragraph in Husák's mammoth speech. It said:

> '... the central committee is of the opinion that those who were not active representatives of right-wing opportunism, who work well and prove by their deeds that they firmly and sincerely uphold the positions of socialism and our friendship with the Soviet Union, and who actively support the policy of our party, can become once again eligible for new admission to the party, while every individual case has to be considered separately'.[70]

Not a word about lifting the impositions on the 'ghetto' or about discontinuation of at least some apartheid conditions in employment and education. But then, according to the official line, there was no discrimination. Addressing a district party conference in Prague before the congress, Husák said that most of the ex-members had already realised how bad Dubček's policy had been and how good the present one was. All citizens had equal rights and everyone could anyway be active in a 'mass organisation'. No one was discriminated against.[71] The problem was solved by saying that it did not exist.

Indeed, the congress brought few surprises, if any. As Husák put it when announcing that the entire party praesidium, except Ludvík Svoboda, was re-elected: 'You do not change horses in mid-stream'. Bilak and Indra did not even address the congress but remained members of the praesidium. Brezhnev did not come. In his stead and on his behalf, the policy of the Czechoslovak leadership received the desirable blessing from A. P. Kirilenko:

> 'Thanks to a Marxist-Leninist approach to the development of society, thanks to a consistent struggle against right-wing opportunism as the main danger, and thanks to the cementing of the leading role of the party and its links with the people, your party has consolidated your society and ensured Czechoslovakia's transition to a new stage of economic, social and cultural development'.[72]

All the ingredients were contained in that little paragraph. What has proved to be so right in the past cannot be wrong for the future. The three categorical imperatives would continue to govern Czechoslovakia's progress: Marxism-Leninism, struggle against reforms, and more power for the party leaders. In other words: ideology, militancy, dictatorship. Under this safe umbrella, the coalition of radical and not so radical conservatives can easily survive, and Husák can go on presiding over it. Kirilenko said:

'. . . an important official of the international working-class movement, a firm Marxist-Leninist, an internationalist, a great friend of the Soviet Union—comrade Gustav Husák.'[73]

All people in Czechoslovakia over the age of fifteen have to carry an identity card, a smallish red book containing all kinds of useful information for the authorities about the bearer as well as a number of free pages for rubber stamping by successive employers, health authorities etc. At the beginning of April 1976, the month of the 15th congress, two thousand young people in Prague were identified in a frantic police search (others may have gone undetected) as having torn out page 15 out of their identity cards. Some had even decided to make do without page 25. Was it not the year of the Soviet Communist Party's 25th congress as well? The growing up generation was displaying signs of disaffection. Most of them had been too young in 1968 to appreciate the meaning of the Prague Spring then. Why should they reject the ideals of 'normalisation'?

IDEOLOGY SUPREME

Ideological vehemence has been the highlight of the leadership's prescription of how party and government should behave. Campaign followed campaign, designed to restore the tenets of Marxism-Leninism to their full power, such as they did not even enjoy in the last six years of the Novotný regime. A pragmatic approach may have been considered satisfactory in the working out of the basic social contract whereby the public would not meddle in politics in exchange for a steady supply of consumer goods and entertainment, but this was to happen to the accompaniment of the ideological drums.

In 1970 there was a saturation campaign on Lenin's centenary, in 1971 the Czechoslovak party celebrated its 50th birthday, held its 14th congress and masterminded a general election. In 1972 new cultural unions were at long last properly set up and the party central committee held a special session on ideology which set in motion intensive propaganda activity in all organisations. In 1973 the high-light was the 25th anniversary of the communist takeover, celebrated in Brezhnev's presence, and the focus fell on education and youth at another central committee session. The following year it was the mass media which received a massive dose of ideological guidance at several conferences and a party document on the social sciences saw the light of the day. 1975 brought the 30th anniversary of liberation, the national Spartakiade (a mass display of gymnastics and athletics) and a renewal of attacks on revisionism at a grand scale. 1976 featured several high points: the 15th congress, another general election, Gottwald's 80th birthday anniversary, and the communist summit in East Berlin.

Throughout the period no stone was left unturned to declare emphatically the party's allegiance to Soviet theory and practice of socialism, no less than its absolute loyalty to Soviet foreign policy and the Soviet party's stand in the international communist movement. The Brezhnev doctrine was embraced, diligently elaborated and incorporated in state treaties with the USSR and East Germany. China, Solzhenitsyn, Israel and the junta in Chile were attacked again and again as a composite enemy number one. Detente was interpreted strictly on class terms and in impressive unison with Soviet views on the subject. In castigating Eurocommunism the disciples even sur-passed their masters.

After the early 1950s, the 'normalisation' period has been the most militantly and blatantly ideological phase of modern Czechoslovak history. The impact of it all cannot be measured. According to visitors and the opposition circles, large segments of the public have developed immunity to official propaganda.

The evolving ideological patterns reveal that the regime has been concerned above all with the following general issues:

1. Continuity with pre-reformist communist past, so that the Prague Spring can be presented as an aberration, a dangerous blemish on the essentially beautiful face of communism.

2. Direct descendance of the 'normalising' regime from the Leninist form of Marxism whose theory and practice fit Czechoslovakia like a glove after all.

3. Inextricable linkage of Soviet and Czechoslovak communist experiences in all their forms: the salvager-salvaged role in the 1938–1945 period; the teacher-pupil relationship in the stage of socialist construction; the benefactor-beneficiary type of economic interdependence; and the leader-led configuration in the great anti-imperialist ventures of the present and the future.

In its more specifically mobilising aspects, the ideological offensives have concentrated mainly on imbuing the hard core of the party with the notion that it is legitimately, by the law of history and the fact of power, entitled to be in command of the society in which it operates. Education and indoctrination of the young received a high measure of priority with the aim of drawing a line between the generation of parents who fell for the ideas of the Prague Spring and the age groups who would spend their formative years in conditions of revivified orthodoxy. After the ex-reformers have died out, the 'normalised' youth will take over and never again allow the true communist dream to succumb to democratic, reformist, revisionist, imperialistic on-slaughts. Or, to put it differently, even after the present 'normalisers' have passed away (they too, alas!, being mortal), the younger generation will rise and go on normalising.

Education

The progress of 'normalisation' in the educational system was from top to bottom. As we have already said, the universities were the first target of purges, class selection of entrants, strengthening of Marxist-Leninist teaching and pruning of curricula. In 1971–72 the focus shifted towards secondary schools, with the same pattern of restricting teachers who had been outspoken during the Prague Spring, and manipulating admissions to exclude children from reformist families and to give preference to working-class pupils. Para-military (or pre-military) education was introduced in September 1971 and so was the old-new subject of 'civics', better described as 'political instruction'. In 1973 the much heralded experience of the early 1950s with one-year training courses for under-educated workers' children was re-started. The idea was to compress secondary education into an intensive boarding-school type course which would provide automatic entry into a university.

In 1974 the indoctrination process reached the kindergarten level. This admittedly was found a tall order even for avid proponents of orthodoxy, but they did cope. At the softer end of the effort, the idea of collectiveness (not quite the same as 'teamwork') was singled out as worthy of being inculcated in the three-to-five year olds, while the more forward educators came out with the theory of 'key concepts' with which the children ought to be familiarised, such as 'Lenin', 'party', 'Soviet Union', 'Red Army', 'October Revolution'. They were to evoke correct associations, a notion somewhat reminiscent of the Pavlovian conditional reflexes in dogs. At about the same time the Ministry of Education decreed the extension of pre-military education into kindergartens. The connecting element between military goals and the psycho-physical disposition of a child was discovered in the 'play-toy' sequence or, in plainer words, the kindergartens were supplied with toy tanks, rifles and rockets, and the instructors were there to provide the requisite comment on the importance of socialist military preparedness. As one writer put it:

> 'This goes beyond the negativist attitude as characterised by the non-class and non-historic statement in the *Educational Dictionary* of 1965 which said that children educated in socialism and communism shall not be given toys simulating devices designed for destruction'.[74]

We have a letter from a teacher in Prague describing what it is like in a secondary school these days. (The letter was written in 1974, but little has changed.) She considers herself lucky because 'her' pupils have confidence in her and so far she has been able to trust them. 'I appear before my class and, as ordered, I recite things which I do not agree with. My students know this and also disagree but they keep silent'. A kind of make-believe which this particular class is playing for the benefit of those absent from it. 'But this is exactly where my situation becomes painful; I have to feel ashamed in front of my children and at the same time grateful to them but I cannot help worrying about the kind of character traits they are developing and about what they are going to be like as future citizens of this country'. The situation is wrought with fear. The pupils repeat everything after the teacher, some apathetically, others with obvious disgust which she pretends not to notice, and still others in a mocking manner which underlines the absurdity of the whole affair, but she still pretends not to see it and only worries lest the class bursts out laughing or begins making faces.

'Suppose these nice students of mine start boasting somewhere what a brick their teacher is and what she allows to be said in her classes; someone will blab and I will be in trouble again . . . Or perhaps a parent will want to take revenge on me for a poor grade . . . It has happened that parents with a so-called "healthy cadres record" have put a casette recorder into their children's briefcase instructing them to record what the teacher says. Inducing a child to become a snooper may be quite attractive for a foolish youngster, since suddenly he has a secret power over the teacher's fate'.

The superiors, trusted headmasters and inspectors, tend to call students away from their classes and enquire about what the teacher said about this or that political subject. 'Is this anything else but just another, officially fostered, form of snooping?' Or take the fixed quotas for transfer to higher grades of secondary schools. They were set high for children from politically reliable families and also, seemingly without political designs, for girls as against boys. Talented boys are supposed to go to vocational training centres and, if lucky, obtain secondary education there. Admissions to universities are governed by still stricter political criteria.

'. . . this regime has devised a punishment hardly known even in the dark Middle Ages: to punish children for the alleged sins of their parents. . . . On the other hand, the children of political functionaries were accepted even if they were completely stupid and some of them, who originally did not even intend to go to university, were encouraged to apply at a later stage, even to faculties which had several times more applicants than places, i.e. a very high percentage of rejections.'

This teacher concludes her letter by saying that the 'normalisation' regime has committed many outrages: it has ruined people's careers and allowed science, culture and the economy to be pervaded by incompetence. It has squandered money on bureaucracy and the coercive forces and it has put innocent people in jail. 'But all this means nothing compared to the crimes committed against our younger generation, against out children'.[75]

Another testimony about education was sent from Prague to UNESCO with a request for help in 1976. Signed 'Helena Trojanová', it contains facts about discrimination of applicants for university admission. The author is familiar with the procedures and has undertaken unofficial enquiries among education functionaries involved in the process. She says that the 'complex assessment dossiers' of prospective entrants (which listed political information next to school records) are no longer used to substantiate rejections but application forms still contain questions on the political affiliation of parents (previous and present) and their public and political involvement. (Most recent information, sporadic and not quite clear, would seem to indicate that in preparation for the 1977–78 admissions, these questions have been deleted, possibly as a result of the spotlight which Charter 77 threw on this practice and in view of international protest.) According to Trojanová, lists of prospective university entrants were being sent well in advance to Regional National Committees which processed them in conjunction with the educational departments in Regional Party Committees. When these lists were returned to the respective faculties, some names had the letter N in green ink appended to them and others an A. The N's were not recommended for admission while the A's stood for 'accept unconditionally'. The former turned out to be children from 'suspect' families, victims of the purges, while the latter came from families of office holders and loyal supporters of the regime. A university official told Mrs Trojanová: 'Those who were marked N could not be accepted under any circumstances whatsoever, even if at the entrance examinations they performed like young Einsteins.... And conversely, those who had been given an A by the regional party committees were accepted even if they performed abominably before the examining boards and if their results were quite inadequate'. She noted that applicants for places at technical faculties were assessed less stringently, especially since it would cause great problems if young people without adequate mathematical or other basic skills were admitted simply on grounds of their parents' political commitment. But negative sifting to weed out 'stigmatised' candidates applied to these faculties as well. (Between the N's and the A's a certain leeway was allowed to the universities to choose from 'unmarked' candidates who fitted neither of the two categories.) Mrs Trojanová attempted an estimate of how many children from non-conformist families had been discriminated against in either secondary school promotion or university entrance, and came up with the figure of between 200,000 and 300,000 from 1970 to 1976. This would include either straight rejections or forcible re-orientation towards 'safer' disciplines than the ones originally applied for.[76]

What, then, are the university students like, after seven to eight years of normalisation? One of them sent a letter abroad in June 1976 describing the ideological pressures to which they are exposed. At the admission stage, assuming they passed through the sifting procedure before meeting the examination board (there are interviews at universities before matriculation is allowed), they are told that a contribution to the faculty's political life was expected of them. Membership of the Youth Union (and the party) is increasingly presented to them as a condition of obtaining a good career assignment on graduation. (Graduates are generally sent to work at specified places, not allowed to find jobs themselves.) Yearly assessment sessions are held, and students are of course obliged to attend courses in Marxism-Leninism. Male students have to take part in 'military preparation' (one day a week for two years) and female students and invalids must go through civil defence courses, both containing ideological classes as well. The author of the letter estimates that only about five to ten per cent of students are not members of the Youth Union, while another 10 to 15 per cent are functionaries and 'committed' activists. (This group could be further subdivided into 'genuine believers' and 'careerists', he says.) The remaining 80 per cent are 'passive Union members' whose duty is to attend meetings and 'actions'. Almost anything can become a Union 'action': joint visit to a theatre or a football game, a table-tennis tournament, a tour of Prague 'in the footsteps of the workers' movement' (a good opportunity to call at several working-class pubs), a party to celebrate the beginning or the end of a semester, a wedding party. 'Actions' are added up and reported in 'activity sheets' which then make up for 'socialist competition' between various Union groups. The author of the letter believes that the vast majority of students would once again support a reform movement. 'Considering how much effort has been expended by the regime, students have succumbed to pressure and demoralisation to a minimum extent only'.[77]

As from 1974–75 school-year the authorities have embarked on a comprehensive reform to the entire educational system. (Reforms have been numerous since 1948.) At the lowest level the reform involved shortening of the five-year elementary cycle to four years, as was done in the Soviet Union, the starting date for the new system being set as 1 September 1976, after pilot operation in some schools. Many educationalists opposed the scheme, but the authorities had their way in the end. Subject matter in four-year elementary schools is divided as follows: mother tongue and writing, 42·5 per cent of teaching time; mathematical training, 21·1 per cent; basic instruction on nature and society, 12·1 per cent; aesthetic education, 11·1 per cent; polytechnic and manual skills training, 4·4 per cent; physical education, 8·8 per cent.[78]

For the secondary schools the option eventually taken eschewed Soviet practice (which would require restructuring the entire educational system) but sought to achieve identical aims by bringing all the different types of school closer together insofar as curriculum imposition was concerned. Differences between the various types of secondary school, including vocational training centres, were scaled down, and elements of polytechnicism were strengthened throughout the system.

At university level the reform returned to shorter courses (mostly reduced from five to four years of study). In this reform 'the focus of the educational process is shifted from the informative system of instruction to a methodological one designed to teach the student how to learn, to acquire the ability to generalise his experience, to make use of the modern technology that surrounds him, and to lead him to independent thought with regard to form, but at the same time to orient him accurately as far as content is concerned'.[79] As a corollary, increased emphasis on training in the ideological and moral-political sphere *(Weltanschauung)* was once again demanded.

Scholarship

Attention which the 'normalisers' paid to social science even after the initial sweeping dismissals of dissenters from research institutions and teaching positions and after the imposition of a total ban on the publication of anything they wrote before, during and after the reform, has had the dimensions of a saturation attack. Its pattern would seem to be something like this: the banishment of dissenters is total and perpetual including complete exclusion of their books from all libraries (one case of abject public recantation is known, of philosopher Jiří Cvekl in August 1970); the first and foremost task of social scientists who passed the screening is to analyse and repudiate views and theories expressed in the 1960s and during the Prague Spring; then they must proceed to link their respective disciplines to the policy of the party so that scholarship becomes utilitarian; utmost care must be paid to what is taught, researched and published so that 'incorrect' views are no longer propagated; close cooperation with scholars from the Soviet Union and other Comecon countries must become a constant feature, including division of labour in the tackling of problems jointly set by the political leaderships of the socialist countries; to this process Czechoslovak scholars must contribute their experience of struggle against revisionism, liberalism and democratic socialism.

Judging from the special document on 'The Development, Present Stage and Tasks of the Social Sciences' promulgated by the party praesidium on 3 May 1974, and the accompanying spate of articles in the daily press and scholarly journals, something was really rotten in the social science sector even after the wholesale dismissals and the other prophylactic measures against revisionism. Consider what one of the chief 'normalisers' in this area had to say about the situation in the second half of 1974:

> 'Negative factors which survive to this day include, above all, lack of purpose and barren academism, under-estimation of social needs, contemptuous attitudes to ideological, political and organisational work, fragmentation of projects, unhealthy ambition, élitism, mutual grudge and formation of cliques. A number of scholars have shown interest in pushing foward their personal promotion and various kinds of élitisms. Behind positive results achieved by politically mature and scientifically erudite workers, there often hide people who have stood

still in their development or, for other reasons, are incapable of promoting scientific knowledge and joining in the investigation of topical, ideo-politically committed themes and problems. Unprincipled liberal attitudes of leading workers in social science institutions *vis-à-vis* such people make it then impossible to admit new workers with the requisite qualifications for scientific work'.[80]

The author evidently spoke with knowledge and was familiar with problems the existence of which we can only surmise from the thrust of his onslaught, which is not quite clear but unmistakable. No wonder then that the party praesidium, while issuing the above-mentioned document also ordered 'a re-examination of the personnel structure of institutions engaged in social sciences' and decreed that measures must be taken to improve their political profile.[81] And so another expurgation campaign was started. The extracts of the Document, as they appeared in *Rudé právo*, in fact single out almost the same gamut of sins as the author of the above article. The Document also called for enhancement of the party's supervisory capacity in social science institutions and for stricter planning of scholarly work. Both basic and applied research were said to be unsatisfactory: the former in failing to treat of such important topics as economic management and planning in an advanced socialist society, and the latter in failure to provide practical economists with studies, expertise and forthright recommendations. Next to economics, sociology and law were singled out for criticism, but elsewhere in the Document and other materials from the same time, practically all other disciplines got an unfavourable mention. The Document ended by enumerating four areas of research on which social scientists were obligated to participate with vigour and dedication: 1. The nature of the present stage of the construction of socialism. 2. Theory of the party. 3. Development of economy and economic policy. 4. Education of a socialist man, including his protection from bourgeois and petty-bourgeois ideology.

It is difficult to say to what extent the 'normalisation' policy worked in the social science field as a result of this second round of concentrated attention from high party quarters, accepting that it had not quite worked between 1969 and 1974. To give credit where it is due and to express some surprise that economics were so heavily criticised in the party Document, one should say that several important books by economists were published in 1974–1976 and a major economic study was undertaken and completed in the Economic Institute of the Academy of Sciences.[82] Indeed, the topic of economic reform began once again to be discussed in 1975.

Also deserving attention are a few books of party history, mainly devoted to specific aspects of certain developments of periods rather than a synoptic overview.[83]

In sociology an attempt was made (but presumably not completed) to continue a major project started in 1966 on the stratification of modern Czechoslovak society. The team leader, Pavel Machonin, and several of his collaborators were now *non gratae*, but the results of a large survey of data which they assembled were used by others.[84]

A judgment on the state of the social sciences would of course have to take into account the publication of a large number of books and articles which were far below the standards of the comparatively few quality works. Another criterion would have to be the potential of Czechoslovak social sciences as shown in the 1960s; it was most certainly not being put to full use in the 1970s. Furthermore, even the top works tackled only a small range of topics while extensive target areas of research remained closed to serious investigation or were reserved to hack writing. Neither can a student of the period ignore the persecution of so many talented people among the community of scholars and scientists. Even if those that remained active produced only gilt-edged works, they would still be tarred by the consideration of what their less fortunate colleagues were forbidden to produce.

Academician Ivan Málek, formerly vice-president of the Academy of Sciences and holder of the International Lenin Peace Prize, himself a victim of the purge, addressed a letter to the Academy's praesidium on 25 June 1975. The letter had a very calm and dignified tone and the writer stressed his concern for the fate of science in Czechoslovakia, not his personal predicament. He pointed out the banishment of scientists, politically-biased recruitment of new researchers and placement of unqualified people into positions of influence in scholarly institutions as the main reasons why the institutes and departments had been seized by an atmosphere of fear and uncertainty. In spite of the planned nature of social development, science was not being pursued and directed so as to ensure its advance in terms of time over the applied fields which it should serve. And the international links, even inside the community of socialist states, were being impeded by bureaucratic and ideological barriers.[85]

Culture

The basic institutional network in the field of culture, such as would correspond to the principal 'normalisation' aim of restoring party control, was in existence from the constituent congresses of the new cultural unions in 1972. This in itself, as we have said earlier, presented the party with considerable problems because of the degree to which commitment to autonomy had pervaded the cultural community.

The setting up of a new Czech Writers' Union, for example, went through several laborious stages under the direct control of the Minister of Culture, M. Brůžek. Until the end of 1970 he ruled by decree and through *aktives*, i.e. *ad hoc* assemblies of those willing to play the new game, often functionaries rather than writers. Then a preparatory committee of the new union was set up in December 1970, headed by the poet Josef Kainar and, as his secretary, Donát Šajner, formerly an official of the Ministry of the Interior. This committee held two meetings in 1971, in May and September, before a conference of the whole union could be called on 18 November of the same year. Kainar died of a heart attack two days earlier and the man who stepped into his shoes and has remained the leading figure in the 'normalisation' process to this day was Jan Kozák, erstwhile an employee of the party *apparat* and a political writer. He steered the frail structure of the new union to a constituent congress in May–June 1972 at which under 100 members were registered. (the Slovak Writers' Union had 210 members at the same time, as against the joint membership of some 610 for both unions in 1968. All membership figures are approximate because once again the offical information is inconsistent and fragmented.) From the latter part of 1969 to the autumn of 1972, there were no Czech literary magazines, as against five journals run by the old union. In October 1972 the new union at long last began to publish its one and only journal under the title *Literární měsíčník* (Literary Monthly) and no more have been added since. Since May 1975 *Literární měsíčník* carries newsletter-type reports about the Union's activity. (*Měsíčník* is not really a monthly because only ten issues appear every year. The circulation is not known but presumably does not exceed a few thousand copies. In comparison the old union's weekly *Literární noviny* printed 150,000 copies and during the Prague Spring even more.)

All the new unions had considerably fewer members than their rebellious predecessors in the 1960s. This was not only due to the reluctance of individual artists to join, but also to the determined vetting procedures. More and more emphasis was being placed on selectivity, with the criterion of active political commitment to the new course an over-riding prerequisite for admission. When the unions were first created after the communist takeover in February 1948, the selectivity principle had also been applied but gradually it became eroded as the unions acquired the character of professional sectoral organisations, (Some people remained outside the unions throughout.) Now the directive was evidently to go back to the original élitist concept, even though officials did remark now and then that non-members would not be prevented from practising their art or profession outside the emergent organisational framework provided of course that they showed loyalty to the regime. For some unions this was more true than for others. Actors, for instance, could (and can to this day) be active members of theatre companies, or perform on television, without belonging to the Drama Union, provided they have no great aspirations. Artists, non-members of the Fine Arts Union, find it more difficult to have their work exhibited than their organised colleagues, but they can still survive, say in ornamental or industry-orientated applied art. Writers, once again, have found the going rough. Those dubbed enemies had all publishing outlets closed to them. Gradually, as the new Writers' Union cemented its organisational foundations, it began to exercise patronage over young authors (or those who had not published previously) without admitting them to membership right away.

The new unions' activity began to gather momentum rather slowly and for the first year or two was explicitly political. For instance, the Czech Writers' Union busied itself with the revival of international contacts with counterpart unions in the communist countries, notably the Soviet Union, as its major 'task' in 1972–73. It also sought to project its image into the provinces by organising speaking arrangements and 'study trips' for its members. Formal meetings have been held rather infrequently, even of the committees, and full-scale congresses take place only once every five years. Most of the current business is conducted from well-endowed secretariats. The unions also administer various facilities, such as publishing houses (with varying measure of direct responsibility), clubs, recreational (or 'creative') houses and special funds to finance their members' activities through grants, exhibition expenses etc. Some endeavour has been made to set up regional branches and thus ensure a better organisational hold on provincial artists. The Writers' Union has evolved what it calls 'work with young authors', attracting newcomers, arranging seminars for them and giving them publication space in *Literární měsíčník*. Activities of the other unions are less well known but can be assumed to evolve on similar lines. Many people tend to view the new unions, illegitimate as their origins on the ruins of the defeated liberal structures were, as simply instruments of ideological overlordship over the cultural and artistic life of the country. This assessment is inescapable, and it has also to do with the re-introduction of 'socialist realism' as the mandatory profession of faith, although it has been cautiously recognised that it ought to be understood as 'a method', not 'a new genre'.

Having followed the Czech literary output (not the Slovak) of the 'normalisation' years fairly closely, I feel compelled to interject a brief paragraph of personal evaluation. Czech literature has suffered badly in language, style and content. Literary criticism is for all purposes dead. Among the officially published books and short stories the proportion of strong party-minded literature is relatively small but there is a great deal more of ideological appendage to works which are otherwise indifferent. The overall impression is one of clumsiness, both in the quality of writing and the way in which political dues are paid. At the same time one discerns a desire to eschew total identification with political command (except in perhaps two dozen books) by escaping into the time-honoured thematic fields: history (both in the sense of historical novel writing and in a going-back to the early days of social conflict), and light entertainment. In the latter genre, there has been a proliferation of detective stories, adventure yarns and romance. The target area that has remained singularly under-represented is the inner life of man; books and stories in this vein have either been literary failures or aroused the wrath of the authorities. No truly great writer as a commentator on the social and human predicament of Czech society of today has emerged and is unlikely to emerge in the near future. But there is promise among the younger writers, clearly discernible in some, barely fathomable in others. And if we allow ourselves the luxury of stronger imagination than is customary, it would appear that the most promising are those who write in the style and spirit of their exorcised predecessors of the 1960s, while the party commandments are best obeyed by those who would even under different circumstances remain hacks. The 1970s may yet come to be remembered as an intermezzo, tragic for many and costly for Czech literature as a whole, but still only an interlude.

About 150 writers were 'put on an index' as the Czech expression goes, and the damage done to literature, not to mention the liberal spirit, by their exclusion is immeasurable. Several artists committed suicide (Jiří Pištora, Stanislav Neumann, Jan Alda, Vladimír Burda and Vladimír Heller) and several recanted, some publicly and others in the more private bulletin of the new Writers' Union. The way in which these recantations were worded is not without interest. For Jiří Šotola the ten years since he became first secretary of the old Writers' Union until his attempted expiation in April 1975 were long enough to make him realise the difference between genuine and false values. A writer cannot go on writing without knowing whether he will have an audience. Šotola refused to play the role of an embittered individual standing outside the living organism of human society. He would like to recover his contact with the readers and be useful to them, to the country, to socialism and to the party. He would henceforth write historical novels.[86]

Bohumil Hrabal gave an interview rather than a statement. For Czech writers, he said, it was more important to know what the readers thought about them rather than what some foreign radio station said. He would like his readers to realise that he wished them and socialism well. He had not written much recently but he would liken his texts to a game of football, to the beautiful tension on a green pitch. He would confine himself more and more to the role of someone sitting on the line and watching the young play football, and he would applaud them because they have a big heart and much enthusiasm even if they remained as yet anonymous.[87] On the whole the self-criticising writers did not do too well in the way of publication. Save for one or two books in a small number of copies and a few extracts in magazines, their comeback simply did not take place. They are rarely if ever mentioned.

Others refused to surrender and especially after the abortion of the attempt to organise a socialist opposition became increasingly active as critics of the regime. The Czech literary samizdat was born: dozens of books and short stories, especially of the *feuilleton* kind, began to circulate in typewritten copies. In 1973 they even founded their own unofficial publishing series, the so-called Padlock Edition *(Edice Petlice)*, which has reached nearly one hundred titles by the time of of writing.[88] *Petlice* differs from traditional Russian samizdat and the Czechoslovak authors are anxious to point out the difference. Individual items, ranging from 50 to 700 pages, are fully attributed to their authors, signed by them and released for circulation in type-written form, paper-bound, only in a limited number of 'authorised copies'. They are marked on the front page with a warning: 'Further re-typing of the manuscript is explicitly forbidden'. This makes the volumes 'legal' in the sense that they must be regarded as private first drafts, unedited texts circulating among friends and profes-sionally interested members of the public with the aim of soliciting their opinion which the authors might take into account when preparing the manuscripts for proper publication, whenever it may become possible. The authors do not accept that this activity is against the law and although the secret police have confiscated volumes found during house searches, the prosecutors do not appear to have yet found the right paragraph in the Criminal Code to institute pro-ceedings. The 'silenced' writers have also had their works published in translations elsewhere in the world and even won several significant awards. Many of them have given interviews to Western newspapers, radio correspondents and even television stations, although such activity has been not infrequently considered by the authorities as a ground for prosecution. They have also sent protest letters to Western cultural personalities, for example when their manuscripts were con-fiscated. In all, the Czechoslovak literary community, though de-prived of all official outlets, exposed to incredible harassment and chicanery and spoken to by the authorities only through members of the secret police, has remained active both as a group of writers, creating new works of literature and finding a limited audience, and as proponents of liberal ideals with which they identified themselves in the past twenty years. The existence of a dual literary culture in Czechoslovakia is a fact.[89]

Culture is of course more than just the writing and publishing of books, one way or another. Czechoslovakia has for at least two centuries been a country where indigenous cultural achievement comprises a complicated system of creation, mediation and consumption. It has been renowned for its musical life and high standard of theatrical production. People are eager 'consumers' of cultural products and the demand has long acted as a stimulant on the creators and purveyors. Statistics are not a good guide to understanding what is really going on because of their inability to express quality, one of the key indicators in this field of human activity, but they show that people have not stopped reading books, going to the theatre, listening to concerts, visiting exhibitions. Some of the 'normalisation' trends, as reflected in official statistics, can be summarised as follows: the number of weekly and monthly periodicals in the fields of culture and scholarship has registered a decline; in book publishing there was a sharp rise in the number of political titles and a decline in fiction; fine artists were able to arrange fewer exhibitions through their union and fewer people went to see them; more people on the other hand have taken interest in music by way of concert attendances; the number of theatrical performances has remained steady while attendances slightly declined; cinema-going has continued to slacken, perhaps more than the natural trend would warrant; and film-making has been steady, with some forty full-length feature films made every year.

In 1977–78 there was a veritable surfeit of cultural unions' congresses. Not only did every union hold a separate Czech and Slovak congress but the long-delayed formation of joint Czechoslovak unions at last came to fruition. Until then joint affairs, mainly of a formal character anyway, were looked after by coordinating committees. It is not easy to predict how the existence of bi-national unions will foster contact on other than committee level, or at quinquennial congresses, but the federative organisational shape obviously called for this climax to the 'normalisation' effort.

In the end, however, culture is a matter of quality, innovation and identification between the man who creates and the one who receives. Cultural unions are accidental to the process. Even when they assumed the role of protagonists in a movement of spiritual liberalisation in the 1960s, they did so on a plane which was not congeneric with the acutal creation of literary and other art values. The less so can they play the part of begetters of culture today when their main mission lies in the realm of pomp and circumstance. Much of the cultural continuity has been maintained in spite of the hardliners, not because of them. The only chink in the wall of ideological supererogation is in that little place in the sun which the unions and their political patrons have to yield to young newcomers. Therein a ray of hope for the future may be shining through.

215

Religion

As already noted there have been few good reasons why the post-reformist regime should sustain a steady and determined anti-religious and anti-church campaign, other than the self-imposed ideological command. The Jews have been a small, old and politically inactive community for a long time. The Christian churches have on the whole realistically assessed their own strength *vis-à-vis* the successive communist regimes and have refrained from aspiring to more than the Christian values of offering spiritual comfort to those who called for it. Proselytising has been modest and mild, and for twenty years it was the believers who had to go out of their way to obtain pastoral assistance rather than the priests and preachers actively seeking out new flocks. When the 'normalisers' tightened party and state supervision over religious life in the wake of the tolerance of 1968, it could have appeared to some observers as an ostentatious yet temporary gesture in line with the general escalation of ideological vigilance. Live and let live, may soon return as the obvious course for a regime which anyway will have a great deal of worries in other departments, such as the economy, for the smooth functioning of which the services of the believers would be needed. Far from it. It became clear in 1971 and especially in 1972, after the 'ideological' meeting of the party central committee in October, that next to reformism, religion was to constitute a target on which the party activists would once again sharpen their ideological tools.

There were at least three reasons why this should be so. Firstly, in a country like Czechoslovakia it was relatively easy to score ideological triumphs over religion and the churches, unlike in Poland. In combating religion, the 'normalisers' could prove themselves in the eyes of their supervisors to be 'normalising' vehemently, without compounding economic and political problems too much. No great resistance could be expected and no great risks would be run. Neither the churches nor the believers would rise to defend themselves in a way which would put in jeopardy the other objectives of 'normalisation'. Secondly, with the reduction of anti-religious pressure at the time of the Prague Spring, the expectations of some churches and some believers were running higher than previously. Religious and church life did revive somewhat in comparison with the first twenty years of Czechoslovak communism, for example in the number of people who wished their children to receive a modest form of religious instruction, or who preferred to have an ecclesiastical dignitary officiate at the traditional three high points of birth, marriage and death, or who intended to make priesthood their institutionalised vocation. This probably did cause discomfort to the 'normalisers'. In reality, as all indicators testify, the 'religious awakening' of the Prague Spring was more than modest and could only be thought excessive with regard to a deliberately determined low base line, such as had been established in exceedingly oppressive conditions in the first place. The excess was in previous oppression, not in the moderate reaction to it. Thirdly, out of protest and defiance and often for reasons other than faith, a number of people, young among them, adopted some of the outward signs of religious belonging to taunt the authorities who had deprived them of other, secular means of expressing disagreement with the way things were going. Hence the crosses around young people's necks, the large attendance at midnight masses, and performances of church music, and the white weddings.

Thus out of action and counter-action, but very much more the former than the latter, militant atheism has once again entered the scene and has been kept there until the present day. The anti-religious theatre of war has three main battlegrounds: propaganda, restrictive practice and relations with the Vatican.

Propaganda itself has been conducted in three main areas: in institutions (not the least in the communist party itself, against religious or lax members, but primarily in state institutions where upholding of religious views disqualifies people from attaining or retaining responsible positions), in schools (where teachers are duty-bound to perform sustained atheistic work among the pupils), and in the media.

Lest anyone wondered about religious freedom being conceded in the consititution and endorsed by the Czechoslovak government in international documents, the justification of atheistic campaigns was made clear from the start. The issue was one of ideological struggle, itself an 'objective phenomenon', and not interference with the private lives of individuals. Moreover, the party stands for 'scientific' atheism which by definition constitutes 'an objective tool' for the acquisition of knowledge indispensible for social management.

The Department of Scientific Atheism, which had existed at the Institutes of Philosophy of the Czechoslovak and Slovak Academies of Sciences from 1959 to 1967, was revived in Slovakia in March 1971, though not in Prague. From the beginning of 1973 it began to publish a bi-monthly journal called *Ateizm*, intended as a theoretical base from which scientific workers should draw inspiration when encountering 'problems of religion and atheism'. Many contributions, especially in the first issues were translations from the Russian, and even included articles specially written by Russian authors for the Slovak journal. This would indicate a certain paucity of domestic writers willing to tackle the subject, but it should be noted that fraternal assistance was being rendered by Soviet ideologues in a similar fashion to other areas of the class struggle.

'Principles of Scientific-Atheist Education in Schools' were issued by the Czech Ministry of Education in 1972 to spell out six aspects of religion which the teachers were duty bound to combat among their pupils: religion as an idealist look at the world, as an ethical set of directives, as ideology of the inimical class, as a component of man's emotional life, as a cult, and as an institution. Methodological principles of the teacher's requisite behaviour were also enumerated and stress laid on comprehensiveness: teaching and extra-curricular activities as well as the family influence should be harnessed for the struggle. Coercion was, however, ruled out and *ad hoc* campaign-making pronounced ineffective.[90]

According to directives of the Ministry of Culture, dated 30 July 1971 and superseding a previous ordinance of 22 October 1968, all approved churches and religious societies enjoyed the right to instruct children in religious matters, provided it was done in the premises of state schools. (Control is easier.) Both parents have to sign an application form of enrolment. Evidence that school and other authorities discourage one or both parents, and even 'work on them' after they have signed the forms, can be derived even from official press reports. It is more than corroborated by private reports. Only 'state-reliable' priests or other vetted persons can teach religion: priests must do so without pay while lay teachers must be paid by the church in question at no more than Kčs 10 per hour. Only children under the age of 12 can receive religious instruction and the number of periods per week depends on how large a group enrolls in the particular school. If 16 or more children attend, they can have up to two periods a week; a group of nine to 15 gets one hour; five to eight pupils one hour every two weeks; and if only two to four children are admitted, they have to remain content with one hour per month. There are other administrative procedures to observe.[91]

As for the media the campaign started in 1971–72 and reached a new peak in the autumn of 1975. It was widespread, sustained and manifold in the sense that it ranged from anti-religious jokes to attacks on individual priests and the clergy collectively, and to the publication of special issues of scholarly journals with contributions by leading theorists of 'normalisation'. When concern was expressed in the West, *Rudé právo* retorted angrily that to speak about suppression of churches and religion in Czechoslovakia was a malicious lie and, if there were a God, he would have to punish those who disseminated it. Indeed, it was the churches which attacked the socialist system in an effort to bring back the pre-socialist state of inequality in society. If things went as the Catholic Church wished they should, the Czech and Slovak peoples would still be living under feudalism and paying tithes. Taken together the apparatus of all the churches in the country was larger than that of the communist party. But the priests bore no responsibility for the running of the country and could devote all their time to exerting ideological influence on the people. Religion was reactionary and offered false guidance to man.[92]

The brunt of the campaign was borne by the Catholic Church, the largest in the country. (Religious affiliation has not been entered in Czechoslovak censuses, or indeed any personal documents, since the communist takeover, so that the number of believers generally and of members of the individual churches could be only estimated with gross inaccuracy.) The Evangelical (Protestant) Church of Czech Brethren and the Jewish Religious Communities were also not spared, while the Russian Orthodox Church was hardly ever mentioned and the Czechoslovak Church (also known as the Hussite Church) received lenient treatment because of the loyalist attitudes of its leaders. Altogether 18 churches and religious communities are allowed to operate legally in Czechoslovakia, but most are small and not enough in the public eye to warrant exposure.

The war was not one of words alone. A number of restrictive policies have been vigorously applied to contain and diminish religious beliefs among the population. (It goes without saying that as part of the campaign the party exposed and punished its own members who 'had not yet rid themselves of religious prejudice', but believers joining the party could hardly complain about something which had been quite obviously in the statute book.)

Many restrictions were applied to the clergy. A number of priests were arrested and jailed for a variety of reasons, arising from the exercise of pastoral activities. Some Western sources say that about one hundred have suffered this fate. Some of them belonged to the reputed 500 out of the total of some 3,500 Catholic priests who had been banned from performing priestly duties either by not being given the requisite assent on ordination or by having it withdrawn later. As state employees, priests were being retired at the age of 60, the official pensioning-off age, although they wanted to go on serving, not the least because of the general shortage of clergy. A strict *numerus clausus* was in operation at all faculties of theology and students knew that, should they get through the sieve, they would be under constant political supervision and exposed to all kinds of harassment. They still applied in at least treble the numbers that were admitted, even though non-acceptance excluded them from possible entry into another institute of higher learning. One of the Roman Catholic faculties, in Olomouc, re-established in 1968, was phased out by 1973. Table 9 shows the diminishing number of first-year students.

The remaining members of religious orders, mainly in Slovakia, were arbitrarily moved from one place to another, including to what looked like detention centres, and forced to work in menial jobs. No regular monastic life was allowed and neither was admission of

Table 9. Day students in faculties of theology 1966–1977 (A = students total. B = first-year students.)

Year	Catholic Litoměřice A	B	Catholic Bratislava A	B	Catholic Olomouc A	B	Czech Brethren Prague A	B	Evangelical Bratislava A	B	Czechoslovak Prague A	B	Orthodox Prešov A	B
1966–67	83	22	97	26	—	—	43	14	26	8	18	11	28	12
1967–68	112	28	110	26	—	—	49	17	27	7	24	6	25	4
1968–69	237*	10*	184	94	—†	—†	67	23	44	19	53	9	15	3
1969–70	161	29	278	111	120	46	75	22	50	17	50	26	15	4
1970–71	161	44	291	45	118	0	87	17	50	11	56	25	15	4
1971–72	161	39	260	31	117	0	93	19	48	8	55	12	18	3
1972–73	216	26	265	35	83	0	80	10	45	2	70	22	15	5
1973–74	125	26	199	20	42	0	77	14	35	4	52	9	18	3
1974–75	137	25	147	22	—	—	64	11	27	3	46	10	17	4
1975–76	119	16	133	22	—	—	63	13	23	6	35	5	15	4
1976–77	112	22	119	26	—	—	62	15	22	6	27	8	10	4

* including first-year students at Olomouc
† first entrants included in Litoměřice numbers

Source: Statistical Yearbooks, various issues.

novices. Western estimates put the numbers at 1,200 monks and some 5,000 nuns, mostly working in nursing homes for the mentally and physically handicapped and old people's establishments. In 1968 the government stated that there was no valid legal reason why religious orders should not exist, but a great majority of monks and nuns were old survivors of pre-1948 orders.

A virtual ban on the publication of religious literature was imposed and the two religious publishing houses, the Catholic *Caritas* and the Protestant *Kalich* were mainly confined to publishing calendars in which offical state holidays were described at greater length than religious ones. As a special achievement, however, an ecumenical group of translators comprising religious scholars from the three largest churches, the Catholic, the Hussite and the Czech Brethren, had prepared for publication four of the 14 books of the Old Testament and the Four Gospels in one volume. The latter was published at the beginning of 1974. This was the first collective translation of the Holy Scriptures (from the Greek) since the Kralice Bible in the 16th century and the first ever ecumenical translation of the New Testament into Czech.[93] It is not know how widely this edition was sold (or the number of copies) but the momentous achievement received next to no publicity.

Religious periodicals were gradually led to diminish the religious content of their pages and to write up the same secular items as all the other press. Some contributions on religious matters were apparently so heavily edited that the authors decided to abstain. The pro-regime organisation of Catholic clergy, *Pacem in Terris*, virtually took over *Katolické noviny*.

Chief Rabbi Richard Feder died in November 1970, and as his one and only potential successor, trained for the high office at the Rabbinical Seminary in Budapest, remained in the West after the invasion, the Jewish community is without a religious leader. After protests against a press campaign which accused long-dead Jewish leaders of collaboration with the Gestapo and complicity in the murder of rank-and-file Jews in Theresienstadt during the war, the leadership of the Jewish Council in the Czech Lands was forced to resign in 1974 and a more trustworthy chairman was appointed. By 1975 it was estimated that only about 5,000 to 7,000 Jews remained, 1,200 of whom lived in Prague, and practically all nearing the winters of their lives. There had been some 350,000 Jews in pre-war Czechoslovakia where they lived for a thousand years. One of the survivors told a Western visitor: 'I am afraid the Golem has let us down once too often. Like him, we seem to be destined to return to lifeless clay. But what beautiful monuments we are leaving behind!'[94]

The Catholic dioceses in Czechoslovakia suffered badly because episcopal vacancies have remained unfilled. Three bishops died in

1972 and the state consent was withdrawn from another one in the same year. The only Cardinal (Štěpán Trochta) died in 1974 of a stroke after a reputedly provocative and tough visit by a regional official. Other bishoprics had been vacant for a long time and yet others were under the charge of apostolic administrators rather than bishops proper. The situation became desperate and early in 1973 the first accord between the new regime and the Vatican was concluded whereby four appointments were made, two of apostolic administrators and two of resident bishops. All four dignitaries, as all priests, had to take an oath of loyalty to the regime. One of them is an active functionary of *Pacem in Terris* and the other three take part in pro regime activities more sporadically. It seems that the Vatican came rather worse off from the agreement. but it was induced to seek it by the dire state of pastoral hierarchy in Czechoslovakia.

There are fourteen Catholic dioceses in the country: six Roman Catholic episcopal sees in the Czech Lands, six in Slovakia (two of the sees in the Czech Lands are archbishoprics), one Greek Catholic diocese in East Slovakia (vacant since the last bishop died in prison in 1960), and one Old Catholic diocese in North Bohemia (vacant since consent was withdrawn from the resident bishop in 1972). After the death of Cardinal Trochta, nine dioceses were without an incumbent, two had resident bishops and three apostolic administrators.

Several rounds of talks followed between the Holy See and the Czechoslovak Office for Church Affairs. Monsignor Casaroli, the Holy See's 'foreign minister', was in Prague in February 1975. Then the Pope named František Tomášek, the apostolic administrator of Prague (who does not partake of pro-regime activities in *Pacem in Terris* and had in fact been the chairman of the Council Revival movement during the Prague Spring), cardinal *in pectore* in May 1976 and the appointment was announced a year later. Husák even sent a letter of congratulation. (It is not without interest that Document No. 9 issued by the Charter 77 movement in April 1977, just before the announcement of Tomášek's elevation to the curia, concerned infringement of religious beliefs.) Further negotiations with the Vatican, conducted by both parties in confidence, produced an agreement in September 1977 which appears to have been ratified in January 1978 and at the time of writing awaits implementation and clarification. Not all provisions are known at the moment, but it seems that the Vatican is making what it must consider a major concession, possibly in exchange for more episcopal appointments. (Cardinal Tomášek was installed as archbishop of Prague in March 1978.) The concession concerns an issue dating back to 1918 when the Holy See showed little enthusiasm for the secular nature of the newly born Czechoslovak state and the protestant beliefs of its founding father, T. G. Masaryk. The Vatican refused to re-draw the boundaries of some

Czech and practically all Slovak dioceses so as to coincide with the new state's frontiers, and some bishoprics have nominally continued to be under the ecclesiastical suzerainty of apostolic dignitaries in Hungary and Poland. Now a new church province and a new arch-bishopric are to be created in Slovakia, with the seat at Trnava, for the Latin rite dioceses, while the Greek Catholic bishopric in Prešov is to remain independent and directly subordinate to Rome. This could signify a turning point towards a more relaxed state-church relationship, but it is too early to judge possible impact on the other vexed questions affecting the lower reaches of religious life and the clerical profession.

ECONOMIC ADVANCEMENT

A system based on political command has no difficulty in affecting economic changes which require no more than a simple issuance of decrees. It was comparatively safe to effect re-centralisation after 1969 because the hold of the reforms was still weak and because counter-reformism was not a step into the dark; a centralised system had existed in Czechoslovakia before, and was simultaneously in operation in most fraternal countries under Soviet control. Nevertheless, political tension did underlie economic decisions from the start, mainly because of the projected conflict of views within the leadership as to the degree of severity with which 'normalisation' ought to be effected. The intransigents believed that behind economic reforms, no matter how much they were watered down, there lurked the hydra of political counter-revolution. The more moderate conservatives, more aware of the need for economic change and hopeful that Moscow would tolerate a cautious progress in this direction (as it did in Hungary), were confident that a mild economic reform could be kept sufficiently isolated from possible obnoxious repercussions in other fields.

The resolution of the 14th congress stated that 'exceptional importance was being attached to improving and consolidating the system of planned management based on democratic centralism'. In doing this, the party and the state would 'base themselves on principles approved at the January 1965 central committee session as re-affirmed by the central committee in January and December 1970, and on the requirements of economic development, results of measures adopted since April 1969 and experience of fraternal countries, especially the Soviet Union, as postulated at the 24th congress'.[95] In short, the 'years of distortion' were to be taken out of the continuity context which in their stead would be enriched with the centralising measures passed after Husák's accession to power. Lubomír Štrougal, who delivered the main economic address at the 14th congress, made this point clear: 'Basing ourselves on what we have already achieved in the national economy, we can continue with an economic reform purged of the layers of revisionism'.[96]

It was on the basis of this mixture of centralism and hazily defined reform that the government issued guidelines for economic management in August 1971.[97] They reflected predominance of command over initiative. According to them, the central planners were once again made fully responsible for issuing directives and checking on the implementation of obligatory planning indices, foreign trade, wages and prices. Investment activity was also to be controlled from the centre while part of it was to be paid from enterprise and production unit funds. In accordance with the Soviet move towards a middle link of management *(ob"edineniya)*, the guidelines also provided for a three-tier system, investing the intermediate units between enterprises and the centre with wider powers. Such intermediate units have of course always existed, under different names, and the 1968 reform conceived of their continuance as voluntary associations to which the enterprises would cede certain of their own powers should they consider it beneficial. It took over three years to implement the reorganisation of 'production-economic units' under the new emphasis on middle-level administration within an essentially centralised economy. The new scheme came into operation on 1 January 1975.

Adaptation of the wage system took the same length of time. It started with an experiment in 73 enterprises in May 1972 and, compared to the 1968 reform, contained a much greater emphasis on the validity of centrally determined tariffs. The need for differentiation and for a stimulating effect on the basis of achieved results, found reflection in the structuring of central tariffs according to the sector to which they were to apply, the occupational category, the qualification (training) criterion, and performance.

Wholesale prices were to be reorganised so as to bring about their overall reduction by 10·4 per cent as of 1 January 1976. This was to be a major operation involving re-calculation of hundreds of thousands of items and aiming at an even distribution of profit margins. (It is perhaps worth noting that in a self-professed Marxist economy the 'law of the value' ought to be a safe yardstick, reflecting the amount of labour—necessary and surplus—which goes into every item manufactured for sale between state-owned enterprises. In reality the central planners, or price setters, do not even attempt to measure the labour content. Also, wholesale prices in a communist economy differ from those under 'capitalism' in that their effect on retail prices is only tenuous.) In the end the impact of certain dramatic price increases on the world and Comecon markets from 1974 onwards, together with the complexity of the entire operation, led to a delay in the reorganisation of the wholesale price system by a year and the actual overall reduction was only less than a quarter of what it was intended to be.

By the second half of 1974 the success of the initial administrative measures began to wear off, and the perennial problems of a centrally planned economy were seen to reassert themselves. Investments were rising, material inputs would not be curbed, quality of manufactures was below competitive standards, efficiency was low, unsold stocks were piling up, and the foreign trade balance grew worse and worse. The pre-reform plague was back, amplified by adverse terms of foreign trading. A half-hearted attempt was once again made at the close of 1974 to reconcile modernisation demands with the fear of a decentralising reform. A campaign to promote 'rationalisation' was launched, with an emphasis on efficiency criteria for decision-making at all levels. It was in fact a somewhat nebulous search for a reform which would be neither market-orientated nor fully technocratic but in which a limited technocratisation would fit into a commanded framework. It did not produce the expected results.

The entire Czechoslovak economy, fairly complex and advanced, has since then been geared towards compliance with just two basic requirements: to keep the price level of basic commodities down in order to preclude material grievance from acquiring the dimension of a political irritant, and to meet commitments to Comecon undertakings.

Perhaps somewhere along the way which the Czechoslovak economy has covered since the abandonment of the reform, a measure of political leniency towards the ex-reformers and dismissed managers may have been suggested, such as at the central committee session in October 1972 (of which very little was released for public information) and again in November 1974 in connection with the 'rationalisation' campaign, but this move must have run into the implacable opposition on the part of the hardliners and ideologues, because it came to nothing. Many of the designers of the economic reforms were still sweeping the streets and an estimated 40 per cent of 'reform managers' of enterprises had been demoted to positions without authority. Very slowly some of those theoretical economists who remained in the Academy of Sciences and the ministries, as well as the young ones who joined them in the intervening years, have begun to show appreciation of the reformist tenets once again. At the time of writing the inner conflict between differing political attitudes to economic theory and practice has not been resolved. Signals have been received from Prague that economic pressures may lead to personnel upheavals in the high party echelons: scapegoats are being allegedly looked for and replacement cadres are being sized up. It remains to be seen whether any changes along these lines can generate an atmosphere of courage for economic steps, some of which will have to be unpopular while others will have to revert to reformist thought advocated ten and more years ago.

Let us look at some of the problems in greater detail. Throughout the 'normalisation' years global output, a very rough and general indicator, has evolved rather steadily at the same pace as in 1968 and 1969. The average annual growth rate from 1968 to 1975 was 6 per cent; it then dropped to 3·8 per cent in 1976. Created national income (also called NMP, 'net material product') has been growing more slowly than in the 'crisis years' (7·2 per cent in 1968 and 7·3 per cent in 1969), but without deviating either way too sharply. Its average annual rate of 6·1 per cent from 1968 to 1975 however declined to 3·5 per cent in 1976. A preliminary set for 1977 indicates a slight improvement over 1976, with figures for global output and NMP standing between 4 and 5 per cent.

The conclusion is simple: the plans have been on the whole fulfilled, people have not stopped working and producing goods, and the economy has not come to a grinding halt. In spite of the absence of economic reform and, some would say, the unpopularity of the regime's ideology, the Czechoslovak economy has remained an impressive organism in which sufficient strength has been found to sustain quantitative improvement. These general data do not, however, reveal internal tensions and disproportions. Neither is the series automatically boding well for the future. The late 1950s were equally, if not more, impressive before the plunge of the early 1960s. Even so, success is impossible to deny. What should be remembered is that 1968 and 1969 were also successful, and even the traumatic invasion by foreign powers did not produce more than a temporary slackening of growth. By crediting the economy with success after the advent of 'normalisation' one does not necessarily adduce that the success has been due to the 'normalising' practices.

Investment data give cause for concern. After a deliberate slowdown in 1970 and 1971, the increase of monies sunk into investment projects from 1972 to 1975 was much too high. The leaders of Czechoslovak economy appear to have forgotten the accusations which they hurled at the reformers, and indeed their own avowed intentions. At the 14th congress they resolved to keep the ratio between investments and NMP within the 29–30 per cent band. By 1976 they have reached the staggering proportion of 35·5 per cent, and we do not quite know how much more money has been tied in projects outside Czechoslovak territory, for example in developing raw material extraction in the USSR and Poland. Annual rate of increase of investment was 8·1 and 9·7 per cent in 1968–1969, then was brought down to 5·9 and 5·7 per cent in 1970 and 1971, only to start climbing to 8·7 per cent in 1972, 9·2 in 1973 and 9·3 in 1974. In 1975 it levelled off at 8·3 per cent, and was brought down sharply to 3·6 per cent in 1976, the danger signs being obviously too strong to be ignored. Even this adjustment was insufficient to stop the ratio of investment to NMP from climbing another 0·1 per cent to 35·5.

The trend in investment towards 'productive' and 'unproductive' sectors is also instructive. (Services and social spending form the bulk of 'non-productive' investments.) Whereas under the reform plans, the former was to rise more slowly than the latter, the logic of a command economy calls for a reverse ratio. In reality, the Husák regime injected a massive investment dose into the non-productive sector in 1970 while cutting productive investments in the same year substantially (21·1 per cent growth over 1969 in non-productive, and 0·4 per cent in productive investments), evidently to forestall a slump in material standards. In 1971 productive investments grew faster than non-productive ones, but in 1972 the opposite happened. Since 1973 productive investments were consistently higher than non-productive ones, and in 1976, when funds were generally made scarcer for new projects, the saving was almost entirely achieved at the expense of non-productive investments. They grew only by 0·1 per cent over 1975, whereas productive ones increased by 5·0 per cent.

In a country like Czechoslovakia this over-reaching of the investment potential is an unmistakable sign that official bets are being placed on 'extensive' development, such as most economists, reformist and otherwise, have long vowed to terminate in favour of 'intensive' practices. One has to note that project completion time is long, with many painful delays, and that manpower resources are diminishing, so that even the existing capacities can be manned only with difficulty. The shift-working coefficient stands at 1·33 and has been falling for some time, despite desperate efforts to arrest the decline. Productivity per worker is low. As much as a quarter of working hours is allegedly spent not working, according to private accounts. As the leadership was demonstrably aware of all these dangers at the beginning of its reign, and in fact kept the overall investment rate down in 1970 and 1971, one can only deduce that something or someone changed their mind in 1972. Whatever that may have been, the investment policy cannot rank among their economic success stories.

One final point to note: large sums of money have been sunk into the development of coal production in an effort to relieve expenditure on imported oil and gas. The coal sector being 'productive', it obviously accounts for a certain percentage of the growth of investment rates. In 1973 investment into coal mining and processing reached over Kčs 5,100 million against 2,370 million in 1969, and an additional 5,295 million were committed to the production of electricity and heat.

Personal consumption reveals a slow-down of the improvement registered in 1968–69, especially since 1975. The average rate of growth from 1968 to 1974 was 5·7 per cent; in 1975 it fell to 2·7 and in 1976 to 2·6. Expressed in *per capita* terms, the figures were 5·3 per cent from 1968 to 1974, as against 1·9 in 1975 and 1·8 in 1976. Both prices and the cost of living indices confirm the trend.

The highly favourable results in price stability testify to the potential of a centrally managed economy which can divorce wholesale and world prices from domestic retail price levels, at least to a large extent and for a certain period of time. Price fixing is done from the centre which also holds funds needed to subsidise those commodities which it is politically expedient to sell cheaply. The extent of price subsidising in Czechoslovakia has long been staggering, and more recently acquired unbelievable proportions. One can look at this process as a thoroughly uneconomical way of running a national

Table 10. Price subsidies 1967–1976 (in million Kčs)

Year	Price subsidies	Intervention, price differences, discounts
1967	7,481	2,611
1968	3,436	2,446
1969	8,380	4,463
1970	8,725	4,271
1971	9,789	4,468
1972	8,739	4,974
1973	7,249	8,349
1974	7,636	8,744
1975	16,604	8,733
1976	17,862	9,064

Source: Statistical Yearbook 1977, p. 144.

:onomy no matter whether one accepts the supply-demand principle
r the Marxian notion that prices express roughly the value of things.
ut then one can also argue that in being able to afford such subsidies,
nd in being ready to grant them, the regime shows its truly popular
naracter. In the last instance of course it is not the party's money, or
ne government's, that is used for the purpose. Let us look at the two
ems which comprise price subsidies in Czechoslovak statistics, the
rst directly and the second through *ad hoc* intervention. Both
olumns in Table 10 include an unknown amount of subsidies to inter-
nterprise and foreign trading, and have to be regarded as indicative of
ne size and the trend. The jump in 1975 in the first column must be
elated to the dramatic increase in the cost of oil imports.

It should be clear now why the Western criteria of measuring
nflation along the wage-price spiral simply do not apply to an
conomy run on these lines. Using money obtained from the people
irectly and indirectly, the state soaks up pressure which higher
roduction costs or higher prices of imported raw materials exert on
omestic retail prices. Neither are prices forced up by trade union
ressure for higher wages. First of all, it is not within the unions'
emit to do such a thing, their main assignment being to make
vorkers work harder and to dispense to them some fringe benefits
ı return. Secondly, wages are fixed centrally and there could be only
ne bargaining table for the whole of the country, should such a state
f affairs be allowed. In 1968 this was how the wage-bargaining
·rocess was to be inaugurated. The government sees to it that wages
nd monetary incomes in general (on which it has much more direct
nfluence than in any 'capitalist' country) rise only to the point where

229

the annual incremental sum total can be matched with availabl
commodities.

Thus a determined effort to keep down the prices of basi
commodities, particularly food, and to keep the goods themselves i
adequate, if unimaginative, supply has produced satisfactory results s
far. The retail price level (goods and services) increased by 1·1 per cen
in 1968, 4·2 per cent in 1969, 1·7 per cent in 1970, whereupon it fell b
0·3 per cent in 1971 and again in 1972, before beginning to climl
slowly by 0·3 per cent in 1973, 0·5 in 1974, 0·6 in 1975 and 0·8 in 1976
In 1976 the overall price level was 8·9 per cent higher than in 1967
Over the same period the cost of living of non-farmers' household
increased by 7·9 per cent.

Nevertheless, the government has not been fully successful in it
endeavour to match availability of goods with money in people'
pockets. A large amount of unsatisfied purchasing power has evolve
in the form of savings. Panic buying is possible and projects itself int
the funds held by the savings banks, as it did several times during th
'normalisation' period. It would be of course wrong to interpre
savings as no more than a threat to the government's effort a
preserving an equilibrium of the market. Money in savings bank
includes sums set aside for purchases of more expensive items an
holidays, a perfectly natural thing in a society that makes do largel
without hire-purchase and other forms of credit buying. Also there i
the healthy trend of new strata of the population reaching the saving
age and learning how to manage their own financial affairs. At the sam
time the savings levels do show that saturation points in the equipmen
of the population with various durable commodities and services ar
being reached and that the logical progression will be (or already is
towards a wider range of such values which the present system may no
be able to provide readily. Figuratively speaking, the stage of washin
machines, refrigerators, local cars and holidays in Bulgaria has bee
attained, and the era of automatic washing machines, freezers
Western cars and Western holidays is on the horizon.

The total sum of money held by savings banks for members of th
public amounted to Kčs 126,110 million in 1976.[98] This is a vas
amount which, under the volatile conditions of an artificially main
tained equilibrium between supply of goods and demand for them
would wreak havoc on the economy should it be thrown onto th
market. That danger point is, however, not the main headache becaus
it could always be pre-empted by the imposition of a freeze or
'currency reform'. What is more pertinent is the steady pressure on th
supply of goods and services which this pile of unspent money exerts
In socialism it cannot be invested into business privately and it i
therefore always on call. It cannot be easily siphoned off because th
economy does not seem able to produce a sufficient amount o

desirable exchange values. An all-round price rise of sufficient magnitude appears unthinkable for political reasons.[99] So, when the price of coffee is raised by 50 per cent, as it was in 1977, the demand for coffee does not really diminish (or soon picks up again) because people simply dip into their savings and keep drinking the dearer stuff—which still has to be imported for hard currency. In other words, the fine tuning of the economy through slight and selective price adjustments is rendered less effective by the presence of the saved money mountain.

But the price level does rise, and just about every visitor to or from Czechoslovakia can confirm it, despite statistics and official assurances. Some goods have been made dearer officially and fairly openly, such as gold, furs, petrol, coffee, chocolates, spare parts for cars, building materials and others. Some prices have been creeping up with minimum publicity: fruit in 1976 was 23 per cent and vegetables 38 per cent dearer than in 1967.[110] Furniture has become appreciably more expensive and even some babywear, the pride of price setters as an example of social policy reflected in retail trade, has grown in price considerably. Services and eating out are dearer. Often the quality standard is lowered for the sake of keeping the price down (water content in butter) or, still more often, a new product is introduced at a higher price on account of sometimes barely discernible improvement while the old one quietly disappears from the shops. Finally and perhaps most importantly, both persistent and erratic shortages and bottlenecks have given rise to the emergence of a 'second market', never so highly developed according to eye witnesses as during the 'normalisation' period. This is the sphere of tit-for-tat services, under the counter sales of coveted items, bribery in kind and in cash, an all-pervasive *modus operandi* in which prices are higher, commodities better, services prompter and even the impossible becomes possible. Unavailable medicines, recommendations for the child's admission to a secondary school, speedy repair of a cracked toilet, allocation of a room in the old people's home for aging granny, spa recreation vouchers—you name it and you can have it, for money or in return for another service which you yourself can offer. A man writes from Prague:

> 'Never has this "second market" combined with corruption been so widespread as during the past eight years. Today even a member of the government will take a bribe, and so will a party official who holds power, and a university professor no less than the sales and purchasing managers, medical doctors and shop assistants. They will take money in order to be able to bribe others. They will take money because their superiors do the same. They will take money in order to be able to pass it on to their superiors in exchange for their favours'.[101]

Table 11. Selected agricultural indices 1968–1977 (million tonnes)

Item	1968	1969	1970	1971	1972	1973	1974	1975	1976	1977
Harvest of:										
cereals	6·9	7·4	6·7	8·2	8·0	9·0	9·8	8·4	8·6 ⎫	
maize	0·4	0·5	0·5	0·5	0·6	0·6	0·6	0·8	0·5 ⎬ 10·4	
potatoes	6·5	5·2	4·8	4·6	5·0	5·0	4·5	3·5	4·2	3·8
sugar-beet	8·1	5·8	6·6	5·8	6·9	6·1	8·2	7·7	5·2	8·3
fodder (root fodder and hays)	14·2	13·2	14·1	12·4	14·1	12·3	13·4	13·2	10·6	n.a.
Meat on the hoof	1·275	1·211	1·234	1·305	1·370	1·413	1·489	1·538	1·398	1·462

Source: Statistical Yearbooks, various issues. Figures for 1977 from *Rudé právo* 27/1/78, p. 3.

It would therefore seem that lower prices are being maintained at a price, such as is paid when human character is going awry. At the same time it is true that the basic needs cost little more today than they did in 1970. The difficulty may be in defining what is basic. Expectations have risen beyond bread and butter.

Czechoslovak agriculture is a success story without doubt; it has been so since 1966, and in the process it has offered invaluable assistance to the 'normalisers' who cannot really claim, although they do, that the success is theirs. Feeding of the population has become less of a problem, to the point where imports of both grain and meat could be substantially reduced and 'self-sufficiency' is the order of the day. Money thus saved comes in handy when every heller spent abroad must be counted twice. Weather has had less influence than previously, and the seasonally caused weaker harvest in 1972 did not lead to great problems. In 1977 bad weather did not stop a record crop from being brought in, except that the moisture content was high. Not everything is rosy, however, and as Table 11 shows the crops of maize have stagnated and that of potatoes, sugar-beet and fodder is declining. In 1976 enormous quantities of feedstock had to be imported at great expense, including 750,000 tonnes of maize from the United States.

It can be argued that the common denominator of all the causes that led to good agricultural results is the party leadership's realisation—in the middle of the 1960s—that farmers are best left alone to decide what to do and·how to do it, once industry was allowed to produce the goods they need and they were allowed to go out and buy them. The overseers of ideological rigidity in the 1970s could not have been unconcerned that one field of human activity had been permitted to extricate itself somewhat from the minute surveillance imposed by the party on just about everything and everybody else. Hence the resolution of the party central committee secretariat, published in January 1974, which enjoined all communists to step up their influence 'on the processes through which our agriculture is passing'.[102] Good results were said to derive from correct party policies but it was still necessary to strengthen party organisation and control in and over farming. Party branches throughout the agricultural sector must be reinforced as regards their unity, capacity for action, ideological standard and direct subordination to district committees. Indeed, more party branches must be set up in order to implement the leading role comprehensively over 'fulfilment of tasks, . . . accomplishment of party policies . . . and influence on life in villages'. Political help must be despatched to cooperative farms that had shown political weaknesses, such as in admitting new members. Some districts had been slipping away from party control where the farms themselves had set up coordinating councils on economic and organisational rather than party-political lines. This must be remedied by the establishment of party cells in these councils, more regular party meetings and a general drive towards party-mindedness.

Fortunately for Czechoslovak agriculture and for the 'normalisers' themselves, this invitation to interference has not led to much. The campaign has been allowed to peter out without causing great damage, but more was in store.

The success of collectivised farming was too good not to be capitalised on and new agricultural taxes were introduced with effect from 1 January 1975 with the avowed pupose of pressing for higher efficiency and reduced cost while evening out differences in profitability between farms operating in different natural conditions. Profit became the taxable base instead of gross production. One of the impositions was a punitive tax of 50 per cent on 'rewards' (in fact wages) which the farm might pay to its members in excess of a government-set limit. It was stated before the introduction of the new law (just one law covering all kinds of taxation) that about half the collective farms would pay the same or lower taxes under its stipulations.[103] Quite evidently the other half was paying considerably more as shown from the following sequence of agricultural tax proceeds (in million Kčs):

1968 . . . 1,209	1973 . . . 2,335	1975 . . . 4,747
1969 . . . 1,162	1974 . . . 2,525	1976 . . . 3,100[104]

It had also been promised that any higher proceeds would be used towards agricultural investment or to pay for bonuses to less favourably situated farms.

Another parallel development which can only be described as opportunist was the new collectivisation drive against the few remaining private farmers, especially in the mountainous regions of East Slovakia. Czechoslovak agriculture had long been collectivised: in 1967 only 695,000 hectares of the total agricultural acreage of 7,132,000 hectares were in private hands, including 454,000 in Slovakia. A slight increase in private holdings occurred in 1968 and 1969 not because of a flight of members from cooperative farms but because new strips of land were allowed to be added to some existing private farms. Then the ideological eager beavers started a campaign in the second half of 1971; it probably originated with orthodox party functionaries in East Slovak districts after they had reclaimed their offices from ousted reformers. (East Slovakia is Vasil Bilak's home ground.) It was all done the old way, including quotas of farmers to be collectivised being cited at party conferences, except that this time no resistance was on record. The people involved were mostly old and ailing, they knew that they were beaten once the idea got officially under way. (A large percentage were probably Ruthenes.) And so in the summer of 1972 *Rudé právo* could already report that in many villages the peasants needed little persuasion. Some even voluntarily requested permission to start a cooperative undertaking. It was left to *Tribuna* to provide the ideological charm. The paper wrote that in fact further collectivisation would not bring the state any benefit because private farmers had not kept their farms well and new additions would only cause headaches to the cooperatives which took them over. No cooperative farmer would use the scythe or horses to plough up and reap grain in inaccessible and difficult fields as the private farmers did. But the private farmers had been taking advantage of all the revolutionary achievements of the working class without accepting the basic principle of socialism, namely collectivisation of the means of production. Society could not go on giving benefits to citizens who were only interested in socialism insofar as it rendered them social advantage.[105]

Whatever the real reason, the number of private farmers in the country as a whole decreased from 147,000 in 1969 to 92,000 in 1972 and 59,000 in 1974 (the last figure available). The campaign must have affected the Czech Lands as well without much public notice because there the numbers went down from 39,000 in 1969 to 28,000 in 1972 and 17,000 in 1974, while in Slovakia the trend was from 108,000 to 64,000 and 42,000. We have a full run of figures for private agricultural and arable acreages (the latter as part of the former) which shows a decline from 705,000 hectares in 1969 to 367,000 in 1976 in agricultural land, and from 339,000 hectares in 1969 to 146,000 in 1976 in arable land. It should be noted that only 48 per cent of land held by private farmers in 1969 was suitable for sowing, and that this percentage declined to 40 per cent in 1976; the organisers of the drive were evidently more interested in the richer among the poor.[106]

The irrepressible desire to follow dogmatic precepts against the run of things came to a head at the end of 1975 with the passing by the Federal Assembly of two acts, both with effect from 1 January 1976, on cooperative agriculture and on transfer of land between cooperative and state sectors.[107] The first one strengthened still further the powers of the state over matters which hitherto had been at least to some extent in the hands of the cooperatives. Thus the government was given authority to lay down principles of intra-cooperative financing, including distribution of proceeds and other incomes. Cooperative farms became less free to initiate new lines of economic activity and to set up joint undertakings with other cooperatives. The Cooperative Farmworkers' Union, surviving since 1968 without much meaningful activity or impact, was completely bypassed by the law. The law on land transfers facilitated takeover of cooperatively tilled land by state farms.

As other official sources testify, such as articles in law journals and

235

Table 12. Foreign trade balance 1967–1976 (in million Kčs at frontier)

Partner	1967	1968	1969	1970	1971	1972	1973	1974	1975	1976
Overall	1,326	−517	182	700	1,225	1,676	−483	−2,761	−4,065	−3,859
Comecon	470	−1,065	−1,060	688	869	1,465	366	−874	−2,243	−837
USSR	85	−203	139	92	−251	795	451	261	−889	−534
Western advanced	19	−555	−123	−359	−1,052	−809	−1,376	−2,300	−3,244	−4,461
Developing	429	673	883	833	1,238	917	325	338	1,200	1,007

Sources: Statistical Yearbooks, various issues. Figures vary slightly in other sources, e.g. Zahraniční obchod No. 1/1974, pp. 8–11 gives trade balance with Comecon as +820 in 1971 and +1,440 in 1972.

speeches by state agricultural administrators, the intention of the government is to bring about the ultimate ideological feat of ending the double-line ownership status in agriculture by way of changing all cooperatives into state farms, possibly to be called 'all-people farms'. Czechoslovakia may be aiming to becoming the first socialist country in the world to accomplish this final solution.

The Law on Cooperative Agriculture mentions in the preamble the process whereby 'the two forms of socialist ownership in agriculture are gradually coming closer together' and a high government official was quite explicit on this score: the cooperative and the state ownership are in the process of transformation into all people's ownership. Absolute cooperative ownership does not exist in Czechoslovakia anyway. Cooperative farms have already been assimilated into the system of central planning, including command over their structures, supplier-customer relations, prices and wages. They do not have freedom in conducting economic transactions either with each other or with the state-owned sector.[108]

It will be interesting to observe whether *étatisation* of Czechoslovak agriculture in the 1980s by way of industrialisation and erosion of the remnants of cooperative enterprise can be accomplished more smoothly than its collectivisation in the 1950s.

Foreign trade has been a problem from the start of 'normalisation'; from 1974 it has become a nightmare. Czechoslovakia must import vast quantities of raw materials which she does not have, above all oil, iron ore and non-ferrous metals. She does so almost exclusively from the USSR. From 1975 even this good friend has had to charge higher prices and issue warnings that in future it could not be relied on to continue increasing supplies. The goods which Czechoslovakia manufactures are no longer of sufficient quality to be automatically accepted throughout Comecon as they were in the 1950s and a good part of the 1960s. The less so are they competitive enough to earn hard currency in Western markets, such as would enable Czechoslovakia to buy all the desired modern machinery there or even that part of oil which she needs but the USSR potentially cannot provide. The only consistently positive balance of trade occurs with the developing countries where it is suspected, however, that a great deal of exporting is done on long-term low-interest credit and may in fact entail a large proportion attributable to arms sales.

From 1973 Czechoslovakia has been running an overall trade deficit, from 1974 it has had a deficit in trade with the Comecon, and from 1975 with the USSR. With advanced 'capitalist' countries the sequence of deficits extends back to 1968. The 'normalisation' years have shown a number of variations some of which probably conceal small and interesting mysteries, but for our purpose we shall confine Table 12 to enumerating the overall balance and the balances with the four main groups of countries: Comecon (including USSR); Soviet Union in a separate line; advanced Western countries; and developing countries.

According to the Deutsche Bank[109] Czechoslovakia's debt in hard currency with Western countries has reached US$ 1,700 million at the end of 1976 which, measured by the mean official exchange rate of Kčs 5·77 to the dollar represented Kčs 9,809 million. This was less than any other Comecon country. (Bulgaria $2,400, GDR $5,500, Hungary $2,500, Poland $11,000, Romania $2,700 and USSR $14,000, all in millions. For 1977 the debt is likely to have increased by $6,000–8,000 for the Comecon as a whole.)

Oil prices are obviously the biggest single factor causing the unfavourable balance, but considering the amount Czechoslovakia has to import (there are virtually no domestic deposits), the deficit with the USSR since it started to charge more is not so great. The inability to step up export production dramatically (even to the Comecon area) must count as another major factor. The chronic inability to break into the Western markets compounds the problem still further. The increase in Czechoslovakia's oil bill can be seen from Table 13.

Price per tonne increased by 91·03 per cent in 1975 and another 7·96 per cent in 1976, but because of rising deliveries Czechoslovakia's oil bill in 1976 was 135·47 per cent higher than just two years earlier. The fact that the oil price hike contributed most to the country's trade deficit is obvious. It is equally obvious that Czechoslovakia would have to import oil and pay more for it even with a reformed economy. In fact, it might have then had to pay even more, because some oil would probably be imported from other sources, and the Soviet price is still considerably lower than the current Western price. On the other hand, the exporting capacity of Czechoslovak industry would almost certainly have been higher after a few years of the stimulating influence of an enterprise-based system. A conjecture as to how the increased earnings could match higher expenditure would, however, not be in order here.

Taking into account all that has been said about economic developments in the past eight years, the fact remains that the 'normalising' leadership has so far been able to keep certain priorities which benefit the ordinary man in the street. In addition to stable prices of basic commodities and a steady growth of real incomes, a number of social measures were enacted and implemented. Already in September 1971 maternity and childbirth allowances were raised as were pensions for some categories. As from 1 January 1973 family allowances were increased generally and so was supplementary assistance to invalid children. On 1 April of the same year a scheme of low-interest state loans to newlyweds was enacted whereby a portion of the loan is deducted from the repayment plan on the birth of each child. From

Table 13. Import of oil from the USSR and prices paid 1970–1976

Year	Amount of crude imported (tonnes)	Total amount paid (Kčs)	Price per tonne (Kčs)
1970	9,402,000	1,150,106,000	122·32
1973	13,046,000	1,649,173,000	126·41
1974	14,291,000	1,801,518,000	126·06
1975	15,503,000	3,733,551,000	240·82
1976	16,316,000	4,242,080,000	259·99

Sources: Columns 2 and 3 from *Statistical Yearbooks*, various issues. Price per tonne calculated from this data.

January 1976 most old-age pensions were increased and otherwise improved (e.g. discontinuation of taxation). Parity of old-age benefits was introduced between wage-earners and cooperative farmers. The average increases of an old-age pension amounted to 10 per cent. From 1 January 1976 there is full equality between wage-earners and cooperative farmers in health insurance benefits.

All in all, the 'normalising' regime has not however succeeded in constructing a healthy, harmonious and forward-looking economy. Partly because of its own dislike of innovation parallelled by the commission of sins long known to plague centralised economies and partly as a result of international circumstances beyond its control, a number of structural and conceptual problems still await solution as they did in the 1960s. These may generate pressures for a more imaginative and radical set of reform measures than have been allowed so far. The present situation is almost uncannily reminiscent of the late 1950s, just before the slump which compelled even the timid and the diehard to show a little green light to innovation.

At the same time, the leadership has abided by its promises to make the lot of the people materially better. Measured by bread alone, the Czechoslovak citizen is better off now than he was ten years ago. If there is grumbling, then it is because expectations are higher, not because past living standards were. Nevertheless, it is against expectations and international comparisons that governments and populations evaluate their material predicaments in these modern times.

A Czechoslovak citizen is reasonably satisfied with his material standing and cares little for what the economitsts, or some of them, see as dangerous tensions and signals inside the economic mechanism. He has, relatively, enough money, and he does not have to work too hard to earn it. He is assured of his job as long as he does not show deviation from the official political line. He knows that for his money he can buy relatively good food and adequate merchandise, but he is not happy about the narrow choice, shortages, growing prices of other than the most basic things, and he has reason to complain about inadequate housing and unavailability of more adventurous foreign holidays. He knows that next to the state-owned and controlled market there is escape into a tolerated semi-private market. And he is grateful for the chance to enjoy himself in his recreation hut, by going for sports and by consuming light entertainment. A reasonably well fed and clad citizen, devoid of political aspiration and interest, is the product of economic 'normalisation'.

SOCIAL POLICIES AND PROBLEMS

In 1970 a political alarm sounded: the country was getting older! What the demographers had known for long, became a political issue and a matter on which the leadership's care for the national welfare could be measured. Due to low natural increments of the population during the war years, reflected in smaller numbers of women in childbearing age, and the general trend in modern families to remain small, fewer children were being born while the post-productive age groups were growing. The nadir was in fact reached in 1968 with 213,807 live births, 153,271 deaths and 60,536 natural increase, i.e. 4·2 per thousand. The average family had 1·9 children. The pre-productive age bracket in that year (children aged 0–14) comprised 3·4 million persons, while the number of people in retirement age (women over 55 and men over 60) stood at 2·8 million. The size of the post-invasion emigration outflow must have sunk home, no less than the realisation that the economic system, newly embarked on after the abandonment of the reforms, with its reliance on 'extensive' elements of development, would not be getting a regular supply of new manpower which its functioning required so badly. The problem was real enough and any government would have to tackle it, although the sense of urgency might have been less dramatically presented and the long-term prospects would be seen in a less alarming light. Also, the progress towards a solution would probably lie elsewhere. The official policy in all communist countries within the Soviet orbit (in contrast to China) has, however, always been to present a high birthrate as a national achievement, a thing to be proud of. The virtues of motherhood in general and of large families in particular have always been extolled, and the reluctance of urban couples to have more than one or two children has been frowned on. Now, in the 1970s, a sequence of determined and expensive social measures has been adopted with the declared aim of arresting the unfavourable trend. When this happened, the success got first-class publicity. Political officials and demographers gave credit to the regime's pro-natality policy.

Demographers will know how difficult it is to identify a single cause of what in fact is influenced by several factors. Without casting aspersion on the social policy of the 'normalisers', it must be said that the span of growing birth-rate from 1969 to 1974, with the levelling off figures for 1975–77, has an uncanny resemblance to the period from 1946 to 1956. Most children are born to mothers in the 20–24 age group, more particularly around the age of 23. This tallies exactly. About 140,000 girls were born in 1946, and about 106,000 children were born in 1969 to mothers aged 20–24. In 1953 the peak was passed

Table 14. Selected birth-rate indicators 1946–1958 and 1968–1977
Live births. Natural increment per thousand.

Year	Number of girls born		Natural increment (boys & girls)
1946	est.	139,069	8·6
1947	est.	142,491	12·1
1948	est.	139,889	11·9
1949		133,932	10·5
1950		138,873	11·8
1951		138,552	11·4
1952		135,749	11·6
1953		131,441	10·7
1954		129,158	10·2
1955		128,450	10·7
1956		127,471	10·2
1957		122,047	8·8
1958		114,338	8·1

Year	Number of children born to mothers aged 20–24		Number of children born to all mothers	Natural increment (boys & girls)
1968		101,667	213,807	4·2
1969		106,287	222,934	4·3
1970		110,236	228,531	4·3
1971		113,393	237,242	5·0
1972		119,274	251,455	6·3
1973		127,457	274,703	7·3
1974		133,568	291,367	8·1
1975	est.	130,204	289,342	8·0
1976	est.	129,210	287,134	7·8
1977	est.	126,900	282,000	7·3

Sources: Statistická příručka ČSR 1948; Statistical Yearbooks, various issues from 1957 to 1977. Natural increment for 1977 calculated from preliminary reports in Rudé právo, 27/1/1978, p. 3. Breakdown by sex for 1946–48 and by mothers' age for 1975–77 is not available and has been extrapolated from percentages and their conversion in absolute figures.

(with some vacillation in previous years) and in 1975 the same downward movement occurred in the more recent trend. If this correlation is correct, the years 1980 and 1981 should witness a more substantial drop in the birth-rate, notwithstanding the social policy of the day. Let it be understood that this argument does not disparage social measures which almost certainly help offset a number of factors militating in a modern urban society against child-bearing and genuinely raise the living standards of many families. The conclusion does, however, go counter to the claim that social policy was the primary cause of the high birth-rate in the 1970s. The trend after all began in 1969, not in 1970 when the first of these measures was adopted. Let us compare notes in Table 14.

Czechoslovak demographic experts were of course aware of the boost which the strong fertility years 1947–1956 provided for the current birth-rate and the view was expressed that the number of live births should eventually stabilise at around 250,000. It is difficult to project this static estimate into the future as it would represent a birth-rate sliding down as the population grows, and a fairly rapid decline in the natural population increment as the number of deaths increases.

The number of marriages has been increasing since 1967, with a particularly high jump in 1972 and then again in 1973, but a tailing off after that. This is also partly due to more people reaching the age in which marriages are mostly made, and partly to the financial rewards granted to newlyweds by the state. In Table 15 the figures are

Table 15. Marriages and divorces 1967–1977

Year	Marriages	Divorces	Divorces per 100 marriages
1967	119,896	19,889	16·6
1968	122,947	21,641	17·6
1969	125,285	23,936	19·1
1970	126,585	24,936	19·7
1971	129,952	28,074	21·6
1972	135,108	26,582	19·7
1973	141,288	29,458	20·8
1974	140,437	30,415	21·6
1975	141,045	32,308	22·9
1976	138,876	31,561	22·7
1977	138,000	32,500	23·6

Sources: Statistical Yearbooks, various issues. Figures for 1977 are preliminary and the rate has been calculated from approximates as given in *Rudé právo*, 27/1/1978, p. 3.

juxtaposed with the number of divorces and the rate of divorces per 100 marriages.

According to a law of 1957, termination of pregnancy had been relatively easy and legal. Abortion figures reached their peak in 1969 (127,232 against 222,934 live births) and then began to decrease in number due, among other things, to the adverse social climate. The government stepped in to speed up the anti-abortion tendency in July 1973 when the 1957 law was amended to restrict the grounds on which permission for an abortion could be obtained. The lowest number was recorded in 1973 (111,465) whereupon it rose again slightly.

Government assistance to children, mothers and families, as already mentioned, has been deliberate and massive. Whatever the reasons for it, if I were to choose the one aspect of Mr Husák's governance which appeals to me most, this would be it. Not everything is without hiccups and the process of rearing children in Czechoslovakia does not consist of delights only, but the size of financial support given from public funds can be the envy of every country in the world. It is a matter of regret that the 'normalisation' record cannot be measured on accomplishments of this nature alone. Historically speaking, the discrepancy between progress in society's care for mother and child and the retention of dictatorial political and ideological practices is surely not unavoidable. Compared with the vindictiveness of the purges, the devastation of Czech literary life, the *Gleichschaltung* of education, the persecution of religious people, the eradication of free speech and the chicanery of dissidents, the material benefits lavished on the family looked as if they came from a different world. It should be noted, however, that progressive social legislation has always been Czechoslovakia's strong point, even if it was commensurate with the determinants of each particular period, and that communist governments before the present one had a largely good record on this score. The reformers were also equally dedicated to pursuing social policies. The attainments of the period of 'normalisation' are therefore not surprising on account of their innovation, but rather their extent.

Social measures in this field can be divided into four categories. *First*, there exist direct financial grants linked to prospective, actual and effected child-birth. Maternity leave is of 26 week's duration on 90 per cent average pay. (75 per cent of women in Czechoslovakia are in gainful employment.) A balancing contribution compensates prospective mothers for lower earnings while at work during pregnancy. On giving birth, the mother receives a lump sum about equal to an average montly wage in 1971 when the allowance was fixed at Kčs 2,000, double of what it had been before, and about 85 per cent of the average wage in 1976. (The average wage of employed women is about one-third lower than men's.) Family allowances, already fairly high, were increased as of 1 January 1973 with a steeper progression for second and subsequent children, and women caring for two or more children below the age of two receive a special allowance of Kčs 500 per month. Special support is also due to parents who look after children that are ill for a long time. *Secondly*, a range of measures provides for direct assistance to other than 'ordinary' families, e.g. with a disabled child, single-parent, fostered, neglected and orphaned children. *Thirdly*, indirect benefits accrue to all families with children either across the board or depending on parental income. Thus there are deductions from the payroll tax and from rents; caring for women in maternity hospitals and for children in infant-care institutions is free; public transport fares for children (also school-going) are low; and subsidies go towards nurseries, kindergartens, school meals and prices of children's clothing and footwear. *Finally*, as already mentioned, from 1 April 1974 low interest loans to newly married couples allow them to pay for the purchase of a flat or furniture. Of the borrowed sum, Kčs 2,000 is written off after the birth of the first child and another Kčs 4,000 for every subsequent child that reaches the age of one year. Theoretically, the highest borrowable sum of Kčs 30,000 could be entirely written off if eight children were born in quick succession, discounting interest. To all this must be added outlays for expanding paediatric health services and investment into pre-school and school facilities.

It seemed that the growing number of children caught some of the state-owned industries and planning organs by surprise, which it should not have done in a planned economy and if the social campaign was as intentioned as it was presented. Soon complaints were heard, and they persisted, about 'temporary difficulties'. Maternity hospitals were said not to be able to cope with the large intakes, and vacancies in crèches and kindergartens were insufficient so that tens of thousands of applications had to be turned down.[110] National committees and some enterprises were lax in building up new facilities or expanding existing ones. Manufacture and marketing of an adequate supply of children's clothes and footwear, beds, cots, carriages and some items of baby food did not keep up with demand and thus made the new mothers' lives more difficult.

Lack of housing for newly founded families has been and still is a perennial problem. As many new marriages were being concluded as there were new flats commissioned for use, and of course, far from all of these could be allocated to young couples. Simple replacement of decaying houses swallowed up a large portion of the increase. The housing situation, while improving slowly, is near disaster point. There is no free market in housing and families wait for years to have a dwelling allocated to them. Only 'social cases' receive housing free (but then have to pay rent), while a growing proportion have to pay considerable sums which still do not obviate long waiting lists. Neither is the floor space per person improving fast enough. As an example, 138,876 new marriages were concluded and 138,802 new flats built in 1976. Of the latter figure 28,225 flats (or 'dwelling units'; most housing is in flats, but there is growing 'individual construction' of family houses in the country) had to be used to replace old flats. An average new flat had 2·2 rooms (i.e. all rooms other than kitchen, bath and indirectly lit small corridors) and the surface area of 39·3 square metres. New flats are well appointed: all are of course connected to the electricity mains, 81 per cent (in 1976) had gas, 99·9 per cent running hot water, 99·6 per cent central heating (from district thermal plants), and 95·7 per cent were in houses with communal laundry rooms. All flats in Czechoslovakia have been double-glazed for many decades if not a century and more. But there is a shortage of housing and over-crowding; many new families have to live with their parents.

The improving population trend has had a serious effect on employment. Women make up nearly 48 per cent of the total labour force, but in 1974 over 300,000 were absent from work because of maternity leave. If they wanted to take up gainful employment again (which they are guaranteed to be able to do, in the same job which they left when going on maternity leave), they had to place their children in some kind of institution and there they would run into the problem of few vacancies. The state is as interested to have women in work as they are themselves to supplement family income, and perhaps more. This problem relates to the wider issue of manpower.

Tautness in the manpower 'market' has been caused by a variety of developments. There are fewer young people in the age of first employment from 15 to 19, because of lower birthrates in the second half of the 1950s, and this trend will continue at least until the 'baby boom' of the 1970s begins to project itself in the latter part of the 1980s. The transfer of village population into industrial employments has all but ended; only a trickle can still be expected from that quarter. Practically all employable women already hold jobs. Despite efforts to the contrary, the administrative range of job opportunities has grown at the expense of industrial workers' jobs. The type of economic expansion through investment into new capacities which was chosen by the 'normalising' regime because of the short-term success it promised and for fear of a new reformist upsurge, has meant unceasing pressure for additional manpower from practically all branches of industry. It is common knowledge, though only indirectly reflected in statistics (such as in the amount of shift working), that under-utilisation of working hours perhaps by as much as one-fourth, has come to be regarded as a kind of fringe benefit by the workforce, a part of the social contract between government and population, which is being criticised but cannot be removed. Finally, compulsory military

Table 16. Selected manpower indicators 1968–1976

Item	1968	1970	1972	1974	1976
Age group 15–19					
in thousand persons	1,297	1,282	1,247	1,178	1,096
in % of population in productive age	16·4	15·7	15·0	13·9	12·8
Women at work					
in thousand persons	3,141*	3,286*	3,145†	3,199†	3,209†
annual balance in thousand	+78	+75	+54	+30	−5‡
Shift coefficient§	1·360	1·351	1·337	1·329	1·323
Number of foreign workers in thousand persons	n.a.	15	17	22	17

Source: Statistical Yearbooks, various issues
* These figures include women holding jobs but temporarily absent on maternity leave
† These figures do not include women temporarily absent on maternity leave
‡ 5,000 fewer than at the end of 1975
§ As against possible three shifts per day

247

Table 17. Patients in psychiatric wards 1967–1976

1967	1968	1969	1970	1971	1972	1973	1974	1975	1976
36,370	36,367	36,318	40,226	40,741	41,333	42,159	42,573	42,758	44,484

Source: Statistical Yearbooks, various issues.

Table 18. Suicides 1967–1974 (More recent data not available)

Item	1967	1968	1969	1970	1971	1972	1973	1974
Completed suicides	3,415	3,516	3,350	3,627	3,486	3,567	3,259	3,361
Suicides per 100,000 inhabitants	23·9	24·5	23·2	25·3	24·2	24·6	22·4	22·9

Source: Statistical Yearbooks, various issues.

service ties up young people for two years from the age of 18 to 20. (Selected manpower indicators shown in Table 16 are meant to serve as an illustration of the scene rather than a complete documentation.)

Two other tendencies ought to be mentioned as indicative of the quality of life in a modern society. The number of patients in psychiatric wards jumped up in 1970 and has been slowly climbing since then, as shown in Table 17.

Suicides have always been numerous in Czechoslovakia, possibly because the record-keeping was so good in the 'suicide belt' of Hungary, Austria and Czechoslovakia, all successor states to the Habsburg empire. The pre-war numbers were higher than post-war. (In 1936, 4,220 cases were recorded, or 27·79 per 100,000 inhabitants.) Even so, the 1971 rate of 24·2 per 100,000 contrasts sharply with 11 per 100,000 in the United States. A jump in 1970 is also noticeable in Table 18.

The three countries mentioned, Hungary, Austria and Czechoslovakia, are also among world leaders in the consumption of alcohol. In this respect it must be said that the years of 'normalisation' coincided with a spectacular rise in consumption, an increase in the number of offences committed under the influence of drink (an aggravating circumstance in Czechoslovak law) and a growing number of persons in the 'heavy drinker' and 'alcoholic' categories (which cannot however be followed in available statistical series). A warning is in order; one should not jump to conclusions easily. While many writers believe that the combination of relative material prosperity and political frustration has driven people to drink more than before, and made drinkers into alcoholics, the rising tendency is not peculiar to Czechoslovakia. It can be observed in the other communist countries of Eastern Europe (with the Poles aspiring to the championship), but also in all advanced Western countries. The motivation is obviously a composite of causes and inducements, many of which transcend political boundaries. Even so, Czechoslovak health officials have recognised that alcoholic consumption has shown 'an accelerated increase' since 1968.[111] Statistics certainly bear this out. It is interesting to note that drinking is heavier in Slovakia which is less urbanised than the Czech Lands and supposedly has suffered less political and ideological depression under the post-reformist regime. (In Table 19 selected indicators are given.) Overall consumption is expressed in 100 per cent pure alcohol to which all kinds of alcoholic beverages (such as hard liquor, wine and beer) are statistically translated to permit international comparison (although some other East European governments follow different practices). 'Spirits' on the other hand means hard liquor expressed in alcoholic content of 40 per cent, the most popular 'strength' of all the rums, *slivovice* and vodkas on the domestic market. It is equal to about 72 proof on the

249

Table 19. Per capita consumption of alcohol and indictment of offences under the influence of drink 1967–1975 (In litres where applicable)

Item	1967	1968	1969	1970	1971	1972	1973	1974	1975
Czechoslovakia (100% alcohol)									
Czech Lands	7·0	7·2	7·8	8·4	9·0	9·1	8·7	8·8	9·2
Slovakia	6·5	7·0	7·3	8·0	8·6	8·6	8·1	8·2	8·6
	8·2	7·9	8·8	9·3	9·9	10·1	10·1	10·2	10·6
Spirits (40%)									
Czech Lands	2·6	3·4	4·1	4·2	3·9	4·2	4·4	4·6	5·0
Slovakia	5·6	6·9	8·9	9·5	10·5	10·9	11·5	11·3	11·8
Beer									
Czech Lands	140·2	144·8	151·6	154·1	160·7	160·2	157·9	156·1	157·3
Slovakia	105·3	106·3	108·2	109·3	115·0	119·1	118·1	113·9	113·9
Offences thousand persons	35·9	27·0	36·8	47·4	42·3	48·7	47·6	47·0	43·4*

Source: Statistical Yearbooks, various issues.

* In 1976 the number of offences under the influence of drink was 46,600.

250

British scale. In 1976 offences under the influence represented 27·8 per cent of all indictments.

Czechoslovakia pioneered sobering up stations and anti-alcoholic clinics after the war and the efforts were stepped up in the period under examination. In 1973 there were 51 sobering-up places with 450 beds catering for appoximately 30,000 persons every year (usually brought in by the police); 212 anti-alcoholic centres whose services were considered 'completely unsatisfactory' but which were keeping a register of 130,000 persons; 20 specialised anti-alcoholic departments in hospitals with 1,000 beds; and two 'centres of prophylactic anti-alcoholic treatment' opened in 1972.[112] By 1976 the number of registered alcoholics evidently increased to 155,000 but this number probably understates the case because the same source appears to have mentioned the figure of 300,000 alcoholics in the Czech Lands alone a few months earlier.[113] If the latter figure is correct and if Slovakia with about 32 per cent of the total population, but greater consumption of alcohol, is extrapolated as having 120,000 alcoholics, then the overall number of 420,000 would mean that about 3·7 per cent of the population above the age of 15 were considered 'alcoholics'. The 1973 source cited above stated that 2·3 per cent of the Prague population 'had a card in an anti-alcoholic centre'; if children's age groups are deducted, the percentage would approach the one for the country as a whole and confirm our speculative estimate.

The authorities have tried to create a social climate adverse to heavy drinking through legal measures (such as the ruling which gave enterprise officials the right to check the alcohol content in the blood of workers suspected of intoxication) and a propaganda campaign pointing both to the ill-effects which are injurious to an individual person's health and the social consequences in terms of lost production etc. The valid legislation dates back to 1962 (Law No. 120/1962 'On Struggle against Alcoholism') and its general overhaul and tightening was much spoken about throughout the years, especially in the second half of 1976. A government decree (No. 121/1973) listed specific measures to be taken in education, the health service, material production and distribution, and there are of course appropriate passages in the Highway Code, the Labour Code and the Criminal Code. There is also in existence a Central Anti-Alcoholism Board (as well as a separate one in Slovakia). In 1976 the public was told about some stipulations to be included in the new general Law against Alcoholism, but the time of writing early in 1978 the new legislation has not been put on the statute book.

The government is of course facing the dilemma of governments throughout the world: how to kill the alcoholic goose but still allow it to go on laying golden eggs.[114] About one-fifth of all expenditure on food and beverages goes towards alcoholic drinks. Not that the money would be lost to the treasury coffers if re-directed towards other items in the family budget, but it might thus aggravate the already strong pressure on the production of commodities which the economy simply cannot provide. So, the prices of alcohol have been slowly rising but the imbibing public absorbed every increase with relative ease. The Czechs are great beer drinkers, second to West Germany only in the world, and the Slovaks consume a great deal of wine, but the danger lies obviously in the consumption of hard spirits. So far there has been no indication that the government might contemplate a dramatic price increase, say ten-fold, such as would have a permanent effect on consumption.

To explain why people are drinking heavily in a society which has purportedly gone a long way towards educating 'a new socialist man' and liberated him from the everyday oppressive worries of capitalism, is a tricky proposition, especially after thirty years of socialism. Some blame can be put on Western ideological infiltration, but on the whole those who address themselves to the problem of alcoholism publicly evade motivational search. Neither of course would it be right to seek only those causes that are somehow associated with the communist system of government as practised by the present Czechoslovak leadership.

Czechoslovakia has not developed a drug-abusing sub-culture although a small number of offences are being committed, possibly revealing an upward trend. Importation from non-communist countries is obvious from the fact that now and then foreign nationals are apprehended smuggling narcotic substances through or into Czechoslovakia. Occasionally concern is officially expressed about the use of hallucinatory drugs or substitutes, such as glue sniffing or detergent inhaling, but the number of addicts is almost certainly very small. A Czechoslovak Press Agency report of April 1977 admitted that since 1965 the number of addicts had been increasing but stated that strict handling by the courts forced the trend down. It also said that deaths from narcotics occurred in nine cases in 1973, eight in 1974, 25 in 1975 and 18 in 1976. Drugs used were hashish, marijuana and barbiturates, and only to a very small degree heroin.[115]

In a rare case of public reporting on a drug case, *Rudé právo* noted in November 1972 that a 23-year old man from North Bohemia had brought with him from a legal trip to West Germany hashish and LSD which he then was dispensing to young people. Sometimes as many as thirty boys and girls attended 'a sitting' and there were 22 such sittings. The accused and his helper got away with surprisingly mild sentences of 16 and six months respectively.[116] At about the same time it was said that the Bratislava city police estimated the number of drug addicts in the Slovak capital at one thousand in 1971 but that the actual number was probably greater, mostly young people in the 15–17 age group. They allegedly associated in gangs.[117] This is a high estimate and for once the police information was probably an overstatement.

The already quoted article on alcoholism of August 1973 had a passage which would seem to indicate that there was cause for concern. It said that in view of an increase in drug-taking, special 'anti-addiction centres' ought to be opened at regional level and that hospital departments for long-term treatment of addicts should be established. Only one such centre was then in existence, in Prague, where it was opened in 1971. Its equipment and number of staff were stated to be no longer adequate.[118] It is also known that the newly proposed anti-alcoholism bill, now presumably held up at the committee stage, will include provisions relating to other toxicants. Soaring use of painkillers and tranquilisers can be considered another symptom in the same broad category. One newspaper wrote that the consumption of painkilling drugs quintupled from 1964 to 1974.[119]

Where some people seek oblivion in the bottle, whether it contains *slivovice* or tablets, others opt for the path of crime hoping that it would pay more. Practically from the start of the communist regime in Czechoslovakia, and certainly as time went by, offences of an economic nature have been committed with ever greater ease of conscience. The summary heading under which such offences are categorised reveals something of why this should be so. They are dubbed 'misappropriations of socialist property' and include everything from petty larceny, through pilfering, to complex large-scale conspiratorial operations, all with the common denominator of having the state as their target. The property in question has no visible, apparent, identifiable owner, and if it does, he is not thy neighbour but an anonymous and nebulous national enterprise.

Statistical evidence exists but is inadequate because by definition it contains only 'uncovered' cases which are brought before the courts. It is generally believed that real figures of persons involved and damage caused are much higher; occasionally officials confirm this. Jan Němec, the Czech Minister of Justice, answered questions in April 1975 on the subject and said that of persons sentenced by district courts in 1974, 16 per cent were tried for economic offences, including three-quarters for misappropriation of socialist property. After traffic offences, economic crime was the most frequent. Sentences were not light, up to five, ten and even fifteen years in jail, depending among other things on the amount of damage caused. The minister warned all potential offenders, greedy men, embezzlers and advocates of the various 'new' economic theories of 1968–69 vintage to watch out: sentences would grow stricter and stricter.[120] Why he should wrap up economic reformers into the same parcel as pilferers is not quite clear, but as a well-tried hardliner he could afford to take liberties, especially since the men of the Prague Spring were anyway commonly being

Table 20. Selected crime indicators 1967–1976
(Number of offences cited in verdicts.)

Offence	1967	1968	1969	1970	1971	1972	1973	1974	1975	1976
All except traffic	109,765	83,917	101,933	149,891	181,090	183,717	158,180	170,565	151,077	167,649
% increase over previous year	+0·6	−23·5	+21·5	+47·0	+20·8	+1·4	−13·9	+7·8	−11·4	+11·0
Misappropriation of socialist property	20,294	17,390	18,340	15,422	14,317	14,852	14,802	13,265	12,901	11,802
Injury to another person (brawl)	10,846	7,556	9,686	13,027	13,783	14,752	14,048	13,814	11,271	12,152
Hooliganism, disturbance of peace	3,154	1,941	2,160	3,047	3,437	4,605	5,385	7,725	10,003	10,592
Parasitism	2,906	1,631	2,161	3,129	4,437	5,476	6,097	5,833	6,327	6,293
Theft, fraud etc.	19,848	18,784	19,137	12,904	10,600	11,330	11,199	10,149	8,295	8,524
Rape, sexual abuse	2,365	1,807	1,437	1,679	1,857	2,247	2,475	2,217	2,196	1,887

Source: Statistical Yearbooks, various issues.

accused of all kinds of cardinal sins and another absurd invective did not matter.

Let us look in Table 20 at the incidence of crime in the light of official statistics, leaving aside traffic offences, misdemeanours and such low-figure offences as abusing the powers of a public official, non-payment of alimony, speculation and infringement of duties. (Political crime will be discussed later.)

Officials claimed that the slump in the crime-rate in 1968 was due to inadmissible leniency on the part of the then reformist leadership which affected courts of justice. On the other hand, rising crime in the years of 'normalisation' did not necessarily mean that people were committing more offences, but that the powers of detection had improved under a more vigilant and militant guidance. In a system which proclaims class justice as its foremost legal principle and assures the party of a leading role in its dispensation, such arguments cannot be taken lightly. They obviously have some validity. Nevertheless, even if we disregard the difference between 1968 and subsequent years, other features of the sequence are of interest.

First of all, incidence and/or detection of offences jumped up substantially in 1970, the same year that witnessed increases in other contexts, such as the number of suicides, persons committed to psychiatric wards and offences committed under the influence of alcohol. It will be remembered that this was the year of the political purges. Only two of the major types of offences went down in 1970: misappropriation of socialist property and ordinary theft. Could it be that the powers of detection were slacker in these respects because offences of this kind are less 'political' than affrays, hooliganism and parasitism? (The latter can serve as a peg on which work evasion is often hanged, work being a duty and unemployment non-existent.) Another noteworthy thing is the unevenness of the series. Within the space of ten years the number of prosecuted cases changed from one year to the next by 47 per cent once, by over 20 per cent three times and by over 10 per cent another three times. This kind of fluctuation over and below the average must surely reflect on the methods of detection and sentencing guidance rather than actual commission of crime. (The same uneven pattern is seen in the number of misdemeanours not given in our table.) Furthermore, the perennial offence of thieving state property shows a fairly steady tendency, slowly declining over the ten observed years to some 58 per cent in 1976 of what it was in 1967. Similarly, ordinary theft—by one man from another, i.e. of private property—has gone down from 100 per cent in 1967 to 43 per cent in 1976. (Sexual crime also appears to be receding.) Inconsistency in the prosecution of offences which *can* or *do* have political connotations seems to be contravened by judicial success in bringing to heel the more traditional offenders. Perhaps the trends reveal the law and order consciousness of the coercive authorities of the state with particular emphasis on public order, such as tends to be breached when more people congregate, for whatever purpose, lest the situation gets out of hand. Alternatively, the figures may prove that it is this last type of crime, breaches of public order and peace, that has an increasing tendency, as is the case in non-socialist countries.

If one were to read the statistics without trying to fathom any hidden attitudes and directives which may underlie them, the conclusion would have to be something like this: 'Normalisation' has distinguished itself by a massive increase in crime, above all crime of violence. People steal less from the state and from each other, and have about the same interest in violent sex as before; but they fight more, cause injury to their fellow men, disturb the peace, behave in a hooliganish manner and more of them lead a parasitic existence. The authorities combat traditional infractions fairly successfully but have shown considerable inconsistence towards violent crime, such as may be indicative of a lack of policy in this respect, or frequent changes of policy. Fluctuations are of an order which in a democratic society would call for public enquiry or a resignation of the Minister of Justice.

Perhaps a dissertation in one of the law journals can throw some light on this somewhat puzzling divergence. A lady jurist wrote that socialist legality was primarily a political method of implementing the functions of the state through law. Legal awareness was closely connected to political ideology and the former could not exist without the latter, just as law could not exist without politics. Legal norms must conform to the political, legal and ethical views of the people. (At this stage she said that if they did not, the ruling class was obviously weak, but she produced a pre-war 'bourgeois' example and made no reference to the current crime wave in Czechoslovakia.) She went on to square the circle dialectically: whereas the courts were an autonomous component of the mechanism of the state, this did not mean in any way that either the judges or the courts could be above the classes or non-class. A judge could not be a non-political personality, could he? He interprets and employs a law which is a political act and an expression of class will, reflecting as it does the political power of a class.[121]

At this stage we must introduce a continuation of Table 1 in which we gave the numbers of political offences from 1967 to 1971. It should be noted that the category of 'Petty Offences' ceased to be used in 1970 and was replaced in the same year by 'Misdemeanours' (*Přestupky a provinění* as against *přečiny*). They do not entail only political misbehaviour, but we do not know how many do.

The inferences are that fewer cases of an explicitly political nature have been tried as 'normalisation' progressed. From the highest number of such cases in 1970 (again!) the trend was solidly down-

Table 21. Offences of a political nature and misdemeanours 1972–1976

Year	Against the Republic	Assault on public officials	Misdemeanours
1972	582 (59)	5,496 (160)	48,081 (8,106)
1973	279 (9)	5,860 (168)	36,730 (4,954)
1974	272 (10)	5,631 (178)	48,214 (6,709)
1975	206 (7)	5,308 (195)	41,966 (4,623)
1976	223 (18)	4,656 (109)	54,384 (5,664)

Figures in brackets are for juveniles.
Source: Statistical Yearbook, various issues.

wards. The more spontaneous offence of assaulting a public figure, such as a policeman or a party functionary, stayed rather constant until 1976 when it fell. Most of the assaults were once again committed (or prosecuted, or both) in 1970. Misdemeanours oscillated wildly. A comparison of Tables 20 and 21 would suggest that both the notoriously non-political and the notoriously political offences have declined, while a sharp increase has been registered in the categories which may but need not involve political motivation or undertone. This would be in line with the successive re-writing of laws so as to permit the presentation of political offences as ordinary criminal infractions.

When both chambers of the Federal Assembly convened on 5 April 1977 in response to the Charter 77 campaign for the preservation of human rights in the country, the ostensible concern was with legality as such. The highest legislative body in the country did not adopt any laws on this occasion, only a resolution. It reiterated that the social achievements of the Czechoslovak people were in fact their rights and freedoms. Everyone had the right to work, to receive a decent wage, to have paid holidays, to enjoy free medicine and to draw a pension. Through the good offices of social and political organisations of the National Front, the citizens could also put to use freedom of speech and assembly. Whoever violated the law must expect to be exposed and prosecuted, and the Assembly called on the Procurator General to mete out just punishment to all who might come into conflict with the law of the land. Thus social advancement, legality and their political meaning were lumped together in the Federal Assembly's resolution as they are in this chapter.

INTERNATIONALISM

That proletarian internationalism begets fraternal assistance by the Soviet armed forces to foreign comrades in trouble has been demonstrated beyond doubt. The Brezhnev Doctrine works at a time of crisis. Is it sustainable over prolonged periods when the comrades progress from strength to strength? Or, in other words, can Soviet bayonets be sat on even when it is not really necessary? According to a Czech author, principles of equality and sovereignty are neither an end in themselves nor do they form the essence of proletarian internationalism. Freedom of national decision-making cannot be stripped of its class content.[122] To put it differently but no less succinctly, 'consolidation of the leading role of the party is the international duty of every socialist state, not just a purely internal matter. Whereas general international law considers sovereignty as its key principle, socialist international law recognises socialist internationalism as its leading tenet.... The internal and external aspects of sovereignty cannot be separated'.[123]

So there they were, Czechoslovakia and the Soviet Union, breathing relief that the worst was over but not letting go. At first the 'temporarily' stationed troops were put to use with terse but telling publicity. A military exercise was actually held when discussions about Dubček's replacement by Husák and the initiation of a tough 'normalisation' course were in progress in early April 1969. A spate of manoeuvres followed in May ('Vesna 69'), July, August (both a Warsaw Pact airforce exercise and ground games) and October 1969. Physical presence of the Warsaw Pact was emphasised by the holding of high-level meetings including that of the Political Advisory Committee in January 1972 and an assembly of generals and other high officers in June of the same year. The Military Council of the Pact was in conference in Prague in October-November 1973, and the Pact's Defence Ministers sat there in November 1975. Czechoslovak leaders regularly paid visits to commanders of Soviet units stationed in the country or received them in their offices, these events always getting prominent but not extensive publicity. Gradually the various party and state agencies and social organisations were setting up contacts with the troops at lower levels by way of exchanging social visits. Soviet soldiers would occasionally be sent to work for little or no money on 'brigade' assignments in Czechoslovak enterprises or farms. It is estimated that some 50–70,000 troops have been variously stationed in military compounds and smaller garrison towns, about half of them in the Czech Lands. The Central Group, as they became know, has its headquarters at Milovice, near Prague, in an old military

258

camp. On the whole a low profile but not total secrecy was being maintained. Rank-and-file soldiers are rarely seen outside their compounds, although in provincial towns their presence is inevitably seen and heard. Officers and their wives do go out more, almost always in pairs or small groups. The population showed dislike and animosity to them at first, but as things settled down and they became a part of the scenery, the attitude became one of studied ignorance. The Czechoslovak armed forces are working in close cooperation with the Warsaw Pact command and it is believed that guidance of a much tighter kind than existed before the invasion is being dispensed through permanent observers and advisers as well as the military staff now physically present in the Central Group headquarters.

On balance, however, the military is plainly not the main instrument of control over the making of internal political decisions and their implementation. Several times during the 'normalisation' period it looked as if part of the troops might be actually withdrawn from Czechoslovakia to indicate Soviet satisfaction with consolidated conditions. After all, the early post-invasion documents did stipulate such withdrawal, and the treaty on their stationing did refer to 'temporary' deployment. While some people may have interpreted a possible reduction in the number of troops on Czechoslovak territory as heralding a relaxation of the regime, it was clear to the majority that no more than a formal gesture would have been made. The bayonets are literally there, but few people believe that the 'normalised' structures would crumble without them, especially since they could be reintroduced within hours. Nevertheless, neither the Russians nor the Czechoslovak leadership have taken any chances. No withdrawal has been announced and in fact the word 'temporary' has been dropped from public references to Soviet troops altogether. They are there 'just in case' and as a constant reminder of the continued validity of the Brezhnev Doctrine. Also, a reintroduction, should it become necessary, would carry a certain omen and that kind of discomfiture can be averted by the simple precaution of keeping the troops there. It is understood that the Warsaw Pact combat and logistic structures and plans have been reworked on the basis of a permanent Soviet military presence in Czechoslovakia.

Controls are exercised mainly outside the military remit, even if some hardliners in the ruling coalition and outside have been repeatedly trotting out to see Soviet generals at Milovice. Soviet advisers function directly in the Ministry of the Interior and some are present at interogations of dissidents. The KGB probably maintains a vigilant network in the country. The main thrust, however, is once again through the channels that have been painstakingly built up from the end of the 1940s, namely high-level meetings, regular consultations between party leaders, inter-party connections between central committee secretariats in Moscow and Prague, cooperation between social organisations of all kinds, and the Soviet Embassy. To this must be added the enhanced integration policy of the Comecon which may not appear a spectacular success, but which fairly effectively limits the scope of economic action of Czechoslovak ministries and enterprises. The outstanding new feature of the economic relationship is the recent investment of Czechoslovak funds, together with those of other Comecon countries, into the extraction industries on Soviet territory.

Foreign policy of the 'normalisation' regime has been totally subordinated to Soviet foreign aims and the conduct devised in Moscow towards their attainment. There is throughout the period not a single instance of deviation on record or even reluctance to perform as expected. (The re-establishment of diplomatic relations with West Germany, around which a disputation possibly evolved, is discussed below.) Czechoslovak foreign policy has consequently lacked innovation and character, and has come to be accepted by the non-communist countries as no more than an exercise in repetition. After the initial three or so years of noticeable coolness and absence of all but the most formal contact, the Czechoslovak regime has undertaken an effort to rejoin the detente-inspired dialogue between East and West and has achieved some success in this respect, especially under the directorship of Foreign Minister B. Chňoupek. Exchanges have become more frequent and trade has picked up, largely as a result of cautious Czechoslovak effort to acquire Western technology and a more determined endeavour to step up exports to the developing countries. Four geographical areas received increased attention: the Middle East where the main partners are Libya and Syria; India where a notable cooling off came about after the fall of Mrs Gandhi's government; West Germany where trade has been significant but not dramatic and political relations have not risen beyond the formal level; and Austria where strained relations were badly in need of repair with regard to outstanding financial issues and a certain improvement was actually achieved. As for Czechoslovak involvement in the African continent, visits by leaders of several revolutionary movements have been noted, but on the whole relations appeared to remain at the less publicised level of trade, possibly in military commodities.

The travel pattern of the leaders, although not a reliable barometer, shows that by far the most important objective of Czechoslovakia has been to prove her loyalty to the Warsaw Pact countries and to put a seal of pomp and circumstance on it.

Husák's publicly announced journeys outside Czechoslovakia between 1969 and 1977 included 26 trips to the Soviet Union, i.e. almost three visits every year. He has regularly taken his holidays in the Crimea, usually in the second half of July or first half of August, to meet Brezhnev and often other travelling Warsaw Pact leaders. In

Table 22. Number of foreign ruling communist leaders' visits 1969–1977

1969 . . . 2	1972 . . . 4	1975 . . . 0
1970 . . . 5	1973 . . . 6	1976 . . . 4
1971 . . . 7	1974 . . . 2	1977 . . . 1

addition he went to East Germany and Poland eight times, to Hungary six times, Bulgaria four times, Romania three times (for the first time in 1971), and made one trip each to Yugoslavia (in 1973), Mongolia, Cuba and North Korea. Of the non-communist countries he visited only India in 1973, Finland in 1974 and again in 1975 to sign the Helsinki Final Act, and Iraq in 1977. Finally, after several postponements, he visited West Germany in April 1978. For whatever it may be worth, his travel was rather heavy in 1969 (twelve trips) and in 1970, 1971, 1975 and 1976 (eight trips each year), medium in 1973 (six) and 1977 (seven), and light in 1972 (three) and 1974 (four trips).

The frequency of return visits by other communist leaders (of the ruling parties) has been uneven. Sometimes, such as when congresses are held, a cluster of leaders descend on the country in question, and we know little about the proportion of formal and working elements in their visits. Table 22 lists the number of visits by foreign leaders in Czechoslovakia.

Figures for 1971 and 1976 include presence at the 14th and 15th party congresses, in 1970 at the 25th anniversary celebration of the end of the war (whereas in 1975 the 30th anniversary drew high-level visitors, e.g. Kirilenko, but not the top leaders), and in 1973 at the 25th anniversary of communist takeover (in comparison the 30th anniversary of this event in 1978 was a subdued affair with ambassadors only). Counterposed leader by leader the picture looks as shown in Table 23.

The Czechoslovak Prime Minister also travelled extensively and even ventured to non-communist countries: Cairo in 1970 (to attend Nasser's funeral), Finland in 1973 and again in 1975 (Helsinki agreement), Syria, India and Kuwait (all in 1974), Libya and France in 1975, Turkey and Iran in 1976, and Austria in 1977. Vasil Bilak's publicised travels have taken him to all the communist countries, often as Czechoslovak delegate to international communist consultations, and also to some Western and developing countries, sometimes as delegate at the local communist party's congress. He was in France in 1970, Egypt in 1971, Algeria and Syria in 1972, Syria again in 1975, Portugal in 1976 and Austria in 1977.

The Soviet Union has rendered Czechoslovakia ideological guidance and assistance and was assured of Czechoslovakia's support in

Table 23. Exchange of visits between G. Husák and other communist leaders 1969–1977

Name of leader	Number of visits in Czechoslovakia	Number of Husák's visits to country of visitor
Brezhnev	4	26
Gomulka/Gierek	7	8
Kádár	5	6
Zhivkov	5	4
Ulbricht/Honecker	5	8
Castro	2*	1
Ceauşescu	1†	3
Tsedenbal	1	1
Tito	0	1
Kim Il-sung	0	1

* One of them a stopover
† Termed 'unofficial' in 1973

the international communist movement. At first the Czechoslovak representatives successfully assisted Moscow in parrying attempts, however half-hearted they were, to make the intervention and subsequent 'normalisation' a subject of discussion at international communist gatherings. The Czechoslovaks said that the matter was being resolved in comradely cooperation between Prague and Moscow and its internationalisation would only serve the enemy who was waiting to exploit the potentially divisive issue. If the dissenting parties opposed a discussion of the wrecking policies pursued by the Chinese party, how illogical it was of them to want to talk about 'normalisation' in Czechoslovakia where the leadership's sole aim was to cement the movement's unity. The Czechoslovak party, now under new management, must be given time to prove itself as a real communist party, capable of leading the country in an orderly and ideologically sound way. The past was the past, and to open up an examination of it on an international forum would hamper progress into the future.

Once the 'Lessons from the Years of Crisis' had been adopted in December 1970, the Czechoslovak leaders could claim that now a Marxist-Leninist analysis of what had gone wrong was available and the chapter was closed. More than ever the concern must be with the new pressing tasks of the communist movement, not with successfully resolved problems. This line of argument was on the whole accepted and no discussion of the Czechoslovak developments before, during or after the Prague Spring took place at any international communist meeting. A few Western communist delegates made a remark or two, disproving the invasion, or questioning the need for it, at the early meetings in 1969 and 1970, and stronger opinions may have been expressed in bilateral meetings with the Soviet leaders, but the movement as a whole acknowledged that the issue was best left to be dealt with by Moscow.

Prague was in fact chosen as the background to international conferences at which the Moscow line in the movement was propagated in front of delegates of communist parties from all over the world. In the absence of a centralist structure of the Comintern or Cominform type, the role to dispense ideological guidance was assigned to the editorial board of the journal *Problems of Peace and Socialism* under K. Zarodov, who have their seat in Prague.

Problems is no mean undertaking. Published in 30 languages and 525,000 copies, it is distributed in 145 countries. Nearly half of the circulation goes to non-socialist countries as against 15 per cent when the journal was launched in 1958. At that time eleven parties had been represented on the editorial board; now there were 51 with 30 others cooperating regularly. As Zarodov put it disarmingly, *Problems* is not an organ of a communist guiding centre because, as is known, such a centre does not exist. It is simply published by those parties that wish to act in unison. Not that the journal imparts any directives to its readers or aspires to work out a joint strategic line, but it does assume that class struggle continues and ideological cooperation between the two systems is impossible. The journal aims at strengthening the unity of communist parties on the basis of Marxism-Leninism and proletarian internationalism. *Problems* is determined to propagate proletarian internationalism widely because, as Brezhnev said, to abandon it would mean to give up a strong and well-tried weapon.[124]

Attendance at conferences organised by *Problems* appeared to be voluntary and indeed at some meetings it was rather small, insofar as one can judge from incomplete public information, but every three years a general conference in the presence of Soviet party praesidium member B. N. Ponomarev has been held, commanding a wide audience at the level of central committee secretaries or similar high officials. The first of these, in 1971 (14–16 December), was attended by representatives of 62 fraternal parties, the second, in 1974 (7–9 January) by 67, and the third, in 1977 (27–29 April) by 75. The same number were present in June 1977 when the theme was 'The Great October Revolution and the World Today'. Other subjects over the years included internationalism, the Third World, class struggle under capitalism today, women in capitalism, guest workers in Western Europe, economic integration, the contest between capitalism and communism, the media in capitalism, unity of anti-imperialist struggle, scientific and technical revolution, racism and Lenin's threory of imperialism and present-day reality. Altogether there was one such conference in Prague in 1970 and again in 1971, four in 1972, five in 1973, four in 1974, three in 1975, one in 1976 and two in 1977. Occasionally they were held in other East European capitals.

Czechoslovak leaders and propagandists evolved into the most ardent advocates of proletarian internationalism and critics of Eurocommunism, sometimes exceeding and even preceding Soviet spokesmen, so that they have been suspected of inflating the trial balloons of ideological militancy such as even Moscow would not dare to float. Pride of place must go to Vasil Bilak who has also become notorious for criticising Romania and Yugoslavia at private party meetings from which leaks were allowed or arranged.[125]

In the crucial question of internationalism, whether proletarian or socialist, the attitude of the Czechoslovak leadership was determined by the following tenets: (1) While the practical considerations of the period of detente make the existence of a structured and centralised communist movement inexpedient, it is the principle of proletarian internationalism that holds it together. (2) The international qualities of the movement must never be subordinated to national exigencies, although there is room for tolerating certain formal 'peculiarities'. (3) Underlying the notion of internationalism is the recognition of the 'laws of development' which govern the building of socialism throughout the world. They are as follows: the working masses shall be led by the working class, the core of which is a Marxist-Leninist party; a proletarian revolution and the enthronement of the dictatorship of the proletariat shall be obligatory aims of the movement; workers shall ally themselves with the bulk of the farming population and other working strata of the public; capitalist ownership shall be liquidated and socialist ownership introduced in its stead; agriculture shall be gradually socialised; economic advancement shall be planned so as to raise the standard of living; a socialist revolution shall be accomplished in ideology and culture; all nations and nationalities shall enjoy equality and be free of oppression; socialist achievements shall be defended against internal and external enemies jointly with the other socialist countries.[126]

When the Eurocommunist tendency grew stronger and the communique at the East Berlin communist summit was signed in the summer of 1976 without using the term 'proletarian internationalism', the Czechoslovak politicians and ideologues hastened to explain away the underlying controversy by implying that the words might be different but the essence of the movement was still the same. He who ignores this does so at his own peril. Practical implementation of the principles of proletarian internationalism may be influenced by different conditions in various parts of the world and in different countries, but the dominating tendency is still that of interdependence. The law of a single historial orientation for all components of the movement asserts itself even more strongly. Internationalism is not obsolete, it is only richer, deeper and has more facets than before. World communism must continue to comprise a united purposeful force which pursues its activity on an international scale as a factor of the class struggle which itself is international. Of course every communist party must first of all work within its national environment, but its leaders must not forget such realities of life as the existence of the Soviet Union, the socialist commonwealth and the movement as an international phenomenon, not just a sum total of national parts. One must not lose sight of the forest when looking at a tree. The communist parties need a united attitude and coordinated policy.[127]

By the same token detente was seen primarily and often exclusively as simply a new milieu in which the perennial communist struggle for world domination was being waged. Apart from a brief description of some bilateral deals with non-communist countries and one flat sentence of seventeen words about the Helsinki conference, the East-West relationship was summarised in Husák's main speech at the party's 15th congress in 1976 as 'a programme of peace elaborated at the 25th congress of the Soviet Communist Party'. It was the relentless 'struggle for peace' that had influenced international relations in the teeth of the cold-war warriors. 'Thus favourable conditions are being widened and strengthened for the building of socialism and communism, for peace and social progress'.[128]

Detente is neither a static division of the world into zones of interests nor a policy of open door through which imperialism can infiltrate the socialist fortress. Detente is a state of affairs in which military confrontation can be avoided while the fundamental class conflict goes on, transposed into a more moderate form, that of a struggle between ideologies.[129]

> 'The policy of peaceful coexistence between socialism and imperialism is not—from the viewpoint of the communist parties and socialist states—a pacifistic desire, but rather a revolutionary, anti-imperialist policy, the objective of which is to eliminate imperialism, to liberate the nations, to ensure their advancement, to make socialism flourish and to achieve its triumph throughout the world. All this in the most favourable conditions, without another world war'.[130]

The logical consequence of this attitude is exhortation to vigilance so as to minimise the side-effects which the overwhelmingly favourable international climate may produce. Special attention has therefore been paid to preventing the penetration of inimical arguments. Everything associated with the non-communist world is looked at with doubly suspicious eyes. The Prime Minister asked in the Federal Assembly: 'How are we to pursue economic cooperation with the capitalist countries and reduce to the minimum any possible risk of ideological erosion?' He answered himself by stipulating that 'the condition of conditions' and 'the categorical basis' of all pursuits of detente must be an ever closer cooperation with the USSR and the other socialist countries. The right-wingers of the Prague Spring, he added in a by now customary sortie against the ill of all ills, had sought to improve relations with the capitalists while eroding alliances with the socialist countries. 'We are going, and shall be going, in exactly the opposite direction'. Did he really mean that his government was keen on getting Western technology (this was two days after the signing of the treaty with West Germany) but would at the same time 'erode' relations with those who could provide it? Hardly, but the blindness of his remarks was typical of the ideology prophylactic approach of the leadership to detente. He went on by naming a second condition: cementing and enhancing the leading role of the party in every possible manner. And finally: we must weigh the content and forms of cooperation with the West very vigilantly. Flexibility is all right, but in all fields we must accurately know the borderline beyond which cooperation could evolve into an instrument of alien penetration.[131]

A lurid picture of the hazards of detente was painted in many press articles. Through films, television, advertising, glossy magazines, luxury goods and pornography, capitalist propaganda was seen reaching out to the socialist countries in an attempt to impress on their citizens petty bourgeois ideas. A great deal of this propaganda is carried out by Western tourists who are invariably well-clothed and possess enviable cars and large sums of money, thus conveying the impression of a standard of living much higher than the actual average in their countries of origin. The remainders of petty bourgeoisie in Czechoslovakia are especially vulnerable to this kind of ideological warfare as are the inexperienced young people who do not know the shady sides of capitalism. As interaction between cultures and individuals cannot be arrested, it is imperative to step up ideological work and concentrate on the formation of an appealing model of the socialist man and a socialist style of life.[132]

Czechoslovakia is probably the most rigid of all the East European countries in keeping away Western books and newspapers, jamming radio broadcasts and operating a tight surveillance over the movement and activities of foreigners in the country. There is minute checking of behaviour by Czechoslovak citizens when abroad and after return through a series of debriefings and lengthy questionnaires. Trusted scholars and scientists at the few conferences in the West which they are allowed to attend report daily to the head of the Soviet contingent at the conference and write long accounts of what happened for the authorities when back at home.[133] Any international developments which to an observer not sufficiently trained in dialectics may seem to indicate that detente goes too far, are allowed by extensive and intensive interpretative campaigns.

When Richard Nixon went to Moscow in May 1972, the Czechoslovak party journal noted that some people thought ideological struggle was being relaxed. By no means, the paper retorted. Incidentally, this was what the imperialists would like to see happen. In fact they are only compelled to negotiate compromises (which are in fact compromises only from their point of view) because they are militarily inferior to the socialist countries and must respect the latter's economic and political strength. Soviet-American agreements change nothing in the nature of imperialism and they are being negotiated only to prevent the irreconcilable antagonism from being resolved through a nuclear conflagration.[134] Similarly, on the eve of Brezhnev's trip to the USA in June 1973, before he actually went there, *Rudé právo* told its readers not to fall victim to illusions: America was weak and the Soviet Union was strong, hence the former had to talk to the latter, but Brezhnev will be guided by class and internationalist principles when seeking to avoid a nuclear holocaust.[135]

The Helsinki Final Act, an event widely and rather pompously reported (this was Husák's first major international undertaking in his new capacity as president of the republic), was equally accompanied with comment designed to give it its place in the historical scheme of things as seen through Marxist-Leninist eyes. Even when the protracted negotiations were still in progress, the citizens were warned not to forget that the capitalists were not as good as their word. The talks and the eventual agreement would still have class limits.[136] The signing of the Act was welcomed as the creation of a platform on which economic, scientific and technical cooperation could evolve. The Act was seen as an agreement between two blocs, and the West was said to have committed itself to lifting cold-war impositions, such as economic discrimination, something which the East had not been guilty of anyway. The public should not conclude however that East-West cooperation leads to class truce or conciliation. Economic competition after all *is* a form of the class struggle too.[137]

Some comment on 'peaceful coexistence' (a term preferred by some ideologists to 'detente', although 'relaxation' was also frequently used) went as far as to be undistinguishable from sabre-rattling. Thus a propagandist reminded his readers that coexistence could only be properly understood in conjunction with the Marxist-Leninist notion that history evolved from a lower to a higher socio-economic formation. Coexistence represents a certain phase in this process which will lead to the establishment of communism all over the world. Coexistence and revolution were not mutually exclusive. The USSR 'and other communist forces in the world' did not reject wars altogether even though now it was coexistence which could best promote a world-wide socialist revolution. Even if a solid mechanism for the peaceful resolution of conflicts were to be established, the Marxist-Leninists would still support the waging of just wars, liberating and revolutionary wars.[138] And another writer exclaimed: 'We are not pacifists!' Only the complete elimination of capitalism can prevent wars from breaking out. And only when people take matters into their own hands and are willing to defend peace to the end, can socialism be built.[139]

The 'normalising' regime in Czechoslovakia was certainly better suited to wage ideological wars inside and outside the country than to engage in a practical exercise of detente. The one outstanding case which it had to attend to in the early 1970s to fall in line with the Soviet foreign policy designs, concerned West Germany. At first it looked a simple enough operation involving a formal establishment of diplomatic relations and putting trade between the two countries, which had evolved even previously, on a firmer basis in order to regulate its growth. It turned out to be a protracted and at times agonising process in which practical exigencies battled with ideological preoccupation and even caprice. It is hard to say to what extent did Czechoslovak intransigence and Soviet pragmatism clash or whether the diehard stand was part of Moscow's plan to make practical detente look difficult. Briefly the story is as follows.

Attempts at a rapprochement between the two states were made at the end of the 1950s and already at that time the formal hitch was found to be a differing attitude to the Munich Treaty of 1938, concluded between Britain, France, Germany and Italy, i.e. without Czechoslovak participation, but ruling on the German seizure of extensive tracts of Czechoslovak territory. West Germany, considering itself the inheritor of the German legal order, was of course willing to declare the Munich Agreement 'no longer valid' or, as the British had done, to say that it had been invalidated by the occupation of Czechoslovakia in March 1939. This was not enough for the Czechoslovaks who insisted on a declaration that the Agreement was invalid *ab initio* as it had been signed under false pretences and without Czechoslovakia's consent, and that no consequences arising from it even hypothetically would have any practical meaning. (President Beneš and the Czechoslovak government of the day did however formally accept the Agreement in 1938.) During the Prague Spring when conditions for an amicable settlement existed, the reformers deliberately abstained from forcing the issue for fear that it might exacerbate their relations with the USSR and East Germany. At the pre-*Ostpolitik* time, only the Soviet Union and Romania, a maverick, maintained formal ties with the Federal Republic. With the advent of Chancellor Brandt's coalition government in October 1969 and its opening to the communist countries of Eastern Europe, and once the general principles of international detente regained momentum in Soviet foreign political thought after the subsidence of the ill-effects of the invasion into Czechoslovakia, relations between Eastern Europe and West Germany acquired a special meaning. Everyone was joining the bandwagon in expectation of a favourable position on the West German trading list.

With respect to Czechoslovakia the negotiations were the most protracted ones and lasted from preliminary consultations in October 1970 to the ratification in July 1974. Until the autumn of 1971 the Czechoslovak side insisted on the Munich Agreement being called 'invalid from the start, with all its attendant consequences'. This the Germans were unwilling to accept as it left open the question of reparations and made possible to challenge the former Czechoslovak Germans, now citizens of the Federal Republic, with regard to their action between October 1938 and March 1939. When the Czech side finally agreed to drop the vague reference to the 'attendant consequences' or 'consequences deriving from it', the haggling about the *ab initio* clause continued for another year and it was at this time, during 1972, that some signs of Soviet impatience with the Czechoslovak negotiating stiffness could be detected. This coincided with rumours about Soviet criticism of the course of 'normalisation' (passivity of the masses, profiteering and hypocrisy) and especially of the state of Czechoslovak economy which the Russians allegedly wanted to move ahead more rapidly in order to step up deliveries to Comecon and the developing countries.[140] Towards the end of the year Brezhnev allegedly sent an emissary to question one of the deposed reformist leaders, Josef Smrkovský, about alternatives to the tough course of the Husák leadership. It is difficult to make head or tail of the story which lacks essential factual ingredients, but the fact remains that reference to the *ab initio* clause was first dropped in a Zhivkov-Brezhnev and a Kádár-Brezhnev communique in November 1972. From then on the Czechoslovak-West German negotiations progressed more rapidly in the direction of a compromise formulation. The text was initialled by the two Foreign Ministers on 20 June 1973. It declared the Munich Agreement immoral, null and void but qualified the statement to the effect that the present treaty did not affect the legal consequences deriving from legislation applied from 30 September 1938 to 9 May 1945 except those laws that contravened the principles of justice. The treaty also left unaffected the state citizenship of both living and deceased persons insofar as it derived from the legal system of either of the two parties, and material claims by Czechoslovakia or her individual citizens were ruled out. The treaty further renounced the use of force or threats, proclaimed territorial integrity of both parties and inviolability of their frontiers, explicitly stated that neither party had territorial designs on the other, and stipulated development of cooperation in economy, science, technical fields, culture, anti-pollution measures, sports and transport.[141]

The story was not to end there, as the problem of consular representation of West Berlin, unacceptable to the Czechs in the German formulation, once again delayed the signature ceremony for three months and had to be resolved through Moscow's indirect good offices by an exchange of notes outside the treaty itself. Another two letters from the Czechoslovak Foreign Minister were handed over as supplementary to the treaty which was eventually signed in Prague on 11 December 1973 by Herr Brandt and Herr Scheel and their Czechoslovak counterparts. The ceremony coincided with the 30th anniversary of the Czechoslovak-Soviet treaty of 12 December 1943 and shared the limelight on the front pages of Czechoslovak papers with it. A treaty with West Germany, and unbreakable friendship with the Soviet Union. Western press reports said that the atmosphere during Herr Brandt's brief visit in Prague was subdued and cool.

As if to underline the point, when it came to ratification by the National Assembly on 15 July 1974, several speakers uttered tough words. One warned that peaceful coexistence between the two countries must be considered a long-term relationship of states based on different social systems, implying that import of Western ideology through the Federal Republic has not been agreed, and another said that the treaty should not cover up the Nazi atrocities of the past and the existence of the German Democratic Republic. The Foreign Minister minced his words more, had praise for the 'political realism' of the West German leaders but warned about 'certain circles' and 'revanchists'.[142] Husák was present in the Assembly when the treaty was ratified. Not long afterwards a Czechoslovak-West German long-term agreement on economic, industrial and technical cooperation was hammered out and then signed in Bonn on 22 January 1975.

The era of practical detente for Czechoslovakia had been launched. With it came new problems, while several old ones would not go away. A large number of people was still at the wrong end of apartheid rather than the right end of relaxation. Detente abroad, oppression at home? Once again the early sins of Husák's reign were taking their toll. If only the purges had been conducted in a conciliatory manner. By now the new climate of international cooperation would have added credence to the 'normalisation' claims and made people think about the Prague Spring as a dream of the past rather than a continuing grievance. A conflict between the international commitments contiguous on detente and the conduct of internal politics need not have arisen.

In an atmosphere of ideological militancy the Czechoslovak leadership felt, however, secure enough to ratify the United Nations covenants on civil and political rights and on economic, social and cultural rights which were signed way back in October 1968 when Dubček was still precariously holding on to some of the reformist concepts of the Prague Spring, the observation of human rights among them. The ratification was effected on 11 December 1975. In March 1976 the covenants became legally binding inside Czechoslovakia.

Part Four

The way of the Charter

1971–1976

TRIBULATIONS OF DISSENT

In the summer of 1972, when the leaders of the Socialist Movement of Czechoslovak Citizens were put in jail, the idea that the regime can be opposed by a structured, semi-communist movement, died. Those who considered it their moral duty not to lay down the arms of active dissent had to look for less organised yet, so they hoped, more effective forms of protest.

Before the new forms of democratic opposition got under way, a last flicker of hope kindled the imagination of one of the great men of communist renaissance in Czechoslovakia, Josef Smrkovský. He was given to understand that Moscow contemplated cutting down the zestful 'normalisation' practices of the Husák leadership in favour of a more moderate pursuit. Some of the men of the Prague Spring might even be called back from the cold to help put the country on a footing which would be acceptable to the world at large in this period of detente. Information about this episode, for that is what it turned out to be, is naturally scant but such facts as are known allow a certain measure of evaluation.

It all began with an unnamed Soviet visitor to Czechoslovakia, allegedly an Academy of Sciences official (not too high, not too low), calling towards the end of 1972 on an unnamed Czech person, currently in disfavour, and asking him about the measure of popularity still enjoyed by the aces of the Prague Spring, men like Dubček, Smrkovský, Černík and Císař. He was referred to Josef Smrkovský, who by then had already expressed his criticism of 'normalisation' in an interview to an Italian communist paper (in September 1971), and was just about to decline an invitation from the French Socialist Party to attend a seminar in Paris (in November 1972), which he would not be allowed to accept anyway. Among the top leaders of the reformist experiment, he was something of an elder statesman. With forty years of communist activity behind him and without direct implication in the opposition group that had just been put behind bars, he was indeed a good contact. He was ill with cancer. He also had enough personal integrity not to be counted among the opportunists who might be waiting for a beck and call to resume badly missed public activity and the attendant comforts of office. We know from Smrkovský's 'memoir' (published in the West in 1975) that Brezhnev had already once before tried to win him over, in the spring of 1968, as a replacement for Dubček whom the Soviets had then begun to suspect of weakness. At that time Smrkovský declined, but he kept the offer to himself in order not to make Dubček's life more difficult. Later in 1968 Smrkovský's standing in Moscow's eyes fell sharply and he was the first of the 'inner four' (Dubček, Svoboda and Černík being the other three) who had to be dropped after the invasion, though it did not happen immediately.

So the Soviet emissary went to see Smrkovský several times in the first half of 1973 and told him that Moscow thought the mass expulsions of 'pro-socialist forces' from the Czechoslovak Communist Party had gone too far. What did Smrkovský think should be done about it? Some of the few friends to whom Smrkovský confided the unexpected development warned him that the whole thing could be a provocation, but he decided not to miss a chance even though it was suspicious and certainly tenuous. In the summer of 1973 the Soviet contact suggested that Smrkovský should outline his view of the Czechoslovak situation in a letter to Brezhnev. He was told that the Soviet party praesidium planned to reopen the Czechoslovak question precisely because 'normalisation' was not producing the requisite results. Smrkovský wrote the letter in July, took one copy personally to the Soviet embassy and despatched another to Berlinguer with the request that it should be delivered to the Kremlin.

Here the known version of the story has the first logical hiccup: why should the Soviet emissary not have collected the letter in the first place himself? Nonetheless, the Soviet embassy passed its copy to the Czechoslovak Foreign Ministry which returned it after a few days to the sender without any accompanying note. Both institutions must surely have xeroxed the document so that it is not quite clear why Smrkovský should have waited for another two months before sending a carbon to Husák (in September), according to the information available to us. In the meantime, we are told, the Italian communist leader did forward Smrkovský's letter to Brezhnev allegedly with an appended recommendation of his own that it should be given serious consideration. There was no reaction from Husák but the mysterious Russian contact materialised again in October and hinted that the letter had been positively received in the Kremlin and that important new steps would be taken within a few months. Smrkovský died in January 1974, perhaps mercifully without learning that nothing would happen.

In his letter to Brezhnev, Smrkovský said that the severity of the 'normalisation' policy was casting a shadow over the process of detente which had got under way. The invasion of Czechoslovakia had belonged to the pre-detente era and was now anachronistic. Should the whole affair not be turned from an impediment to a stimulus of international relaxation? If the Soviets showed initiative in this direction, some members of the present Czechoslovak leadership would welcome it and so would a large number of the purged victims. Perhaps the Soviets should initiate a round of talks about a solution with all the interested parties, including the exorcised communists.

Smrkovský himself would be prepared to dedicate himself to such a quest for an equitable settlement.[1]

One has the feeling that Smrkovský might have misread the information which his Soviet source was feeding him, obviously in an oblique fashion. It is unlikely that a Soviet official, even one from the Academy, would call on the 'enemy' without some kind of commission from high quarters, but Brezhnev was hardly the man to seek enlightenment from a pariah. The message might have been one of invitation for Smrkovský to change sides, join the 'normalisers' and renounce his former reformist associates. A public expiation would certainly come in useful from someone of Smrkovský's stature, but a change of policy, which Smrkovský appeared to be suggesting, was simply not on.

What is interesting in the whole affair is the linkage between the further progress of 'normalisation' and the developing detente which Smrkovský perceptively identified in his letter to Brezhnev. Soviet intervention in Czechoslovakia in 1968 certainly delayed East-West rapprochement, but Moscow very soon began making peaceful noises again and especially since 1971 it was in effect saying that the unpleasant episode was over and done with. Czechoslovakia was under 'normal' rule and the great powers could return to the business of detente. Smrkovský's argument to the effect that not only the military intervention itself, but also the internal policies in Czechoslovakia which derived from it, ran contrary to the spirit of international relaxation, foreshadowed the attitudes of Czechoslovak opposition as they crystallised in the wake of the destruction of its organised attempt in 1971–72. Communist treatment of dissidents in their own countries was being raised by Smrkovský to the level of an international touchstone of goodwill and honest intentions.

Several more statements were published in the name of the Socialist Movement of Czechoslovak Citizens after the incarceration of its leaders but those oppositionists who remained at large have not endeavoured to create a new organisational structure. They too pinned hopes on the international dimension. In a proclamation which they issued shortly after the political trials, on the fourth anniversary of the Warsaw Pact invasion, there was the following passage:

> '...European security cannot be assured through a pact between governments who simply undertake not to attack each other.... European security can only be founded on mutual under-standing, open discussion, exchange of views, ideas and experiences, mutual confidence and open international relations. The advantages of socialism cannot be safeguarded through closed borders, imprisonment, labour camps, jamming of foreign radio stations, an ideological defensive and fear of the spreading of information'.[2]

Growing awareness of the international dimension (which for example was still not evident in the Short Action Programme) was matched by another process in the oppositional ranks. Ex-communists began to shed the tenets and precepts which their party had taught them to consider sacrosanct and which they still tried to implement, albeit in modified form, when launching the Socialist Movement. For example, the perception of the oppositional 'front' as a hierarchy consisting of the leadership ('vanguard of the vanguard'), the party ('leading political stratum') and the masses ('membership base') crumbled. Less communism in theory also meant easier cooperation with social-democratic and liberal oppositionists. The Socialist Movement of Czechoslovak Citizens, insofar as it still existed (more as a concept than an organisation), ceased to be a kind of alternative communist party, with many of the typical party features preserved, such as the righteous belief in its own infallibility and suspicion that all non-believers were either dumb or 'non-scientific' or both. A freer approach to the practical issues of the day gradually prevailed. An ex-communist in Prague commented on this process as follows:

'We have stopped worrying about the attachment of labels.... It is not easy to divest oneself of verbal symbols into which so much chiliastic faith, pragmatic effort, hate and anger had been invested. These symbols used to have the validity of vouchers exchanged for power and privileges of all kind while on the other hand stigmatising the powerless people and sometimes even rubber-stamping their consignation to jail: a communist, a non-communist, an anti-communist, a no-more-than-socialist, an advocate of socialist democracy or democratic socialism, a Social Democrat or a Masaryk man... These and similar words were and for some still are overloaded to a point well below the draught line on which safe navigation in the political waters is possible.... Ships overloaded in this way are visibly fewer and forced confessions are heard less and less frequently. Occasionally a debate will produce a few sparks but conflicts come to an end as quickly as they flare up....
Confessional disputations, let alone preoccupations with political trademarks of the future, are of no interest to anyone, and by the same token divide no one among us who...have not given up, regardless of our present or past party membership and outlook.'[3]

As a direct corollary to the blunting of ideological edges, no more action programmes were being formulated. The opposition became pragmatic:

'There is not enough desire to manufacture thorough programmes and for people to associate or close ranks around them.... The aspiration to address oneself to fundamental issues, even if only in friendly chitchats, to identify what true socialism is and what it is not, to make decisions about a final taking of sides with and against other people, to compile platforms and hoist political banners, however honest they may be—all this is in the Czechoslovakia of 1975 an increasingly foolish stance, even less commensurate with reality. Even the language which for decades corresponded to precisely this kind of endeavour, and not only among the reform communists, is vanishing. . . . Ideological charades appear less and less fascinating. . . . The totalitarian regime of today presents the thinking man constantly . . . with a heavy barrage of practical problems, politically coloured in this or that shade. And since personal attitudes must be adopted to them, albeit on a trial and error basis, it transpires that all ready-made prescriptions and unequivocal answers are worth nothing; they melt like a handful of snow thrown on a hot kitchen stove'.[4]

At the heart of these processes whereby the opposition became more pragmatic and less ideological was an unwitting exchange of concessions between the two main components of the oppositional striving, the ex-communists and the non-communists. The former gave up the concept of the leading role of the party and the latter readily acknowledged the social democratic framework of the anti-regime protests. This is not to say that the ex-communists ceased to be socialists (although some did), or that the opposition started to advocate an ideal democratic alternative to the Czechoslovak political system without regard to the realities which were inescapable in that part of the world. The contention was no longer between two communist parties, one in power and the other underground, nor between 'pure' communism and 'pure' liberalism.

The proclamation issued on behalf of the Socialist Movement of Czechoslovak Citizens on the fifth anniversary of the invasion, on 21 August 1973, drew attention to the international aspect first and then to a series of problems which called for solutions: continuing victimisation of hundreds of thousands, political imprisonment, tensions underneath the economic investment programme and technology transfer from the West. On the nature of the society towards which steps ought to be made it had the following to say:

'Czechoslovakia, a country with a highly developed culture, could evolve in a few years' time into a society of contented citizens whose aim it is not just to consume things but to create a modern socialist commonwealth. . . .A country with deeply rooted democratic traditions, which could stand in the front ranks of progressive European lands by implementing democracy within a socialist framework even in relation to the freedoms of its citizens, has so far shown itself to be a grim society of silent and indifferent people, intimidated by the arrogance of the powers that be who show contempt for public opinion, display a police-based arbitrariness and hold their prisons full.'[5]

Political prisoners, those sentenced in the trials of summer 1972 and also many others, including the victims of prosecutions in the provinces, on which there was less information, were the immediate concern of the opposition. It was known that conditions in prison were harsh, even if much better than in Stalin's time.[6]

The cells were small, two by four metres, shared with an ordinary criminal. The prisoners had to work in them, sewing buttons on cardboard, sorting pins and glass beads, manufacturing artificial flowers, doing wicker work. The work norms were high which meant that they had to spend ten to twelve hours a day fulfilling them. Failure to meet the quota was punishable by, for example, reduction of food portions. Wages paid to political inmates were about half those of criminal convicts and about one-fifth of the average wage in the country. Some 80 per cent of the wage was deducted as compensation for board and lodging. Only Kčs 20–40 were given to the prisoner per month to supplement food rations; he was forbidden to receive any money from his family. Sanitary conditions were bad: lack of fresh air, inadequate health examinations, inferior food. Only one food parcel of three kilograms per three months was allowed from the outside but permission to receive it tended to be withdrawn as a penalty. Visits were allowed only for one hour every three months for two adults and children. Correspondence with family was limited to one letter per week and censorship was strict. Many letters got inexplicably lost. Families were also victimised: dismissals and demotions affected wives and close relatives, and children were not admitted to senior secondary and higher education. As the status of 'political prisoner' officially did not exist, cultural isolation was felt very badly. In some prisons only one copy of a newspaper and one book were allowed for each cell every week, and the choice was the warder's. No specialised, foreign-language or Marxist literature was permitted, and no notes could be taken. Many prison guards indulged in petty chicanery of political prisoners.[7]

In spite of complaints and petitions by relatives and friends, and notwithstanding two general amnesties and the good behaviour which most of them demonstrated, the political prisoners had to serve the entire duration of their sentence or had only a few months remitted. Twelve of those sent to jail in 1972 were released on 21 December 1973, all having been sentenced to less than three years' imprisonment and after spending at least two years inside, including pre-trial detention. Jan Tesař was released in October 1976 after serving four years and nine months of a five-year sentence. Four were released before Christmas 1976 (Hübl, Šabata, Müller and Rusek). Vladimír Škutina, a writer, was let out two months before the expiry of his long sentence of four years and four months, with broken health. Neither were the international protests heeded, although the protesters included members of communist parties in Western Europe. Several new cases of blatant political persecution followed, for example of the writer from Ostrava, Ota Filip, who had already spent fifteen months in detention. In 1973 he was extensively interrogated in connection with a novel of his which was published in West Germany, and threatened with all possible and impossible consequences. Eventually the police forced him to emigrate. Dr J. Krejčí, also from Ostrava, a secondary school teacher now working as a manual worker, was sentenced to three years' imprisonment for subversion and misappropriation. The latter charge consisted of 'unjustified wage claims' which he had made against his employer, and the former included the writing of appeals against his daughter's non-admission to a grammar school, some private correspondence, and the authorship of an unpublished study on 'The Socratesian Strategy of Absolute Enmity' and two other essays, all designed for publication abroad. (Dr Krejčí is in exile now.) There were other instances in the constant war of nerves and the entire question of political incarceration remained an irritant and a barrier to some kind of a *modus vivendi* between the regime and the large disaffected community of intellectuals.

The grave of Jan Palach, the student who burned himself to death in January 1969 to protest against the continuing occupation of the country and capitulation of many of its politicians, was a place of pilgrimage to many. Fresh flowers and candles were interpreted by the authorities as inadmissible political demonstration and finally, before the fifth anniversary of the invasion in 1973, the grave was fenced off and Palach's mother was pressured into agreeing (in October) that the body of her son should be exhumed and cremated. This happened surreptitiously and for a long time no one knew to where the urn had been removed. Even so, people were still decorating the old grave with candles arranged to form Palach's initials after another body, of an old and poor woman without relatives, had been buried there.

Josef Smrkovský died on 14 January 1974 and the regime took complicated steps to prevent the funeral from becoming a demonstration of resistance. They were not quite successful: over a thousand people took part, including workers' delegations from factories and even some members of the lower echelons of the present establishment, next to hundreds of friends and acquaintances. Dubček's letter to Mrs Smrkovský has already been mentioned; the telegram informing him about the death and the funeral was not delivered. In March 1974 the police informed Smrkovský's widow that the urn with his ashes had been stolen from the grave in Prague, presumably by enemies of socialism in order to be smuggled out to the West. The police said however that they found the urn at the men's lavatory in a South Bohemian railway station when the Berlin-Vienna express train was passing through. Two Prague journalists were interrogated in this connection, but eventually the purpose of the morbid and suspicious machinations became clear when Mrs Smrovský was told that the police could not 'keep watch' over the urn at the Prague cemetery and that it better be buried in Smrkovský's home village.

Throughout the years many people were exposed to police surveillance, house searches and interrogations. The ex-reformers were not left alone, unmolested, in the ghetto created for them and their families as a result of the purges. One has the impression that their existence was being used to justify the perpetuation of the class struggle. First a large community of disaffected people was created and then an extensive police apparatus mobilised to keep an eye on them. It was a matter of action and reaction. The dissidents would not sit still, or many of them would not. When the attempt to organise themselves failed, they resorted to other, more individual forms of protest.

They began to write open letters to leading officials of the party and state, and either publish them in the samizdat press or release them for publication abroad when no satisfactory action was taken. Two main clandestine broadsheets were appearing in Czechoslovakia: *Národní noviny* as the organ of the Socialist Movement of Czechoslovak Citizens, and *Fakta, připomínky, události*, a survey of events including acts of injustice at home and reports on developments abroad.[8] Increasingly, especially since 1973, the silenced writers and intellectualls have also been granting interviews to Western media correspondents and addressing statements to the Western public, notably the socialist and communist parties of Western Europe, but also individual cultural personalities in the West.

Among the open letters, proclamations and other forms of individual and small-group protest in 1972, Dr František Janouch, a nuclear physicist, expressed to the president of the Czechoslovak Supreme Court concern about miscarriage of justice in the political trials of the summer of that year, and sent another letter to all the leading legislative and juridical authorities suggesting changes in the legal system of the country 'because some laws either do not respect at all or do not quite respect the constitutional rights of citizens', and because some subsidiary decrees and ordinances contravene the existing laws. Dr Janouch also informed the Czech Minister of Education that the Rector of Charles University acted unlawfully when prohibiting the publication of books or articles by scholars and scientists who had been expelled from the party or dismissed from the university for political reasons. Dr Janouch informed the Procurator General that such a ban was unconstitutional and asked him to take action. Karel Boček, formerly general manager of the Czechoslovak Uranium Industry, told Husák in an open letter that his statement to the effect that there were no political trials in Czechoslovakia was a lie. Boček himself had been arrested, interrogated and scheduled for trial when he managed to escape and eventually find his way to the West. Karel Kosík, Jiří Lederer and Rudolf Slánský Jr filed a suit at the end of 1972 against the police who searched their homes and confiscated books and manusripts there.

In 1973 Ludvík Vaculík and Pavel Kohout, both writers, gave interviews about cultural and literary oppression to Western journalists (*Die Zeit*, West German and Austrian television). Kohout also sent an open letter to the Czech Minister of Culture on the same topic; he said: 'statements by leading European writers, including for example Heinrich Böll and numerous communists, such as Aragon, to the effect that fruits of creative work in our country are being destroyed and their authors persecuted, are true'. Jan Tesař, one of the political prisoners, managed to address a letter from jail to the president of the Supreme Court in which he related his own case to the general suppression of civil liberties in the country. Věra Šťovíčková, a journalist, wrote the party central committee about her dismissal from an inferior job in a museum because of 'lack of class awareness'. For half a year she tried to find employment in vain, until she was finally taken on as a charwoman in a hostel but as soon as the personnel officer realised who she was—a proscribed journalist—she was fired once again. 'I an probably the first cleaning woman ever to have been sacked for political reasons.' Associate Professor Ján Mlynárik, Ph.D. and Candidate of Sciences, then employed as a stage hand in the National Theatre, complained to Husák about the behaviour of the Theatre's manager who abused him verbally and 'promised that...he would sack me from the Theatre without any reason'.

In 1974 Jiří Hochman, a former journalist, wrote a letter to Vasil Bilak asking him to 'take the police off my back'; Hochman had been in jail, was seriously ill and could not cope with constant harassment and chicanery. (He eventually emigrated to the USA.) The Socialist Movement issued a statement on the fifth anniversary of Husák's accession to power. In the summer, thirty political prisoners, now released, addressed a letter to the Lawyers' and Jurists' Union in connection with the Union's protest against illegalities in Chile after the putsch that swept away Allende's government. The Czechoslovak political prisoners expressed their solidarity and support for progressive Chileans but denied the Union the right to do the same. 'We do not know of a single instance of the Union's protecting human rights, civic freedoms and observation of legality in our own country...' Associate Professor Bohumil Peleška, Doctor of Medical Science, published an open letter to the World Federation of Scientists in *Nature* (London) describing how he had been dismissed as director of the Institute for Electronics and Modelling in Medicine, deprived of all opportunity to study, research and publish, and refused a permit to work abroad.

The year 1975 witnessed a great increase in the number of protest statements, partly because of the impending crowning of European cooperation talks in Helsinki. In February Zdeněk Mlynář protested to the editor of a party journal against his being associated with Zionism. At the beginning of April Václav Havel, the writer, addressed a long open letter to Husák with a scathing criticism of the moral state of the country where political rule is based on fear, intimidation and corruption.[9] Karel Kosík wrote to Jean-Paul Sartre (who replied, also publicly) that the police confiscated a thousand-page manuscript of the new philosophical work he was writing during a house search. 'Was this an attempt to foist on society a new custom and new normality—the regular confiscation of manuscripts? Could not this custom, in the land of Franz Kafka, become in a short time such a matter of course and indoctrinated need that authors themselves will phone the police to come and collect their freshly completed works?' Pavel Kohout mentioned the same topic in his open letter to Heinrich Böll and Arthur Miller: 'Does this not create a kind of precedent permitting the police from now on to enter everywhere and take everything?' Fifteen dissidents asked the president to take advantage of the 30th anniversary of liberation and set free all political prisoners. 'We ask you to regard this petition... as part of a general effort for humanisation and democratisation...' Academician Ivan Málek conveyed his concern about detrimental practices in the administration of scientific research to the praesidium of the Academy of Sciences. Ludvík Vaculík sent an open letter to the UN General Secretary who had come to Prague in April in April 1975 to receive with great pomp a *honoris causa* doctorate from Charles University. At about the same time the police were confiscating a manuscript, books, notes, photographs, tapes and other things from Vaculík's flat although no formal legal proceedings had been instituted against him. Should Herr Waldheim be an ordinary doctor of Czechoslovak jurisprudence instead of just an honorary one, he might be called upon to send Vaculík to jail for up to five years simply because the manuscript could be said to contain political subversion. Vilém Prečan sent a letter to the World Congress of Historians in San Francisco, drawing the world's attention to well over a hundred names of Czechoslovak historians who had been banned from research, teaching and jobs in their field. An open letter from Karel Kaplan to the party secretary Vasil Bilak was a general denunciation of the political system based on revenge in connection with Bilak's interview to an American communist paper in which he claimed that most of the purged people had been allowed to retain their positions. Zdeněk Mlynář and Jiří Hájek gave an interview on detente to Swedish television. František

Kriegel congratulated Academician Sakharov on the award of the Nobel Peace Prize. Věra Chytilová, the film director, explained to Husák the ordeal which she had to go through as a politically suspect person: in a truly absurd and grotesque fashion she was not allowed to make any films, and not given employment because she was making no films. Thirty-five Czechoslovak dissidents signed a protest against the garrotting of five Spanish revolutionaries. 'May the democrats of Europe show their solidarity whenever a dictatorial hand tightens the iron collar around the neck of democratic freedoms in any European country. It would be a dignified tribute if the revolutionary memory of Spanish patriots was commemorated by the proclamation of a year of political freedoms in which not a single political prisoner would be left lingering in jail. We appeal to the Czechoslovak government to take the first step in this direction'. Seventy-five signatures from among the oppositionists were collected under a congratulation to Dolores Ibarruri, the Spanish communist veteran, on her 80th birthday: 'You represent for us a party which plays an important role in the world revolutionary movement and holds attitudes to developments in our country as well as to the situation in the international workers' movement most of which are close to ours'. Three open letters in connection with detente, as it then culminated in Helsinki, were sent to the Czechoslovak leaders: by the former Foreign Minister Jiří Hájek, by the historian Karel Kaplan and by three veteran communist parliamentarians, František Kriegel, Gertruda Sekaninová-Čakrtová and František Vodsloň. When the regime decided to abolish the designation of 28 October, the day when democratic Czechoslovakia was established in 1918, as a public holiday, twenty-eight persons signed a proposal to the Federal Assembly chairman that this decision should be rescinded. 'It is an explicitly politically motivated decision. It shows extreme lack of sensitivity for the national awareness and feelings of our peoples, expecially the Czechs, and also a patently contemptuous attitude to the importance of our statehood'.

In 1976 the emphasis on the Eurocommunist dimension grew stronger. When fourteen former members of the party central committee signed a new petition for the release of political prisoners, they said: 'The citizens whose release from prison we are requesting were jailed because they pleaded publicly for a link between socialism and political democracy, thus holding a view very close to the official programmes of the French, Italian and other communist parties'. Zdeněk Mlynář sent an open letter to the 'communists and socialists of Europe' in which he argued that 'some of the political concepts put into practice by the holders of power in Czechoslovakia today are not only damaging to the development of socialism in this country but also a serious threat to the prospects of socialism in the whole of Europe'. Fourteen signatures appeared under a letter to the central committee of the Italian Communist Party expressing disagreement with the dismissal by the Czechoslovak authorities of eight Italian communist employees of Radio Prague who refused to cooperate with the Czech secret police in reporting their foreign contacts. Oldřich Jaroš, a historian, protested to the Ministry of the Interior and other organs against their arbitrary and rude action which prevented him from visiting Alexander Dubček who he had known for many years. Věnek Šilhán gave an interview to some Western newspapers critically evaluating the so-called 'small pardon' offered by Husák at the 15th party congress to those who fully retracted their reformist views. Thirty-six people signed an open letter to the French Committee of Mathematicians and the French Communist Party Central Committee whose public rally in defence of political prisoners in Paris was attacked in the official Czechoslovak press with the remark that one of those mentioned in Paris, the former student leader Jiři Müller, had been sentenced because of preparing an armed putsch and the physical liquidation of public figures. A number of protests and declarations was issued in connection with the arrest of several young pop-musicians who were sent to jail at separate trials in Pilsen and Prague, ostensibly because they used vulgar words and incited base insticts in the audience, but in fact as members of an underground non-conformist counter-culture. Professor Arnošt Kolman, an 84 year old philosopher, was allowed to visit his daughter in Sweden (after four years of asking for a permit and sixteen rejected applications) and used the opportunity to ask for political asylum. He sent an open letter to Brezhnev announcing his departure from the Soviet Communist Party. Kolman, a Czech by birth, had joined the Soviet party 58 years ago, was acquainted with Lenin and held high posts in the Comintern and the Soviet Communist Party Central Committee. 'I have reached the firm conclusion that to stay in the ranks of the Soviet Communist Party would amount to a betrayal of the ideals of social justice, humanism and a new, better society which I have striven for throughout my life in spite of all my mistakes and errors of judgment'.

Even this very incomplete look at the topics which the Czechoslovak opposition chose to advocate publicly from 1972 to 1976 reveals a confluence of three thematic backgrounds: continuing infringement of human rights, incompatibility of such practice with international detente, and kinship of Prague Spring ideas, which the opposition still upheld, with Eurocommunism.

HUMAN RIGHTS

That the question of human rights should be brought into focus in the middle of the 1970s is no wonder. It sometimes appears to have been conceived by the Carter Administration in the United States whereas of course every critique of totalitarianism and authoritarian precepts has always included a consideration of the relationship between man and his government. The spotlight which now is shining so brightly was switched on as a result of three developments: the conclusion of a twenty-year process in the United Nations whereby the Soviet Union had to allow full citation of political and individual rights alongside social, economic and collective rights in two legally binding international covenants; the institutional completion of an important stage of international detente, first started with other goals in mind, whereby rights and liberties were made components of an indivisible *modus operandi* package at Helsinki; and the suppression of dissent, reformism and rebellion inside the Soviet Union, Czechoslovakia and Poland at the end of the 1960s and first half of the 1970s with the use of methods that directly curtailed the human rights of large segments of the local population.

Communist theorists claim that because capitalism and socialism are antagonistically different, like hell and heaven, so must be their respective approaches to rights and freedoms of man. First of all, freedoms and rights under communism are not inalienable. They comprise a commodity which the party leadership has appropriated together with political power. It can then allocate them, as it does with the more tangible consumer goods, for temporary use by individuals and groups of people in exchange for other commodities, such as political obedience or even money. The exchange value of rights and freedoms is realised on a seller's market. Marx would rejoice seeing his theory of value extended into this field, or he might get angry, depending on how one understands him.

It transpires that the haggling in Geneva, Helsinki and Belgrade cannot alter this quintessential relationship because the negotiations are not about a transformation of the communist system into a non-communist one. They can only achieve what business meetings are about and for, that is induce the communist governments to lower the price they are exacting from their citizens for the conditional enjoyment of some rights and freedoms.

Over the years the numerical scope of the list of rights and freedoms has grown substantially. Franklin Roosevelt needed just four concepts to formulate the essence of his 'Four Freedoms' address in 1941: freedom of speech and worship, and freedom from want and fear. The

United Nations Charter spoke against discrimination on grounds of race, sex, language and religion, and the Universal Declaration of Human Rights of 1948 contained both political and social rights in 31 articles. The two most recent United Nations covenants contain more than sixty derivatives of the original four synoptic expressions.

It has often been asked why did the communist states sign all these documents and indeed press for their elaboration and international promulgation. It would seem that the recognition by the post-Stalin leadership of the importance of the emerging Third World states was initially responsible for the process which eventually led to the adoption of the Covenant on Economic, Social and Cultural Rights and the Covenant on Civil and Political Rights in 1966. The possibility of changing the voting balance in the United Nations must have played a role in the USSR's embracing once again the cause of *national and collective* rights and freedoms, such as are associated with anti-colonialism, self-determination, exploitation of natural resources, anti-racism, safeguards of humane living conditions, etc. Moscow probably underestimated the capacity of domestic dissent and opposition in Eastern Europe to turn the tables on their rulers. It did not expect the Prague Spring to happen when the covenants were being negotiated, and it was confident that domestic dissent in Russia could be handled as it had been previously. Similarly, almost ten years later, the economic and technological advantages of detente appeared to be too good to be missed and the risk of consenting to the inclusion of human rights provisions into the Helsinki Final Act seemed manageable, especially as the thrust of Basket Three was towards controlled exchanges. It should be noted that cooperation under the so-called Basket Three, while based on the exercise of certain rights and freedoms, remains largely within the institutional jurisdiction of extant authorities. Recognition of the applicability of individual rights derives from Principle VII in Basket One.

In the Soviet view, however, collective and social rights are superior to individual and political rights, and such rights as are recognised are superior to freedoms. The 'right to work' occupies a pivotal position in the Soviet interpretation; without it the other rights allegedly have little sense. But 'right to work' is not associated with 'freedom to choose one's work', just as 'right to education', commendable as it is, does not entail 'freedom to choose education'. Above all, man as an individual cannot claim a right or a freedom either from the theory of natural law or from supra-national conventions to which his government, not he, is a party. Hence all rights and liberties are conditional on official consent and derive from the state.

As a Czech legal theorist has put it: 'The adoption of both covenants [on human rights] and their promulgation do not mean that the arrangement of the legal status of an individual in a particular, organised society, i.e. in a state, has ceased to be a matter essentially subordinated to the internal jurisdiction of the state'.[10] And two others added that from the international covenants 'there do not follow entitlements and obligations for the area of relations between the state, the agencies of the state, the citizens and their organisations inside the state.... These relations—including human rights—are codified exclusively through the valid legal system of the state in question'.[11]

The Czechoslovak opposition questioned the validity of an argument which put the state as an obstacle between the citizen and the applicability of human rights. But they could also point to the fact that the Czechoslovak legal order itself, including the constitution, while containing a great deal of individual laws which curtail the validity of human rights and liberties, still reflects a certain adherence to them. Some articles of the constitution were circumscribed by various limitations. For example, freedom of speech and the press is said to be guaranteed only insofar as it is 'consistent with the interests of the working people' (Article 28), leaving it of course to the authorities to decide what was or was not the working people's interest. Article 24 states that 'all citizens shall have the right to education' and there is no circumcision of this entitlement, even though a subsidiary paragraph proclaims that 'all education and schooling shall be based on the scientific world outlook', i.e. Marxism. Some other stipulations are free of any riders. Thus every citizen has the right to submit proposals, suggestions and complaints and the state agencies are even obligated to 'take responsible and prompt action' in response (Article 29). 'Inviolability of the person shall be guaranteed' and 'offenders can be punished only by due process of law' (Article 30). 'Inviolability of the home, the privacy of the mails and all other forms of communication, as well as freedom of domicile shall be guaranteed' (Article 31). And 'freedom of confession shall be guaranteed' although the practising of religious beliefs is tolerable only 'insofar as this does not contravene the law' (Article 32).

It must be clear from the account of 'normalisation' so far that the critics of the regime voiced their protest against the violations of rights and freedoms from very early on. They were also aware that by insisting on their rights, they might be breaking those legal provisions which had been introduced precisely in order to curb them. In July 1973 one of the political prisoners who had been jailed for complicity in the Socialist Movement of Czechoslovak Citizens, the historian Jan Tesař, sent a letter to the Supreme Court from prison. In it he said:

> 'The verdict of the Czech Supreme Court [according to which he was ordered to jail] therefore logically expresses a denial of both the right of civic involvement and the right of disagreement with the government; both of these rights belong to the most precious values created by

European civilisation, rights which cannot be relinquished. I was found guilty because I exercised the inalienable rights of a man and a citizen as they were proclaimed two centuries ago; as early as one hundred years ago they became a reality in our country and they were then exercised to a much greater extent than they are today. I have never denied and I do not deny even now that in the process of exercising my rights I violated some Czechoslovak laws (e.g. by disseminating information and printed materials from abroad). I was aware of what I was doing. Such is the dilemma of free people living in those unfortunate countries—Czechoslovakia is one of them—which base their administration on the principle of the so-called leading role of the party, in our case the Czechoslovakia Communist Party... This is the dilemma of a citizen under a government and a system of justice which considers it normal for a developed country to be in a position where one political party unilaterally assigns "tasks" to the whole of society, where "fulfilment of the party's tasks" is seen as the rationale for the existence of the state organs, and the only possible form of civic involvement'.[12]

DETENTE

The mainstream of Czechoslovak opposition has always professed a positive belief in the beneficial nature of international detente and even when expressing scepticism about this or that of its aspects, the Czechoslovak dissidents had little doubt that the alternatives were not preferable. The birth of the Czechoslovak reform movement had been connected with the relaxation of tensions in Khrushchev's time. When the reforms gathered momentum in the middle half of the 1960s, interchange with the West in economy and culture became part and parcel of the overall pattern of change. The Prague Spring embodied pursuance of detente in the various action programmes as one of the fundamental principles of Czechoslovak foreign policy. Those responsible for such emphasis were now in opposition and did not see why their attitude should change.

For one thing, they appreciated the strength of the new regime's hold over the oppressive apparatuses and knew that the launching of large-scale persecution and even terror on the Stalinist lines was still possible. The instruments were there. Only two things stood in the way: the leadership's unwillingness to go to the extreme, for a variety of reasons, and the accessibility of international public opinion which Moscow could not afford to ignore completely. Should the second of these obstacles disappear under the impact of a cold war, the first one would almost automatically become much too precarious to rely on for safety. The present victimisation and infringement of human rights is still preferable to Stalin-type persecution. Over a hundred thousand people served time for political reasons in prisons and labour camps of one kind or another in Czechoslovakia from the communist takeover in 1948 to the early 1960s. Tens of thousands were physically tortured. Thousands died in jail. And perhaps three hundred were executed. This memory became associated with the notion of a cold war, the opposite of detente. Compared to it, the 1970s were still relaxed.

Secondly, even if the only alternative to detente were not to be a full-scale cold war but only a withdrawal of the state from other than just commercial agreements with the democratic West, the present state of affairs was still to be preferred because political and cultural involvement of the government in the international arena forced it to enter into commitments whose implementation at home could then be demanded and infringements exposed. The Soviet Union signed the General Declaration of Human Rights in 1948, a cold war year if there ever was one, but no one inside the East European countries could really make the Declaration a term of reference against which the regime would score plus or minus points for its behaviour *vis-à-vis* the

291

domestic population, largely because the signing of the Declaration was not followed by detente. On the other hand, the ink on the signatures of the Helsinki Final Act had not had time to dry before the Czech dissidents took their government to task for not abiding by its provisions.

What admittedly seems to be lacking in the various pronouncements on detente by the Czechoslovak oppositionists is the drawing of distinction between detente and appeasement, something that a number of Soviet dissidents commented on. As if the possibility of having a bad detente, a one-way street in which the West provides the goods and the East reaps the benefits, including freedom to persecute large sections of its populations, was not a real one. And yet, the Czechs in particular should have in their historical memory a special place for wariness against international appeasement; the detente of the 1930s between Britain and France on the one hand and Hitler on the other hand has been nearly fatal to the Czechs as a nation and fully fatal to the independence of their state. Perhaps the domestic opponents of the regime do not want to be castigated as warmongers, as Sakharov has been, and what they anyway mean when preaching international cooperation is detente with a spine.

The proverbial man in the street, not in the limelight either as a pro-regime activist or an outspoken dissenter, is understandably somewhat less circumspect in venting his true feelings. A sociologist conducted an unofficial opinion poll of 187 persons on detente in February and March 1975. The question 'What do you expect of the Helsinki conference' was answered by 138 respondents spontaneously: 'Nothing'. Some added: 'That is, nothing for us, for our country'. Another 33 said they expected withdrawal of Soviet troops and restoration of full sovereignty. (A surprisingly high percentage of rather simple perceptions. But then, I remember from the days of the invasion a chalked inscription on a Prague wall: 'Don't despair! United Nations will help!') Only one respondent in the poll, which was of course conducted under camouflage, a 60-year old functionary, stated that the conference would have to confirm the frontiers dividing the two camps. Some of the comments are worth quoting: 'I do not believe the West will achieve anything. It is not united and the Russians will always dupe them.' 'The West will die of too much democracy and naïveté. The world will just have another declaration on paper. And in a few years' time the Austrians, Yugoslavs and maybe one of the Scandinavian states can expect internationalist assistance from Soviet troops. The Washington-Moscow red line will then glow hot and the Americans will fire off a warning to the effect that should the Russians do the same thing again in the future, the next summit meeting will not take place.' 'The West will play into the hands of the Russians because it is glad that they are leaving them alone—for the time being. . . . Perhaps only China has the small nations' fate at heart'.[13]

When the Final Act was signed, an anonymous report from Prague was a little more accommodating:

> 'If we disregard our subjective feelings and views . . . we must admit that the results of the European security conference, although no more than a beginning, are still promising. Even the few new things that the West succeeded in incorporating into the document could represent a step forward, provided they will be complied with. . . . Fot the USSR this kind of politics carries certain risks. It leads to a certain opening of the system and, through it, its erosion. Perhaps the turn of Czechoslovakia will come in the course of this process—in the long run'.[14]

The fullest expression of the opposition's attitude to international detente is contained in an interview which Zdeněk Mlynář and Jiři Hájek gave to a Swedish radio and television correspondent in Prague in September 1975.[15] They first offered an explanation of why the harsh Moscow Protocol of August 1968 was accepted by the majority of the Dubček leadership. Apart from the consequences which a repudiation would carry for the people of Czechoslovakia, 'we were also concerned lest the solution of the conflict rendered impossible peaceful coexistence in the Europe of the future'. They subordinated their own interests to those of Europe. Or so they thought. 'There must not arise in Europe a perpetual focal point of tension which would impede the emergence of provisos for an international policy of the kind which has recently led to Helsinki. Every relapse into a cold war appeared to us unacceptable.'

This is a rather striking line of reasoning, and although it comes straight from the horse's mouth one is reluctant to accept it at face value. Nonetheless, Mlynář was obviously right when pointing out that 'the very substance of our political reform presupposed, and still does, a completely different atmosphere in Europe than that which is associated with cold war'. Both Mlynář and Hájek (who was Czechoslovak Foreign Minister during the Prague Spring) welcomed the results of Helsinki and wished to 'dissociate themselves from attempts to minimise and denigrate them'. Then came another unusual argument: although Soviet military intervention in Czechoslovakia slowed down the relaxation process by lowering the credibility of the interventionists, it also contributed 'to the manner in which the principles of inter-state relations were formulated at Helsinki. Czechoslovakia's tragic experience and the lessons deriving from it were surely in the background of formulations about the equality and sovereignty of every country, about the right of every nation to choose its economic, social, political and cultural system and regime without outside pressure, and about the impossibility to justify the use of force in inter-state relations'. Finally, Mlynář and Hájek suggested—with a good amount of wishful thinking, one feels compelled to add—that the Helsinki Final Act should have retroactive validity. It should obligate the signatories, at least morally, to make amends for such actions in the past which were demonstrably in contravention of the Act. Reiteration of the principle of non-use of force at Helsinki could even be understood as self-criticism of its violation in the past.

The two ex-reformers were treading on firmer ground when relating the signing of the Final Act to the current and future behaviour of the signatories. 'Hundreds of thousands of people who advocated these principles in face of military intervention are still being excluded not only from political life but also banned from practising their professions. . . . A curious situation has arisen: the secretary general of the Czechoslovak Communist Party has solemnly signed his name under the same principles for which others are being expelled from his party and from society'.

Already then, in the autumn of 1975, Hájek and Mlynář expressed three ideas which were to become part of the philosophy behind the drafting of Charter 77: that the Helsinki document acknowledged every individual person's right to have his place in society respected by the power of the state, that principles adopted in international dealings have their validity inside each participating country, and that the Final Act recognised the existence of common European cultural values and humanitarian traditions. 'It contravenes the spirit of Helsinki if some European nations and states keep alive elements which are contrary to European civilisation and cultural foundations'.

The Mlynář and Hájek attitude can be seen as a political approach on a general level, such as could conceivably be accepted by Moscow and Prague and still leave the scope of implementation at their discretion. They did not elaborate what it would specifically mean if the principles of the Final Act were really to be translated into life in the communist states.

Karel Kaplan, a historian, spelled out the details and from his enumeration of the desiderata one can see how absurd it is to expect that a regime based on premises which consider human rights irrelevant to the fulfilment of its purpose would feel duty bound by an international undertaking to change these premises. Kaplan's open letter to the party praesidium, the Federal Assembly and the Federal Government, dated 20 October 1975, does not mean that its author expected all this to happen. To act on his eight proposals would be logical in terms of the Final Act, but against the stronger logic of a one-party state. He suggested that in view of its signature under the Final Act, the Czechoslovak government should do the following:

1. Expand economic relations with the West and readjust Czechoslovakia's place in the international division of labour.

2. Release and fully rehabilitate all political prisoners and discontinue victimisation of others; permit free promotion of one's own views; amend the criminal law accordingly.

3. Give a passport to every citizen and abolish special exit permits.

4. Stop censoring and impeding international cultural exchanges for political and ideological reasons; abolish political discrimination over the creation and dissemination of cultural and literary values at home.

5. End discrimination against researchers and scholars; make scientific information generally available; guarantee freedom of publication at home and abroad; permit international contacts of scientists and scholars.

6. Abolish state monopoly in the field of information; end censorship; admit the foreign press freely; stop jamming radio stations.

7. Before armament expenditures are cut, troop numbers reduced and conscription period shortened, the inner life of the armed forces should be democratised; by granting civil rights and liberties, the state will no longer need a part of its police force.

8. All legal-political acts passed after the 1968 invasion ought to be annulled and their substance freely debated anew.[16]

In two statements the human rights aspect of detente was singled out as evidently corresponding best to what the opposition believed would be of genuine benefit to Czechoslovakia. František Kriegel, Gertruda Sekaninová-Čakrtová and František Vodsloň, all leading communist veterans and victims of the purges, suggested to the Federal Assembly on 8 November 1975 that it should at long last ratify the two United Nations covenants and political rights and on economic, social and cultural rights which had been signed seven years earlier. (This was actually done in December of the same year.) They further proposed that in the light of Helsinki the Federal Assembly should open talks with the USSR on the removal of Soviet troops which, after all, had been stationed in the country only temporarily. In connection with human rights inside the country the three reformers called for the release and rehabilitation of all political prisoners, termination of repressive measures and victimisation against adults and children, and amendment of such laws that are in contravention of the Helsinki Act, the Declaration of Human Rights, the United Nations covenants and the Czechoslovak constitution.[17]

In a similar vein, Jiří Hájek wrote to the Prime Minister on 1 October 1975:

'The Czechoslovak president's signature under the Helsinki Final Act and the Czechoslovak government's statement of 8 August 1975 that it would consistently comply with the undertakings deriving from that document, mean that all agencies accounting to this government have been obligated to ensure that no person adhering to these principles and applying them to the specific situation in Czechoslovakia since 1968 is on account of such views deprived of such employment as corresponds to his qualification, that he should not be denied the opportunity to pursue creative work in the art, science, technical development, economic organisation, health care and cultural life, that his children should not be on account of such views and attitudes prevented from learning at secondary and higher schools if they show the requisite ability and talent, and especially that no one should be prosecuted and jailed for views based on such principles or for their dissemination, and that such acts of persecution and discrimination should be stopped, their continuation prevented and the damage caused by them redressed'.[18]

All this is recited here at length and in some detail to show that the signing of the Helsinki Final Act represented a powerful impetus to oppositional activity in Czechoslovakia and that the human rights component of the Final Act, notably as expressed in Principle VII, had direct relevance to the Czechoslovak situation and was identified as such by the victims of persecution and their spokesmen. An emigre source evaluated the upsurge of protest and criticism in 1975 and came to the conclusion that Alexander Dubček and his followers had not become oppositionists in order to plunge into a political adventure. They were what they had been in 1968: advocates of democratic socialist reform. Neither were they alone. They were joined by liberal non-communists and young people who had experienced the Prague Spring as their first political lesson, or had even been too young for that. Helsinki in particular and detente in general offered them the possibility to demand with renewed vigour an annulment of the intervention and its consequences.[19]

Given that this was so, and the evidence is amply bearing it out, it seems rather surprising that a more profound study of the meanings of detente has not emerged from the oppositional circles. (Perhaps it has, but it is not available to the writer.) One would have expected the theorists of Prague Spring to come out with a somewhat more realistic view of what the West could and should attain and what the East was willing to concede. They could have asked for detente to be understood as an active policy, not just an aim already achieved, a concession already made and a public relations exercise deftly arranged. They could have exhorted the Western partners of the Soviet Union to go on showing initiative after Helsinki and to promote detente as both a sequence of measures and a public dialogue. Detente should not be only a matter of diplomacy of the traditional type. Quiet deals behind closed doors would obviously go on being made, but the ex-reformers could have called for non-abandonment of an open international political dialogue, such as the communists call 'ideological struggle'. They might have also stressed that detente should be more than a matter of international public law regulating relations between states, and that the governments involved should seek to provide a favourable space and frameworks not only for themselves but also for non-governmental groups and individuals. It is in this transcendence that the governments should discharge one of their primary functions with which they had been enjoined in the 'social contract', that they should exist for the benefit of the people who they govern. Detente should be populist in the good sense of the word. The communist governments are obliged to take account not only of their own interests but also of those of their Western partners and of Western public opinion. Conversely, the Western governments have every right to conceive and formulate their detente-inspired policies while taking into consideration governmental *and* popular feelings in Eastern Europe, of which the latter are to an extent articulated by non-conventional means. The partners should comprise both the governments and the people. Detente between governments makes sense, but detente between governments and between people is more valuable. Detente should be understood as neither just a bilateral Soviet-American arrangement nor a simple exercise in inter-bloc politics. Detente is multi-lateral. It should be evaluative because its accretion is only partly due to an intrinsic momentum; more significantly it grows by volition. The West has no reason to accept an ideological conception of detente as the best way towards communist domination at a lesser cost than a world war would command. Hence the need for a periodic look-back to assure that the edifice is not being undermined by spurious deeds.

It appears as if the Czechoslovak opposition accepted detente in a static fashion. Here it is, so let us say what it means for our governments. But detente is many things to many people, it is man-made, not an 'objective law', and the Western participants have been in need of a reasoned argument from East European oppositions as to how they think it ought to be pursued. As any other international state of affairs, detente can obviously turn sour, peter out or terminate abruptly. The dangers should be kept in perspective: the alternative to a successful and sustained period of detente is not war. Several intermediate stages lie between the very good and the disastrous. One can have a not quite satisfactory detente or even a thoroughly bad one; it can be seen working in one area and fail in another; and it can meet the expectation of one or several partners while failing others. Even a 'cold war', obviously objectionable, does not necessarily spell the end of the world. The world has been there before. Every one of the thirty-five Helsinki signatories severally, and all of them jointly, would probably have enough strength to survive and surmount a 'cold war' period. How far does one go before sacrificing detente?

The danger is not so much in detente not working to perfection as in its taking the path of appeasement. There does not seem to have been enough warning from Czechoslovak oppositional circles against another Munich. The Helsinki Final Act and the international covenants on human rights represent a checklist of obligations against which the opposition can measure the performance of its government. But detente is more than that. It is about human rights, the primary concern of the oppositionists, but it is not only about human rights. It is also about East-West deals in weapons and trade, a complex relationship which involves danger to the Western world. Detente has been neither created nor accepted for the sake of oppositions in Eastern Europe. Can the interests of dissenters and of Western governments be reconciled? How?

EUROCOMMUNISM

There are good reasons why a special relationship should have developed between the Czechoslovak democratic-socialist opposition and those Western communist parties which have become known as Eurocommunist.

The broad contours of East European reformism, of which the Prague Spring represented a culmination, have taken shape concurrently with the evolution of 'polycentrism', that nucleal notion of Eurocommunism. Some Eurocommunist theorists place the origins of their variety of communism further back into the past, at Gramsci's prison door and the Popular Front policy in Spain and then throughout the Comintern-dominated movement. This can be accepted in honesty only inasmuch as communism has always produced groups, strands and tendencies of great variety. Every anarchist, New Leftist, terrorist, centrist, moderate, democrat, liquidator, *Salon-kommunist*, every Maoist, Stalinist, Trotskyite, Bukharinite and Leninist of today can claim the right to an ancestry line extending back to either the venerable fathers themselves or to some of their venerable disciples. What is more, nearly every one of the descendants will claim that his is the one and only legitimate lineage. What matters is not so much the assertion of historical continuity, given that dialectics can justify just about everything, as the more recent confluence in time, method and objective. In this sense, 1956 and de-Stalinisation are the name of the game. When some of the West European communists began to question international centralism in the movement, some of the East European communists began to evolve reformism. The Czechoslovaks were fortunate to bring the reformist spiral in Eastern Europe to the fullest expression in 1968, in good time for some Western communists to be ready to do the same thing in their own way. The difference between Prague Spring and Eurocommunism, apart from the obvious fact of the one happening in and around a ruling party and the other in and around several non-ruling parties, was in no more than the set of priorities. The Czechoslovaks placed emphasis on reforms first, and greater autonomy *vis-à-vis* the Soviet Union later, whereas the Eurocommunists started from the other end. Hence the basic cause of affinity. By the time the Czechoslovak reformers became oppositionists, their Eurocommunist brothers had strengthened their determination to the point of making a public stand of it.

But the story did not end there because the 'normalisation' regime in Czechoslovakia was perpetrating precisely those sins which the Eurocommunist leaders had been trying to avoid, namely subservience to Moscow, orthodoxy in theory (including such crucially important questions for Italy, France and Spain as militant atheism), and blatant disregard of human rights. These happened to be also the sins which the socialists, Christian Democrats and others had been accusing the communists of. The Czechoslovak regime was even creating apartheid in their country just when South Africa and Rhodesia became the whipping boys of every decent progressive in the West and when the hot summers in America's black ghettos had not quite yet died away. Not enough of that, the Husák-Bilak coalition was doing to its defeated adversaries essentially the same injustice as the Chilean junta to the supporters of Allende, even if not with equal Latin American cruelty. And finally, the end of the three last authoritarian regimes in non-communist Europe—in Portugal, Greece and Spain—came about during the same period. Berlinguer, Carrillo and eventually Marchais could no longer prevaricate even had they wanted to. This was the time, and God only knows when a more suitable moment would offer itself. They had been disposed to seeking autonomy from Moscow's spell before, there is no denying them uneasiness at least since 1956, but fate has certainly thrown them together with the Czechoslovak ex-reformers in the 1970s. Brezhnev and Husák made them Eurocommunist as much as Togliatti.

Had Czechoslovakia been 'normalised' differently, on the basis of a Husák-Dubček moderate scaling down of the reforms under benign Soviet tutelage, the Eurocommunist dimension in the movement would have evolved more slowly.

As it were, the Czechoslovak oppositionists of the reform-communist variety soon began to point out the kinship between their beliefs and those of their West European comrades, and to address their protest statements either to West European communist organisations and committees directly or to 'the communists and socialists of Europe' generally. Zdeněk Mlynář was the most active proponent of the Eurocommunist link. In one of his public statements (an open letter) he drew the following parallel:

'In the Czechoslovakia of today the problem is not only that of the so-called dissidents; not only individuals who express their critical views and discontent ... are being silenced. Suppression and persecution affects hundreds of thousands of people who for many years advocated, and still do, a certain tendency in the European communist, socialist and democratic movement. This tendency is very similar and sometimes completely identical with the tendencies that are increasingly and positively asserting themselves in the European working class movement, especially in the recent political evolution of the communist parties in Italy, France, Spain, Great Britain, Sweden, Belgium and elsewhere. It is also very close to the tendency represented for many years by the Yugoslav communists and in some questions it comes near to the political attitudes of Romanian communists. . . . I am convinced that if the European socialist movement is genuinely concerned in safe-guarding the aims expressed in the political platform of the Helsinki conference, it cannot evade giving help to the restoration of political democracy in Czechoslovakia'.[20]

The last sentence in this quotation shows that expectations were running high between Helsinki in the summer of 1975 and the European communist summit in East Berlin in the summer of 1976. Czechoslovak ex-reformers wished for the Eurocommunists to take up a cudgel on their behalf. In the Mlynář-Hájek interview on Swedish television, the 'attitude to Czechoslovak reformism and its sup-pression' is presented as 'one of the strongest differentiation factors in the international communist movement after the Second World War', and Mlynář specifically referred to the forthcoming meeting of communist leaders: 'The conference can hardly pass over in silence the fact that the further evolution of socialism was profoundly disrupted in our country and that a way out of the closed situation must be sought'.[21]

Such expectation of a debate directly concerned with Czechoslovak 'normalisation' was futile and Mlynář may have assessed the chances wrongly. (After his arrival in the West from Czechoslovakia in June 1977, he admitted that this was the case.) For one thing, the communist summit was no place for any debate. All discussions took place at the ten preparatory sessions of the 'editorial commission' (five in 1975 and five in 1976) which was drafting a document to be signed at the conference, and although information is scant, there was at no time any intention to bring focus on specific instances of policy. All the wrangles centered around general issues of 'proletarian and socialist internationalism', the role of the Soviet Union in the movement, the nature of inter-party relations and the significance of such things as 'common principles' of the Marxist-Leninist legacy for the movement as a whole. When the 29 leaders assembled in East Berlin, they just read out their speeches and signed a joint statement. In the end the only mention of Czechoslovakia was a bracketed reference in Berlinguer's speech to the continued disapproval of the Italian Communist Party of the military intervention in 1968. Even this criticism was directed at the invasion, a matter of the past, and not the 'normalisation'.

But of course the difference in views as to the unity of the movement under one centre or even one set of mandatory principles bore directly on the policies advocated by the ex-reformers in Czechoslovakia. Mlynář was aware of this broader context already in 1975:

'On the whole we hope that the European communist conference will reflect new conditions in which the communist parties pursue their policies. It is necessary to give up the idea that communists in Europe can work according to a standard prescription and that they can have a single directing centre. Equal and democratic relations must be introduced into the communist movement at long last. No party should be castigated for advocating a specific policy, and equally criticism of a party should not be regarded inadmissible. The unity of the future can only be contemplated as unity in diversity, full of logical differences and contradictions. To claim that what has so far been implemented in the socialist countries is generally valid and binding on others is theoretically a poor proposition'.[22]

There is no doubt, however, that Mlynář expected more. He wrote a book-length manuscript in 1975, *The Czechoslovak Reform Attempt*[23], which went into great detail to counter Soviet accusations and to explain the reformist policy of 1968, including its mistakes. Its 50-page last chapter dealt with the 'international context of the Czechoslovak reform in relation to the European socialist states and the international communist movement'. In it Mlynář went a long way to meet even those Soviet objections to the Prague Spring which were later encapsulated in the Brezhnev Doctrine: he acknowledged that the 'fate of socialism' in every country was the legitimate concern of every member party of the communist movement. The communist parties of the Soviet orbit had a right to be interested in Czechoslovak developments in 1968 and even to criticise them, but had no right to intervene. Mlynář had to say this if he wanted to be logical, because he then went on to suggest that by the same token 'normalisation' ought to be subjected to an international communist examination by those parties which staked their future on theories and policies symptomatic of the Prague Spring.

The argument is noteworthy and evidently hinges on what exactly is entailed in the 'right to be concerned' and where in the process of being concerned the other key principle of Eurocommunism begins to operate, notably that of the 'ultimate right' of every communist party to do as it pleases, even if this means going contrary to the 'concern' of others. This argumentation can, however, retain some validity only as long as there is a 'communist movement', however hazily one defines it, which associates both orthodox and non-conformist parties. As soon as a party decides to step outside such a movement, and is allowed to do so, the 'concern' of others about its policy would presumably have to be much less. The shades of dissociation differ and logic does not always apply: Yugoslavia is presumably still in the movement, albeit loosely, and Soviet 'concern' about its theoretical foundations and practical policies is expressed only mutely and sporadically, whereas China holds no track with the movement (except by proxy, through her links with Romania, which in itself is not a very clear case) and vicious criticism of her internal and foreign policies is the staple diet of Soviet and bloc propaganda.

Be it as it may, the playing of the Eurocommunist card was a natural thing to do for the Czechoslovak reformist opposition on grounds of theoretical kinship and practical exigency. It also revived the use of concepts and language symptomatic of the communist movement, such as had been on the wane in the oppositional circles at home from 1972 to 1975. This too showed a remarkable resilience of the communistic spirit in the ex-reformist constituency, but was not accepted entirely without misgivings by their partners who had a straightforward non-communist background, or those ex-communists for whom the lessons of Czechoslovak communist 'construction', from the February 1948 takeover to the 'normalisation' practices of the 1970s, were sufficient encouragement to free their minds of the faith.

One could argue, as I have often done in this context, since politics are the art of the possible, and there is no sign of the Soviet hold over Eastern Europe crumbling, that the association of systemic criticism with the tenets of reform communism represents the only faint hope of political relaxation inside the Soviet orbit, irrespective of the ideal preferences of the critics. In the second half of 1976, after the communist summit failed to exert any visible influence on the course of 'normalisation', while at the same time confirming the inner division of the movement, the question for Czechoslovak oppositionists was whether the continued violations of human rights against the backdrop of detente and the Eurocommunist criticism of such practices could make the individual expressions of protest coalesce.

THE CHARTER

As is so often the case, great things have simple beginnings. Not even the Czechoslovak secret police apparently know who was the first to come forward with the idea of a Charter. The story, as related from Prague, is really very modest and it takes us as close to the truth as we dare to go.

'We stood in the kitchen door and she said "Something ought to be done about it" and made three more steps and turned on the tap to make water run over our voices, crouched into whisper as they had been anyway. That sentence, just prior to the cascade, had neither an exclamation nor a question mark appended to it. It had nothing at the end except the falling trickle of water but it presaged a debate on civic and political rights. The day was Thursday, 11 November 1976, when they began selling *Collection of Laws* No. 23 which contained among other things the Foreign Minister's ordinance of 10 May 1976, numbered 120 and bearing a title full of hope: International Covenant on Civil and Political Rights and International Covenant on Economic, Social and Cultural Rights. Price per copy Kčs 2·60—a lot of citizen's rights for almost a trifle, not counting slightly higher running water rates incurred during the debate.

'The afore-mentioned covenants were opened for signing in New York on 19 December 1966 and on behalf of Czechoslovakia were signed in the same New York on 7 October 1968, forty-seven days after the entry of friendly armies into the country. The Federal Assembly gave its consent to both covenants on 11 November 1975, seven years after their signature in New York. The president of the republic ratified them and the appropriate documents were deposited with the United Nations secretary general on 23 December 1975. The international covenant on civil and political rights came into force on 23 March 1976 and became effective for Czechoslovakia on the very same day. The international covenant on economic, social and cultural rights came into force on 3 January 1976 and also became effective for Czechoslovakia on 23 March 1976. The ordinance No. 120 was published in the Collection of Laws on 13 October 1976 and reached the stalls, as has already been made known, at Kčs 2·60 per copy, on the day when the memorable sentence "Something ought to be done about it" was spoken and supplemented with the turning on of a water tap.

'The preamble to the covenants says that "recognition of the inherent dignity and of the equal and inalienable rights of all members of the human family is the foundation of freedom, justice and peace in the world" and that "the individual, having duties to other individuals and to the community to which he belongs, is under a responsibility to strive for the promotion and observance of the rights recognised in the present covenant". With regard to the recognition of inherent dignity and inalienable rights, the preamble says nothing about the need for running water during discussions of the said dignity and rights. But we have developed certain habits.

'Thus the idea of "doing something" was born and because the heads which generate such ideas were undoubtedly more numerous than our official signatories of covenants could ever imagine, the Proclamation of Charter 77 came into being . . . Peace to people of good will. Christmas is here and, as calendars go, the year 1977 is drawing nearer, the one that was named the Year of Rights of Political Prisoners. Christmas is here and man is somehow closer to his fellow man, they give presents to each other and usually exchange best wishes for health and happiness. This is what Charter 77 aspires to be . . . a modest best wish for everyone. How will it be received? . . . Approving signatures under the Charter grow in number. Happy and merry new year—the seventy-seventh!'[24]

The Charter is a combination of a statement, a petition and a declaration of intent. It was to be delivered to the government, the Federal Assembly and the Czechoslovak Press Agency but the police arrested those carrying the appropriate copies to their destinations. It can be legally argued that by falling into the hands of the police, in clearly addressed envelopes, the act of delivery was completed and since no crime could have been suspected (see Article 29 of the constitution guaranteeing the right of every citizen to submit petitions), the police were obliged to transmit the consignments to the addressees. Also confiscated were envelopes with copies meant for mailing to the individual signatories.

The Charter was signed by 243 persons, one of whom withdrew his signature on 25 January. It was intended for publication, as witnessed by the fact that one of the prime copies was addressed to the Czechoslovak Press Agency. The Western press reported the Charter on 7 January (some West German media on the night of the 6th).

The document begins by referring to the two United Nations covenants and the Helsinki Final Act. It says in a calm and dignified tone, characteristic of the text as a whole that the rights and freedoms underwritten by these international acts constitute 'features of civilised life for which many progressive movements have striven throughout history'.[25] And it welcomes Czechoslovakia's accession to the agreements. Regrettably, many basic human rights exist in Czechoslovakia on paper alone.

Then comes the longest section of the Charter in which the various instances of infractions of human rights in Czechoslovakia are described and referenced to the appropriate articles of the two covenants and to the way they are expressed in Czechoslovak legislation. The covenants are the basic term of reference.

The following areas of human activity are mentioned:

Freedom of expression. Here, two categories of infringements are specified: 'tens of thousands' are prevented from working in their own fields because they hold dissenting views, and 'hundreds of thousands' of others are denied 'freedom from fear' because they risk unemployment and other penalties should they voice their own opinions.

Right to education. The Charter says that countless young people are prevented from studying because of their own views or even their parents', and innumerable citizens fear that their children's right to education might be withdrawn 'if they should ever speak up in accordance with their convictions'.

Freedom of information and public expression. He who seeks to exercise this right is prone to be subjected to extrajudicial and even judicial sanctions, as in the recent case of young musicians. [This is a reference to the trials of several proponents of 'underground culture', already mentioned. This case had a special importance in the period immediately preceding the issuance of the Charter for several reasons. It was after some time once again a blatantly political persecution that reached the court stage and received publicity. It had an intimidatory character, and a 'united front' of the opposition emerged in defence of the young musicians, embracing their most vehement supporters with New Left leanings, ex-communists, liberals, Christians and others.] The Charter points out that centralised control of all communications media, publishing and cultural institutions makes it impossible for people to exercise their freedom of expression outside the narrow scope of officially endorsed tenets. Neither can they defend themselves against 'attacks on their honour and reputation'. Scholars and writers in fact suffer today for legally publishing their works many years ago.

Freedom of religious confession. This is being continually curtailed by interference with the activity of churchmen, by financial and other sanctions against believers and by constraints on religious education.

In the above sections the Charter criticism is directed against what one might call straightforward infractions, such as could conceivably be set right without the regime ceasing to be communist. There follows a passage which goes beyond the confines of a reformed, democratised communism, such as for example was striven for during the Prague Spring.

Leading role of the party. The Charter identifies as 'one instrument for the curtailment or in many cases complete elimination of many civic rights' the system whereby all institutions and organisations are de facto 'subject to political directives' from the *apparats* of the ruling party and to decisions made by powerful individuals. [The word *apparats* was presumably inserted not to make the Charter appear anticonstitutional. The leading role of the communist party, but not specifically of its *apparats*, is embodied in the Czechoslovak constitution. The difference may seem semantic but it is important in the context.] Such directives and personal decisions have no force in the constitution or the law of the land, and yet in reality they have precedence even before the law. 'Where organisations or individuals ... come into conflict with such directives, they cannot have recourse to any non-party authority, since none such exists'. Thus they cannot exercise their freedom of association, the right to take part in the conduct of public affairs and the right to equal protection by the law.

The Charter then reverts to less systemic rights and duties. *The right to establish trade unions and the right to strike* cannot be implemented.

Three paragraphs are devoted to *violations of rights and duties by the police.* These are said to include interference with privacy, family, home and the mails, intercession with employers to secure job discrimination, pressure on the judicature and the mass media, and violation of the rights of defendants before courts, and of political prisoners. 'This activity is governed by no law and, being clandestine, affords the citizen no chance to defend himself', the Charter says with regard to the influence which the Ministry of the Interior has over decisions by employers, judges and journalists in relation to politically proscribed persons.

Right to leave the country. This is continually violated and subjected to various unjustifiable conditions. Foreigners are also hampered from entering the country [the only oblique reference to the Helsinki Final Act] because of their personal or professional contact with those of Czechoslovak citizens who are discriminated against.

Then the authors of the Charter defined their own position in face of the situation. They feel co-responsible 'for the conditions that prevail and accordingly also for the observance of legally enshrined agreements, which are binding upon all individuals as well as upon governments'.

'It is in this sense of co-responsibility, our belief in the importance of its conscious public acceptance and the general need to give it new and more effective expression that led us to the idea of creating Charter 77, whose inception we today publicly announce'.

The Charter is defined, with an eye on the restrictive rules governing the association of citizens in organisations, as 'a loose, informal and open community of people of various shades of opinion, faiths and professions, united by the will to strive individually and collectively for the respecting of civil and human rights in our own country and throughout the world'. Everyone who agrees with its ideas and participates in its work, belongs to it.

The Charter 'does not form the basis for any oppositional political activity. Like many similar civic initiatives in various countries, West and East, it seeks to promote the general public interest. It does not aim, then, to set out its own platform of political or social reform or change, but within its own field of impact to conduct a constructive dialogue with the political and state authorities . . .'

It is said that the 'constructive dialogue' clause has been inserted against the objection of some of the more radical oppositionists who, however, agreed to abide by the moderate and legalistic philosophy of the manifesto.

The Charter's authors stated their intention to discharge their civic duty especially in five ways: they would draw attention to individual cases of human rights infringements; they would document such grievances; they would suggest remedies; they would put forward proposals of a more general nature to strengthen rights and freedoms and the mechanisms designed to protect them; and they would act as intermediary in situations of conflict.

A brief paragraph says that Charter 77 has taken a symbolic name in connection with the Year of Political Prisoners and the Belgrade follow-up conference to Helsinki.

Finally three spokesmen for the signatories are named: Professor Jan Patočka, a philosopher, Dr Václav Havel, a writer, and Professor Jiří Hájek, a political scientist and former Minister of Foreign Affairs. They would represent the Charter *vis-à-vis* the authorities and the public at home and abroad, and their signatures would attest the authenticity of the Charter documents. Others would help them.

'We believe that Charter 77 will help to enable all the citizens of Czechoslovakia to work and live as free human beings'.

The main characteristics of the Charter would then seem to be the following:

It did not introduce new subject matter into the continual conflict between the regime and a large section of the public; instead it summarised and generalised protests that had been made before.

It has a firm focus on the human rights dimension, one of the key problems in 'normalised' Czechoslovakia; its authors chose this concentrated approach rather than discussing the whole range of questions pertaining to the country's economic, political and cultural life.

By the same token, the Charter is not a political programme in the sense that groups or parties formulate their views and proposed solutions in an all-embracing platform; it has, however, the nature of a programme in the self-proclaimed confines of the endeavour to expose the government's failing in the field of human rights.

In relation to socialism the Charter is neutral; it neither explicitly endorses nor condemns it. This is presumably because of the belief held by the signatories that for the observance of human rights the socialist or non-socialist nature of the state is irrelevant. A socialist state ought to be able to recognise the inalienable rights and freedoms of its citizens without doing harm to itself.

In relation to a communist one-party state the Charter is critical in the sense that it questions the right of the monopoly party to issue orders binding on non-party citizens outside and even above the legal framework. This is deplored inasmuch as it is the doing of party *apparats* or individual power holders. The Charter remained within the law of the land as it stood after more than eight years of 'normalisation'. Its authors did not use formulations that could be interpreted as illegal and neither did they in the slightest sense ask the public to break the law. In fact the essential thrust of the Charter is to uphold the laws, including of course international commitments. It does not criticise those 'normalisation' laws, exposed by the oppositionists in their individual statements of protest, which go contrary to rights and liberties and international stipulations.

Thanks to its scrupulously legalistic character, the sharp focus of its argumentation on a question which had been a sore point for many years, and its ideological neutrality, the Charter was signed by an unnusually high number of people from all walks of life and of all political persuasions, except the loyal followers of the communist teaching as professed by the incumbent regime. By the end of 1977 the number of signatories rose to over 800. Several oppositional groups which claim clandestine existence (for example of the New Left variety, but also Christians) and which had not directly cooperated in the drafting of the Charter, endorsed it in separate statements. Among the first 242 signatories the members of the intelligentsia predominated, most of them victims of the purges and subsequent discrimination. As new signatures were being added, the numbers of three categories of supporters were seen to grow: workers, young people and those who had not been affected by the successive waves of discrimination or were only affected marginally.

An accurate tally or breakdown is impossible: some signatories did not give their occupation, just name, others gave their pre-purge occupation. Where does one classify a person who had been a warehouse keeper for six or seven years before signing, while his original training and profession was that of an historian? The Charter has also become a movement in the sense that an unspecified number of supporters, themselves not signatories, helped to promote the Charter's message in other ways, for example by distributing the text and collecting new signatures.

In October 1977 the Charter spokesman, Dr Jiří Hájek, gave an interview to the Swedish daily *Svenska Dagbladed*[26]. He admitted that 'a great number among us are intellectuals because they have above all experienced the contradictions of "normalisation" and valid laws on their own skins. They can neither publish nor speak up publicly, they are being silenced and turned into non-persons. That is why men of culture, expelled reform communists and Christians comprise the main groups associated with the Charter. Insofar as workers are concerned, I think that a full one-third of the 800 persons who have signed the Charter so far, are workers. They include not only those on whom a workers' occupation was forced by "normalisation" but also those who have always been workers'. According to Hájek, the signatories comprise an adequately representative cross-section of the population, with the exception of Slovakia:

'In Slovakia the "normalising" repression has been substantially more moderate than in the Czech Lands. Slovaks are the smaller of the two nations in the federation. People are closer to each other there and solidarity between them is stronger. Furthermore, the political leaders in Bratislava are evidently wiser than their colleagues in Prague. They do not want to destroy their creative intelligentsia. In Slovakia, repression after the defeat of the Prague Spring has been almost exclusively directed against active reform communists, not large sections of the non-party population. And communists have never been as numerous there as in the Czech Lands. In addition, as is known, federalisation of Czechoslovakia has been retained as the only large reform dating back to the Prague Spring. It represented great progress for the Slovaks which has continued under "normalisation". The Slovaks do not have a national cause to feel that their hopes were frustrated as the Czechs do'.

In another interview Hájek suggested that under-representation of farmers among the signatories was due to the fact that they were materially well off and probably felt the restrictions of the civic freedoms less acutely than other strata of the population.[27]

For reasons which are not quite clear, the official response to the Charter initiative was furious and vicious. Mlynář evaluated it, while still in Prague, as a reaction which was 'influenced by irrational factors (anger, fear, vengeful aggression) and resembling a Pavlovian dog more than the behaviour of a thinking politician. Subconscious reflexes prevailed, acquired a long time ago in another situation and other conditions: reflexes of the 1950s. Not to say what it is really about. Not to discuss, not to negotiate. Suppress. Let loose the police to track people down. Arrest one, dismiss from work another. Slander all. And organise popular support for the regime—resolutions, statements, signatures demanding punishment on this earth and in hell'.[28]

That there would be official rejection and condemnation is not surprising. Not even the Chartists themselves could have expected otherwise. It is the extent of the anti-Charter campaign and the amount of venom in it that seemed to defy explanation. After all, far more uncompromising and aggressive texts had been sent to the various authorities before, and simply ignored by them. Many circulated in samizdat form at home and through foreign media. The Charter's subject, human rights, was not new either. The reason for the outburst can possibly be found in the combination of three factors. The regime must have watched the growth of oppositional activity in 1975 and 1976 with increasing hostility and unease and could have been waiting for a suitable opportunity to pounce on the protesters. Secondly, what must have been disconcerting was the number of signatories; five, ten, twenty persons signing a protest or a petition is bad enough because it indicates collusion, but 242 is positively dangerous and alarming. If the Prague grapevine is anything to go by, Husák was not pleased with his police officers who failed to uncover the Charter 'plot' when it was being hatched. Collecting signatures in an unauthorised fashion smacked too much of Prague Spring practices. If unchecked by a massive intimidatory campaign, the signing could spread and become a habit. Other documents in the future might again command popular support. Thirdly, in spite of protestations to the contrary and careful formulations, the Charter must have been regarded by the guardians of orthodoxy as a nucleus of a potential oppositional organisation. The Socialist Movement of Czechoslovak Citizens, having been kicked out of the door in 1972, was returning through the window. Moreover, it was doing so in a 'popular front' formation, in conjunction with liberals, Christians and social democrats, not just as a refomed communist party in disguise.

Let us analyse the contradictions in the official re-action to the Charter a little further.

The text has never been published in the official media or shown to people or read out in full. After a few weeks party officers are said to have read at members' meetings a statement from the central committee secretariat, condemning the Charter and instructing party members as to the line of argument they should take when speaking about the Charter to non-party people. This statement allegedly contained excerpts from the actual text of the Charter, but since the statement is not available the proportion between direct quotations and comment cannot be adjudged. It seems that the text proper was considered so explosive that even the propagandists writing against it were not allowed to see it, unless of course their words were part of a disinformation trick. A *Rudé právo* article of 15 January said that 'the bourgeois press has revealed that the signatories appointed three spokesmen'.[29] This fact was clearly given in the text of the Charter itself. The same article made clear that the Charter would not be published:

'Let us say it loud and clear to friend and foe alike: our press is not a mouthpiece of the reactionaries and the less so will it offer publicity to a junta of counter-revolutionary self-appointed impostors. Not even the naivest of all naive people can expect us to give the floor to wreckers throwing calumnies on our socialist society. To disseminate anti-state materials is an anti-social and punishable activity'.

This quote also shows some of the juiciness of language which was typical of much of the official comment on the Charter. About a week later another *Rudé právo* writer confirmed that there should be no question of publishing the Charter as it was 'an echo of petty bourgeois socialism' and quotes presented to the party meetings were sufficient.[30] Vasil Bilak also alluded to non-publication when he told an *aktiv* of various central Bohemian functionaries on 7 February, 'I will not comment on this piece of infamy as you all know it'.[31] But they did not, and he did comment on it after all, saying that not one counter-revolutionary had been put on trial after 1968 although they had been preparing a bloodbath; now they interpreted this magnanimity as a sign of weakness and raised their ugly heads again. There was a lesson in all this: revisionism must be combatted at all times.

The clearest comment, albeit made at a closed meeting, purportedly comes from the Minister of the Interior, Jaromír Obzina. He was reported by Western agencies to have told the Political Party School that the Charter 'has been compiled by the best brains of the opposition and is so cleverly formulated that some 90 per cent of the public would not realise wherein lies the danger if it was published'. Perhaps one or even two million people might actually sign the Charter if it were not for the campaign against it.[32]

Given that the Charter could not be published in the official press and that large-scale intimidation was needed to stop the infection from spreading, the form of the campaign was really quite logical. A few arrests, many more police interrogations, about a hundred dismissals from jobs in blatant contravention of the labour law and the covenant on economic rights, fire and brimstone in the media, and a forceful mobilisation of the public to sign either individual condemnations or various forms of 'anti-Charters'. How else can people be discouraged from supporting something which the regime feels, provided Obzina's remarks are correctly reported, they would support if left to their own devices?

It did seem, however, that there was a certain measure of disunity as to how vehemently the campaign was to be conducted. The evidence is slight, if one discounts Bilak's statement at the above-mentioned meeting to the effect that there was no disunity at all and that comrade Husák enjoyed great authority in the central committee, the entire party and the people. This statement was reported publicly and of course put everyone immediately on guard. At about the same time, early February, the media attempted a switch from negation to a positive phase: what had to be said about the Charter had been said, and now the authorities would speak primarily through new creative deeds and successes. This also coincided with a four-day visit in Prague by Ivan Kapitonov, a secretary of the Soviet Communist Party central committee and there was speculation that the drive was being adjusted to Moscow's wishes. At about the middle of February the press ceased to publish 'angry letters and resolutions' condemning the Charter and chastising its signatories, and a new tone was added in the form of heavy criticism of the Western countries for what harm they were doing to human rights. It did not take long, however, before the daily barrage was resumed. The occasion was the visit of the Dutch Foreign Minister, Max van der Stoel, who found the time in between official engagements to receive one of the spokesmen for the Charter movement, Professor Jan Patočka, in his Prague hotel. As a consequence Husák refused to see Stoel at the end of his visit and the Dutch politician was heavily censured in *Rudé právo* after his departure. Patočka was then subjected to several interrogation sessions and after one that reportedly lasted over ten hours collapsed and died a day later, on 13 March, of brain haemorrhage. *Rudé právo* blamed his friends who had known he had a heart condition and was weak but still pressed him to the fore.[33]

A West German journalist reported that Vasil Bilak, representing Czechoslovakia at a conference of ideological secretaries of ruling communist parties in Sofia (2–3 March), exhorted his colleagues to launch a common drive against dissidents through harsher repressive measures. He allegedly also demanded intransigence towards Euro-communism. The proposal was rejected by the Hungarian, Polish and Romanian delegates and finally even by Boris Ponomarev, the Soviet party secretary. They turned the tables on Bilak and were said to criticise the Czechoslovak leadership for not being able to keep the situation at home under control and then reacting in a ham-fisted way.[34]

The campaign gradually grew more sporadic and its anti-Western edge became more pronounced than the thrashing of dissenters at home. On 6 April a specially convoked session of the Federal Assembly was all devoted to legality in the sense of proving that everything the government was legally obligated to do, it was doing. In an enlightening paragraph, the Foreign Minister explained why it was the duty of the international community to castigate violations of human rights in some countries, while foreign criticism of Czecho-slovakia amounted to meddling in her internal affairs:

'Only in the case of a state grossly and systematically violating human

313

rights and non-observing fundamental principles laid down in international law and the afore-mentioned international documents [the UN covenants and Helsinki], does the question of human rights cease to be its exclusive internal affair and becomes the target of justifiable interest on the part of the international community. Such is the case of the gross violation of human rights by the fascist and racist regimes in South Africa, South Rhodesia, Chile, Israel and elsewhere, which leads to the infringement of friendly relations and peaceful cooperation between states and, in its consequences, creates conflict situations which threaten international peace and security'.[35]

Finally, after Husák himself spoke of the Chartists as the most rabid enemies of the regime who no longer dare to preach the return of factories to the capitalists and therefore have resorted to the Trojan horse tactics of calling for an 'improvement of socialism',[36] the campaign in the media died away, flaring up only occasionally afterwards. Accusations against the West have however become a permanent feature of the media in Czechoslovakia and the whole of Eastern Europe.

As the Charter was once again the work of the intellectuals, the regime considered it imperative to prove before the public eye that the mass of the intelligentsia was in fact opposed to the Charter. (It has become fashionable in some circles in the West too, to show a degree of contempt for protest documents which are thought up and issued by Soviet and East European writers, scholars and other 'brain workers'. It is difficult to share a view which judges an act of courage not by its content and effect but by the social status of its protagonists. Some appeals for workers' solidarity with the Charter were issued[37] and in many factories workers were said to have refused to sign anti-Charter resolutions individually. This was then done 'on their behalf' by trade union and party committees.)

Especial attention was focussed on the five art unions: now the time had come for them to prove that they would mobilise their respective constituencies. Artists from all over the country were summoned to a massive meeting in the Prague National Theatre on 28 January ostensibly to prepare for the congresses of their unions, to be held later in the year. The highest official present was Josef Havlín, a party central committee secretary. Speeches were made, some attacking the Charter directly, others dropping a hint obliquely and yet others not mentioning it at all. Finally a proclamation 'For New Creative Deeds in the Name of Socialism and Peace' was read out and signatures collected under it. Some names were apparently transferred from lists of those present, signed before the performance. The proclamation itself was somewhat long-winded, mixing patriotic sentiment with traditional communist phraseology. It is not quite clear from the text why it was being adopted at all, and a future historian who may stumble over it will be inclined to classify it under 'Rhetoric, Empty', should he not be aware of its context. Everyone in the hall, and those appending their signatures later, willy or nilly, knew of course that this was the *Anti-Charter*, to be bandied about for a long time to come as a proof of the true feelings of the cultural community. There is in fact one sentence which lets the cat out of the bag. It comes towards the end of the text (about 1,600 words against some 2,000 of the Charter) and runs as follows:

> 'That is why we hold in contempt those who in irrepressible pride, vain haughtiness, selfish interest or even for a base penny, wherever in the world they may be—and even in this country a small group of such renegades and traitors emerged—separate and isolate themselves from their own people, their life and true interests, and who, under the merciless logic of things, turn into a tool of the anti-humanitarian forces of imperialism and, in their service, become preachers of disintegration and quarrels among the nations'.[38]

The sluice gate was opened and 'nearly one thousand signatures' under the Anti-Charter were reported on 31 January, and about 7,500 by 11 February. In retrospect and under a cool eye, the engineers of the campaign may have made an erroneous judgment. A less verbose and more purposeful statement by a well-selected group of say fifty famous people, such as film and television actors who are best known to the public, would probably have had greater effect. Documents signed by thousands, endless columns of small print, name after name, are by definition not given much credence. People know how they are masterminded. In the end just about everybody in the wide world of culture, from National Artists to broadcasting technicians in a provincial radio station, signed. The man in the street knew this could not be right. The overkill became counter-productive, even though some bitterness lingered on with regard to several signatories of the Anti-Charter who, people thought, did not have to climb on the wagon.

Like the media and the cultural unions, the police played a memorable part in the orchestrated campaign, to the point that some Chartists joked about having called for a constructive dialogue and getting it—with police officers. The three spokesmen were interrogated for a week, being allowed to go home every evening, presumably so as to circumvent the rule that a person can only be detained without being declared a suspect for 48 hours. Václav Havel was however arrested 'properly' on 14 January and held until May. He was not charged in connection with the Charter but eventually tried and sentenced in October, with three others, Ota Ornest, František Pavlíček and Jiří Lederer, on charges of maintaining contacts with emigres. Ornest had not signed the Charter and after his trial criticised himself twice on television whereupon his three-and-a-half years' sentence was reduced by one year. Lederer got three years, Pavlíček 17 months suspended for three years, and Havel 14 months suspended for three years. On his release from detention on 20 May, Havel resigned from his function as spokesman for the Charter because he would not be able to discharge it properly pending judicial proceedings against him. To indicate how difficult it was to breathe in the atmosphere created around the Charter spokesmen, one could quote from Havel's statement of 21 May. He said he had offered the procurator general an assurance that he would no longer 'take part in activities which could be qualified as punishable by law' and that he would 'avoid public political action'. At the same time he put it on record that he 'is not renouncing—and will never renounce—his signature under Charter 77 or the moral obligation deriving from it, namely to defend people who fall victim to unlawfulness, and that he will try to make use towards this aim of all opportunities which he will consider effective, constructive and in accordance with the Czechoslovak legal order'.[39] Since Dr Hájek, the only remaining spokesman, was exposed to such a saturating level of surveillance and harassment that his activities became impeded, two new spokesmen were nominated in September 1977, Dr Ladislav Hejdánek, a philosopher, and Miss Marta Kubišová, a pop-singer.

The Charter itself was described by members of the general procurator's office as being 'in conflict with the law' and Hájek and Patočka, then still alive, were warned on 1 February that there would be criminal proceedings if they did not quit, but the only known case in which the Charter was invoked before a court was during the trial of Aleš Macháček and Vladimír Laštůvka in Ústí nad Labem in September 1977. They were convicted on charges of having in their possession, and lending to others, foreign literature. Each received a sentence of three years' imprisonment for subversion because they were said to be 'deeply hostile' to the regime. This was said to have been proved among other things by their keeping at home copies of the Charter and, in the case of one of them, by speaking up at a factory meeting against a resolution condemning the Charter.

Probably all the signatories were questioned by the police at one time or another and for varying lengths of time. Some were picked up from their home at 4 a.m., others were interrogated, sent home and, as soon as they got there, summoned again. House searches became frequent. Surveillance over some of the better known signatories was absolute: one policeman at the door to the flat, two at the main entrance to the house, and a car with three more at the ready in the street. All visitors had to show identity cards, their arrival and departure were recorded, some were sent away before they could ring the bell or were even taken to the police station for questioning. An innocent passer-by who might ask a Charter signatory, unbeknown to him, what was the time, would be taken to the station, had a mug-shot taken and registered in a suspect file. Jiří Hájek jogs every day and once, when his 'bodyguards' could not keep pace and he refused to slow down, they sprayed his face with some kind of noxious substance. Hájek is very shortsighted and has suffered from an eye illness for many years. A suspected professor who travelled to Prague from Slovakia was bundled into the nearest return train, without getting further than a few yards away from Prague Central Station, but not before his own money was used to buy his return ticket. Charter signatories running cars had their licenses withdrawn on spurious grounds. Their telephones were disconnected without explanation. Some even more disquieting things happened: mysterious shots were fired, fires started in weekend chalets, anonymous letters threatening to maim and kill were received and one or two people were mugged under strange circumstances. None of these could, however, be conclusively traced to the authorities. A 22-year old worker who had signed the Charter committed suicide in October 1977. In a farewell note he said that he would have to resist conscription on grounds of conscientious objections. (Several cases were reported in 1977.) As a sick man, he would not survive the prison term which was inevitable, and so he chose to take his own life.[40]

An offer to expedite emigration was made repeatedly and forcefully to several leading oppositionists. At first rejected, it was eventually accepted by some when all means of their earning a living in Czechoslovakia appeared to have been closed, or when health reasons demanded it, or when the possibility to work for the cause in exile was distinctly promising.

It is estimated that about one hundred signatories were dismissed from employment and had either to look frantically for a menial job or remained unemployed. Others were demoted and yet others affected in a variety of ways, for example by not being paid bonuses which non-signatories were receiving as of right. Dismissals also affected several people who, not having signed the Charter themselves, refused to sign its condemnation. Justifications bordered on the ludicrous: 'Public indignation at this act of yours is of such a nature that your further stay here would disrupt the creative atmosphere of the working collective.' '... one of the essential conditions for the proper discharge of all functions—including yours—is a devotion to the socialist society and the state system; the political stand you have taken has proved that you do not meet this requirement.' 'In doing this [i.e. signing the Charter] you have infringed the working discipline in so grave a manner that your continuing in employment... is not possible without jeopardising the working discipline.' '... your present stance [i.e. refusing to condemn the Charter] negatively influences not only the public but also your colleagues and students, and consequently it is not desirable for you to continue working as a teacher and educator of our society's younger generation'.[41]

Taken together, the media campaign, police harassment and persecution in employment, have accomplished their purpose, if that is what they were supposed to accomplish, notably to prevent the ripple-like spreading of the circles of Charter signatories and the evolution of the Charter into a semi-permanent organisation of the opposition. Anti-Charter action also gave a fresh sense of mission to the agencies of the state, above all the police which once again had frantic activity to undertake and fat dossiers to compile. For half a year the propagandists had an interesting new target to shoot at and could exercise their pens in a militant fashion on well-known domestic adversaries. Criticism of the Western governments for their failures to observe human rights has emerged as a permanent preoccupation. The Carter administration above all, notably the President's Security Adviser Z. Brzezinski, for long a *bête noire* of the 'normalisers' for his alleged complicity in the Prague Spring (he gave a lecture at a Prague institute in 1968), was seen as legitimate prey on this score and few stones remained unturned here, even after direct exposure of the Charter has subsided.

Vehement publicity had of course the undesired but inevitable effect of taking the message of the Charter to those who otherwise could be reached by the oppositionists only with difficulty. The Charter became the talk of the nation and just about everyone knew of its existence and had at least an idea of what it was about. The knowledge that a fairly large group of people refused to accept the fate meted out to them lying down must have given heart even to those who chose to do nothing themselves. Everywhere in the world the timid take vicarious pride in the deeds of the brave. Dr Hájek spoke in one interview about private visits and apologies proffered by those who let their names be appended to anti-Charter forays. Such reports as are available, for example from Charter signatories who emigrated to the West and from Western visitors to Czechoslovakia, speak of undoubted good feelings for the aims of the Charter and its very existence among the public. But they also convey a certain amount of bitterness when contrasting the risk which some people were taking just as others opted for the proverbial bowl of potage. And they speak about the symptomatic attitudes of people for whom material survival, in relative comfort, has become a programme. Why should the perennial grumblers continue to carp and cavil? Why don't they just keep quiet and make good as best they can, like so many of us do?

Alexander Dubček, the man whose name will forever remain associated with the most comprehensive attempt to date to reform communism from within, did not sign the Charter. Since his recall from ambassadorship in Turkey in 1970 and subsequent expulsion from the party, he has lived quietly in a small house in Bratislava, going unobtrusively about his duties as an official of a forestry administration. He sent some private communications to the authorities and spoke up publicly twice: in a letter to the widow of Josef Smrkovský after his attendance at the funeral of his old comrade-in-arms had been made impossible in January 1974, and in the autumn of the same year when he wrote to the authorities a long complaint about police surveillance and an explanation of his disagreement with 'normalisation'. It would not be proper to speculate on the reasons that have made Dubček stay out of the other oppositional undertakings, although one can easily surmise that he did not wish to expedite the desire of some 'normalisers' for a massive clampdown on a 'conspiracy' with him as its head. His refusal to recant had been generally known and perhaps his silence spoke more eloquently than words would have done.

When the Charter campaign got under way, the pro-Moscow Austrian communist party newspaper *Volksstimme* suggested that Dubček disagreed with the Charter. Perhaps it would be best to quote in a full message which has reached the West in this connection:

'The following information has been received from the circle of Alexander Dubček's friends in Bratislava: Dubček had been astonished at the way in which the *Volksstimme* correspondent took the liberty of interpreting his present views, feelings and attitudes, considering that he did not speak to Dubček personally or to any member of his family or another person who might have been enjoined by Dubček to express his views. The *Volksstimme* assertion of 30 January and then again 2 February to the effect that Alexander Dubček allegedly disapproves of Charter 77, its content and publication, does not correspond to the truth and is contradictory to the views which Dubček communicates in this matter to his friends and even the "appropriate" authorities. After all, Dubček's own letters of 1972–75 expressed a general criticism of the prevailing conditions, including similar demands for a restoration of civil rights. At present Dubček has been disconcerted by a series of police interrogations, house searches and the entire propaganda campaign; he is particularly disturbed by the fact that those arrested include the playwright František Pavlíček, a member of the party central committee in 1968, who is known by his defence of Dubček's post-January policies at central committee plenums. Dubček also rejects quite unequivocally the attempts of the Husák leadership to deport several of its critics abroad; this resembles Husák's similar attempt of 17 April 1975 to silence Dubček himself in the same fashion. There can therefore be no doubt about Dubček's opinions and attitudes in matters of this nature.

'Insofar as *Volksstimme* has headlined Dubček's name with the assertion that he has refused to sign Charter 77 when it was submitted to him, such a statement does not correspond to reality. Nothing of the kind has occurred. It is well known that a politician chooses the moment and the form of his public pronouncements according to his own deliberations, and from this point of view the absence of Dubček's signature under Charter 77 has a purpose. It can certainly not lead to deductions which the *Volksstimme* editor insinuates to his readers. Well-informed friends of Alexander Dubček say that attempts to misuse Dubček's name in the campaign against the signatories of Charter 77 could create a situation which might compel him to take a public stand, despite the limitations which he has so far imposed on himself, in order to set the disinformation straight and to show the people who spread it wherein they are wrong'.[42]

The Charter had an unusually wide and sustained international publicity and response. Even though a human rights initiative had been maturing in Czechoslovakia for a long time and fed primarily on domestic repressive practices, its promulgation coincided with the onset of the Carter Administration and its programme in the same field. The State Department and the President criticised Prague for its human rights record in connection with the Charter, and so did many other Western governments, parliaments, organisations and individuals, including the Eurocommunist parties. China issued several tough comments: the *People's Daily* said that the Charter 'had the effect of upsetting the Kremlin colossus and making it jittery' and continued optimistically that 'the activity focussing on Charter 77 is a mere spark of the great struggle of the Czechoslovak people against the Soviet occupation and domination and for freedom and democratic rights.... The spring of independence and freedom will dawn on the banks of the Vltava at long last'.[43]

It is impossible to say to what extent foreign criticism impeded the regime's hand in its anti-Charter pursuit. One would be inclined to say that not too much, considering the duration and profundity of the campaign and the fact that the main political trial of 1977 (Havel *et al.*) took place at the time of the Belgrade conference. On the other hand, one cannot say what else might have been in store. The authors of the Charter themselves said several times that they welcomed foreign support from those to whose hearts the aims of the Charter were close. Eurocommunist endorsement of human rights as inseparable from socialism was of particular relevance. Dr Hájek was asked by a Swedish reporter whether Eurocommunism meant 'something immediate and specific' for the Charter. He replied:

'Of course. It is no secret that Eurocommunism is my strongest trump when dealing with the representatives of power. I am telling them: "Do you really think that Charter is anti-socialist? And what then about the articles and statements in the Italian, Spanish and French party press? Are these communist parties also anti-socialist when giving us support?" The authorities have no answer to these questions'.[44]

As the Prague Spring contributed to the treasure box of reformist experience in the entire Soviet bloc, so did the Charter take a little further the oppositional stream which had been evolving along similar lines in the Soviet Union and, after the 1976 price riots, in Poland. Solidarity statements were made by dissident groups virtually throughout the bloc. Human rights advocacy, already strong in some countries, has received an added impetus. In Bulgaria and Romania the case of the Charter seems to have called into existence groups of human rights activists which had not existed previously. There is no record, however, of collusion between any of the East European groups or individuals and the authors of the Charter either before or during the campaign. In the autumn of 1977 the Polish Committee of Public Self-Defence and the spokesman for Charter 77 exchanged messages of solidarity.[45] Historians of the future are well advised to take note of this act: it is the first direct communication between dissidents in different East European countries (as distinct from solidarity declarations). Charter 77 may yet come to be regarded as a factor which set in motion the internationalisation of opposition in Eastern Europe. With the impediments being what they are, such a contact is however extremely difficult to sustain. Cross-fertilisation of ideas and mutual learning from experience are, of course, another matter. News cannot be stopped from spreading nowadays, and ideas never could.

One of the great things about Charter 77 was that it did not remain just one proclamation. While its range of objectives has been fairly narrowly defined from the start—the area of human rights—the treatment it gave to it was dynamic. This was mainly achieved through the pursuance of one of the aims the Charter set itself at the start, namely 'to document grievances and suggest remedies'. The Charter has issued statements on individual and collective infringements of rights and freedoms, supported by documentary evidence. These are the so-called *Documents* of the Charter, which appeared in a numbered sequence. The Chartists have also addressed queries and petitions to various authorities, and they put out communications of other kind, mostly about their own activities.

Documents Nos. 2, 5, 8, 11 and 14 contained lists of new signatures under the Charter. The others concerned the state of human rights observance in various fields.

321

Document No. 1 was the Charter itself.

Document No. 3, dated 15 January 1977, expressed disagreement with the initial response of the government to the Charter through police persecution and a mendacious media campaign. The authors of the Charter, convinced of the legitimacy of their initiative, want to conduct a dialogue with the authorities on how to resolve practical problems, not to be reviled as enemies.

In this connection the spokesmen issued a juridical analysis of the Charter on 3 February in the form of a letter to the Federal Assembly, concluding that the manifesto was not at variance with Czechoslovak law and that the procurator general was wrong when claiming it was a punishable criminal offence.

Document No. 4 of 23 January concerned 'one of the most burning problems in the area of human rights in Czechoslovakia', notably the 'persistent discrimination in the selection of young people for secondary schools and universities'. This is a tightly argued criticism of discriminatory rules and practices, including the banning of some and promotion of other children on the basis of non-educational reasons. A committee of enquiry is demanded. An official ministerial ordinance is enclosed as an illustration: it categorises applicants for study in five groups with 'class-political criteria' being the first consideration in each of them.

Small groups of young people throughout the country, spontaneously reacting to the educational ban, have begun to congregate in private flats to hear talks by scholars who were themselves dismissed from university and other posts for political reasons. Professor Jan Patočka was one of those who willingly and with dedication discussed moral and philosophical problems with them. After his death in March 1977 they have named this exercise in uncensored education the Jan Patočka University. It continues to this day.

Document No. 6 of 15 February again relates to the persecution of the signatories and their supporters, this time in detail and with extensive citation of individual cases. It gives the names of people whose houses were searched, who lost their jobs, whose health was put in jeopardy as a result of police action, who are recipients of threatening letters, who were being forced to apply for emigration permits, and who did not sign the Charter but refused to condemn it and suffered the consequences.

Zdeněk Mlynář, one of the signatories of Charter 77, addressed an appeal to West European communist and socialist parties already on 16 January, informing them about the persecutions. He wrote:

> 'At present the problem is whether the democratic and socialist forces in Europe will allow the defenders of internationally acknowledged pledges to be brutally silenced for the second time in one decade in

Czechoslovakia. . . . Help us before a great many democrats, socialists and communists are hunted down, before the arrogance of power gives rise to new illegal political trials based on fabricated accusations! Help us so that the reason which prevailed over the arrogance of power in Helsinki in 1975 may win again in Prague in 1977!'[46]

Document No. 7, dated 8 March, examines in detail the violation of social and economic rights in Czechoslovakia, in contravention of various international agreements. This was an analysis of considerable importance because it tackled the one area of the human rights checklist which the communist governments regard as their strong point. It has four parts, dealing with the 'right freely to choose or accept work', the right to a just reward for work (including the question of discrimination against employed women), the prevalence of political criteria in work placement and promotion, and the non-existence of a right to organise independent trade union activity.

Document No. 9 of 22 April is about the freedom of conscience, thought, expression and, above all, religious belief and pursuance of religious practices. It exposes the various restrictions officially imposed on the churches, their clergy and the believers.[47]

Document No. 10 of 29 April sums up the anti-Charter campaign in juxtaposition to the great support the movement received at home and abroad, and suggests that the costly and undignified campaign should be stopped, that the international covenants should be republished for all citizens to see what their entitlements are, that citizens' complaints against infractions should be attended to by the various agencies of the state under the close supervision of the Federal Assembly, that laws incompatible with human rights stipulations should be amended, that the dialogue with Charter signatories and spokesmen should be conducted responsibly, not in the interrogation rooms of the secret police, that Czechoslovakia should accede to the optional protocol to the international covenant on civil and political rights and recognise the competence of the international human rights committee to receive and consider communications from individuals, and that officials, such as journalists, policemen and others, who have abused their powers or the law in the course of the anti-Charter crusade should be brought to justice.

Document No. 11 of 13 June gives a list of 133 new signatories but also has a brief preamble which refers to a letter, including documentary enclosures, sent by Dr Hájek to several representative institutions in the matter of violations of Czechoslovak labour legislation. The preamble also states that Dr Hájek will in the meantime continue alone as the spokesman but that 'suitable alternatives' have been prepared in case the legal activity of the Charter is curtailed.

Document No. 12 of 30 June concerns discrimination and victimisation of writers, and contains a list of 130 names of Czech writers who have been persecuted or banned from publishing their works. Mention is made of the speech against the blacklisting of Slovak writers which Miss Hana Ponická wanted to deliver at the Slovak Writers' Congress earlier in the year but was prevented from doing so. [She was expelled from the Union and her books and film scripts withdrawn from circulation.] In this connection another 25 names of Slovak writers are cited as being on the prohibited list.

'A Communication from the Charter', dated 21 September, sums up the results of the Charter so far: it has been successful in bringing the observance of human rights to the forefront of public attention and in inducing the authorities to take the civic initiative into account; it has also gained support from many citizens at home and wide circles of public and institutional opinion abroad; it has, however, not been able to give much individual help to people whose rights and freedoms were trampled on; some of the signatories are not in touch 'with the focal points of the Charter's activity'; the public is not adequately informed about the work of the Charter and some people do not even know that the Charter is still alive. That is why many signatories have agreed on the following: 1. The Charter is not concerned with its own prestige and henceforth will give support to the manifold civic initiatives which have emerged outside the Charter. 2. Individual signatories will develop their own initiatives, according to the command of their conscience, and not all of these need necessarily involve the Charter as a whole. 3. Groups of signatories may come together to pursue specific initiatives in accordance with their knowledge, preoccupation or special interest. 4. These informal groups may wish to maintain mutual contact and nominate their own spokesmen. 5. The Charter as a whole will continue to function and be represented by three spokesmen: Miss Marta Kubišová and Dr Ladislav Hejdánek have been appointed in addition to Dr Jiří Hájek. As the Charter is not an organisation, the spokesmen can hand over their responsibilities to other persons, if need be, without formality. It will be the main objective of the 'central' spokesmen of Charter 77 to strive for a constructive dialogue with the state and to go on publishing the main

Document No. 13 of 20 November 1977 deals with the lack of freedom in the field of popular music and the arising conflict between a section of the younger generation and the state. 'A police truncheon can sustain real authority only speciously'.[48]

There were other documents, worth noting, that originated from within the Charter circles. Several signatories have addressed a letter to the West German public in connection with the so-called *Berufsverbot*, i.e. a West German regulation whereby extreme political activists cannot be employed in the state's service. Thirteen Czech intellectuals asked prominent Western writers to seek international

documents on behalf of the Charter as a whole.
support for the recognition of works which cannot be published in one's own homeland. The Charter also commented on the trial of Ornest, Havel, Pavlíček and Lederer in October 1977. Lederer's son addressed an individual request for help to his father to the French communist leader Marchais in November 1977. (In his reply, Marchais restated his party's critical attitude to the trial.) And there were several documents by clergymen, both Catholic and Protestant, sent either to the authorities or issued as open statements.[49]

Five days before his death, Jan Patočka wrote:

'Maybe that the powerful of this world will slowly set out on the road of premeditating their intended deeds so as to adjust them to the script of the covenants. This alone will be a certain success; if such a course becomes habitual, it will be beneficial to all. The Charter has never expected to act in other than an educational manner'.[50]

And Jiří Hájek concluded:

'It all goes slowly, at a snail's pace, but still in the right direction. We proceed forward, relying on the laws, as the Bible says: "Think not that I am come to destroy the law or the prophets; I am not come to destroy but to fulfil". And so I think that we have reached the point when the Charter cannot be eradicated. It has emerged in the midst of this society and it is here to stay'. [51]

The new spokesman, L. Hejdánek, in 'Letter to a Friend' wrote:

'The aim of the Charter is not to collect as many signatures as possible, it is to win over the greatest number of people to our idea that it is possible and desirable to behave towards the state as free and courageous citizens, and on the other hand that it is possible and desirable to behave towards one's compatriots as friends, as companions, as comrades'.[52]

The question remains whether it has all been worthwhile and whether what has been and may yet be accomplished is much or little. Not wishing to have the last word of evaluation, this writer would leave it to the readers to provide their own answer.

CONCLUSION AND PROSPECT

It should have been possible to destroy Czechoslovak reformism in a more amicable way. One part of the process, the winning of the population's neutrality through the provision of a fairly high level of consumerism, has gone without a hitch so far. No alternative solution was probably possible in this respect, and the only fear must remain whether material satisfaction can go on matching expectations. But it is the age-old story of not by bread alone. The parallel process of weeding out the propensity to reformist striving among the politically active elements of society has been pursued by way of a prolonged war on large numbers of people. This has antagonised them and made them into more permanent adversaries of 'normalcy' than they would have been otherwise. The Hungarian example of 1956–1968 has not been followed. Here there *was* an alternative.

Husák probably tried to set out on an alternative course several times. He may have expected to keep Dubček and a number of his followers in the ruling coalition. He may have wanted to keep some reforms going at a moderated level and pace, such as the federalisation of the party and the economic reform. He may have wanted to devise the party purge as a more lenient exercise in expiation. He probably did not want to carry expurgation into such lengths in the non-party fields, such as culture, science and education. And he may have desired to stop the purges before they inflicted lasting damage on society.

On each of these points he lost out and then pretended to be in complete agreement with the rigid policies that were actually adopted. What might have been a moderate Husák policy has disappeared in the process and he must know, weary after all the battles with political friend and foe, and with his own conscience, that others have imprinted their stamp on the history of the past decade through his good offices and over his signature. If a policy associated with his name is to go into history books, it will be one of constant retreat before left-wing extremism. Pity.

But why should it be so? Two answers offer themselves. Either the combined pressure of the intransigents and the 'ultras' was consistently stronger than his own capacity to resist, or Moscow always upheld them when it mattered because in the Soviet scheme of things a modestly reforming Czechoslovakia, next to a modestly reforming Hungary and Poland, was incompatible with the long-term plans which the Kremlin designed for Eastern Europe in the wake of the Prague Spring and contiguous on 'detente' with the West. It is my guess that Husák could have dealt with the local diehards relatively easily in 1969–1970. The ultimate responsibility, it seems, must be

Moscow's. It makes sense but it does not absolve the local executors of the Soviet will, whether they be from the Husák camp or that of his coalition partners.

For several good reasons annexation of Eastern Europe to the Soviet Union, Baltic states fashion, is not yet the order of the day. What then about the scenarios for the 1980s?

One possible course of events, as far as Czechoslovakia is concerned, would be reminiscent of another sequence in the country's post-war history. The Prague Spring can be likened to the co-existence of communism and democracy from 1945–1948. The purges of 1970 are not unlike the communist takeover in February 1948 and the ensuing persecutions. The oil price rise and the heavy investment programmes of today are causing similar economic trouble to those which the country experienced from 1958–1963. And Charter 77 is like the liberal stirring of 1956–1963. It follows that the 1980s may well witness a reception of the reformist developments of the 1960s.

The need for economic reform can become imperative and be at long last recognised as such by a majority in the leadership. Then the thesis would once again be mooted that economic change should entail some measure of political liberalisation. If this happens, the intellectuals (Chartists) will obviously give their support to both economics and political relaxation and express willingness to cooperate with potential reformers in the Establishment, as their disaffected predecessors did in the last five years of the Novotný regime from 1963–1968.

The grassroots and the lower echelons of the party will probably look on sympathetically but stay impassive and wait for the leaders to make a move. In a command system initiatives to be pursued by the *apparats* originate at the top. If the new course is not nipped in the bud, some of the hardliners in the leadership may cross the lines and join the change-seekers for a variety of essentially selfish reasons, while the rest of the 'sound core' at the top would find themselves blamed for economic difficulties and pressed into increasing isolation.

The next logical development would be to transform the sense of change into a more specific blueprint, possibly by enjoining the economic theorists with the task of designing a new reform plan. As this might happen concurrently with an economic depression in the USSR and a boom in Western economies, the general atmosphere would be conducive to reform ideas, not unlike the 1960s. The reform plan would, however, be watered down by the more ideologically minded people in the leadership and as a result of inherent fear of radical transformations.

The Young Turks in several cultural unions would by then have asserted themselves sufficiently to push out the old guard and to express liberal thought beyond the confines of economic theory. One or two cultural journals would become bolder in what they print, and one or two censors more uncertain in what they should or should not pass. Cultural liberalism would meet with open-hearted support among the students.

The Slovaks would once again take advantage of the state of flux and claim more power in economic planning and in administration to undo the effects of the re-centralisation of December 1970. They would probably be less interested in political and cultural liberalisation.

Inside the party the build-up of a change-seeking mood would help the neo-reformers (the Štrougals?) to outvote the ideologists (the Bilaks?) in the praesidium and secretariat. The leadership would announce that a reform of rigid practices was overdue because the current system was no longer able to cope with the modernisation challenges of the last years of the century. They would say that centralisation had been necessary to overcome the 1968–1969 crisis but now outlived its usefulness.

In such context national unity would have to be seen desirable in order to help the system get over the difficulties (belt-tightening), and so the divisive effects of the 1970 purges would most likely be repudiated. The victims of the purges would, however, only be admitted to positions of lesser influence and authority, and control over the new reform would stay in the hands of people who either conducted the 1970 purges, or did not oppose them, or were too young to take part in them.

In short, Czechoslovakia can become a reformist country again. If it happens, the leadership will seek to maintain the will for change in manageable, Hungarian, proportions. Should it fail to please Moscow in this respect, the possibility of Soviet military intervention would once again arise. The story is open-ended. And of course a completely different scenario can be played out. Grey is all theory, but green is the tree of life. Prophesying about Eastern Europe is an unrewarding preoccupation.

NOTES

Part One

1 For two of the latest accounts see Pavel Tigrid, 'The Prague Coup of 1948: The Elegant Takeover' in T. T. Hammond, ed., *The Anatomy of Communist Takeovers*, New Haven, Yale University Press, 1975, pp. 399–432; and Vladimir V. Kusin, 'Czechoslovakia' in M. McCauley, ed., *Communist Power in Europe 1944–1949*, London, Macmillan, 1977, pp. 73–94.

2 John Erickson, 'International and Strategic Implications of the Czechoslovak Reform Movement' in V. V. Kusin, ed., *The Czechoslovak Reform Movement 1968*, Santa Barbara, ABC Clio Press, 1973, pp. 31–49.

3 'Mluví Josef Smrkovský', *Listy*, 2/1975, pp. 4–25. 'Informace o osudné noci' *Rudé právo*, 23/8/1968; in English in R. Littell, ed., *The Czech Black Book*, New York, Avon Books, 1969, pp. 24–29. Zdeněk Mlynář's book about his involvement in the reform movement and about the invasion, currently being written, is not available to me at the time of writing, but I talked extensively to another high party official present during the crucial night in and near the conference hall.

4 Bilak is reported to have told a meeting in June 1969: 'They did not want to enter Prague at all, as the Soviet comrades explained to us in Moscow later. Had such a resolution not been adopted in the party praesidium, they would have not entered Prague and remained on the outskirts. Originally, as they told us in Moscow, the intention was to send in just four divisions. But when they saw what happened, that even the praesidium, the government and the National Assembly were against, they probably thought that the Americans and the West Germans would take advantage of the chaos, and so they threw 29 divisions on us and were determined to roll over into West Germany because as they had told us in Moscow in May [1968] we must realise that they would never let Czechoslovakia go ... even if it meant risking some kind of a third world war'. Quoted from a district party publication in Topolčany by *Listy*, 1/1978, p. 23. Interesting as this information is, it must be taken *cum grano salis*. The one thing it *could* explain is the delay between flying in troops to Prague and seizing the high offices. Could they have been waiting for a favourable or at least neutral statement from the praesidium after all?

5 Jiří Pelikán, 'The International Communist Movement' in V. V. Kusin, ed., *The Czechoslovak Reform Movement 1968*, p. 304.

6 Only Piller and Barbírek of the seven who voted against the invasion remained at large. Among the other prominent reformers, Čestmír Císař was apprehended but either released or allowed to escape later in the day.

7 'Mluví Joset Smrkovský', *Listy*, 2/1975.

8 *ibid.*

9 *ibid.*

10 The Vysočany congress was well described elsewhere. See references to books by Pelikán, Hejzlar, Skilling and Golan in the *Further Reading* section.

11 *Rudé právo*, 25/8/1968. The statement is dated 23/8/1968.

12 Dušan Havlíček, 'Mass Media and Their Impact on Czechoslovak Politics in 1968' in V. V. Kusin, ed., *The Czechoslovak Reform Movement 1968*, pp. 256–7.

[13] *Zprávy v boji proti kontrarevoluci*, Prague, Svoboda, 1971. This is a collection of 64 articles reprinted from the original broadsheets. It is said that *Zprávy* had a circulation of 300,000. Eye-witnesses know how many were burned in bundles and otherwise disposed of.

[14] 'Mluví Josef Smrkovský', *Listy*, 2/1975, p. 19.

[15] *ibid.*, p. 20.

[16] In English in Pavel Tigrid, *Why Dubček Fell*, London, Macmillan, 1971, pp. 210–4.

[17] Typescript summary of the meeting.

[18] *Der Spiegel*, 1/1978, quoted in *Listy*, 1/1978, p. 4.

[19] See for example Jiří Pelikán in V. V. Kusin, ed., *The Czechoslovak Reform Movement 1968*.

[20] *ibid.*, p. 301.

[21] Typescript of confidential report.

[22] Santiago Carrillo, *'Eurocommunism' and the State*, London, Lawrence & Wishart, 1977, pp. 131–2.

[23] Alexander Yanov, *Detente after Brezhnev: The Domestic Roots of Soviet Foreign Policy*, Berkeley, Institute of International Studies of the University of California, 1977.

[24] See for example Vladimir V. Kusin, 'Československo a konstitučně-demokratická opozice v SSSR', *Proměny*, July 1972, pp. 4–14.

[25] See N. Gorbanevskaya, *Red Square at Noon*, London, Andre Deutsch, 1972 and *Natalia Gorbanevskaya: Poems, The Trial, Prison*, Oxford, Carcanet Press, 1972.

[26] *Khronika tekuchikh sobytii*, No. 5, 25 December 1968, in *Posev*, 1st Special Edition, August 1969, p. 43.

[27] From among the many treatments of the notion of limited sovereignty I would single out Boris Meissner, *The Brezhnev Doctrine*, Kansas City, Park College Governmental Research Bureau, 1970.

[28] R. A. Remington, *Winter in Prague*, Cambridge, Mass., M. I. T. Press, 1969, p. 414.

[29] *ibid.*, p. 415.

[30] *Statistická ročenka 1970*, Prague, SNTL, 1970, p. 421.

[31] The report was made out by a Dubček sympathiser who attended the meeting incognito.

[32] J. A. Piekalkiewicz, *Public Opinion Polling in Czechoslovakia 1968–69*, New York, Praeger, 1972, p. 27.

[33] *ibid.*, p. 264.

[34] *ibid.*, p. 265.

[35] *ibid.*, p. 28.

[36] *Rok šedesátý osmý*, Prague, Svoboda, 1969, p. 236.

[37] Pavel Tigrid, *Why Dubček Fell*, p. 218.

[38] For several articles on self-management in Czechoslovakia see for example *Studie*, 50/1977. This journal, in Czech, is published by Křestanská akademie, Rome.

[39] V. Mastny, ed., *East European Dissent*, Vol. 2, 1965–1970, New York, Facts on File, 1972, p. 168.

[40] Zdeněk Hejzlar, *Reformkommunismus*, Cologne, Europäische Verlagsanstalt, 1976, p. 312.

[41] 'Mluví Josef Smrkovský', *Listy*, 2/1975, p. 25.

[42] Hejzlar, *op. cit.*, pp. 329–30.

Part Two

[1] *Rudé právo*, 5/1/1978, p. 3.

[2] Two instructive and factual articles are G. Wightman and A. H. Brown, 'Changes in the Levels of Membership and Social Composition of the Communist Party of Czechoslovakia 1945–1973', *Soviet Studies*, July 1975, pp. 396–417; and 'The New Czechoslovak Communist Party Central Committee', Radio Free Europe Survey, 25/6/1971.

[3] Speeches delivered at the September 1969 session of the central committee were published in Czech in *Svědectví*, 38/1970, pp. 207–30 and 267–94. These include full texts of speeches by Dubček, Bilak, Kolder and Svoboda and extracts from speeches by Smrkovský, Miková, Prchlík and Černý. Dubček's speech appeared in English in W. Shawcross, *Dubček*, London, Weidenfeld and Nicolson, 1970, pp. 274–98.

[4] 'Poučenie z krízového vývoja v strane a spoločnosti po XIII. zjazde KSČ' in *Svedectvo dokumentov a faktov*, Bratislava, Pravda, 1975, p. 37.

[5] J. Lenárt, Speech at Slovak Party Congress in May 1971 in *ibid.*, p. 171.

[6] *Rudé právo*, 1/7/1970, p. 3.

[7] 'Likvidace důstojnického sboru čs. armády', *Listy*, 3/1976, pp. 16–8.

[8] *Práce*, 19/2/1971, pp. 1, 5.

[9] *Obrana lidu*, 17/4/1971, p. 2.

[10] *Obrana lidu*, 26/6/1971, p. 4.

[11] Gustav Husák, *Projevy a stati, duben 1969-leden 1970*, Prague, Svoboda, 1970, p. 81.

[12] *ibid.*, p. 390.

[13] *ibid.*, p. 313.

[14] *ibid.*, p. 398.

[15] *ibid.*, p. 399.

[16] Gustav Husák, *Vybrané projevy, květen 1970-prosinec 1971*, Prague, Svoboda, 1972, p. 156.

[17] *Rudé právo*, 18/4/1970, p. 1.

[18] *Rudé právo*, 15/12/1970, p. 3.

[19] *Rudé právo*, 13/9/1975, p. 2.

[20] *XV. sjezd KSČ*, Prague, Svoboda, 1977, p. 106.

[21] G. Wightman, A. H. Brown, *op. cit.*

[22] *XIV. sjezd KSČ*, Prague, Svoboda, 1971, p. 91.

[23] Josef Smrkovský quoted in *Der Spiegel*, 14/11/1968.

[24] See Leonard Schapiro, *Totalitarianism*, London, Macmillan, 1972, p. 55.

[25] *Rudé právo*, 29/4/1970, p. 3.

[26] As quoted in *The Czechoslovak Trade Unions*, Brussels, International Confederation of Free Trade Unions, 1970, p. 28.

[27] *Rudé právo*, 10/11/1970, pp. 1, 2.

[28] *Mladá fronta*, 4/3/1971, p. 2.

[29] *Tribuna*, 31/3/1971, p. 9.

[30] *Rudé právo*, 17/6/1971, p. 2.

[31] *Právník*, 6/1971, pp. 529–31.

[32] For a detailed description from Prague oppositional circles see a series of articles entitled 'Social Sciences in the Vice of "Consolidation"', *Listy*, 3/1974, 4/1974, 5–6/1974 and 1/1975. In Czech.

[33] *Listy*, 4/1973, p. 18.

[34] According to Antonín Kapek in *Tvorba*, 28/4/1971, p. 5.

[35] *Učitelské noviny*, 30/4/1970, p. 3. The quotation is condensed.

[36] *Rudé právo*, 19/2/1970, p. 2.

[37] *Učitelské noviny*, 17/12/1970, p. 1.

[38] *ibid.*, p. 7.

[39] *Učitelské noviny*, 16/7/1970, pp. 1, 3.

[40] *Učitelské noviny*, 23/9/1971, p. 1.

[41] *Učitelské noviny*, 25/6/1970, p. 4.

[42] Gustav Husák, *Projevy a stati, duben 1969-leden 1970*, p. 27.

[43] Vasil Bilak, *Pravda zůstala pravdou*, Prague, Svoboda, 1974, pp. 261–3.

[44] *Novinář*, 2/1971, as quoted in Radio Free Europe Situation Report, 7/4/1971, p. 6.

[45] *Rudé právo*, 27/6/1970, p. 3.

[46] For full texts of such ordinances, which were not openly published in Czechoslovakia, see for example *Listy*, 2/1971, p. 21; 4–5/1971, p. 33; 3/1972, p. 29; 5–6/1973, p. 54; 1/1974, p. 28.

[47] *Listy*, 2/1971, p. 24.

[48] *White Paper on Czechoslovakia*, Paris, International Committee for the Support of Charter 77 in Czechoslovakia, 1977, pp. 167–9.

[49] *Rudé právo*, 16/12/1969.

[50] *Rudé právo*, 19/12/1970, p. 1.

[51] Milan Zubek in *Nová mysl*, 8/1970, pp. 1111–9.

[52] Lumir Hanák on Radio Prague, 14/12/1969, and in *Pravda*, Bratislava, 4/1/1970, as

quoted in Radio Free Europe Situation Reports 16/12/1969, pp. 4–5 and 9/1/1970, p. 4.

[53] *Katolické noviny*, 16/8/1970, p. 2.

[54] *Listy*, 3/1972, p. 5.

[55] *Rudé právo*, 1/9/1970, p. 2.

[56] *Nová mysl*, 12/1970, pp. 1658–68.

[57] *Kostnické jiskry*, 9/12/1970, p. 4.

[58] All quotations from the text of the laws in *Sbírka zákonů* 1969. See also H. Frank, 'New Repressive Legislation in Czechoslovakia', Radio Free Europe Research Report, 10/2/1970.

[59] Gustav Husák, *Projevy a stati, duben 1969-leden 1970*, p. 7.

[60] *ibid.*, p. 30.

[61] *ibid.*, pp. 255–6.

[62] Leonard Schapiro, *op. cit.*, p. 31.

[63] It is fair to say that while the party leadership's will is superior to the script and spirit of every individual law, the existence of a legal *system* does reduce the arbitrariness of action somewhat. This point is noted and well elucidated in Schapiro, *op. cit.*, p. 31. Nevertheless, in moments of crisis, which the party leaders regard as potentially lethal to their hold on power and which can last for prolonged periods of time, the considerations of the legal system are set aside and activities expedited which would stand no scrutiny in more normal times.

[64] Both the Revolutionary Socialist Party and the Ten Points Manifesto will be discussed in part three.

[65] *Rudé právo*, 16/10/1971, p. 3.

[66] *Listy*, 3/1971, p. 8.

[67] *Listy*, 1/1972, p. 28.

[68] *Listy*, 2/1971, p. 9.

[69] Gustav Husák, *Projevy a stati, duben 1969-leden 1970*, p. 40.

[70] *ibid.*, p. 106.

[71] *ibid.*, p. 298.

[72] *ibid.*, p. 388.

[73] A good juxtaposition of the original legislation and the 1970 amendments appears in Jíři Grospič, *Československá federace*, Prague, Orbis, 1972.

[74] *Statistické přehledy*, 11/1971, p. 349.

[75] There were 10,625 Czechs in Bratislava as of the same date.

[76] Robert W. Dean, 'Three Years of Czechoslovak Federation', Radio Free Europe Research Report, 1/3/1972. See also his *Nationalism and Political Change in Eastern Europe: The Slovak Question and the Czechoslovak Reform Movement*, Denver, University of Colorado Press, 1973.

[77] L. Štrougal in his address at the 14th party congress. *XIV. sjezd KSČ*, p. 129.

[78] *Sbírka zákonů* No. 47 of 23/12/1969, Law No. 153.

[79] Calculated from *Statistické přehledy*, 1/1969, p. 22.

[80] *Statistická ročenka 1970*, p. 467. This is in fact 0·2 per cent more than given in *Statistické přehledy*, 2/1969, p. 62.

[81] *Statistické přehledy*, 11–12/1970, p. 237.

[82] *Hospodářské noviny*, 4/9/1970, pp. 1, 4, 5.

[83] *Hospodářské noviny*, 11/9/1970, p. 3.

[84] Calculated from *Statistické přehledy* for 1968, various issues.

[85] *Hospodářské noviny*, 11/12/1970, p. 1.

[86] Calculated from *Statistické přehledy* for 1968–1972, various issues.

[87] Calculated from *Statistické přehledy* for 1970–1971. There may be an error in the Soviet tally where two figures are shown differently in subsequent issues of the publication.

[88] *Hospodářské noviny*, 1/10/1971, p. 2.

[89] *Listy*, 3/1973, p. 1.

[90] *Rudé právo*, 29/9/1970, p. 3.

[91] *Rudé právo*, 29/8/1970, p. 2.

[92] Speech in Ostrava, *Rudé právo*, 12/10/1970, pp. 1–2.

[93] *Rudé právo*, 3/10/1970, p. 3.

[94] J. Houfová in *Rudé právo*, 18/9/1970, p. 2.

[95] *Rudé právo*, 8/9/1970, p. 2.

[96] *Obrana lidu*, 10/10/1970, pp. 1–2.

[97] 'Poučenie' in *Svedectvo dokumentov a faktov*, p. 46. The 'Lessons' were translated into English in *Information Bulletin*, 2/1971, Prague, Peace and Socialism.

[98] *Pravda*, Bratislava, 31/12/1970 as translated in R. W. Dean, 'The Situation in the Czechoslovak Party after the December Plenum', Radio Free Europe Research Report, 18/2/1971, p. 5. Another perceptive paper by Mr Dean.

[99] His speech at a National Front conference on 27/1/1971. Gustav Husák, *Vybrané projevy, květen 1970–prosinec 1971*, p. 219.

[100] *XIV. sjezd KSČ*, p. 563.

[101] *ibid.*, p. 565.

[102] *ibid.*, p. 566.

[103] *ibid.*, p. 568.

[104] *ibid.*, p. 567.

Part Three

[1] The English translation of the Ten Points Manifesto was published as an appendix to Jiří Pelikán, *Socialist Opposition in Eastern Europe*, London, Allison & Busby, 1976.

My references are to a carbon copy of the Czech original. For a history of criminal prosecution that followed the Ten Points, but was not consummated, see Luděk Pachman, *Jak to bylo*, Toronto, 68 Publishers, 1974. This is Pachman's memoir, very readable and illuminating.

[2] Aleš Křemenda and Ludvík Teufelwald, 'Nových dva tisíce slov: výdělek, nad kterým se pláče', *Svědectví*, 38/1970, pp. 195–200.

[3] 'Hovoří Sibylle Plogstedt', *Listy*, 4/1972, pp. 27–31.

[4] R. A. Dahl, 'Introduction' in R. A. Dahl, ed., *Regimes and Opposition*, New Haven, Yale University Press, 1973, p. 13.

[5] *Svedectvo dokumentov a faktov*, pp. 20 and 27.

[6] *Tribuna*, 15/9/1971, p. 9.

[7] Jiří Pelikán, *Socialist Opposition in Eastern Europe*, pp. 40–44.

[8] *Listy*, 1/1971, pp. 3–5. In English in Jiří Pelikán, *Socialist Opposition in Eastern Europe*, pp. 125–34.

[9] All quotations from the full text in English in *ibid.*, pp. 135–56.

[10] *Rudé právo*, 2/12/1971, p. 2.

[11] *Rudé právo*, 8/12/1971, p. 2.

[12] *Tribuna*, 22/12/1971, p. 5.

[13] *Rudé právo*, 12/1/1972, p. 2.

[14] *Rudé právo*, 18/2/1972, p. 2.

[15] Valerio Ochetto's 'Open Letter to the Procurator', *Il Giorno*, 3/8/1972.

[16] Jiří Pelikán, *Socialist Opposition in Eastern Europe*, p. 66.

[17] An excerpt from Indra's speech is quoted in *Svědectví*, 39/1970, p. 333.

[18] *L'Humanité*, 18/2/1972, as quoted in Devlin-Hajek-Niznansky, 'The Czechoslovak Trials and CPCS Relations with Western Communist Parties', Radio Free Europe Research Report, 14/9/1972, p. 6.

[19] *Giorni Vie Nuove*, 16/9/1971.

[20] *Svědectví*, 44/1972, pp. 568–9.

[21] *Rudé právo*, 16/8/1972, p. 3.

[22] *Večernik*, 22/9/72, p. 1.

[23] *Rudé právo*, 28/8/1972, pp. 1–2.

[24] Devlin-Hajek-Niznansky, *op. cit.*, p. 6.

[25] *Morning Star*, 10/8/1972.

[26] Jef Turf, 'Procès en Tchécoslovaquie', *Drapeau Rouge*, 4/8/1972, as quoted in Devlin-Hajek-Niznansky, *op. cit.*, p. 11.

27 *Listy*, 2/1973, p. 3.

[28] *Pravda vítězí! Bulletin of the Committee to Defend Czechoslovak Socialists*, No. 6–7, undated, p. 20.

[29] *Rudé právo*, 16/12/1972, pp. 1–2. See also *Tvorba*, 20/12/1972, pp. 2, 6.

[30] *Rudé právo*, 20/2/1970, p. 1.

[31] *Demografia*, 4/1972.

[32] As quoted in Radio Free Europe Situation Report, 24/1/1973, p. 8.

[33] For a perceptive assessment of successive emigration from Czechoslovakia see Pavel Tigrid, *Politická emigrace v atomovém věku*, Cologne, Index, 1974.

[34] Milan Matouš, *Fronta bez příměří*, Prague, Svoboda, 1974.

[35] *Ústřední věstník ČSR*, Part 2, 1/6/1977.

[36] Both quotations from 'Mandát těm venku', *Listy*, 2/1973, pp. 8–10.

[37] *Rudé právo*, 15/4/1971, pp. 1–2.

[38] *Pravda*, Bratislava, 17/7/1971, p. 4.

[39] *Rudé právo*, 25/11/1971, p. 2.

[40] *Pravda*, Bratislava, 23/12/1971, as quoted by R. W. Dean in 'The Problem of Slack Party Discipline', Radio Free Europe Research Report, 3/2/1972.

[41] *Tribuna*, 2/2/1972, p. 6.

[42] *Tribuna*, 22/3/1972, p. 6.

[43] *Tribuna*, 1/3/1972, p. 6.

[44] *Život strany*, 4/1972, pp. 29–32.

[45] *ibid.*

[46] *Život strany*, 6/1972, p. 23.

[47] See also *Rudé právo*, 16/2/1974, p. 1.

[48] *Život strany*, 21/1973, pp. 36–7.

[49] *Tvorba*, 29/1/1975, pp. 3, 5.

[50] Unless otherwise stated, data on membership and composition are taken from G. Wightman and A. H. Brown, *op. cit.*

[51] *Život strany*, 3/1974, pp. 8–11.

[52] *Rudé právo*, 26/1/1974, p. 1.

[53] *Život strany*, 23/1973, pp. 14–8.

[54] *Rudé právo*, 3/12/1977, p. 2.

[55] *Život strany*, 22/1974, pp. 19–21.

[56] *Listy*, 4/1974, p. 14.

[57] Thomas E. Heneghan, 'Husak in Hradcany Castle', Radio Free Europe Research Report, 6/8/1975.

[58] *Rudé právo*, 29/5/1975, p. 2.

[59] *Rudé právo*, 28/5/1975, p. 1.

[60] *Rudé právo*, 16/11/1972, p. 3.

[61] *Sbírka zákonů*, *Částka 14*, 3/5/1973. Laws Nos. 44, 45, 46, 47 and 48.

[62] *Rudé právo*, 22/2/1973, p. 4.

[63] *Listy*, 6/1974, p. 11.

[64] Dubček's letter to Mrs Smrkovský, *Listy*, 2/1974, pp. 4–6.

[65] *Listy*, 3/1975, pp. 3–16.

[66] *Rudé právo*, 11/12/1974, p. 1.

[67] *Rudé právo*, 17/4/1975, pp. 1–2.

[68] *Rudé právo*, 18/4/1975, p. 5.

[69] 'O policejním státu neboli fízlokracii', *Listy*, 4/1975, pp. 14–9.

[70] *XV. sjezd KSČ*, p. 73.

[71] *Rudé právo*, 16/2/1976, pp. 1–2.

[72] *XV. sjezd KSČ*, p. 135.

[73] *ibid.*, p. 137.

[74] *Učitelské noviny*, 11/1974, p. 8.

[75] Full text in Czech in *Listy*, 3/1974, pp. 11–13. Extensive extracts in English in *White Paper on Czechoslovakia*, pp. 141–3.

[76] Full text in Czech in *Listy*, 1/1977, pp. 46–7. Extensive extracts in English in *White Paper on Czechoslovakia*, pp. 137–40.

[77] 'Dnešní vysokoškoláci', *Listy*, 4/1976, pp. 12–3.

[78] *Učitelské noviny*, 19/9/1974, pp. 6–7.

[79] *Pravda*, Bratislava, 25/9/1974, as quoted in Radio Free Europe Situation Report, 16/10/1974, p. 9.

[80] L. Hrzal, 'Vývoj, současný stav a úkoly společenských věd v ČSSR', *Filosofický časopis*, 5/1974, pp. 609–16.

[81] The document was published six weeks after it was issued and even then only in lengthy extracts. See *Rudé právo*, 20/6/1974, p. 3. The announcement of a new purge in social science institutions preceded the publication of the document: *Rudé právo*, 18/5/1974, p. 3.

[82] For example: I. Šujan, J. Kolek, K. Gergelyi, *Prognostický model ekonomiky ČSSR*, Bratislava, Alfa, 1974; S. Vácha, *Cíl socialistického podniku*, Prague, Svoboda, 1974; E. Divila, R. Goulli, F. Záhlava, *Zemědělsko-průmyslový komplex v národním hospodářství*, Prague, Academia, 1974; V. Komárek, L. Říha, *Rozbory a perspektivy hospodářského rozvoje*, Prague, SNTL, 1975; J. Vaner, ed., *Československá ekonomika v sedmdesátých letech*, Prague, Academia, 1975; J. Goldman, *Makroekonomická analýza a prognóza*, Prague, Academia, 1975; J. Kolek, I. Šujan, *Ekonometrické modely v socialistických krajinách*, Bratislava, Pravda, 1976.

[83] For example: I. Krempa, *Za internacionálnu jednotu*, Bratislava, Pravda, 1975 (on the formation of the Communist Party in Slovakia and Sub-Carpathian Ruthenia); J. Žižka, *Proti okupantům*, Prague, Svoboda, 1975 (on anti-Nazi activity of the communists from June 1941 to January 1943); J. Tůma, *Na cestě ke KSČ*, Ústí, Severočeské nakladatelství, 1975 (on the anarcho-communist groups from 1918–1925); A. Hájková, *Strana v odboji*, Prague, Svoboda, 1975 (on communist anti-Nazi resistance from Munich to the assassination of Heydrich).

[84] For example, Jaromír Charvát et al., *Sociální struktura ČSSR a její vývoj v šedesátých letech*, Prague, Academia, 1972, and J. Alan, *Společnost–vzdělání–jedinec*, Prague, Svoboda, 1974. Some empirical work was undertaken and published, though not all of it for the open market, by the Research Institute of Culture and Public Opinion in Bratislava, such as a two-year project (1970–71) of investigation into the cultural and social profile of the Slovak village population (*Kultúrny a spoločenský profil dedínskeho*

obyvateľstva na Slovensku, Bratislava, Obzor, 1973). The Prague Institute for the Study of Culture also has some empirical studies to its credit.

[85] *Listy*, 7/1975, pp. 44–8. Two Czechoslovak social scientists, using the pseudonyms Vratislav Prošck and Jiří Žemla, wrote a long situation report on the state of social sciences from 1972–1974. See 'Společenske vědy ve svěráku "konsolidace"', referenced in Note 32 for Part Two. A documentary directory of 146 names of historians who were deprived of the right to stay in the profession and to have their works published was presented to the 14th International Congress of Historical Sciences in San Francisco in August 1975, and appeared as a brochure under the title *Acta Persecutionis: A Document from Czechoslovakia*.

[86] *Tvorba*, 2/4/1975, pp. 7, 12.

[87] *Tvorba*, 8/1/1975, Supplement, p. XIII.

[88] The first fifty titles are listed in *Svědectví*, 50/1975, pp. 412–3, the next 31 in *Svědectví*, 54/1977, pp. 303–4.

[89] A list of writers on the blacklist in Czechoslovakia today is published in *Svědectví*, 54/1977, p. 307, and as appendix to Charter 77 Document No. 12 in *Listy*, 5/1977, p. 45.

[90] *Učitelské noviny*, 11/5/1972, p. 5.

[91] *Věstník Ministerstva školství a Ministerstva kultury ČSR*, 20/9/71, p. 146; *Kathpress*, 13/9/1972; *Pravda*, Bratislava, 29/8/1974; Radio Free Europe Situation Report, 2/10/1974, p. 2.

[92] *Rudé právo*, 22/7/1972, p. 1.

[93] *Český zápas*, 10/3/1974, p. 3.

[94] Malcolm Brown in *International Herald Tribune*, 25/8/1975, as quoted in Radio Free Europe Situation Report of 3/9/1975, p. 6.

[95] *XIV. sjezd KSČ*, p. 576.

[96] *ibid.*, p. 153.

[97] *Hospodářské noviny*, 27/8/1971.

[98] *Statistická ročenka 1977*, Prague, SNTL, 1977, p. 163.

[99] It is rumoured early in 1978 that contingency plans for depreciating deposits have been worked out. They allegedly include an overnight doubling of all prices and earnings, but not savings. In Poland this would be suicidal, in Czechoslovakia it might work—but it will be an admission of at least one failure, if the courage is ever mustered to carry it out.

[100] *Statistická ročenka 1977*, p. 239.

[101] *Listy*, 3–4/1977, p. 20.

[102] *Rudé právo*, 4/1/1974, p. 5.

[103] *Zemědělské noviny*, 24/10/1974, pp. 1, 6. For the full text of the law see either *Sbírka zákonů*, Law No. 103/1974, 23/10/1974 or Supplement to *Hospodářské noviny*, 15/11/1974.

[104] *Statistická ročenka 1977*, p. 143.

[105] *Rudé právo*, 29/8/1972, p. 2 and *Tribuna*, 30/5/1973, p. 14.

[106] All figures from various issues of *Statistická ročenka*.

[107] *Sbírka zákonů* 29/1975, 19/11/1975, Laws Nos. 122 and 123.

[108] František Hamouz in *Rudé právo*, 12/3/1976, p. 3.

[109] As quoted in *east-west*, 22/12/1977, p. 12.

[110] See for example V. Polívková, 'Společnost, podniky a děti', *Svět práce*, 30/7/1975, pp. 1, 4.

[111] *Zdravotnické noviny*, 15/8/1973, p. 5.

[112] *ibid.*

[113] Radio Hvězda broadcast, 2/12/1976 and 10/4/1977, as quoted in J. L. Kerr, 'The Consumption of Alcohol and Alcoholism in Eastern Europe', Radio Free Europe Background Report, 29/11/1977, p. 3.

[114] This metaphor was used in a slightly different wording by J. L. Kerr, *op. cit.*, p. 13.

[115] As quoted in Radio Free Europe Situation Report, 29/6/1977, pp. 4–5.

[116] *Rudé právo*, 2/11/1972, p. 2.

[117] *Večerník*, 1/12/1972, p. 1.

[118] *Zdravotnické noviny*, 15/8/1973, p. 5.

[119] *Rovnost*, 27/1/1976, as quoted in Radio Free Europe Situation Report, 29/6/77, p. 4.

[120] *Rudé právo*, 7/4/1975, pp. 1, 3.

[121] *Právny obzor*, 9/1972, pp. 803–11.

[122] *Nová mysl*, 12/1969, pp. 1471–82.

[123] *Právník*, 8/1971, pp. 663–66.

[124] K. Zarodov, 'Kolektivní tribuna', *Rudé právo*, 13/4/1976, p. 10.

[125] See his comments at the October 1971 meeting of the central committee as quoted in the West. Czech version in *Listy*, 2/1972, pp. 11–14.

[126] B. Němec, 'Upevňování jednoty socialistických zemí', *Nová mysl*, 5/1976, pp. 93–105.

[127] I. Hlivka, M. Štefaňák, 'Nesmrtelný prapor', *Rudé pravo*, 12/7/1976, p. 3.

[128] *XV. sjezd KSČ*, p. 87.

[129] P. Auersperg, 'Zápas za další uvolnění mezinárodního napětí', *Rudé právo*, 11/3/1976, p. 6.

[130] Ilja Šedivý in *Život strany*, 4/1974, p. 10.

[131] *Rudé právo*, 14/12/1973, pp. 1, 3, 4.

[132] *Svět práce*, 26/6/1974, p. 5.

[133] See for example the report of the Czechoslovak delegation of sociologists who attended the World Sociological Congress in Toronto in August 1974 in *Listy*, 1/1975, pp. 16–9.

[134] *Život strany*, 14/1972, pp. 8–10.

[135] *Rudé právo*, 16/6/1973, p. 1.

[136] *Rudé právo*, 4/7/1973, p. 1.

[137] *Rudé právo*, 16/8/1975, p. 3.

[138] *Rudé právo*, 19/10/1973, p. 3.

[139] *Tribuna*, 20/6/1973, p. 9.

[140] See 'Sovětská kritika normalizace', *Listy*, 3/1972, pp. 3–4.

[141] *Rudé právo*, 21/6/1973, pp. 1–2.

[142] *Rudé právo*, 16/7/1974, pp. 1–2.

Part Four

[1] The text of Smrkovský's letter to Brezhnev is in *Listy*, 2/1975, pp. 26–28, and the story about his Soviet contacts in *Listy*, 1/1975, p. 10 and, in a somewhat differently accentuated version, in *Svědectví*, 46/1973, p. 184. Smrkovský himself did not mention the episode in his 'memoir'.

[2] *Listy*, 5–6/1972, pp. 3–5.

[3] Jan Strárek, 'Emigrace a opozice', *Svědectví*, 50/1975, pp. 211–2.

[4] *ibid.*, pp. 215, 217.

[5] *Listy*, 5–6/1973, p. 60.

[6] A book on conditions in Ruzyň prison in Prague was published by Index, Cologne, in 1973 under the title *Motáky z Ruzyně*. The manuscript, by a political prisoner of the 1972 vintage, has been smuggled out from prison and the country. It should be mandatory reading for every student of communism.

[7] See text of complaint by relatives, *Listy*, 3/1976, pp. 3–13, and Jiří Müller's complaint, *Listy*, 5–6/1973, pp. 12–15.

[8] A survey of clandestine publications has been provided in the *Pravda vítězí* bulletin of the Committee to Defend Czechoslovak Socialists in London. See for example bulletin No. 6–7, pp. 19–30. The compilers of the bulletin say that underground publications in Czechoslovakia can be divided into four categories by their content: they provide information about developments inside the communist party; international news, particularly activities of the left parties and movements; documentary evidence about persecution in Czechoslovakia; and statements by opposition groups.

[9] This letter, a penetrating study of the corrupted *mores* of the country, has been translated into English and can be found, for example, in *Voices of Czechoslovak Socialists*, London, Merlin Press, 1977, pp. 90–125.

[10] M. Srnská, 'K ratifikaci mezinárodních paktů lidských práv Československou socialistickou republikou', *Právnik*, 12/1976, p. 1113.

[11] J. Boguszak, J. Mečl, 'K mezinárodní úpravě lidských práv', *Tvorba*, 30/1977, Supplement.

[12] *White Paper on Czechoslovakia*, p. 197.

[13] *Listy*, 6/1975, pp. 11–3.

[14] *Listy*, 1/1976, pp. 33–5.

[15] Czech transcript in *Listy*, 7/1975, pp. 13–7.

[16] *Listy*, 2/1976, pp. 42–4.

17 *Listy*, 1/1976, pp. 44–6.

18 *Listy*, 2/1976, pp. 44–5.

19 Editorial article in *Listy*, 1/1976, pp. 1–3.

20 *Listy*, 3/1976, pp. 41–5.

21 All quotes from the transcript of the interview in *Listy*, 7/1975, pp. 13–7.

22 *ibid.*, p. 17.

23 Z. Mlynář, *Československý pokus o reformu*, Cologne, Index, 1976.

24 *Listy*, 2/1977, p. 10.

25 All quotations from the English text in *White Paper on Czechoslovakia*, pp. 53–6. Other translations have appeared.

26 *Svenska Dagbladed*, 13/11/1977. The quotation is from a typescript of the Czech translation.

27 *Der Spiegel*, 2/1/1978, as summarised in Radio Free Europe Situation Report, 11/1/1978, p. 2.

28 Zdeněk Mlynář, 'První bilance Charty 77', *Listy*, 2/1977, pp. 1–9.

29 Václav Doležal, 'Usvědčují je jejich přátelé', *Rudé právo*, 15/1/1977, p. 2.

30 Stanislav Oborský, 'Nenávist', *Rudé právo*, 22/1/1977, p. 7.

31 *Rudé právo*, 8/2/1977, pp. 1–2.

32 Reuter 19/4/1977, as reported in *Listy*, 3–4/1977, p. 4.

33 *Rudé právo*, 17/3/1977, p. 2.

34 Viktor Meier in *Frankfurter Allgemeine Zeitung*, 21/4/1977, as quoted in Radio Free Europe Situation Report, 27/4/1977, p. 2.

35 *Rudé právo*, 6/4/1977, p. 2.

36 At the 9th trade union congress. *Rudé právo*, 26/5/1977, p. 3.

37 *Listy*, 5/1977, p. 53.

38 *Rudé právo*, 29/1/1977, p. 1.

39 *Listy*, 3–4/1977, p. 31.

40 *Listy*, 1/1978, p. 63.

41 From various documents in *White Paper on Czechoslovakia*. A much more complete record of documentary material associated with the Charter has now become available in Czech, ably edited and prefaced by Vilém Prečan: *Kniha Charty*, Cologne, Index, 1977.

42 *Listy*, 2/1977, pp. 16–17.

43 Hsinhua release No. 012710, 27/1/1977.

44 *Svenska Dagbladed*, 13/11/1977. Here quoted from a Czech translation.

45 Both texts in *Listy*, 1/1978, pp. 28–9.

46 *Listy*, 2/1977, p. 41.

47 A long letter on violation of religious freedom was sent to the Federal Assembly on 7 May 1977 by 31 members of the Church of Czech Brethern. See *Kniha Charty*, pp. 222–48.

⁴⁸ Texts of Charter Documents Nos. 1–10 are translated in full or in substantial extracts in *White Paper on Czechoslovakia*. Documents Nos. 11, 12, 13 and the 'communication' of 21 September in *Listy* 5 and 6/1977 and 1/1978. The same source refers to Document No. 14 as containing names of another 82 signers, bringing the total up to 832. Full texts of Documents Nos. 1–12 also in *Kniha Charty*. Document No. 15 appeared in March 1978. From second-hand information, its subject are contradictions between Czechoslovak legislation and international law.

⁴⁹ For a round-up in English see Radio Free Europe Situation Report, 11/2/1978, and Patrick Moore, 'The First Anniversary of Charter 77', Radio Free Europe Background Report, 3/1/1978.

⁵⁰ *Listy*, 2/1977, p. 21.

⁵¹ *Svenska Dagbladed*, 13/11/1977.

⁵² *J'Informe*, 13/12/1977 as quoted in *Help & Action Newsletter*, 5/1977, p. J1.

BIOGRAPHICAL NOTES

(CPCS = Communist Party of Czechoslovakia)

Vasil BILAK—b. 1917; in Slovak party posts since 1950; CPCS central committee member since 1954; Slovak First Party Secretary from January to September 1968; CPCS praesidium member since January 1968.

Oldřich ČERNÍK—b. 1921; party and government functionary since 1949; CPCS central committee member since 1958 and praesidium member since 1966; Deputy Prime Minister and chief of Planning Office from 1963–1968; Prime Minister from April 1968 to January 1970; expelled from the party in January 1971.

Čestmír CÍSAŘ—b. 1920; in various party posts since 1946; journalist and diplomat; CPCS secretary and chairman of Czech National Council after 1968; expelled from the party in 1970.

Peter COLOTKA—b. 1925; Slovak university teacher and politician since 1956; CPCS central committee member since 1966 and praesidium member since 1968; chairman of Federal Assembly in 1969; Slovak Prime Minister since 1970.

Alexander DUBČEK—b. 1921; in Slovak party posts since 1949; Slovak First Party Secretary from 1963 to January 1968; CPCS First Secretary January 1968—April 1969; chairman of Federal Assembly April—September 1969; Ambassador in Turkey October 1969—January 1970; expelled from the party in 1970.

Martin DZÚR—b. 1919; soldier and officer since 1943; Moscow Military Academy 1952; Deputy Defence Minister since 1958; Defence Minister and CPCS central committee member since 1968.

Jiří HÁJEK—b. 1913; a Social Democratic youth functionary in the 1930s; in Nazi prisons 1939–1945; CPCS central committee member since 1948 (after merger of Social Democratic and Communist Parties); university professor and diplomat; Minister of Education since 1965; Foreign Minister after April 1968; expelled from the party in 1970.

Zdeněk HEJZLAR—b. 1921; in Nazi concentration camp during the war; CPCS central committee member since 1945; expelled from the party and sent to a labour camp in 1952; teacher since 1960; rehabilitated and made director of Prague Radio and CPCS central committee member in 1968; emigrated to Sweden in 1969.

Gustav HUSÁK—b. 1913; lawyer from 1938–1943; Slovak communist party functionary since 1943; chairman of the Slovak Board of Commissioners 1946–1950; CPCS central committee member 1949–1950; arrested in 1951 and sentenced to life imprisonment in 1954 for 'bourgeois nationalism'; released in 1960 and rehabilitated in 1963; researcher at Slovak Academy of Sciences 1963–1968; Deputy Prime Minister April—August 1968; Slovak First Party Secretary September 1968–April 1969; CPCS First Secretary since April 1969, and president of the republic since 1975.

Alois INDRA—b. 1921; in party and government posts since 1948; CPCS central committee member since 1958, secretary since 1968 and praesidium member since 1970; chairman of the Federal Assembly since 1971.

Miloš JAKEŠ—b. 1922; local government and youth union functionary since 1950; studied at Soviet Party School in Moscow 1955–1958; official of Ministry of the Interior 1958–1966 and Deputy Minister of the Interior 1966–1968; chairman of Central Auditing and Control Commission from 1968–1977; party praesidium candidate member since 1977.

Antonín KAPEK—b. 1922; manager of a large industrial enterprise in Prague until 1968; CPCS central committee member since 1958, candidate member of the praesidium since 1962, and full member since 1970; chief party secretary in Prague since 1969.

343

Josef KEMPNÝ—b. 1920; party and local government functionary since 1961; secretary of the CPCS since November 1968 and praesidium member since 1969. Czech Prime Minister since 1969.

Drahomír KOLDER—b. 1925, d. 1972; in party posts since 1948; CPCS central committee member since 1958, and praesidium member from 1961–1968; CPCS secretary from 1962–1968; counsellor of embassy in Sofia 1968–1969, then chairman of Commission of State Control.

František KRIEGEL—b. 1908; a medical doctor; in International Brigades in Spain 1936–1939; in the Chinese army 1939–1945; party and government official 1945–1952; health advisor to the Cuban government 1960–1963; CPCS central committee member since 1966 and praesidium member and National Front chairman in 1968 until the invasion; expelled from the party and pensioned off in 1969.

Zdeněk MLYNÁŘ—b. 1930; jurist since 1955; secretary of the CPCS legal commission 1964–1968; CPCS secretary in 1968 until retirement from politics in November; expelled from the party in 1970; an entomologist in Prague National Museum after 1969; emigrated as Charter 77 signatory in 1977.

Antonín NOVOTNÝ—b. 1904; d. 1975; party official since 1935; in Nazi concentration camp 1941–1943; regional party secretary in Prague since 1945; CPCS central committee member since 1946; praesidium member since 1951 and First Party Secretary since 1953; president of the republic from 1957–1968; dismissed in 1968; party membership suspended in 1968 but probably returned during 'normalisation'; died in retirement.

Josef PAVEL—b. 1908, d. 1973; at Comintern school in Russia 1935–1937; in International Brigades in Spain 1937–1938; interned in France; service in Czechoslovak forces in Britain 1942–1945; party and security official since 1945; CPCS central committee member since 1949; Deputy Minister of the Interior 1949–1950; arrested and sentenced to 25 years in 1951; released in 1955 and later rehabilitated; Minister of the Interior 1968 until the invasion; expelled from the party in 1970.

Jiří PELIKÁN—b. 1923; party and student union functionary since 1948; director of Czechoslovak Television 1963–1968; CPCS central committee member and chairman of the National Assembly foreign committee in 1968; emigrated in 1969; publisher of *Listy* in Rome.

Jaroslav ŠABATA—b. 1927; associate professor of psychology in Brno; CPCS central committee member and secretary of party regional committee in Brno in 1968; expelled from the party in 1969; sentenced to six-and-a-half years for oppositional activity in 1972.

Viliam ŠALGOVIČ—b. 1913; government and economic official in Slovakia 1948–1957; party and security functionary since 1958; Deputy Minister of the Interior in 1968; military attache in Budapest 1969; CPCS central committee member since 1970; chairman of the Slovak National Council since 1975.

Ota ŠIK—b. 1919; in Nazi concentration camp 1940–1945; university professor since 1948; director of the Economic Institute since 1962; CPCS central committee member since 1962; CPCS central committee member since 1962; Deputy Prime Minister in 1968; expelled from the party and emigrated in 1969.

Bohumil ŠIMON—b. 1920; party official since 1948; CPCS central committee member since 1966; candidate member of the party praesidium and chief party secretary in Prague in 1968; expelled from the party in 1970.

Josef SMRKOVSKÝ—b. 1911, d. 1974; at Comintern school in Russia in 1933; party functionary since 1934; underground during the war; party praesidium member 1945–1951; arrested in 1951 and sentenced to life imprisonment; released in 1955 and rehabilitated in 1963; CPCS central committee member again since 1966; Minister of Forestry and Water Conservancy 1966–1968; party praesidium member and chairman of the National Assembly in 1968; expelled from the party in 1970.

Josef ŠPAČEK—b. 1927; party official since 1947; CPCS central committee member and party secretary in Brno after 1966; party praesidium member and secretary 1968–1969; expelled from the party in 1970.

Lubomír ŠTROUGAL—b. 1924; party official since 1955; CPCS central committee member since 1958; Minister of the Interior 1961–1965; party secretary 1965–1968; Deputy Prime Minister in 1968; party praesidium member since September 1968; Federal Prime Minister since 1970.

Oldrich ŠVESTKA—b. 1922; party journalist since 1945; CPCS central committee member since 1962, and praesidium member in 1968; chief editor of *Rudé právo* since 1975.

Ludvík SVOBODA—b. 1895; officer in the Czechoslovak armed forces since 1915, including commander of Czechoslovak troops in Russia 1939–1945; Defence Minister 1945–1950; accountant 1953–1954; head of Military Academy 1955–1956; retired 1959; president of the republic from March 1968 to 1975; CPCS central committee and praesidium member 1968–1976.

FURTHER READING

There is no treatment of the entire past decade of Czechoslovak politics in a single volume.

The period from the invasion to Dubček's replacement by Husák in April 1969 has been well described in the three major works on the Prague Spring, by Skilling, Hejzlar and Golan. H. Gordon Skilling's *Czechoslovakia's Interrupted Revolution* (Princeton University Press, 1976) is massive and as close to a definitive work as can be written without access to Prague and Moscow archives. It is highly recommended to every serious student of the subject and of course a must for every respectable library. The same is true about Zdeněk Hejzlar's *Reformkommunismus* (Cologne-Frankfurt, Europäische Verlagsanstalt, 1976), not the least because of the insider's view it provides and the information from the inner circles of the party it contains. It is an *engagé* reformer's account of Czechoslovak communism in the 1960s. Both books analyse pre-1968 growth of reformism and the Prague Spring as well. Galia Golan's *Reform Rule in Czechoslovakia. The Dubček Era 1968–1969* (Cambridge University Press, 1973) continues in the vein of her first book on the crystallisation of reform and is thoroughly descriptive.

Pavel Tigrid's *Why Dubček Fell* (London, Macdonald, 1971) is a comparatively brief, sensible and readable account of the Czechoslovak reformist attempt, with emphasis on the inevitability of its decline and defeat. However valiant the endeavour, Tigrid believes that communism cannot really be repaired.

Vladimir Horský's *Prag 1968 : Systemveränderung und Systemverteidigung* (Stuttgart-Munich, Klett-Kösel, 1975) has the advantage, from the point of view of our story, of considering in detail the alternatives to military intervention and to the Czechoslovak response to it.

A detailed account of the clandestine 14th party congress has been provided in Jiří Pelikán, ed., *The Secret Vysočany Congress* (London, Allen Lane, 1971). Apart from the full text of the minutes of the congress (transcribed from tapes), its point of interest lies in the outline of reformist plans prepared before the invasion for presentation to the extraordinary congress which was to convene on 9 September 1968.

The only full-length biography of Dubček in English is William Shawcross, *Dubček* (London, Weidenfeld & Nicolson, 1970), perhaps not sombre enough in some judgments but still very informative and with a psychological insight. In German there is L. Veselý's *Dubček* (Munich, Kindler, 1970).

A number of documents pertaining to the early stage of 'normalisation', with Dubček still nominally in charge, have been translated in various publications. Perhaps one ought to refer to that deserving collection by R. A. Remington, *Winter in Prague* (Cambridge, Mass., M. I. T. Press, 1969).

Adolf Müller's *Die Tschechoslowakei auf der Suche nach Sicherheit* (Berlin Verlag, 1977) is about Czechoslovak foreign policy over a longer period of time, but it has a welcome chapter on the foreign political aspect of the Prague Spring and the 'normalisation', a subject not widely tackled in other sources. Another chapter relates Czechoslovakia to European security and cooperation.

Vojtech Mastny has edited a volume on *Czechoslovakia: Crisis in World Communism* (New York, Facts on File, 1972) which is in fact an extensive round-up of events in and around Czechoslovakia as reflected in the world press, and very useful at that. A symposium edited by E. J. Czerwinski and J. Piekalkiewicz, *The Soviet Invasion of Czechoslovakia: Its Effects on Eastern Europe* (New York, Praeger, 1972) has contributions on Soviet, Hungarian, Polish, Romanian and Yugoslav reactions, as well as Ivan Volgyes' comparison of Hungary 1956 and Czechoslovakia 1968.

The post-1969 stages of 'normalisation' or 'consolidation' have so far received only fragmented coverage in the sense that only the oppositional scene is being singled out for attention. Thus there is Jiří Pelikán's *Socialist Opposition in Eastern Europe: The Czechoslovak Example* (London, Allison & Busby, 1976) with its appendix of translations of fourteen oppositional documents originating in the Socialist Movement of Czechoslovak Citizens. (A somewhat different and earlier French edition is *Ici Prague: l'Opposition Interieure Parle*, Paris, Seuil, 1973.) Translations of several materials by the various adversaries of 'normalisation' are also conveniently collected in *Voices of Czechoslovak Socialists* (London, Merlin Press, 1977), and the more literary genres of Czechoslovak samizdat in *Kontinent: Sonderband Prag* (Berlin, Ullstein, 1976). Documentary materials connected with the opposition's view of detente, the regime's reaction to it and Charter 77 have been published as *White Paper on Czechoslovakia* (International Committee for the Support of Charter 77, 3 rue des Lions, 75004 Paris; 1977. English and French versions are available.)

A continuous service of annotated news and background papers is provided by the Czechoslovak Research and Evaluation Unit of Radio Free Europe in Munich. This is a service of generally high quality; researchers like Dean, Hájek, Heneghan, Kratochvil, Nižňanský, Macháň and Trend have written consistently good papers that could be the envy of any scholarly institution.

Much indispensible reading material is in Czech only. The bimonthly *Listy* (Via Torre Argentina 21, Rome 00186) is a repository of documents and comment of primary importance. The quarterly *Svědectví* (6 rue du Pont de Lodi, Paris 6) has a wider cultural-political range but also contains factual information, often from private sources. Both periodicals have maintained a high standard since their inception, *Listy* in 1971 and *Svědectví* in 1957.

Zdeněk Mlynář's polemical and analytical *Československý pokus o reformu 1968* (Cologne, Index, 1975) and Antonín Ostrý's *Československý problém* (Index, 1972) are prime examples of the reformers' interpretative approach to Prague Spring and the 'normalisation' after the defeat of the experiment.

Among the collections of documents in Czech, we should mention four more volumes published by Index in Cologne: *Motáky z Ruzyně* (1973) is a book of letters by a political prisoner to his wife, smuggled out of jail. *Hlasy z domova 1975* (1976) contains seventeen statements and letters written by the dissidents in 1975, many of which have been cited extensively in this book. *Čára na zdi* (1977) is in fact a reprint of a samizdat collection of literary *feuilletons*. The most recent *Kniha Charty* (1978) has all the Charter documents, statements and announcements, as well as other materials associated with the movement for human rights. It has been ably edited and prefaced by Vilém Prečan.

From the official Czechoslovak publications one would recommend the four volumes of Gustav Husák's collected speeches and articles which have been published so far: *Projevy a stati. Duben 1969–Leden 1970* (Prague, Svoboda, 1970), *Vybrané projevy. Květen 1970–Prosinec 1971* (Svoboda, 1972), *Projevy a stati. Únor 1972–Červen 1974* (Svoboda, 1976) and *Projevy a stati. Srpen 1974–Duben 1976* (Svoboda, 1977). Protocols of the two party congresses in 1971 and 1976 appeared under the titles *XIV. sjezd KSČ* (Svoboda, 1971) and *XV. sjezd KSČ* (Svoboda, 1977).

Svedectvo dokumentov a faktov (Bratislava, Pravda, 1975) brings together some of the main official documents, e.g. 'The Lessons of the Crisis' and personal testimonies by several leading 'normalisers' (Bilak, Indra, Švestka, Fojtík, Janík, Hruškovič, Sabolčik). It has the advantage of a Slovak bias over Czech collections of a similar nature.

Vasil Bilak's *Pravda zůstala pravdou* (Svoboda, 1971) includes his speeches and articles from October 1967 to December 1970. A plethora of materials from *Rudé právo* is being periodically collected and reprinted in the paper's special series of brochures. A recent one, entitled *Ztroskotanci samozvanci (Rudé právo*, n.d., but in fact 1978), has a number of articles about Charter 77.

Needless to say, this is only a modest list of reading suggestions.